Faces around the World

Faces around the World

A CULTURAL ENCYCLOPEDIA OF THE HUMAN FACE

Margo DeMello

ABC-CLIO

Santa Barbara, California • Denver, Colorado • Oxford, England

Library of Congress Cataloging-in-Publication Data

DeMello, Margo.
  Faces around the world : a cultural encyclopedia of the human face / Margo DeMello.
      p. cm.
  Includes index.
  ISBN 978-1-59884-617-1 (hardback) — ISBN 978-1-59884-618-8 (ebook)
1. Face—Encyclopedias.   I. Title.
  QM535.D46   2012
  612.9'203—dc23   2011036438

ISBN: 978-1-59884-617-1
EISBN: 978-1-59884-618-8

16   15   14   13   12   1   2   3   4   5

This book is also available on the World Wide Web as an eBook.
Visit www.abc-clio.com for details.

ABC-CLIO, LLC
130 Cremona Drive, P.O. Box 1911
Santa Barbara, California 93116-1911

This book is printed on acid-free paper ∞

Manufactured in the United States of America

Contents

Topical List of Entries

Modification of the Face

Cheek Piercings and Cheek Plugs
Cosmetic Surgery
Ear Piercing
Ear Shaping
Ear Spools and Plugs
Earlobe Stretching
Facial Piercing
Facial Tattoos
Labrets, Lip Plugs, and Lip Plates
Moko
Nose Piercing
Oral Piercing
Permanent Makeup
Teeth Filing

Adornment of the Face

Bindi
Cosmetics
Henna
Jewelry
Kohl

Facial Expressions

Animal Facial Expressions
Evolution of the Face
Facial Expressions

Body Image

Aging
Beauty
Cosmetic Surgery
Disorders of the Face
Facial Symmetry

Thematic Issues

Aging
Beauty
Gender
Sex and Sexuality

Religious Beliefs

Ash Wednesday
Baptism
Buddhism
Christianity
Halo
Image of Edessa
Janus
Judaism
Shroud of Turin
Veil of Veronica
Veiling

Preface

Faces around the World is the first comprehensive reference book that deals with all aspects of the human (and non-human) face. Because the face is the most important feature that we have, and serves as a form of communication, identification, and expression of emotions and character, understanding the face helps us to understand what it is to be human.

This encyclopedia is the first of its kind to take a comprehensive look at the face throughout history and around the world. It addresses the evolution of the face, the role that facial features play, how emotions are expressed on the face, what people read into the face, and the major cultural beliefs and practices associated with the face, by both topic and geographic region.

This volume is aimed at general readers with an interest in sociology and anthropology, because of its coverage of the social and cultural aspects of the face, as well as those with an interest in psychology and evolution. Entries include a list of related topics to explore and a list of further reading on the subject for readers who desire more information, and there is as well a comprehensive bibliography.

There are 132 entries in this Encyclopedia, which cover the biological aspects, social roles, disorders, folklore, beliefs, and cultural practices associated with the face, including makeup, tattooing, scarification, piercing, and cosmetic surgery.

Entries are listed in alphabetical order, and when a subject has multiple names for it, the most commonly used name (i.e., Mardi Gras) will be the name used for the entry, and other names (i.e., Carnival) will include a note directing the reader to the full entry. Additionally, each entry contains cross-referenced items in bold type, as well as a list of related subjects at the end of each entry. Each entry explains the term, gives an overview, and provides any historical or cross-cultural significance.

Acknowledgments

This is the third book that I have published with Greenwood/ABC-CLIO, and I want to thank the people there for their confidence in me, including my editor, Kaitlin Ciarmiello.

I also want to thank the people in my life who have supported me during my writing projects. Criss Starr, Bill Velasquez, and Jeff Hayes have all provided different types of support and friendship during this time, and I thank them for that. Finally, I wish to acknowledge my husband, Tom Young, who patiently endures higher amounts of stress and a much filthier house as I approach deadline, and my parents, Bill DeMello and Robin Montgomery, who have always given me love and support throughout all of my projects.

Introduction

The face is the single most important feature that we as humans use to both comprehend the world around us and to present ourselves to that world. The eyes that we use to see, the nose that we use to smell, the ears that we use to hear, and the mouth that we use to both talk and feed ourselves evolved over millions of years to allow our primitive ancestors to better negotiate the world around them; in fact, four of our five senses are located on our face. Those same features combine to form the most important identifying feature that we now have. Of the over 6 billion people on the planet today, not a single human face is identical to another. Our faces are the visual thumbprints that we present to the world.

But faces are so much more than that. They are the keys to our personal identity and sense of self; they allow us to understand and recognize others, and to represent ourselves. Humans are programmed to perceive and recognize other faces, and within minutes of birth, infants begin to seek out the faces of those around them. We see faces everywhere we look—on clouds, on the moon, and even on cars. We put faces on children's toys—even inanimate objects like trains or telephones have faces on them, and children draw faces before they draw anything else.

Many nonhuman animals also recognize faces just like we do, and recognize that the face is the way in which to best connect with each other, and with us. That is why our domesticated dogs and cats not only gaze into our eyes when they want attention, but sometimes paw at our faces as well. Social animals in particular, like dogs, rabbits, or elephants, need to recognize the faces of those animals with whom they are friendly; just as it is for us, it is a critical social skill for them, and just as in humans, the face in many mammal species is the most distinguishable part of the animal. But most animals, as far as we know, do not recognize their own faces, when seen in a mirror. Great apes can do this, however, and this ability is seen by scientists to indicate that they have, just as we have, a sense of self.

We notice a person's face before we notice anything else about them, barring perhaps the color of their skin. And we do not just notice faces. If the face belongs to a person we know, we draw upon countless images and memories in our brains and quickly are able to recognize who that person is and what they mean to us, all based on their face. If we do not know them, by looking at their face, we *think* we do. We believe that based on the shape of the face, and the characteristics of the facial features and the relationship between them, that we can tell something about the inner character of the person that we see. Are they a good person, a crafty person, a mean person, or a selfish person? Are they naïve, generous, loving, or greedy? All of that can be told, many of us think, from our face. Cartoon caricatures, in fact, began as a way to emphasize not just aspects of a person's facial features, but these cartoons were (and are) also used to emphasize aspects of their inner character, which were thought to be represented through the eyes, nose, or mouth. The eyes, in particular, are thought by many to be the windows to the soul, and can grant immediate access to the true nature of the person into whose eyes we stare. The science of physiognomy and the related art of face reading are both predicated on the notion that you really *can* read a book by its cover, if the face is the cover of the human book. Faces can also refer to other public visages. Buildings can have faces, corporations can have faces, and a wide variety of inanimate objects can have faces, all of which convey to the world what is inside.

Faces also tell the world something about what the person has experienced; an older face, lined with wrinkles or marred by scars, tells something of the life experiences of the person. And tattooing and scarification are both used in many cultures to physically mark on the face (or body) the accomplishments and cultural identity of the wearer. Facial piercings too, and the jewelry and other adornments that we wear on our faces, are visible demonstrations of the cultural and social categories to which a person belongs, including whether they are male or female, married or marriageable, and what religion, clan, or tribe they belong to. Bindis, cheek plugs, lip plates, stretched ears and ear plugs are all ways in which culture, tradition, social position, and beauty are etched upon the face for all to see.

We do not just look at faces, however. We especially like to look at beautiful faces; babies will stare longer at faces considered beautiful than at other faces, and we reward those with exceptional beauty with riches and fame. We love looking at the photos of famous and beautiful people—we watch them on film and television; we buy magazines with their faces on them; and we even put up posters of their faces on our walls. The faces of the famous are on our money, our products, and our billboards and other ads. We even make monuments out of famous faces like Mount Rushmore. We also, apparently, like to stare at those about whom we've heard something bad. A new study confirms this and may explain why we not only like looking at beautiful people but people who have been involved in scandals.

We also stigmatize those who are not beautiful and have created multi-billion dollar industries (the cosmetics and cosmetic surgery industries) devoted to giving people—mostly women—the promise of beauty. And while evolutionary psychologists and others have long felt that beauty can be objectively measured, on the basis of symmetry, for example, the standards of beauty are also cultural and social, and those with power are able to define what is beautiful for any given place and time. Because of the changing and fickle nature of beauty, groups of people who are excluded from the current definition, by virtue, for example, of their ethnicity, are forever shut out of the beauty race and its rewards. Alternatively, they will work harder than others, and employ expensive or dangerous methods to make themselves fit a standard of beauty that was created with others in mind. So skin-whitening products, many of which are toxic, have been used for thousands of years to make women's skin appear lighter than it is, and these products are still popular in Asia and Africa today. Cosmetic surgical procedures are performed on increasing numbers of Asian, African, and Latino women, in order to make their features appear more European and, thus, more beautiful.

Our faces reflect our sex, gender, and ethnicity, and sometimes even our class position. Transgendered people who are transitioning from male to female or female to male often face additional hurdles of social acceptance when their face continues, even after surgery and hormone treatments, to reflect their birth sex, rather than the sex and gender with which they identify. People can, on the other hand, be fooled by faces. If a person presents a convincing enough feminine face, for example, that others think she is female, it could have unpleasant results. Numerous transwomen, or men who are transitioning to become women, have been killed when someone has found out their secret, and realized that they had been fooled.

We can also fool people, sometimes, with our facial expressions. Facial expressions have evolved in order to communicate emotional information to others. The most basic of the expressions—happiness, sadness, anger, fear, and surprise—are all shared by many other animal species who use them in the same way that we do. And we respond to those emotional expressions: seeing someone else smile can make us smile, and seeing someone cry can make us sad. But we can also fake expressions in order to deceive other people or conceal our emotions. In fact, the concealment and control of emotions, and thus facial expressions, are important skills and highly valued in a number of cultures around the world. The British stiff upper lip is an example of this.

Concealing one's emotions and maintaining controlled facial expressions are also examples of what sociologists call *face*. Here, face represents one's public persona or reputation, and losing face, for example, means taking a hit to one's persona. The concern with face in this sense is found especially throughout Asian societies, the very same societies, not coincidentally, to value the concealing of emotions through controlled facial expressions.

The face is so important that people whose faces are disfigured due to injury or disease find themselves socially stigmatized and unable to participate fully in society, even when they are otherwise healthy or normal. But what about when the area of the brain that allows for the recognition of faces is itself damaged? People with conditions that don't allow them to recognize other people's faces also find themselves socially damaged, unable to recognize, sometimes, their own family members. And people with forms of autism like Aspberger's Syndrome can recognize faces but cannot read facial expressions, making interaction with others that much more difficult. Even those with normal face recognition are not equally adept about recognizing all people's faces. We will tend to be conditioned to recognize the types of faces to which we have been exposed. The faces of ethnicities that are foreign to us, on the other hand, tend to appear more alike than different to us. In fact, learning to distinguish between different faces from another ethnic or racial group is one way to reduce racism.

Being able to correctly read the facial expressions of others is one reason why face-to-face communication is so valuable. In recent years, as that communication has lessened thanks to the telephone and computer, new ways of misunderstanding and insulting one another have emerged, as well as new ways to mitigate that. Emoticons, textual or graphical representations of facial expressions, have been developed to help us convey emotions when emailing or texting one another, which helps, at least a bit, to alleviate some of the misunderstandings that are so common in non-face-to-face communication.

In this encyclopedia, we will explore these issues in depth, and will cover the ways in which people adorn their faces, the cultural and religious beliefs and practices about the face, the importance of certain faces, how faces are represented artistically, and even the health problems associated with the face. Ultimately, we will take on the important roles that the face plays in society and culture.

Further Reading

Cleese, John, and Brian Bates. *The Human Face*. New York: Dorling Kindersley, 2001.

A

Acne

Acne vulgaris is a skin condition found in humans resulting in a variety of lesions forming on the skin, known as pimples. It is usually caused when the skin follicles are blocked because the sebaceous gland, attached to the follicle, is clogged with oil or sebum. Acne is most commonly found on the face, back, and chest, and is typically associated with adolescence, when increases in androgen levels cause an increase in oil production from the sebaceous glands, resulting in pimples: whiteheads or blackheads.

Other than pubescent hormones, diet and stress are two other common causes of acne, with some foods, and heightened stress levels, leading to an increase in sebum production. Foods associated with sebum production include chocolate, meat, dairy products, and fried and fatty foods. In addition, foods with a high glycemic index—those foods that cause the body to release large amounts of insulin—can also trigger a release of androgens, which can result in increased sebum production. Thus processed foods—especially foods made with refined white sugar and flour—may be a causative factor. In fact, the Western diet, rich in processed foods, may also be responsible for the earlier age of puberty in western countries, which itself may be linked to higher rates of acne among American adolescents.

People from cultures that consume few processed foods, few fatty foods, and little dairy products, as well as those who favor light oils such as olive or peanut, tend to have less acne than people in the United States, who have an extremely high incidence of acne. A 2002 study looked at residents from two countries, Paraguay and Papua New Guinea, with healthy diets and little incidence of acne. After moving to the United States and engaging in the Western diet, these populations developed acne. Other studies tracked people from Kenya, Nigeria, Japan, and Malaysia, and all found the same thing: when the diet changed from a natural diet to the Western-based diet high in processed and high glycemic foods, acne resulted.

Treatments for acne in the West typically involve chemical treatments such as benzoyl peroxide, which kills bacteria and opens up the pores, or topical retinoids, which prevent blockages, and for women, birth control pills, because the estrogen in the pills combats the testosterone that causes the increased sebum production.

Acupuncture is another treatment for acne, based on the premise that acne is caused by damp heat in the body, which is released by the application of acupuncture needles. Along with acupuncture, Traditional Chinese Medicine (TCM) involves the use of herbs to detoxify the blood as well as cooling foods such as cucumber, squash, melon, and celery (some topically applied, and others eaten), which are intended to counter the body's heat. Finally, many Western doctors and nutritionists advise patients to change their diets to eliminate foods that cause an outbreak, and especially to eliminate processed foods, fatty foods, and dairy from the diet.

See also Acupuncture; Facial Care

Further Reading

Cordain, Loren, Staffan Lindeberg, Magdalena Hurtado, Kim Hill, S. Boyd Eaton, and Jennie Brand-Miller. "Acne Vulgaris: A Disease of Western Civilization." *Archives of Dermatology* 138 (2002): 1584–90.

Juettner, Bonnie. *Acne*. Detroit: Lucent Books, 2010.

Acupuncture

Acupuncture is an ancient Eastern medical technique that uses the insertion of needles into the body to cure illness.

In **China**, where acupuncture is thought to have originated, it has been known as far back as the first millennium BCE. It has also been practiced for thousands of years in **Korea** and **Japan**, and was possibly practiced in Eurasia in the Bronze Age. It was first described in a 4,700-year-old Chinese medical text, *Yellow Emperor's Classic of Internal Medicine.*

Acupuncture is the practice of inserting very fine needles into the body at points called acupuncture points, or acupoints, in order to influence the physiological or emotional health of the body. Shen Nung, a third millennium BCE medical and agricultural scholar, came up with the theories that form the basis of modern acupuncture. He postulated that the body had an energy force running through it known as Qi, which includes spiritual, emotional, physical, and mental aspects. The Qi travels trough the body along special pathways or meridians, and if the Qi is unbalanced or lacks strength, or its travels are disrupted, ill health can occur. Nung felt that the Meridians come to the surface at specific locations in the body, which allowed them to be accessed in order to repair the Qi. These points of access are the acupoints, and can be accessed via the use of needles, as well as through acupressure and moxibustion, the burning of herbs over the skin. By balancing and repairing the Qi, the patient can be healed.

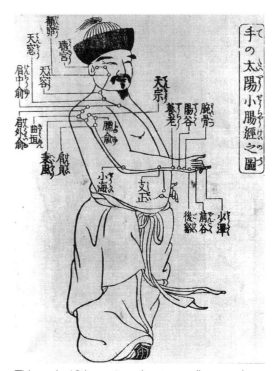

This early 18th-century Japanese diagram demonstrates some of the major acupuncture points, or acupoints, on the body. (National Library of Medicine)

Acupuncture, as well as other forms of Chinese medicine, is based on a very different understanding of health and the human body than Western medicine. The Western approach, for example, is oriented toward disease, with treatments aimed at eliminating or controlling disease, and sees diseases of the mind and body as being separate in origin and nature (and thus in treatment), resulting in a reductionist approach that views the body and mind as constituting a series of parts that can be healthy or sick. Chinese medicine, on the other hand, is a holistic approach that focuses not on disease or pathology but on wellness and balance. It sees the body as divided into several systems of function that correspond to physical organs, and illness is a result of systems being out of balance or harmony. The diagnosis of illness, then, is not associated with a certain organ or part being diseased, but of a systemic disorder, which must be treated on that basis.

Today, acupuncture is practiced not only throughout Asia but throughout the Western world as well, by practitioners who either combine acupuncture with traditional Western methods (in this case, the use of acupuncture is known as a complementary therapy), or those who practice only traditional Chinese techniques.

Acupuncture is used both on the face, and to treat conditions of the face. For example, **acne** is considered in Chinese medicine to be a disorder caused by an imbalance within the bodily organs, and in particular, an accumulation of heat. Acupuncture in this instance is not used on the face; rather, needles are placed on the acupoints that correspond to the organs causing the heat. For instance, the stomach, spleen, and lungs are all thought to produce heat and cause acne; therefore, placing needles onto the points that correspond to those organs (such as in the elbow or behind the knee) is a common approach. In addition, inserting needles into the ear is another way to dispel heat and dampness, and thus to relieve acne. As in Western medicine, stress is thought in Chinese medicine to be a contributing factor to acne; where that is the case, acupuncture needles will be used on the foot and above the ankle to combat stress. On the other hand, in some cases acupuncture needles are placed directly into the lesions, while another approach involves surrounding the lesions with acupuncture needles, which is known as surrounding the dragon.

In recent years, a form of acupuncture known as cosmetic acupuncture has become a popular alternative to a face lift. Known as facial rejuvenation treatments, this includes not only acupuncture but facial massage, herbal supplements, and dietary changes intended to improve the flow of blood into the face. Cosmetic acupuncture is intended to reverse some of the signs of **aging**— such as wrinkles, sagging jaw line, or under-eye bags—that have been caused due to stress, sun damage, poor nutrition, and exposure to toxins. Here, needles are inserted in to the acupoints associated with the face; for example, under eye circles are considered to be caused by weaknesses in the stomach or liver, so needles would be placed into the points associated with those organs. Some practitioners, on the other hand, insert the needles directly into points on the face, in order to decrease the signs of aging, increase blood flow, and decrease the signs of stress on the face.

See also Acne; Aging

Further Reading

Beijing College of Traditional Chinese Medicine. *Essentials of Chinese Acupuncture.* New York: Pergamon Press, 1981.

Ellis, Andrew, Nigel Wiseman, and Ken Boss. *Fundamentals of Chinese Acupuncture.* Brookline, MA: Paradigm Publications, 1991.

Wen, H. "Face Acupuncture." *International Journal of Clinical Acupuncture* 7, no. 3 (1996): 301.

African American

African Americans, or people whose ancestry derives, at least in part, from **Sub-Saharan Africa**, are often judged differently than other ethnic groups in terms of **beauty**, intelligence, trustworthiness, and other characteristics, and these racialized judgments often have to do with their faces.

For example, in the United States, standards of beauty have long emphasized European traits, such as light skin, petite facial features, and straight hair. Consequently, African Americans, whose facial features evolved in equatorial climates and thus tend to not only be dark skinned, but also to have broader noses and lips than Europeans, have been judged as less beautiful than Europeans. As a result of these beauty standards, skin whitening or bleaching products have long been used by African Americans in order to lighten their skin, not so that they could pass for white (although those with more Caucasian features sometimes could), but because going back to slavery, lighter skinned African Americans received better privileges than those with darker skin. This remains true today: studies show that both whites and African Americans continue to favor light skin and Caucasian facial features (yet paradoxically, those characteristics also cause light-skinned blacks to be judged as less "authentically" ethnic to the African American community). A quick look at the most popular African American celebrities also reveals that, for the women, most are relatively light skinned.

For African American men, the issue isn't so much beauty as it is safety. A recent study demonstrated that successful African American businessmen tend to have baby faces, or faces with smaller facial features, and that those features made their wearers seem warmer and less threatening, which led to their success. (The opposite was found to be true for white businessmen.) The results of this study demonstrate that for many whites, African Americans are still considered to be threatening, and it is only when their features are less African that they can be successful.

Throughout the history of the United States, blacks have been seen as threatening to whites, and one way that whites had of mitigating the supposed threat posted by blacks was to create stereotypes and **caricatures** of them.

During the 19th century, the minstrel show was a popular form of entertainment involving white actors wearing makeup to darken their faces, known as **blackface**. In blackface, the face is darkened using black theatrical makeup with the area around the eyes painted white, and the mouth painted red. This exaggerated image of African Americans became the basis of the primary caricature for African Americans, in which blacks were portrayed with inky black skin, huge bug eyes, and large, exaggerated red or pink lips over bright white teeth, and were shown to be lazy, ignorant buffoons. The picaninny, coon, and Sambo are all representations of this caricature, and these images served to shape white perceptions of blacks for over a century. Images like these were common on collectables, toys, kitchen and household items, and were commonly seen in cartoons, ads, and postcards. According to folklorists, these darky images, which depicted blacks as ignorant, primitive, and irresponsible, served to reinforce anti-black attitudes among white Americans. Even today, racist images of President Barack Obama, the nation's first African American president, proliferate, many showing him in exaggerated blackface.

The idea that African American faces are more threatening to whites has been proven in a number of studies that demonstrated that individuals of a variety of racial backgrounds—including African Americans—have a heightened fear response when shown photos of African Americans. Interestingly, one recent study showed that by teaching individuals to differentiate between different African American faces (as well as Asian faces), racial bias was lessened, as well as fear.

See also Blackface; Caricatures

Further Reading

Bond, Selena, and Thomas F. Cash. "Black Beauty: Skin Color and Body Images among African-American College Women." *Journal of Applied Social Psychology* 22, no. 11 (1992): 874–88.

Herring, Cedric, Verna Keith, and Hayward Derrick Horton. *Skin Deep: How Race and Complexion Matter in the "Color Blind" Era.* Chicago: University of Illinois Press, 2004.

Livingston, R., and N. Pearce. "The Teddy-Bear Effect: Does Having a Baby Face Benefit Black Chief Executive Officers?" *Psychological Science* (October 2009): 1229–36.

Russell, Kathy, Midge Wilson, and Ronald Hall. *The Color Complex: The Politics of Skin Color among African Americans.* New York: First Anchor Books, 1993.

Turner, Patricia A. *Ceramic Uncles and Celluloid Mammies: Black Images and Their Influence on Culture.* New York: Anchor Books, 1994.

Aging

All living creatures age, and the signs of aging are found in our bodies and faces. But how we deal with the signs of aging are very different and are culturally and historically specific.

Humans are considered to be old at different times in different cultures. In the United States, for example, we typically mark the senior years with the age of retirement at 65. But long before that time, our bodies are aging, and much of that aging can be seen in our faces.

The signs of aging include wrinkles, sun spots, drooping eyelids and jawlines, dry skin, and turkey necks. Much of this is caused by the changes in skin tone and texture as skin loses collagen during aging, leading to a loss in elasticity. In addition, facial fat begins to move around, leaving hollow pockets on the face that are exacerbated by bone loss. The signs of aging appear at different times for different ethnic groups. For instance, dark skin shows discoloration associated with aging much later than lighter skin, and wrinkles appear later in darker skinned people.

> I think your whole life shows in your face and you should be proud of that.—*Lauren Bacall*

In the United States, aging is seen by many, and especially by women, as something to be avoided. Because women in particular are valued in part by their appearance, aging is viewed very negatively for, and by, American women. The double standard of aging is not universal, however, and applies much more to Western cultures than to non-Western cultures. Many cultures value aging in both men and women because age brings wisdom and thus respect and status. In Japan, for example, reverence and respect for the elderly is a common value; the aging process is much less fraught with anxiety than in the United States. In fact, in most traditional agricultural societies, women and men both age naturally, applying little to no makeup and not attempting to hide their wrinkles. Aging is seen as a natural and normal process, and older people are honored for having lived so long and for the wisdom that they have obtained. Even in the United States, standards for aging differ. In the South, for example, well bred southern ladies maintain a higher standard of beauty than do women in other parts of the country, and that standard is not relaxed as they age. Older ladies are expected to continue to coif and color their hair, make up their faces, and maintain other grooming and beauty standards well into old age.

Two elderly Russian women. In some cultures, which value age over youth, elderly men and women are more respected than in the United States, where the opposite is true. (Magomed Magomedagaev/ Dreamstime.com)

In countries like the United States, there is an enormously profitable market in makeup, pharmaceuticals, and **cosmetic surgery,** which are intended to reverse or slow down the signs of aging on the face. In addition, a number of drugs have been shown to reverse the signs of aging in nonhuman animals, but they have so far not been used in humans. By far the most popular anti-aging products available today are cosmetics and surgical procedures. Cosmetics include anti-aging lotions, creams, and oils, which are intended to rejuvenate the skin and reduce the signs of aging. Surgical procedures include facelifts, brow lifts, botox injections, facial fat transfers, chemical face peels and laser resurfacing, cheek tightening, eyelid lifts, lip enlargement procedures, and injections of collagen or other fillers into the face to fill wrinkles or hollows. Other procedures include hormone injections and nutritional supplements. For the most part, women partake of these procedures, while men are left to age naturally. As with makeup and other ways of hiding the aging process, cosmetic surgery procedures do not actually reverse aging nor do they contribute to longer life; they simply camouflage the external signs of aging.

While the signs of a youthful face—full lips, large eyes, high cheekbones, clear skin—are thought by evolutionary psychologists to be universally appealing to men, because they signal fertility, it is not necessarily true that women exhibiting those signs are universally valued over women lacking them, such as older women. So while older women in other cultures may not be sought out or valued as sexual partners, because of the loss of their youth and beauty, they often achieve higher status later in life, once their reproductive years are over, signaling that physical beauty is not their sole defining feature. Men, on the other hand, do not typically, in other cultures, fear the signs of aging on the face; instead, they fear the loss of power and virility that often come with aging and are not seen on the face.

On the other hand, the fact that cultures around the world feature stories of witches who are almost universally female and old indicates that there is a stigma associated with aging women in other cultures. This is perhaps, because while aging often brings power in other cultures, in men that power is perceived as positive, while in women, it is anti-feminine, and thus masculine and dangerous.

See also Beauty; Gender

Further Reading

Ellingson, Stephen, and M. Christian Green. *Religion and Sexuality in Cross-Cultural Perspective.* New York: Routledge, 2002.

Roper Starch Worldwide and AARP. *Public Attitudes toward Aging, Beauty, and Cosmetic Surgery.* Washington, DC: AARP, 2001.

Animal Facial Expressions

Human **facial expressions**, and the emotions they express, have their roots in animal facial expressions. As early as 1872, Charles Darwin noted that emotions are seen in both the facial expressions of humans and of other animals, and while he was not the first to write on the subject, he was the first to make the claim that human facial expressions were not only universal but shared with other species, thereby proving humans and other animals have a shared genetic history. This claim was revolutionary at the time, given that most people still did not believe there was continuity between humans and other species, and still did not believe, until very recently, that nonhuman animals possessed emotions.

Nonhuman animal facial expressions differ from human expressions in important ways, however. Humans have more musculature (44 different muscles) in the face and scalp, allowing for a greater variety of expressions. In addition, humans have eyebrows, pronounced lips, and a more visible white region, or sclera, of the eye. Most animals, on the other hand, must use body language and vocalizations to supplement their facial expressions, and their faces alone cannot express as wide a range of emotions as ours. Some animals, such as reptiles (that are solitary animals), have virtually no facial expressions whatsoever; the scales covering their faces render them immobile. In addition, as the brain of a species gets more complex through evolution, that species' facial expressions become more complex. Finally, it is especially critical for social animals to express and communicate their emotions to others, as a way to regulate aggression, to maintain social relations, and to ensure reproduction. In fact, among primates, those animals that live in the biggest groups have the most mobile faces, and the greatest ability to read and interpret other animals' faces as well.

> If a dog will not come to you after having looked you in the face, you should go home and examine your conscience.—*Woodrow Wilson*

Social animals, like dogs and primates, need facial expressions in order to convey information to each other and in order to understand the emotions and intentions of other animals. And because humans use the face in this same way, to read the moods, emotions, and even the characters of others, the ability of nonhuman animals to show emotion through their face is crucial to humans' understanding of them and our relationships with them, especially with respect to companion animals.

Nonhuman primates, of all of the animals, can show the greatest range of emotions in their faces, due to their complicated facial musculature; chimpanzees, in particular, have facial muscles that are nearly identical to humans. In addition, in primates we see the shift in focus from the senses of hearing and smell to sight (and a corresponding reduction in the muscles associated with both smell and hearing); the emphasis on sight is another reason why primates' facial expressions are more finely attuned than in other species. (Prosimians, on the other hand, are primitive primates that can make relatively few facial expressions; this may be because they are primarily nocturnal, so seeing each others' faces is not very important to them.) Canines, too, have a wide range of facial expressions and use them, in conjunction with movements of the body, tail, ears, and limbs to demonstrate a wide variety of emotions. One explanation for why humans tend to bond so much more deeply with dogs than with cats lies in the cat's face: cats have fewer muscles in the face and thus cannot make as many expressions as can dogs. We instinctively interpret cats' lack of expressiveness as a sign that they do not have, or display, emotions. (Cats are a solitary species, which means that their need to show emotion on the face is not nearly as important as it is for social dogs.) Alternatively, we use our understanding of dogs' expressions, even when those understandings are incorrect, to better relate to them, because we think that we can detect their moods and intentions. Other species, such as reptiles or amphibians are even harder for us to read—they have extremely limited facial muscles and thus can create no facial expressions.

Chimpanzees, like other great apes, share many of the same facial expressions with humans. (Dreamstime.com)

For example, many dogs display what humans often interpret as a smile: they pull their lips back and show their teeth. Wolves use the smile as a form of submissive behavior, to demonstrate to a more dominant wolf that they are not threatening, and alpha wolves do not do this. Domesticated dogs who smile are probably doing it for the same reason: to demonstrate submission. However, because dogs have co-evolved alongside humans, and have finely attuned their behavior to human contexts, many dogs probably smile because they know humans like it and will reward it with affection. Likewise, pulling the lips back to show the canines serves, in both wolves and dogs, to demonstrate threatening behavior to other animals. Facial expressions like these, whether or not they are combined with body language or vocalizations, are easily read by animals of the same species, as well as animals of different species, including humans. When they are combined with vocalizations, this is known as redundancy, and ensures the message is received. (Some animals go even further and have facial markings that accentuate their expressions and also differentiate between closely related species living in the same region. For instance, the mangabey, an African monkey, has pure white upper eyelids, which make a threatening face seem scarier when the eyelids are closed.)

Since Darwin's time, scholars have been studying the evolutionary roots of both human language and other communication forms, including facial expressions. Studies involving nonhuman primates demonstrate that there is a correspondence between facial expressions and vocalizations, and that primates are able to correlate the proper vocalization with the proper facial expression. This may represent an evolutionary precursor to humans' ability to join human speech with facial expressions.

Darwin himself posited that the facial expressions of humans and other animals all have a functional basis: we show happiness by lifting the face and tightening the upper lip, which derives from preparing for a play bite; while we show anger through tightening the facial and mouth muscles, in preparation for an aggressive bite. Affection is expressed through the lips, whether through kissing, lip smacking, or sucking, and derives from the suckling of an infant to the mother's breast; and surprise is expressed through widening the eyes and the mouth, and rearing back in a protective stance. Darwin called these actions intention movements, or the incomplete or preparatory phase of noncommunicative activities like attack, play, or protection. On the other hand, other expressions are known as reversed signals, such as the submissive gaze aversion that is the opposite of the aggressive stare.

Of the six emotions found to be universally expressed in all humans via facial expression—anger, sadness, fear, surprise, happiness, and disgust—most have a corresponding facial expression and emotion in nonhuman primates, and in particular, in apes. Sadness and anger both have direct correspondences in ape facial expressions, and fear and surprise are found in a number of facial expressions. The human smile has a number of meanings when used by apes—it could indicate fear, submission, reassurance, or affection. On the other

hand, pure happy excitement is shown in the ape's play face, used when the ape is being playful. Disgust may be a purely human expression, however, without a primate equivalent.

And while in animals, as in humans, the expression of emotions via facial expressions is relatively invariable, the context in which those emotions are cued and expressed is very context specific, and has to do with socialization, individual relationships, and other factors. For example, we are able to better read the facial expressions of those with whom we are intimate. In addition, humans can mask our emotions by using a false facial expression, and many animals can do this too, as is seen when an animal with a blank face sneaks up on another in order to pounce on them in a play attack. Finally, like humans, nonhuman animals—especially primates—can mimic the facial expressions of other animals. Orangutans, for example, when playing with other orangutans, will almost immediately respond to a play-smile with one of their own.

See also Facial Expressions

Further Reading

Bruce, Vicki, and Andrew W. Young. *In the Eye of the Beholder: The Science of Face Perception.* Oxford: Oxford University Press, 1998.

Chevalier-Skolnikoff, Suzanne. "Facial Expression of Emotion in Nonhuman Primates." In *Darwin and Facial Expression: A Century of Research in Review*, edited by Paul Ekman, 11–89. Cambridge, MA: Malor Books, 2006.

Darwin, Charles. *The Expression of the Emotions in Man and Animals.* Chicago: University of Chicago Press, 1965.

Fridlund, Alan J. *Human Facial Expression: An Evolutionary View.* San Diego: Academic Press, 1994.

Hauser, Marc D. *The Design of Animal Communication.* Cambridge, MA: MIT Press, 1999.

Anthropometry and Craniometry

Anthropometry is the measurement of the human body from living people and from the skeletal remains of the deceased; while craniometry is the measurement of the skull bones. Craniofacial anthropometry refers to the use of scientific measuring tools to measure the skull and face. Both anthropometry and craniometry derive from physical anthropology and have been primarily used to understand physical variation among humans, although anthropometry can also be used to understand other issues, like human evolution and how nutrition impacts the body. Both have been used to classify people on the basis of **race** and to justify the racial superiority of whites.

Anthropometry has been used by criminologists and those interested in finding a biological origin to criminal behavior. European criminologists once thought that criminal behavior was a biological condition, and that furthermore, a person's physical appearance could indicate their disposition to crime. The idea that a person's character can be interpreted by looking at his or her face is derived from ancient times, but was codified into two 19th-century theories called **physiognomy and phrenology**, which postulated that the shape of the skull and the facial characteristics could reveal an individual's personality and psychological development. But unlike phrenology, which focused on the facial features, anthropometry and craniometry were considered to be more rigorous approaches, involving strict measurements of facial, skull, and body parts. For example, 19th-century criminologist Cesare Lombroso was an advocate of this approach and examined the heads and bodies of hundreds of criminals in order to ascertain the physical characteristics shared by criminals. Not surprisingly, he found that a number of traits, such as a sloping forehead and high cheekbones, were found more commonly in criminals.

Anthropometric measurements of the face were also used to classify people on the basis of race in the early 20th century, and to provide a scientific basis to prevailing theories about the racial inferiority of minorities—especially African Americans.

In Nazi Germany as well, the Nazis measured the size and shape of Jews' skulls, and, using calipers, measured the size of their facial features in order to classify them and determine their background. In the 1930s, prior to the final solution, masks were made from Jews' faces in order to further help with classification. The Nazis believed large facial features meant people were closer to animals; the size of a person's ears or nose (combined with the color of their eyes) could very well determine whether he or she was sent to the concentration camps.

Craniometry, too, was used to justify racial and eugenic theories. Eighteenth century Dutch anatomist Petrus Camper

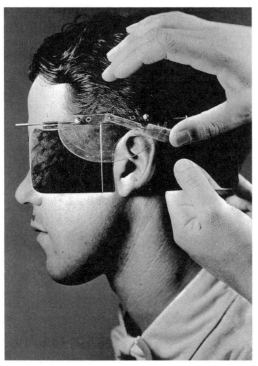

The facial features of a young German are measured during a racial examination at the Kaiser Wilhelm Institute for Anthropology. Exams like these were one way in which the Nazis tried to determine who was of Jewish or Aryan descent. (United States Holocaust Memorial Museum)

gence. His data showed that whites had the largest brains, and thus were the most intelligent, followed by Asians, Native Americans, and Africans. Morton's work was used to prove the theory of polygeny—that the different races of humans evolved separately. It has since been shown that Morton's data were manipulated and even faked to fit his hypothesis.

See also Physiognomy and Phrenology; Race

Further Reading

Dain, Bruce R. *A Hideous Monster of the Mind: American Race Theory in the Early Republic*. Cambridge, MA: Harvard University Press, 2002.

Gould, Stephen Jay. *The Mismeasure of Man*. New York: Norton, 1996.

Lombroso, Cesare. *Criminal Man*. Raleigh, NC: Duke University Press, 2006.

Artistic Representation

Humans have been representing faces in art since humans began making art. But representations of human faces are not universally found in art; some cultures, for example, tend to favor art that is nonrepresentational, and other cultures ban the portrayal of certain faces, or human faces in general.

Cave paintings and petroglyphs from the Upper Paleolithic period represent the earliest forms of artistic representation that have survived today, but interestingly, the oldest of these, the cave paintings found from about 10,000–32,000 years ago in France and Spain, do not contain images of humans at all, which may indicate a prohibition against the representations of

claimed the races could be distinguished by the angle at which the forehead slopes to the nose and jaw; whites had the most refined angle with Africans having an angle closer to apes, demonstrating their evolutionary inferiority. French anthropologist Georges Vacher de Lapouge wrote in the late 19th century that Aryans could be determined by the relatively long, thin shape of their skulls while Jews' skulls were short and broad. Also in the 19th century, physician Samuel Morton collected hundreds of skulls to show different skull sizes (and thus cranial capacities, or brain size) could be correlated to different levels of intelli-

humans at that time and in those cultures. African cave paintings, however, which date between 3,000 and 25,000 years ago, often do represent humans, as do Indian cave paintings, which date to about 12,000 years ago. In neither case, though, do we find close ups of the human face.

Petroglyphs (or rock engravings), on the other hand, do contain images of humans, and have been found in Africa, Europe, Asia, Australia, and the Americas. For example, the Ancestral Puebloan peoples of the American Southwest left thousands of petroglyphs behind, and many do represent, very roughly, the human form and the human face.

The first realistic representation of a human face probably dates to 25,000 years ago with the *Venus of Brassempouy*, an ivory figure found in France. The figure is naturalistic, showing a female figure with long plaited hair, deep-set eyes, and no mouth. It was probably not until the Ancient Egyptian civilization that portraits of individual people—mostly pharaohs and their families—were created.

The representation of the human form in art has been found in the classical civilizations of Mesopotamia, **Egypt**, Persia, Greece, and Rome, as well as in the civilizations of **China, Japan**, **India**, and the pre-Columbian civilizations of **Central America** and **South America**. Other cultures, on the other hand, have never emphasized representations of either the human form or the human face in their art. Islamic cultures, for example, rarely include humans in their art, because it is considered to be a form of idolatry; this is one reason why **masks** are so rare in Muslim cultures today. In addition, Sunni Muslims do not allow visual depictions of the prophet Mohammed; other traditions allow for his depiction, as long as his face is concealed.

> Are we to paint what's on the face, what's inside the face, or what's behind it?—*Pablo Picasso*

When the human face is represented in art, it may or may not be represented naturalistically. For instance, ancient Egyptian paintings and sculptures of the human face were highly stylized, symbolic, and also lacked depth perception. (Foreigners, on the other hand, were represented much more realistically in Egyptian art.) Skin color, for example, was not intended to replicate true skin color, but to symbolize different types of people. Faces were usually captured in profile, with the eyes depicted from the front, a technique known as frontalism. Egyptian faces were always depicted as calm; smiles and other **facial expressions** were rare. Even the classic Greek sculpture or painting represents the ideal standard, rather than real life, with the angles of the face more pronounced than are found in nature. For example, the head of the sculpture of Aphrodite embodies the idealized facial proportions of the Greeks, and the Romans continued with the representation of ideal faces, rather than real faces. Greek art captured, for the most part, deities and not real people. Another common representation of faces from the classical era were the painted wooden portraits found on mummies in Roman-occupied Egypt. These were paintings of the faces of the dead used to cover the faces of the mummified bodies and were rendered in a naturalistic Greco-Roman style, featuring shading to indicate three-dimensionality, rather than Egyptian style. These mummy portraits were among the earliest examples of portraits of individual people.

After the fall of the Roman Empire, Medieval European art emphasized biblical characters representing Jesus, Mary, and other church leaders, using realistic styles. That it was religious figures, which were painted and sculpted most during this period, should come as no surprise because the Catholic Church was responsible for commissioning most of the major artwork of the period.

Art from **Sub-Saharan Africa**, too, has long featured human faces, and those also tend to be represented in a more stylized fashion. For instance, the Segou artistic style of the Bambara of Mali includes distinctively flat faces with arrow-shaped noses. African artwork tends to be sculptural, so three-dimensional representations of bodies and heads are common, and could be of gods, chiefs, and ordinary people. One of the most common forms of African art is the wooden mask, which depicts humans, animals, or supernatural creatures, and would be used for ritual purposes. Whether mask or sculpture, representations of African faces often include common African ornamentation, such as **scarification** or lip plates.

In the New World, a number of civilizations created art featuring humans or anthropomorphic deities. For instance, the Olmec of Central America created tall sculptures of heads, and in Peru, a variety of cultures from the Chavin civilization to the Inca created art featuring human faces.

The Moche, for instance, created vases with life-like, individual human portraits on them, probably representing elites, warriors, and famous craftsmen; and the Chimú, another Peruvian culture that predated the Inca, created portraits in gold and other precious metals.

Human faces have long been captured in the art of Asian countries. Deities were common in Buddhist artwork of Japan and China, with paintings and sculptures of the Buddha an extremely common art form. Japanese art is known to convey faces with very little facial expression, which is most likely linked to the well-known Japanese concern with face, the sociological concept by which people mask their feelings in order to maintain social conventions. Japanese art is also more general—images of faces do not represent particular people, and thus lack defining personal characteristics.

This can be contrasted to Western portraiture that is based on the idea of capturing, as realistically as possible, an individual person's likeness. Whether via painting or photography, Western portraits attempt to represent an individual person as realistically as possible, and usually involve the subject facing the painter or photographer directly. Paintings of individual people—both commoners and royalty—became more common in the late Middle Ages and Renaissance, as new artistic techniques as well as new paints allowed for more realistic portrayals of the subjects, while painters like Leonardo da Vinci emphasized the perfection of the human form in their portraits. Da Vinci, for example, used the rule of fifths when capturing the face, in which the ideal face is divided into

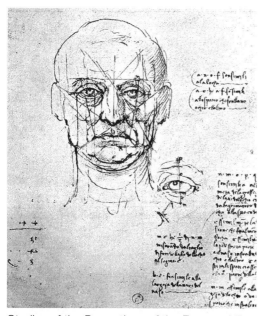

Studies of the Proportions of the Face and Eye, 1489–1490 (pen and ink over metalpoint on paper), Leonardo da Vinci (1452–1519). Da Vinci used the rule of fifths when capturing the face, in which the ideal face is divided into five equal eye widths. (Biblioteca Nazionale, Turin, Italy/The Bridgeman Art Library)

five equal eye widths. Other Renaissance artists followed da Vinci's lead in defining and representing ideal facial proportions in their paintings.

Starting in the 18th century, regular people were able to commission portraits—usually in miniature—of loved ones, leading to the wide dissemination of portraits in Europe and the United States. With the development of photography, photographic portraits soon replaced painted portraits for the middle class, and it soon became the norm for families to have photos of family members in the home. While these photos originally were taken of the whole body or the upper body, they later began to emphasize the face more than the body.

Today, many computer users have an avatar, which is a cartoon, photograph, or animated icon, which represents the user when instant messaging, or posting to blogs or Internet forums. It is often a likeness of the user's own face, but can be an image of a celebrity or cartoon person. When playing computer games, avatars are three-dimensional representations of either the face or the whole body.

See also Egypt; Facebook; Greco-Roman Cultures; Japan; Sub-Saharan Africa

Further Reading

McCormick, James P. "Japan: The Mask and the Mask-Like Face." *Journal of Aesthetics and Art Criticism* 15, no. 2 (1956): 198–204.

Strickland, Carol, and John Boswell. *The Annotated Mona Lisa: A Crash Course in Art History from Prehistoric to Post-Modern*. Kansas City, MO: Andrews and McMeel, 1992.

White, Randall. "The Women of Brassempouy: A Century of Research and Interpretation." *Journal of Archaeological Method and Theory* 13, no. 4 (2006): 250–303.

Ash Wednesday

For Catholics and some Protestants, Ash Wednesday is the first day of Lent, and follows Fat Tuesday, the last day of **Mardi Gras**, which is the celebratory period leading up to Lent. Lent is the 40-day period leading up to Easter when believers fast or deny themselves something as a way of paying penance for their sins and preparing for the celebration of Jesus's resurrection. Ash Wednesday is intended to be a day on which the faithful fast, repent, confess, and contemplate their sins.

On Ash Wednesday, the faithful are anointed on their foreheads with the sign of the cross made of ashes mixed with blessed oil to show the repentance of their sins. This act recalls the ancient Near Eastern practice of sitting in ashes or sprinkling ashes onto oneself as a sign of mourning or repentance. This is seen in the biblical passage in Samuel 13:19, in which Tamar placed ashes on her head while crying, and more specifically, as in Nehemiah 9:1 when the people of Ninevah showed their repentance by wearing sackcloth and ashes. Ashes were also mentioned in Job 42:6 ("I abhor myself, and repent in dust and ashes") and Jeremiah 6:26 ("O daughter of my people, wallow thyself in ashes"). Finally, the placement of ashes directly on the forehead is addressed in Ezekiel 9:4 in which Gold said to a man dressed in linen, "Go throughout the city of Jerusalem and put a mark on the foreheads of those who grieve and lament over all the detestable things that are done in it." God then directed that those without the mark, in other words, those without repentance, be killed. The mark, then, was the mark of the righteous.

Worshippers wear the cross on their foreheads until the ashes wear off naturally. Ideally, the ashes are taken from the palms saved from the previous year's Palm Sunday celebration, in which palm fronds are blessed and distributed to church members, which recalls the Gospel story of Jesus's arrival in Jerusalem on a donkey and the residents laying palm branches before him. *See also* Christianity

Further Reading

Bellinzoni, Arthur J. *The Old Testament: An Introduction to Biblical Scholarship.* Amherst, NY: Prometheus Books, 2009.

Australia and New Zealand

Australia and New Zealand are Oceanic island nations, both colonized by England in 1788. Prior to colonization, aboriginal peoples had lived in Australia for at least 40,000 years, whereas the indigenous population of New Zealand, the Maori, only arrived on that island in about 1300 CE, from the islands of Eastern Polynesia.

Indigenous Australians do not have many traditional practices that relate to the face, with the exception of tooth avulsion, in which one or two of a young man's upper incisors are knocked out during his initiation ritual. Body painting is another example, whereby aboriginal people paint their bodies and faces with ochre in elaborate designs of stripes, circles, and dots—usually linked to social position and clan status—for ritual purposes. While Aboriginal Australian art, which includes sand paintings, petroglyphs, rock paintings, carvings, weavings, sculptures, and bark paintings, does include representations of humans; there is very little representative art that features human faces. However, some rock art in Australia does show people wearing animal **masks**, indicating that the ancestors of modern indigenous Australians may have worn masks, perhaps during Shamanic rituals.

The native people of New Zealand, the Maori, are known around the world for their facial tattooing, known as the **moko**. The moko is the curvilinear facial tattoo worn by Maori men and women as a sign of status as well as affiliation, and only high status Maori and warriors at one time were tattooed.

Aboriginal elder Major Sumner performs a ritual dance in Liverpool, England, May 13, 2009, wearing traditional face paint. (AP/Wide World Photos)

The tattoo design was first drawn onto the skin, and then carved into the skin with a tool known as *uhi whaka tataramoa*. After cutting the skin, pigment was rubbed into the wounds. The procedure was said to be incredibly painful, and caused so much facial swelling that, after tattooing, the person could not eat normally, and had to be fed liquids through a funnel. A woman's moko, which covered the chin and lips, could take one or two days to complete. A man's moko, which covered the whole face, was done in stages over several years and was an important rite of passage for a Maori man; without the moko, a man was said to not be a complete person.

Unlike tattoos in Polynesia and elsewhere, which have designs that are worn by everyone of the same tribe, clan, or rank, Maori tattoos were totally individual. While they did indicate a man's social and kinship position, marital status, and other information, each moko was like a fingerprint, and no two were alike. Maori chiefs even used drawings of their moko as their signature in the 19th century. Because the moko in part signified rank, different designs on both men and women could be read as relating to their family status, and each of the Maori social ranks carried different designs. In addition, some women who, due to their genealogical connections, were extremely high status could wear part of the male moko.

See also Face Painting; Moko

Further Reading

Friedlander, Marti, and Michael King. *Moko: Maori Tattooing in the Twentieth Century*. Auckland, New Zealand: David Bateman, 1999.

Gathercole, Peter. "Contexts of Maori Moko." In *Marks of Civilization,* edited by Arnold Rubin, 171–78. Los Angeles: Museum of Cultural History, UCLA, 1988.

Meggitt, M. J. *Desert People: A Study of the Walbiri Aborigines of Central Australia.* Sydney: Angus and Robertson, 1986.

Nicholas, Thomas, ed. *Tattoo: Bodies, Art and Exchange in the Pacific and the West.* Durham, NC: Duke University Press, 2005.

Simmons, D. R. *Ta Moko: The Art of Maori Tattoo.* Auckland, New Zealand: Reed Books, 1986.

B

Baptism

Baptism is a Christian ritual in which an infant, or, in some traditions, an adult who is converting to the faith, is anointed with, or dunked into, water, in order to be admitted into the Church. It is one of the seven sacraments of the Catholic Church.

Baptism derives from the New Testament story of John the Baptist, who may have been Jesus's cousin, who baptized Jesus by pouring water over him while he stood in the River Jordan. At that time, John baptized Jews as a way for them to repent of their sins. From the time of Jesus onward, baptism became the primary ritual by which someone converted to **Christianity**. The ritual most likely derived from the ancient practice of washing one's hands before a meal, as well as from purification practices found throughout the ancient world, including **Judaism**. Baptism is mentioned in the Gospels, as well as Acts, which recount that after his resurrection, Jesus instructed his disciples to baptize the nations in his name.

Today, the practice of Baptism varies among Christian denominations. While originally, adults were baptized, over time the practice shifted to baptizing children and, ultimately, infants in the Middle Ages. Most Catholic and Protestant groups practice affusion, which means pouring holy water over the head of the disciple, but sometimes aspersion, or sprinkling water

onto the head, is practiced. Immersing the disciple in a body of water is practiced by Mormons, and submersion, in which the entire body is covered in water, is practiced in the Eastern Orthodox Church, by Seventh Day Adventists, and many evangelical and born-again groups. Today, most Christian denominations baptize infants, but Baptists, Pentecostals, Mormons, and a variety of born-again traditions only baptize adults or older children, because only adults are able to profess their faith

Stained glass in a Catholic church in Dublin showing the baptism of Jesus, which forms the basis of the Catholic sacrament. (Jaroslaw Baczewski/Dreamstime.com)

in Jesus. In addition, these groups do not believe that baptism can wipe away sin; it is purely a visible sign of faith.

See also Christianity

Further Reading

Johnson, Paul. *A History of Christianity*. New York: Simon & Schuster, 1995.

Beauty

The concept of human beauty is largely focused on the face. According to evolutionary psychologists, what we call beauty is really just the biological signs of youth, health, and fertility. We can also look at beauty in a cross-cultural context, where it represents cultural values and practices rather than universal norms.

From an evolutionary perspective, there are a number of physical features that both men and women are programmed to find beautiful, including clean, unblemished skin; thick, shiny hair; and symmetrical faces; the Greeks especially valued faces that were symmetrical, in harmony and proportion. The ideal Greek face, for example, was two-thirds as wide as it was high, and was divided into thirds vertically, from chin to upper lip, from upper lip to eyes, and from eyes to hairline. In the Renaissance, a mathematical concept called the Golden Ratio, Golden Mean, or Golden Section was thought to provide the mathematical model for the most beautiful face.

Faces that are average, rather than extreme, also tend to be ranked most attractive in cross-cultural studies. These features are considered beautiful because they signify good health and good genes. Facial features that are unusual are often judged more beautiful than those that are not; rarity then can often indicate beauty. Unusual facial features are certainly noticed more often than those that are average.

From an evolutionary perspective, beauty is simply a combination of features that indicate both youth and fertility. In that sense, beauty is temporary—even the most beautiful woman will become old, losing what made her beautiful. In addition, according to evolutionary theory, men are programmed to find attractive women with full lips and narrow jaws because those features signify low testosterone and high estrogen, which are indicators of fertility. High cheekbones signal that a woman has reached fertility. Large eyes, too, signal youth, and thus fertility. During the 16th and 17th centuries, for example, European women put eye drops from the belladonna plant (*bella donna* means beautiful lady in Italian) into their eyes to make their retinas appear larger; today, it is popular in **Korea** to wear big eye contacts to make the eyes appear larger. And it was popular in Greece, Persia, and Rome to use the powdered form of the metal antimony in the eyes to make the whites sparkle.

Since women are considered beautiful when they display a set of features that indicate both youth (big eyes) and fertility (high cheekbones), they display a combination of adult beauty and baby beauty. Cuteness, on the other hand, refers primarily to baby beauty, and features a small face, big eyes, a small mouth, and a large head. Parental love is triggered by the presence of these features, which is why they are present in all mammal babies. They are also highlighted in some areas of popular culture, and especially pop culture from **Japan**, like anime, manga, Hello Kitty, and Ulzzang from Korea.

Women are thought to look for indicators of high testosterone in men's faces, such as strong jaws, heavy brows, thin lips, and broad cheekbones, which indicate both good genes as well as the propensity to attain high status. However, studies show that women who are not ovulating respond less well to a hyper-masculine face, and that women are attracted to different types of faces when they are looking for short-term, rather than long-term, relationships. Facial **scars**, for example, may be considered more attractive by women seeking short term sexual relationships, although they are generally considered to be a sign of an untrustworthy or dangerous person.

The idea that beauty is universal is demonstrated in studies showing that men and women of many different cultures tend to assess the attractiveness of people in photos very similarly. In addition, other studies have demonstrated that infants, when presented with photos of either unattractive or attractive adults, will spend more time looking at the photos of the attractive people; in particular, they appear to like big eyes, big lips, and clear skin. In fact, scientists have been able to quantify what makes a face attractive. There is an ideal measurement for the space between the eyes, the length of the chin, the height of the eyes, the length and width of the nose, and the width and shape of the mouth. Another feature that some scientists think we look for when evaluating a potential mate is similarity to our own appearance. Apparently, we look for faces that resemble our own.

There is a tremendous variety in the types of features that societies around the world find beautiful, indicating that beauty is also culturally constructed. For instance, in **India**, the traditional ideals of beauty include cleanliness, the graceful use of clothing, how a woman carries herself, whether her skin and hair is well cared for, and the wearing of the **bindi** on the forehead. In many African cultures, on the other hand, unadorned skin is seen as unattractive, and only a woman whose body or face is marked through **scarification** would be considered beautiful—the scars are both beautiful to touch and to look at. Also popular in some African tribes were large plates inserted into the lower lip (and sometimes the upper as well), which made a woman more beautiful and marriageable. While the European long nose came to signify beauty around the world after colonization, people in Malaysia, the Philippines, and Indonesia considered flat noses to be the most attractive. And for hundreds of years in Japan, the ideal of female beauty was symbolized by the **geisha**, who wore thick, white face paint, shaved her eyebrows, and painted on both eyebrows and rosebud lips. Women in a variety of cultures, from Renaissance Europe to Native Americans to the Japanese, also blackened their teeth.

One aspect of culture that plays a strong role in standards of beauty is economics. In many societies, a body that signifies elite status is considered the most beautiful. So very light skin would be considered beautiful when darker skin is a sign of working outdoors; conversely, darker skin became beautiful as wealthy people could afford to travel to warmer climates

Actress Aishwarya Rai arrives for *The Da Vinci Code* premiere at the Palais des Festivals as part of the 59th Cannes Film Festival on May 17, 2006, in Cannes, France. She represents ideal female beauty in the early 21st century. (Denis Makarenko/Dreamstime.com)

during the winter. (Light skin also demonstrates certain illnesses better than dark skin, so light-skinned people would be less likely to conceal illness.) So both Roman and Elizabethan women used makeup made from white lead on their faces. Elizabethan women sometimes would allow themselves to be bled to further whiten their complexions, and in the 18th century, French noblewomen drew blue veins on their necks and shoulders to emphasize the whiteness of their skin. European colonialism heightened the equation of light skin with beauty, but it existed in many cultures prior to colonialism. For instance, in India, the features associated with high castes, that is fairer skin and long, straight noses, have long been considered most attractive and are still sought after in potential brides, while darker skin and rounder noses are considered undesirable. **Skin bleaching** creams and powders have been popular for hundreds of years in Africa, India, and throughout East Asia. The preference for light skin is gendered, however; many cultures prefer men who are darker, even while they value lighter-skinned women. Even with a partial preference for darker-skinned men, the upper classes of most cultures still tend to have lighter skin than the lower classes.

Because of the dominance of Western standards of beauty around the world due to the dominance of Western media, some Western standards of beauty—such as round eyes—are now becoming highly sought after in other cultures. Because of this, some Asian cultures now value Caucasian-looking eyes, making blepharoplasty, a cosmetic surgery procedure to insert a crease into the **epicanthic fold,** a very popular procedure in some East Asian countries today. In Korea, where the standard of beauty means round eyes, pale skin, a sharp nose, and long legs (none of which are naturally found in Koreans), this surgery is so popular that 1 in 10 adults have received it. In addition, many Asians are now having surgery to make their noses longer and more pronounced and to reduce the size of the cheekbones.

Whether beauty is biologically programmed or culturally constructed, it is important in human societies, and not only plays a role in whether a man or a woman achieves a mate, but in contemporary

Western society, beauty plays a role in how much money people earn in their lifetime, how early they will marry, how soon they will be promoted, and whether they will be experience other benefits based on their physical appearance. Studies show, for example, that strangers are more likely to assist attractive people than nonattractive people, and attractive people are less likely to be arrested or prosecuted for crimes. The halo effect shows that in general, beautiful people are judged by others to be smarter, more popular, and better adjusted; those with beauty have a halo around them. Ultimately, this becomes a self-fulfilling prophecy as beautiful people are not only judged more successful and happier—they become happier and more successful because of how they are treated. Because of the importance of beauty, **cosmetic surgery** has become much more popular in contemporary society. In the East, too, beauty is linked to finding a good partner and a competitive job, especially in the business world. For many people around the world today, beauty means happiness.

Beauty is also gendered, in that not only are there different standards of beauty for men and women, but women, especially in modern society, are held to a much higher and more difficult (some would say impossible) standard to attain than men, which explains the multi-billion-dollar **cosmetics** industry and the thousands of products available to make a woman's face appear more youthful and more beautiful.

As women in the past few decades have experienced unprecedented levels of financial, political, and social independence and clout, they have also been assaulted by increasing numbers of images and messages about their appearance. As the messages increase and the standards of beauty became harder to attain, the numbers of eating disorders skyrocket; the diet industry balloons; cosmetic surgery rates take off; and girls' and women's self-esteem plummets.

Today, being deemed unattractive or overweight has very real consequences, as women who don't meet certain beauty standards find that they earn less (about 13 percent less), will get promoted less, and will get hired less often, than thinner or more attractive women. They will also have less luck finding marital partners, while attractive women, on the other hand, will not only be more likely to find a partner, but will be more likely to marry into a wealthy family. Studies show that people view unattractive people unfavorably, while attractive people are thought to be smarter, happier, and better people. Beauty continues to be a major standard by which women are judged, and is associated with a woman's self-esteem, chances of happiness, and upward mobility.

While beauty was once rare, today, because of the rise of cosmetic surgery, it is more easily accessible than ever. The prevalence of beauty today is said to decrease men's commitment to their regular partner because there are so many beautiful women to choose from.

See also Cosmetic Surgery; Cosmetics; Gender

Further Reading

Rhodes, Gillian, and Leslie Zebrowitz, eds. *Facial Attractiveness: Evolutionary, Cognitive, and Social Perspectives.* Westport, CT: Ablex Publishing, 2002.

Scruton, Roger. *Beauty.* Oxford: Oxford University Press, 2009.

Zebrowitz, Leslie. *Reading Faces: Window to the Soul?* Boulder, CO: Westview Press, 1997.

Bindi

The *bindi* is the dot worn on the forehead of Hindu women in South Asian countries like India and Bangladesh. It can be made of powder, makeup, can be adhered with a plastic or felt sticker, or can be a form of jewelry. It is related to the *tilaka,* which is worn by both men and women and, unlike the bindi, is worn as a form of adornment and is used for religious purposes. Traditionally, the bindi, like the tilaka, was most commonly red, but today it can be found in multiple colors.

The word *bindi* is derived from *bindu,* which means drop or round in Sanskrit. Originally, the bindi (like the tilaka) was worn exclusively for religious purposes as well as to mark status on the wearer, with

the earliest recorded accounts of the bindi coming from at least the third century, in such religious texts as the *Puranas.* Bindis were originally made from vermillion or kumkum powder, or sometimes were simply leaves that were cut and pasted onto the head. For instance, married women once wore the bindi to signify their marital status, with red bringing good fortune. Along with the bindi, married women also wore (and still wear) a red mark in their hair part to demonstrate their marital status; this mark was once given by the bridegroom. (These practices may have evolved out of earlier traditions of offering blood sacrifices to the gods.) Widows must stop wearing both red marks after the death of their husband, and many women stop wearing their bindis during mourning for a deceased relative. While wearing the bindi is optional in most of the Hindu world, in some locations it is mandatory for married women to continue to wear it.

The bindi also may have been used at one time to represent ethnic affiliation and other features of social status such as caste

Tilaka

The tilaka is worn by men and women in South Asia (and in South Asian immigrant communities) to demonstrate religious piety, either on special ritual occasions, or every day, and by both priests and lay people. Like the bindi, the tilaka symbolizes the third eye and spiritual enlightenment. Traditionally, the tilaka was most commonly red, but today it can be found in multiple colors, and can be made of sandalwood paste, ashes, clay, or herbs. Different sects, as well as different castes, may wear different colors, and the mark may appear either round or as a line down the forehead and nose. Adherents of the god Shiva wear the tilaka as a series of horizontal lines across the forehead bisected by a vertical line or circle. Unlike the bindi, which can be bought as a sticker or form of jewelry, the tilaka must always be made of paste or powder.

This Indian girl wears a bindi on her forehead. The bindi has religious, social, and decorative functions for Hindus. (Indianeye/Dreamstime.com)

for both men and women. While it is not used as a caste distinction today, it may be that only high status men and women wore a mark on their forehead, or that color or shape distinguished which caste a person belonged to. Even today, priests still wear a mark on their heads to distinguish their own position. In addition, the manner in which the mark was worn may have indicated whether a person was a follower of a particular god.

In the Hindu context, the bindi signifies the third eye or the sixth **chakra**, known as *Ajna*. The sixth chakra is correlated with intuition, clear thinking, and psychic abilities, such as the ability to see into the future. In Hinduism, the seven chakras refer to seven energy centers in the body, and the sixth chakra is where

the body's latent or *kundalini* energy leaves the body. The red bindi worn on that spot retains that energy and increases concentration and protects against bad luck. Today it is still common for priests to mark visitors to a Hindu temple with a mark on their forehead made of red powder.

The bindi is now primarily a decorative item for Hindu women of all ages, many of whom choose the color to match the color of the sari they are wearing. In addition, bindis are now decorated with sequins, rhinestones, and other decorations, and are occasionally worn by non-Hindus, especially in South Asia. They can be in a circular shape, an oval, a triangle, a diamond, or a straight line. According to a Hindu proverb, "a woman's beauty is multiplied one thousand times when she wears a bindi." With the rise of Indian television shows and Bollywood movies, the bindi has been popularized around the world, and American celebrities like Madonna and Gwen Stefani have popularized it in the West.
See also Chakras

Further Reading

Editors of *Hinduism Today* Magazine. *What Is Hinduism? Modern Adventures into a Profound Global Faith.* Kapaa, Hawaii: Himalayan Academy, 2007.

Maheswaraiah, H. M. "Caste Mark." In *South Asian Folklore*, edited by Peter J. Claus, Sarah Diamond, Margaret Ann Mills, 99–100. New York: Routledge, 2003.

Blackface

Blackface refers to the wearing of black makeup, usually by white performers, in order to impersonate and mock African Americans in comedy and musical performances. While the use of dark makeup by white actors to portray Africans goes back hundreds of years to at least the time of Shakespeare, the term *blackface* usually refers to the combination of the makeup with a performance intended to mock blacks. In this sense, true blackface dates back to the minstrel shows that were popular in the United States in the 19th century, and are associated with racism today.

The first minstrel show was performed in the 1830s before the Civil War and became most popular in the next three decades. The shows involved white performers wearing black theatrical makeup on their faces and necks, with the area around the eyes painted white and outside of the mouth white or red. Originally, the black was applied with burnt cork and cocoa butter, but later utilized grease paint. The result was an appearance that was intended to be both comical and monstrous: pitch black faces with huge, bug-eyes, and enormous red or white lips over bright white teeth, and wooly, unkempt hair. One of the stereotypes associated with this stylized appearance was that blacks, who were supposedly always trying to steal chickens and watermelons in the middle of the night, would be given away by the whiteness of their teeth and eyes.

The actors—originally all male—then performed song and dance routines and other musical and comedy skits that were intended to portray blacks as ignorant, childish, lazy, and buffoonish. Common characters in such shows included the genial Uncle Tom, the bug-eyed Pickanniny child, the fat smiling Mammy, the homesick ex-slave, the urban dandy Zip Coon,

and Jezebel, the young temptress, and depicted slavery as a beneficial institution and slaves as happy-go-lucky children who were grateful for the protection that their masters provided. Interestingly, there were a handful of black minstrels who performed during the 19th century alongside white acts and who themselves wore black makeup.

After the end of the war, with the rise of Reconstruction, minstrel shows declined in popularity, but blackface performances did not, and were migrated to the emerging form of entertainment known as vaudeville. Al Jolson was the most famous blackface performer of the 20th century, and made a number of films featuring his performances; films using white actors in blackface were common through the 1930s and served to reassure American audiences that while slavery may be over, relations between blacks and whites would stay largely the same.

Another type of performance that utilized blackface was the medicine show. Medicine shows were traveling shows, like minstrel shows, which featured white actors performing in blackface and featured vaudeville performances along with a fake doctor who used the music and comedy to promote quack medical products. Medicine shows were a popular form of entertainment in the 1930s and 1940s in the United States.

Blackface was also used in more informal contexts as well. During the early decades of the 20th century, whites regularly used blackface—children blackened their faces to perform in school plays; adults wore blackface to attend costume parties; and performers wore blackface at circuses and carnivals through the 1940s.

Al Jolson performs in blackface in the 1927 motion picture *The Jazz Singer*. Blackface is a form of entertainment that dates back to 19th-century minstrel shows and today is associated with racism. (Library of Congress)

The caricatures presented in blackface performances played a major role in shaping Americans' perceptions of African Americans, both before and after the Civil War. The bizarre makeup, grotesque speaking styles, and exaggerated forms of dance led to the rise of a set of long-lasting stereotypes. White Americans—especially those who did not know what black people looked or acted like—could not help but see those stereotypes as true, and blackface performances helped unify whites against blacks. There's no question that those stereotypes played a role as well in the treatment of blacks during the Jim Crow period of legalized segregation that lasted from the 1870s until the 1960s.

Jim Crow laws, which affirmed racial segregation (and which were deemed constitutional in the 1896 Supreme Court ruling *Plessy v. Ferguson*), were, in fact, named after "Jump Jim Crow," the first popular blackface song and show in 1828.

By portraying blacks as ignorant, childish, and crazy, white performers and the white society that embraced the shows, were able to not only create a long-lasting stereotype about blacks, but were able to exercise symbolic control over them, which became increasingly important after the end of slavery. Blacks were seen as dangerous and threatening to white society, but blackface performances provided some relief to audiences, who could assure themselves that blacks were hardly threatening.

On the other hand, the D. W. Griffith silent film *The Birth of a Nation*, while employing white actors in blackface, did not represent blacks as unthreatening. In fact, it depicted blacks during Reconstruction taking over the country from whites, and features black men trying to force white women to marry them, resulting in the death of one white woman who jumps over a cliff rather than submit to him. Unlike the simple "darkies" presented in earlier blackface performers, the blacks in this film were a major threat to white society, and the film confirmed to viewers that blacks could never be integrated into white society.

Blackface became much less popular in films and performances after the 1930s, although the radio show *Amos & Andy* continued to use white performers mimicking blacks until 1960, and a handful of other television shows and movies featured blackface until as late as the 1970s, including the Bugs Bunny cartoons. Performances done in blackface are occasionally performed today, both in the United States and internationally, but they generally result in public condemnations, although there have been a handful of occasions when white journalists wore dark makeup in order to investigate what it is like to live as an African American.

While blackface is most well known in the United States, where it originated and where it continues to signify Jim Crow America, it has been practiced in other countries as well. Generally these international performances were inspired by American minstrel shows that traveled overseas during the height of their popularity.

In many European countries, for example, singers and actors have performed in blackface for years; sometimes those performances are grounded in the same racist stereotypes familiar in the United States, but other times they are used to represent other time periods (such as Art Deco), musical styles (such as jazz), or other cultural influences. However, even when those practices aren't explicitly rooted in the American tradition, they generally emerged out of European slavery, and have often borrowed many of the stereotypes associated with blackface performances in the United States. For instance, a 19th-century Dutch tradition involves a blackface devil named Zwarte Piet who is a servant (or slave) to St. Nicholas and delivers presents to children on the feast day of December 5. During annual celebrations of Zwarte Piet, young men blacken their faces, wear Afro wigs, and adopt many of the stereotypical behaviors of African Americans; these celebrations are seen as racist by American observers as well as by many Dutch.

In Iran, another culture involved in the slave trade, Haji Firuz is a blackface character who ushers in the Iranian New Year, Nowruz, and who some criticize as racist. Even blackface traditions that predate African slavery, such as the English Mummer's Day celebrations, borrow from the American minstrel tradition in terms of music and other terms like "darky."

While blackface is the only tradition in which whites dress up as ethnic minorities in order to mock them publically, Hollywood movies have long used white actors in makeup and racial stereotypes to represent nonwhite actors. For instance, yellowface refers to the practice of using white actors to represent Asian characters. Typically, yellowface involves not yellow makeup, but eye makeup to imply Asian eyes, combined with a heavy accent, a black wig, and stereotypical Asian dress. While these performances predate the cinema, and date as far back as the 18th-century American theater, they were not used in the way that blackface minstrel performances were used—white actors were used in a time when Asian actors would not have been hired by white theater companies. For the most part, yellowface disappeared in the 1970s as Asian actors were hired to play Asian roles, but whites are still occasionally cast as Asians today.

Redface refers to the use of white actors, whose skin is darkened with red or bronze makeup and who wear long black wigs, to portray Native Americans. Redface originated primarily with the American western, when Native Americans were only portrayed by white actors. As with yellowface, redface is less common today than in the past, but is still relatively common.

See also African American

Further Reading

Cockrell, Dale. *Demons of Disorder: Early Blackface Minstrels and Their World.* Cambridge: Cambridge University Press, 1997.

Lott, Eric. *Love and Theft: Blackface Minstrelsy and the American Working Class.* New York: Oxford University Press, 1993.

Strausbaugh, John. *Black Like You: Blackface, Whiteface, Insult and Imitation in American Popular Culture.* New York: Jeremy P. Tarcher/Penguin, 2006.

Braces

Dental braces are orthodontic appliances that are used to straighten teeth that are misaligned, crooked, or to correct malocclusion, the misalignment of the jaw that can result in overbites and underbites.

The use of braces dates back to the mid-19th century when dentists first began experimenting with procedures to correct tooth and bite problems. Today, braces are applied by orthodontists, who are dentists who have completed additional years of training.

Traditional braces force the teeth to move in a desired direction through the use of stainless steel brackets attached to individual teeth, generally with cement, and held together with archwire and rubber bands. Every few weeks, patients must return to the dentist to have the braces adjusted as the teeth begin to move. In the last few decades, newer braces have been developed with aesthetics in mind, such as clear braces, which are made of ceramic or plastic and are held together with white ties, and lingual braces, which are attached to the back of the teeth rather than the front. Often patients must wear retainers made of plastic and metal at night to hold the braces

in place, and the braces must be worn for an average of three years, but as long as six years, to achieve the correct results.

It is most common in countries where orthodontic care is regularly used for braces to be worn by children. However, in recent years an increasing number of adults who were not able to have orthodontic care as children have begun wearing braces, which has led to the development of the newer, less obvious braces.

But while braces have often served to stigmatize the children or adults wearing them, marking them as geeks or nerds, there have been cases where braces have been considered fashionable. In the past five years, news reports began circulating out of Thailand that discussed a fad among Thai teenagers for braces, which are considered cute, like pigtail hairstyles or contact lenses that make the eyes appear bigger. This fad has resulted in the emergence of fashion braces in a variety of colors, which do not correct tooth problems. The media have reported at least two cases of Thai girls who have died from infections that they received from these braces, which they received from untrained amateurs at a cost as low as $45. In China, too, braces have become fashionable, in part because they signify wealth.

The desire for straight teeth and aligned jaws is not culturally universal. For instance, in **Japan**, crooked teeth, known as *yaeba*, are considered to be cute, especially for girls and young women. Apparently, many Japanese women's mouths are relatively small, resulting in teeth—especially the canines—which protrude out of the mouth. This, combined with the fact that the Japanese dental health insurance does not cover braces, is responsible for the country's notoriously bad teeth. But snaggly teeth have only been considered cute since the rise of cuteness, or *kawaii*, in Japanese culture, which emerged starting in the 1970s with Hello Kitty, Pikachu, and other now classic standards of Japanese cuteness. But the fascination with yaeba is not universal among the Japanese however; many women are ashamed of their crooked teeth and cover their mouths with their hands when they laugh, while many older Japanese women are opting to pay for orthodontic care themselves. And while there is no similar love of crooked teeth in Great Britain, the British rank with the Japanese as having the worst teeth in the developed world—perhaps because of the poor British diet, and perhaps because English health insurance only covers braces if the teeth protrude more than five millimeters out of the mouth.

See also Beauty; Dental Care

Further Reading

Proffit, William R., and Henry W. Fields. *Contemporary Orthodontics*. St. Louis, MO: Mosby, 2000.

Rose, Jerome C., and Richard D. Roblee. "Origins of Dental Crowding and Malocclusions: An Anthropological Perspective." *Compendium of Continuing Education in Dentistry* 30, no. 5 (2009): 292–300.

Buddhism

Buddhism was established in the fifth century BCE in **India** and spread, starting in the third century BCE, from India into East Asia, south into Sri Lanka, and west into Central Asia. Today, it is practiced primarily in **Southeast Asia**, **China, Korea**, **Japan**, Singapore, and **Tibet and Nepal**.

Buddhism was founded by Siddhartha Gautama, known as the Buddha to his followers. Born a prince, Gautama became a religious teacher, teaching his followers about how to escape the cycle of birth, suffering, and rebirth, and in particular, about the four noble truths that result in liberation from craving and suffering. While Buddhists do not worship Buddha as a god, some do venerate both Buddha, seeing him as more than a human being, and the bodhisattvas, or beings who have attained enlightenment.

Initially, Buddha was rarely directly depicted in art. Instead, he was represented symbolically, via images like footprints or the wheel. Starting in the first century CE, however, images of Buddha began to appear, in which he often appeared sitting lotus-style with a peaceful expression on his face. No one knows what Buddha looked like so the images, first created hundreds of years after his death, are not thought to be accurate representations of the man himself. Besides the peaceful or meditative expression on his face, Buddha is often depicted with stretched earlobes and with a bump on top of his head, known as an *usnisa*, which represents a bundle of hair tied to the top of his head in a turban. Usually the usnisa is represented covered by a clump of curly hair. Many of the representations of Buddha that have appeared throughout history are not of Gautama himself, but instead are of other Buddhas or enlightened ones, such as the fat, laughing Buddha.

One of the most famous representations of Buddha was the pair of Buddhas of Bamiyan in Afghanistan. Constructed in

This statue of Buddha is typical in that it represents him with a peaceful, meditative expression on his face. (Dreamstime.com)

the sixth century, these monumental statues were carved out of the sandstone cliffs. They were 121 feet and 180 feet high, and were the largest statues of Buddha in the world. The Taliban blew up the statues in March 2001, to the horror of the world community.

In some forms of Buddhism, **masks** may be worn. The form of Buddhism practiced in Mongolia is known as Lamaism, and involves large festivals involving music, dance, and masks. Tsam festivals, for example, are New Year festivals, introduced in the 18th century, during which participants destroy the evil from the previous year. Buddhist monks perform the cere-monies and wear costumes and masks in which they depict Lamaist gods and spir-its, as well as shamanistic spirits, many of whom have been absorbed into the Lamaist pantheon.

In Tibet and Nepal, the use of masks is influenced both by the ancient shaman-istic religions as well as both Buddhism and Hinduism. Today, masks represent the heroes, demons, and gods of these religions, and are worn in dance perfor-mances throughout the region. Buddhists masks are used in dances to invoke guard-ian spirits and to scare off evil ones. For instance, Tibetan monks practice *Chham* dances, which commemorate a Buddhist guru and a Buddha known as Padma-sambhava. In Ladakh, in northern India, Buddhist monks perform annual masked dances in which the monks wear costumes and masks representing the battle between good and evil. Because of their importance as receptacles of spirits, Buddhist masks are treated as sacred objects and kept in monasteries.

See also India; Masks; Mongolia; Shamanism; Tibet and Nepal

Further Reading

Bradley, Lisa, and Eric Chazot. *Masks of the Himalayas*. New York: Pace Primitive, 1990.

Chazot, Eric. "Tribal Masks of the Himalayas." *Orientations* 10 (October 1988): 52–64.

McArthur, Meher. *Reading Buddhist Art: An Illustrated Guide to Buddhist Signs and Symbols*. London: Thames and Hudson, 2004.

C

Caricatures

Caricatures are simple drawings that are intended to represent an individual by highlighting or exaggerating one or more of their distinctive physical traits, such as ears, nose, eyebrows, hair, or lips. While today anyone can have a caricature artist draw his or her portrait—such artists often work on boardwalks or at carnivals or amusement parks—they have primarily been used as a form of political commentary and are the source of the modern political cartoon.

The use of caricature as a form of political commentary developed in London in the 18th century, although artists had been representing people with exaggerated qualities for some time before that. For example, Leonardo da Vinci enjoyed drawing people he saw who had unusual heads or faces, and drew them in such a way as to emphasize their unique physical features. Other artists like Monet and Daumier also drew such portraits. Caricatures were used as an entertaining parlor game by the royal classes of France and Italy during the 17th century, but in the middle of the 18th century, English artists like James Gillray began using caricatures to satirize political figures and the English royal family. This practice soon spread to the rest of Europe, and, ultimately, the Americas and the rest of the world.

Caricatures, as they became used in 18th-century England, became a form of unmasking, whereby the artist, through highlighting a few key features of the subject, was able to make the internal character of the subject visible on the face. By highlighting a person's large nose or bushy eyebrows, a talented caricature artist can shed some light on the personality and temperament of the subject. The art form is related in part to the science of physiognomy, which is the science of reading character traits from facial features. The word itself was first used by 17th-century philosopher Thomas Browne, who was a proponent of physiognomy. Interestingly, while da Vinci did draw what we would consider to be caricatures, today, he was not a proponent of physiognomy. Other artists, on the other hand, like 18th-century portraitist Joseph Ducreux, used physiognomy in their work.

> Who sees the human face correctly: the photographer, the mirror, or the painter?—*Pablo Picasso*

It is not surprising that caricatures emerged during the rise of democratic movements in Europe and around the world, as people clamored to understand more about the politicians who were often deciding their fate. Through distortion of the physical, the internal is supposedly revealed. Most commonly, political caricatures were negative, and were often grotesque; created to highlight the moral failings of the powerful, nose, lips, eyebrows, and jaws could be used to create portraits of greed, lust, sloth, or avarice. Caricatures, and the new art of political cartoons, became not only an effective way to reveal the supposed character or authentic self of politicians, but for the readers of these images, they became an important weapon to attack the wealthy, politicians, celebrities, and even an entire nation or belief system.

For example, Napoleon Bonaparte was glorified in official portraits, but royalists used caricature to lampoon his character, and to challenge his legitimacy as emperor. After Bonaparte's reign, later in the 19th century, Charles Philipon, artist and owner of *La Caricature* magazine, was repeatedly jailed for his caricatures of Louis-Philippe, King of the French, whom he represented as a pear. Philipon's work became so popular that the pear ultimately became the most long lasting symbol of Louis-Philippe and his regime. Another result was that France passed a law banning political caricatures.

In the United States, political caricatures had long lasting impact as well; cartoonist Thomas Nast's images shed light on, and ultimately helped bring down, the corruption of New York City's Tammany Hall political machine. Nast also created the Republican elephant and the Democratic donkey, two of the most iconic political images in the United States.

Caricatures quickly became harnessed to racial ideologies in Europe, but especially the United States. In the 18th, 19th, and 20th centuries, artists have used caricatures to build on racial and ethnic stereotyping, and to create new stereotypes, many of which have had long lasting repercussions. For instance, caricatures of **African American**s were common in American newspapers from the Antebellum era through Jim Crow and into the Civil Rights era. Those caricatures drew on a number of common stereotypes, and included wooly hair, inky black skin, grotesque lips, and bulging white eyes, and often included as well watermelons, alligators, and other items associated with blacks in the popular imagination. Pickanninies, Uncle Toms, Mammies, and Sambos were all variations on this theme, combining distorted imagery with stereotypical behavior patterns, and all served to portray blacks in a negative light and either support the institution of slavery, or in the post-war era, maintain racial segregation.

Other racial groups, too, have been visually stereotyped in this way. Asian Americans, for instance, whether Chinese, Japanese, or from other countries, are usually represented with two primary physical traits: large buckteeth and thick glasses. While it is not common to see such images used today, they were popular for so long that they are firmly cemented in the American imagination. Today, with the first African American president, we have seen a resurgence of racially charged caricatures. While Barack Obama is most often represented with a super skinny neck and big ears—both features of the president—he is also represented with classic racial stereotypes associated with blacks such as big lips; he is also occasionally represented as a monkey or ape. While political cartoons are supposed to be provocative, and even offensive, cartoonists tread a fine line between being provocative and openly racist. Racist individuals and organizations, on the other hand, have no qualms about this and openly create and share such racist material.

Today, the use of caricatures to satirize politicians, the wealthy, and celebrities, is common around the world and is found in all countries in which there is a free press. In recent years, there has been a conflict between the democratic notion of freedom of the press, and cultural and religious ideals about how far caricature should go. The most inflammatory example of this controversy occurred in 2005 when the Danish newspaper *Jyllands-Posten* published a number of cartoons in which Muhammad was represented as a form of political commentary about the fear in many Western nations about criticizing Islam. Much of the Muslim world erupted in protests, both because in Islam (especially among Sunnis) depictions of Muhammad are said to be prohibited, and also because of the disrespectful way that the prophet was treated; in one cartoon, for instance, he was represented as a dog, and in others, he was holding a bomb. Many newspapers refused to reprint the images, while others chose to do so, citing freedom of expression as an important democratic concept, and refusing to censor themselves to appease a religious group. Ultimately, dozens of people were killed in the protests, and a number of death threats were issued against the cartoonists and those responsible for publishing, or republishing, the images.

Other cultures, too, struggle with the question of how much one can satirize through caricature. Relying on racial stereotypes tends to be the most controversial, but lampooning religious beliefs is often dangerous, in Muslim, Hindu, Christian, and Jewish communities. For instance, a cartoon that ran in an Indian newspaper showing the god Ganesh drinking milk from a dairy van (after there were reports of sightings of Ganesh drinking milk) resulted in death threats aimed at the artist.

See also African American; Artistic Representation; Blackface; Physiognomy and Phrenology

A pencil-drawn caricature of U.S. president Barack Obama. Caricatures like these have long been used to lampoon political figures. (Vevesoran/Dreamstime.com)

Further Reading

Rauser, Amelia Faye. *Caricature Unmasked Irony, Authenticity, and Individualism in*

Eighteenth-Century English Prints. Newark: University of Delaware Press, 2008.

Reaves, Wendy Wick, and Pie Friendly. *Celebrity Caricature in America.* New Haven, CT: National Portrait Gallery, Smithsonian Institution, in association with Yale University Press, 1998.

Carnival. *See* Mardi Gras

Central America

Central America refers to the countries and cultures found throughout Mexico and along the Yucatan Peninsula, including Guatemala, El Salvador, Belize, Honduras, Nicaragua, Costa Rica, and Panama. Prior to the arrival of Columbus in the Americas, those cultures included the Olmec, the Teotihuacan culture, the Maya, and the Aztecs. These ancient cultures had a number of traditions surrounding the face.

The Olmec lived in the tropical lowlands of south-central Mexico from about 1,200 BCE to about 400 BCE. There has long been debate about what the Olmec looked like, and whether the huge stone heads that they carved can be considered accurate representations of Olmec facial features. The heads feature faces that are round, with thick lips, and flat noses, and appear similar to some Sub-Saharan African facial features. Whether those features are representative of Olmec people, the Olmec elites, or the Olmec gods is not yet known, and there is a theory that the Olmec actually arrived in Central America from Africa some 3,000 years ago. In addition, other Olmec art appears to demonstrate Asian facial features such as the **epicanthic fold**, leading some to believe that the

civilization was founded by refugees from the Shang Dynasty in **China** in 1200 BCE.

The Maya civilization thrived for almost 2,000 years on the Yucatan Peninsula from about 1000 BCE to 800 CE. After the collapse of the Maya civilization, the people remained, and are now found in a number of communities living in southern Mexico, Guatemala, Belize, El Salvador, and Western Honduras. As with Olmec art, some Mayan art from the highland region depicts faces with African features like larger lips, although contemporary Maya do not have these features. Maya facial features include high, angled cheek bones, dark skin, and broad noses.

Architectural mask from the Temple of the Masks at Kohunlich, Yucatan Peninsula, Mexico. (Dreamstime.com)

The Zapotec culture was found in the Valley of Oaxaca in southern Mexico from about 400 BCE until the arrival of the Spanish in the 16th century. They created elaborate ceramic and stone sculptures of heads, some representing humans, and some representing gods. A number of Zapotec funerary urns have been found with representations of gods and goddesses with mutilated teeth, demonstrating that the Zapotec may have practiced tooth evulsion or **teeth filing**.

The Aztecs were primarily found in central Mexico and thrived from the 14th to the 16th centuries, until the arrival of the Spanish in 1521 brought the end of that civilization. Because the Aztecs oversaw an empire extending through much of Central Mexico, it is probable that the people shared a number of ethnic traits and thus made up a relatively diverse population. After the colonization of Mexico by Spanish Conquistador Hernándo Cortés, the Spanish and indigenous peoples of Mexico began intermarrying, resulting in a population in Mexico today that is largely Mestizo, or mixed.

We know from archaeological evidence that ancient Mesoamericans pierced their ears, noses, and lower lips, and such practices continue to be popular among indigenous peoples in these regions. The Aztecs, Olmecs, and Maya all wore elaborate jewelry, and decorated their faces and ears with a variety of items, including earrings, nose ornaments, lip plugs, and ear spools using gold as well as materials like jade, silver, bronze, obsidian, and copper. Found materials like shells and jaguar teeth and claws were also utilized in jewelry. The Olmec and the Maya also practiced head shaping and **face painting**.

Pierced lips and the wearing of labrets, or lip plugs, was reserved for male members of the higher castes of Mesoamericans. These elaborately designed pieces were inserted into the hole in the lip such that the decorated end, which could resemble a bird, serpent, or another animal, would emerge from the lip opening.

Among the Aztecs, only nobility wore gold jewelry, as it showed their rank, power, and wealth. The main purpose of Aztec jewelry was to draw attention to the wearer, with richer and more powerful Aztecs wearing brighter, more expensive clothing and jewelry made out of gold and precious stones. Commoners, on the other hand, had to wear plain clothing, and either no adornments, or simple adornments made out of bone, wood, shell, or stone.

The Olmec and Maya not only wore earrings in their pierced ears but stretched their earlobes and wore gold, jade, shell, and obsidian ear spools in the enlarged holes. An ear spool is a large cylinder that fits through the ears with a large disk or decorative sheet on the front side. It is thought that ear spools are inserted into the ear by first slicing open the earlobe, inserting the spool, and as the wound heals, the spool is sealed into place. As with the labrets, only high status Maya could wear the larger ear spools. In fact, throughout the Americas, the elaborately large ear-spools were used as a sign of high status.

Upper-class Maya also filed their teeth, and sometimes etched designs onto the surface of the teeth as well, a tradition that has also been found in Africa and contemporary Central America. They also drilled holes into the teeth for the purposes of inserting jewels, a practice that would have been limited to the elites.

Some pre-Columbian Central American cultures also practiced **head hunting**. For instance, the Zapotecs, the Toltec, the Maya, the Aztecs, and the Mixtecs may have all collected human skulls from the victims of war and human sacrifice, and displayed them on public racks known as *tzompantli*, which could contain many thousands of skulls.

Finally, all of the Central American cultures used **death masks** for the faces of royalty, to protect the deceased and ensure their survival into the afterlife. Among the ancient Maya, burial masks were made of jade and other precious stones, and similar masks were also used in Teotihuacan. The Quimbaya, an ancient Columbian civilization, used burial masks made of hammered gold. The Olmec used onyx, jade, serpentine, and other precious stones to construct their death masks.

Masks were also used in celebrations for the living. Ceramic masks found in the Valley of Mexico represented local deities and were worn during agricultural festivals. We know from the murals left at Teotihuacan that priests wore masks covered with feathered headdresses during rituals. Aztec warriors may have also worn animal masks to help make them more fierce.

Today, masks are still used in Central American cultures, although death masks are no longer used. Masked dances were introduced by the Spanish after colonization and remain popular today. In particular, the **Day of the Dead** is widely celebrated throughout Mexico and other parts of Central America, during which participants may wear masks representing skulls or may paint their faces to resemble skulls. Another popular dance in Central and South America is the Dance of the Moors and Christians, or Dance of the Santiagos, which represents the battles between the Christians and the Moors in Spain and Jerusalem. Masks, which are made of papier-mâché, wood, and basket materials, represent Christians, Muslims, demons, clowns, and other characters introduced later. Another post-Columbian dance is known as a Conquest Dance, and celebrates the Spanish conquest over the native peoples of Mexico. Other Mexican masked dances include the Dance of the Old Men, which may relate to an Aztec dance and feature dancers dressed as old men with canes, and the Dance of the Tlocololeros, which predates the arrival of the Spanish and enacts a hunt for a symbolic tiger. Today, Mexican wrestling, or *Lucha Libre*, involves the use of masks and invokes the traditional Mexican masked dances.

See also Day of the Dead; Ear Spools and Plugs; Labrets, Lip Plugs, and Lip Plates; Masks

Further Reading

Bray, Warwick. *Everyday Life of the Aztecs.* New York: Dorset Press, 1968.

Foster, Lynn V. *Handbook to Life in the Ancient Maya World.* New York: Facts on File, 2002.

Chakras

In some practices in Hinduism and Buddhism, it is believed that the human body contains seven energy centers, or energy wheels, from which energy, or *prana*, spins and flows. These *chakras* range from the lower chakras to the human chakras to the divine chakras, each with a different area of the body and spiritual focus. Chakras are used in a wide variety of healing practices like flower essences, **acupuncture**, shiatsu, tai chi, Reiki, and aromatherapy. For example, there is a rough correspondence between the chakras and the meridians used in acupuncture, although there are more meridians than chakras.

In the Hindu Tantric system, there are two different types of chakras: primary, which have no real form and can only be accessed through yoga, and secondary, which take the form of energy and have a specific location in the body. In this system, *kundalini* energy flows upward through the body through the chakras until it ultimately leaves the head at the crown chakra, and achieves union with the divinity. Yoga helps the energy to rise. The lower chakras include the root chakra, found in the coccyx, and the sacral chakra, found in the ovaries and testes; the human chakras include the solar plexus chakra, the heart chakra, and the throat chakra; and the higher chakras include the third eye chakra found between the eyes, and the crown chakra, located on top of the head. The chakras are aligned along the spinal column and each have a different corresponding color.

The chakras were first mentioned in the Hindu philosophical treaties known as the Upanishads, created during the Vedic period from about 700 BCE until about 300 BCE. They thus are a central feature of Hindu practice, but also were adopted by **Buddhism**, and are especially found in Tantric Buddhism.

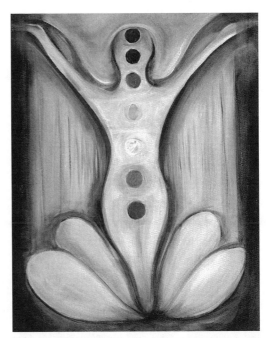

Fine art painting of a body emerging from a lotus with the seven chakras in the center of being. The chakra in between the eyes, *Ajna*, is known as the third-eye chakra and relates to intuition, among other qualities. (Dreamstime.com)

The head has two chakras associated with it: the sixth chakra, located between the eyes on the forehead, and the seventh chakra, located on the top of the head. The sixth chakra, also known as the third eye, is called *Ajna*, which means beyond wisdom. The sixth chakra correlates to intuition, clear thinking, and psychic abilities, such as the ability to see into the future, as well as with the body's endocrine system and lower brain. The seventh chakra is called *Sahasrara*, is where the latent or *kundalini* energy leaves the body, and where the life force is sent into the lower chakras. Intellectually, the seventh chakra is associated with cosmic consciousness and physically with the pineal gland and the higher brain. *See also* Bindi

Further Reading

Macdonell, Arthur Anthony. *A Practical Sanskrit Dictionary: With Transliteration, Accentuation, and Etymological Analysis Throughout.* Delhi: Munshiram Manoharlal, 1996.

Cheek Piercings and Cheek Plugs

Cheek piercings are a form of face adornment, and they are a relatively new phenomenon not found in tribal cultures. The exception to this occurs in Thailand at the Vegetarian Festival in Phuket. During this annual ritual, devotees of Chinese descent enter a trance state and pierce or slice open their cheeks and insert objects like swords, chains, hooks, and guns through the wound. Known as *ma song*, or entranced horses, these men and women engage in a number of self-mortification practices in order to shift evil from the community onto themselves, thus bringing good luck to the community.

Cheek piercing is a relatively uncommon practice even in the body modification community, perhaps because it results

As a form of face adornment, cheek piercings are a relatively new phenomenon and are not found in tribal cultures. The exception to this occurs in Thailand at the Vegetarian Festival in Phuket. During this annual ritual, devotees of Chinese descent enter a trance state and pierce or slice open their cheeks and insert objects like swords, chains, hooks, and guns through the wound. Known as *ma song*, or "entranced horses," these men and women engage in a number of self-mortification practices in order to shift evil from the community onto themselves, thus bringing good luck to the community. (Mark Higgins/Dreamstime.com)

in nerve damage and often causes the cheeks to leak lymph fluid into the mouth. Many people who want the appearance of a cheek piercing opt instead to have a microdermal piercing in the cheek, in which the piercing does not go all the way through the cheek into the mouth. Instead, the **jewelry** sits on top of the skin and the foot of the piece rests beneath the skin. Jewelry is typically a small studded labret.

Much rarer than the cheek piercing is the stretched cheek piercing, worn with a cheek plug. Here, the wearer begins with a simple cheek piercing and begins wearing increasingly larger studs through the hole. Usually this begins by inserting a tapered metal rod known into the hole, and then following that with a larger stud. As the whole gets bigger, larger studs can be worn in the hole until one graduates to wearing a cheek plug, which is a cylindrical piece of jewelry that fits into a large hole, and is sometimes flared at both ends to keep it in place.

See also Ear Spools and Plugs; Earlobe Stretching

Further Reading

Angel, Elayne. *The Piercing Bible: The Definitive Guide to Safe Body Piercing*. Berkeley, CA: Celestial Arts, 2009.

Camphausen, Rufus C. *Return of the Tribal: A Celebration of Body Adornment: Piercing, Tattooing, Scarification, Body Painting*. Rochester, VT: Park Street Press, 1997.

China

China is one of the world's oldest civilizations, and the modern country contains more than 1 billion people making up, throughout its history, hundreds of ethnic and tribal groups. The Chinese have pioneered a number of practices that relate to the face, including **face reading** and **acupuncture**, and share with other cultures a number of traditional customs such as **ear piercing, earlobe stretching, facial tattoos,** and skin whitening. Today, **cosmetic surgery** to change the appearance of the eyes is a very common practice in China, as in **Korea**, **Japan**, and in Asian American communities. In addition, the Chinese share with other Asian cultures a number of beliefs and practices associated with **eye contact** and the sociological concept of face.

The medical practice of acupuncture is thought to have originated in China almost 5,000 years ago. Acupuncture is the practice of inserting very fine needles into the body at points called acupuncture points, or acupoints, in order to influence physiological or emotional health of the body by manipulating the Qi, or the body's energy force.

Face reading is an Asian practice, based on physiognomy and derived from Confucianism, through which one can read the character of a person by analyzing his **facial features**. In Chinese face reading, the left side of the face is the yang, or male; the right side of the face corresponds to the yin, or female; the eyes represent emotion; the lips refer to communication; and the nose represents wealth. Analyzing all of these features, as well as the forehead, the shape of the face, any moles, and the distance between the facial features, can reveal important information about the person.

Both Chinese women and men have worn earrings for thousands of years, and it was very common to stretch the earlobes, as can be seen by illustrations of ancient emperors as well as the large number of illustrations and statues of the Buddha with stretched ears. The length of the stretched ears may have been associated with rank, and perhaps as well with health and longevity.

Facial tattooing was once practiced in China, particularly among ethnic minorities such as the Drung and the Dai. Drung girls were tattooed with geometric designs on the face at puberty as a sign of maturity. Women, who did the tattooing, would draw the design onto the cheeks, around the mouth, on the chin, and between the eyes, with bamboo dipped into ink made of ash and water. The tattooing implement was made up of thorns or other sharp items attached to an instrument; like the Polynesian method, the implement would then be hammered into the skin with another wooden tool. More soot would be rubbed into the wounds in order to create the permanent image. Dai women were also tattooed on the hands, face, or arms as a sign of maturity, protection against evil spirits, and a sign of beauty. The Imperial Chinese also used facial tattooing, along with banishment, as a mode of punishment for criminals.

As in cultures around the world, light skin has historically been highly prized in China. As in the West, in Asia lighter skin was seen as a sign of status, since it indicated that the bearer did not have to work outdoors. In Medieval China, women used skin whiteners made of mercury, or swallowed ground seashell, to lighten their skin further. Even today, skin whiteners are more popular than ever, with hundreds of pills, soaps, creams, and lotions on the market around the world. Many of these products are just as unsafe as those used in the past; in 2002, it was discovered that two whitening creams popular in Hong Kong had extremely high levels of mercury in them.

Another beauty standard in modern China demands round, Western-looking eyes. In recent years, surgery to modify the **epicanthic fold** and to create a crease in the upper eyelid has grown increasingly common in countries like China. The surgery, known as blepharoplasty, is the most frequently performed cosmetic surgery in all of Asia. Other forms of cosmetic surgery popular in China include chin implants, Botox injections in the cheeks, breast implants, leg lengthening procedures, and surgery to reduce the size of muscle in the legs. As Chinese women (and increasingly, men) have more disposable income, much of that income is now spent on such surgeries. The surgeries have become visible signs of wealth, as well as tools to achieve it, since many Chinese see cosmetic surgery as a way to achieve high paying jobs and higher status spouses.

The use of the face to express emotions is somewhat different in China from, say, the United States. China is considered to be a high-context society, in which relationships with others are critically important, while the United States is a low-context society, in which individual feelings and motivations are most important. In China, for example, direct eye contact is interpreted as a challenge, so the Chinese will often look downward when they speak, especially when meeting someone new or speaking to a social superior. In general, Chinese people have an impassive expression on their faces while speaking, so that their emotions cannot be betrayed.

This is related to the sociological concept of face, in which losing face and saving face are important goals to either avoid or achieve. The Chinese words for face, *mian*, *lian*, and *yan*, all mean much more than face. These words are used to mean concepts like reputation, self-respect, prestige, honor, sense of shame, and dignity. For instance, *timian* means "the social front, the ostensible display of one's social standing to the public." For the Chinese, losing face, or losing honor, prestige, or social standing, is a terrible thing and must be avoided at all costs.

China, like many other cultures, has a rich history of mask making. **Masks** in China are primarily used in theatrical performances, but as in other cultures, they probably originated in religious and shamanistic rituals. Ancient Chinese rock paintings depicting people wearing masks suggest early shamanic practices, and today in **Mongolia**, masks are still worn by shamans to communicate with the spirits and gods. And throughout China, rituals are still performed to ask the traditional gods for favor; leaders of these rituals, called *Shigong*, wear masks representing the different gods. Buddhist rituals, which came from **India**, also employ masks known as *Qiangmu* masks, representing the Buddha as well as animals, demons, ghosts, and other spirits. Masks are also worn at rites of passage in China like funerals and weddings. They may be made of wood, papier-mâché, bamboo, or even jade, silver, or bronze. In this context, the mask can ward off evil or bring good luck. Masks are also used at festivals such as the Chinese New Year, when participants will dress up as the animal being celebrated, or during animal sacrifice. Dramatic performances called *Nuo* also use masks. These masks represent spirits and demonstrate that the performer has been possessed by that spirit. Only men can wear or even touch these masks. In addition, masks are worn by the actors in traditional Chinese operas. Finally, there is a type of mask used in China for home protection. Here a mask representing a god or animal is hung over the doorway of a house or at the entrance to a temple or village in order to protect the dwelling or place from evil spirits.

A Chinese boy wears a monkey mask at a temple fair in Beijing on the third day of the Chinese New Year in 2004. Masks like this one are worn at celebrations throughout the Asian world. (AP/Wide World Photos)

See also Acupuncture; Beauty; Cosmetic Surgery; Earlobe Stretching; Epicanthic Fold; Face Reading; Masks

Further Reading

Bond, Michael Harris. *Beyond the Chinese Face: Insights from Psychology.* New York: Oxford University Press, 1991.

Lip, Evelyn. *Your Face Is Your Fortune: An Introduction to Chinese Face Reading.* Singapore: Marshall Cavendish Editions, 2009.

Christianity

Images of the face are common in Christian art and iconography, but differ according to the historical period being discussed or the denomination. For instance, the representation of faces in the Catholic tradition differs from the Greek Orthodox tradition as well as from the various Protestant traditions.

Much of what we would call Christian portraits is devoted to the depiction of the historical figures in the Bible: most notable Jesus, but also Mary and the disciples. Because there is no way to know exactly what these people looked like, artists throughout history have had a great deal of latitude in how they represented their subjects, and in general, carry the ethnic characteristics of the culture portraying them. Faces in much of Christian art lack specific identifying details, and change from artist to artist and time period to time period, even when representing the same historical subject. Even then, Christian art in the late Roman period—starting in about the second or third century—had more facial details than did Christian art in the early Middle Ages; very prominent facial fea-tures, like a beard, were included in such portraits but no real detail. One reason for this may be the change in the nature of the artists at that time, but another explanation may lie in the fear of idolatry among Medieval Christians.

Later, the portrayal of Jesus, Mary, and the disciples became more standardized, with a set of facial characteristics becoming normalized in **artistic representations** over time. While the earliest depictions of Christ, from the Roman period, generally lack the beard and long hair, the full beard and long hair became common in the Eastern church starting in the fourth century and by the sixth century became the norm. (In the West, it was still common to see a beardless Jesus as late as the 12th century.) Still, throughout this period, it was common to see Jesus with the ethnic appearance of cultures around the world, such as a Japanese and Chinese Jesus, a blue-eyed Jesus (in Europe). Some early representations of Jesus made him more explicitly Jewish, and today, those Jewish artists who represent Jesus generally depict him as an observant Jew—with, for example, the leather prayer boxes known as *tefillin* on his head. Even today, Jesus is not portrayed the same throughout the world. The Coptic Church depicts Jesus with dark skin and, in Coptic traditions in Africa, African facial features.

Some of the most important images of Christ are those that are said to have been either painted during his lifetime, or miraculously generated by God. Those include the **Shroud of Turin**, a piece of linen that is said to be the burial cloth of Jesus and that includes a faint negative image of the body of Jesus, complete with bloodstains; the **Image of Edessa**, which purports to be an image showing the face of Jesus, made miraculously after his death and now lost; and the paintings known as Mandylions, which were paintings of Jesus on linen that have been considered at times to also be miraculous images, or acheiropoieta, of Christ.

These images, and the representations of those images, are known as the Holy Face of Jesus, and collectively are worshipped by many Catholics. For instance, the photographic negative of the Shroud of Turin taken by photographer Secondo Pia in 1898 is itself an object of devotion. Worshipping these images is a way to make reparations for the crimes against Jesus before and during his crucifixion, according to a set of visions in which Jesus spoke directly to two nuns in the mid-19th century, telling them (and additional people in subsequent years) that by worshipping his image, they console him. This ultimately led to the creation of medals imprinted with the image from the Shroud of Turin, known as Holy Face Medals.

Jesus's facial features eventually became standardized in the West, and scholar Paul Vignon has identified 15 characteristics common to many portraits of Christ, including a forked beard, a raised eyebrow, large owlish eyes, an enlarged left nostril, and a number of other features, all of which appear on the Shroud of Turin, which may have been found as early as the 14th century. This suggests that if the Shroud was widely known among Christian artists, that it influenced their depiction of him in their work.

Christian traditions have often focused on the face or the head. For instance, **baptism** is a Christian ritual in which an infant or adult is sprinkled with or immersed in water; generally the head is the focus of the ritual, borrowed from other purification rituals, rather than the full body. **Ash Wednesday**, or the first Day of Lent, is also marked with a ritual involving the head; on this day, the faithful are anointed on their foreheads with the sign of the cross made of ashes mixed with oil and blessed to show the repentance of their sins. Marking devotion onto the face probably dates back to the Roman era, when Christianity was illegal. During this period, Christians and other criminals were tattooed on the forehead with a word or symbol indicating their crime. Other Christians, particularly after Constantine's adoption of Christianity as the religion of the Empire, gave themselves voluntary tattoos, which were modeled after the wounds of Christ as a sign of their faith, and as a mark of group membership into the Christian religion. When Constantine became Emperor of Rome and embraced Christianity in the fourth century, he banned the practice of tattooing criminals on the face, because he believed that the human face was a representation of the image of God and should not be disfigured or defiled.

The Bible also has a number of expressions related to the face, which would be related to both **Judaism** and Christianity. For example, "to seek the face" (Ps. 24:6, 27:8, 105:4, Prov. 7:15, Hosea 5:15) is to seek an audience or favor with God, when God "hides His face" (Deut. 32:20; Job 34:29; Ps. 13:1; 30:7; 143:7; Isa. 54:8; Jer. 33:5; Ezek. 39:23,14; Mic. 3:4), He withdraws His protection and favor from man, while "the upright shall dwell in thy presence" (Ps. 140:13) means that the upright shall be awarded God's grace and protection.

A Catholic nun receives the mark of the cross on her forehead in church on Ash Wednesday. The mark represents mourning and repentance. (AP/Wide World Photos)

On the other hand, when men "hide their face" before God (Exod. 3:6; Isa. 6:2; or 1 Kings 19:13 when Elijah "wrapped his face in his mantle"), it means that they are showing humility and reverence before him, as in the traditions of many cultures that demand that social inferiors not make **eye contact** with those who are superior to them. To "turn away one's face" (2 Chron. 29:6; Ezek. 14:6) means to show indifference or contempt to another, while to "recognize the face" (Lev. 19:15) means to show respect to another. Here again we see a connection to other cultures in which eye contact is a way to show attentiveness, or, when it is removed, lack of concern. "To harden the face" (Prov. 21:29; Isa. 50:7; Jer. 5:3) indicates steeling one-

self against an appeal by that person. Finally, "covering the face" (2 Sam. 19:4) is a sign of mourning, while "a face covered with fatness" (Job 15:27) means that one is wealthy and arrogant.

See also Artistic Representation; Ash Wednesday; Image of Edessa; Shroud of Turin; Veil of Veronica

Further Reading

Bellinzoni, Arthur J. *The Old Testament: An Introduction to Biblical Scholarship.* Amherst, NY: Prometheus Books, 2009.

Grabar, Andre. *Christian Iconography: A Study of Its Origins.* Princeton, NJ: Princeton University Press, 1968.

Johnson, Paul. *A History of Christianity.* New York: Simon & Schuster, 1995.

Cosmetic Surgery

Cosmetic surgery is a surgical discipline that is intended to improve the appearance of a person, although some procedures, such as rhinoplasty, can be done for medical reasons as well.

Cosmetic surgery developed during World War I, when doctors began to develop new techniques to repair the bodies and faces of soldiers who were wounded in the war. Today, cosmetic surgery generally refers to procedures that have been developed to repair congenital birth defects such as cleft palates, or disfigurements caused by accidents or injury, such as burns, **scars**, and severe body and facial trauma, as well as to those voluntary procedures that are aimed at making a person look younger or more beautiful.

> God has given you one face, and you make yourself another.—*William Shakespeare*

While cosmetic surgery procedures are performed on the body as well as the face, the oldest and still most common practices are performed on the face, and include nose jobs, facelifts, eyelid surgery, chemical peels, chin augmentations, collagen injections, and botulism injections. In almost all of these procedures, the aim is to make the patient appear younger and, therefore, more beautiful.

Because the standard of **beauty** in Western society demands youth (and slenderness) as the ideal, it is not surprising that these procedures would be so popular with women. According to the American Society of Aesthetic Plastic Surgery, almost 10 million cosmetic procedures (surgical and nonsurgical) were performed in the United States in 2009, at a cost of $10.5 billion. Of those, women had more than 90 percent of the procedures, or more than 9 million procedures that year. On the other hand, in recent years, the number of men seeking cosmetic surgery has been increasing as well, with more than 900,000 men electing to have cosmetic surgery or other procedures in 2009. That same year, 20 percent of all patients were ethnic minorities.

Botulinum injections, known as Botox, are now the most popular nonsurgical cosmetic procedure in the United States, with more than 2.5 million Botox procedures in the United States in 2009. Most users are white, between 35 and 50. No other procedure is done increasingly by doctors or nurses at patients' homes, in what are known as Botox parties. Botox temporarily paralyzes the muscles of the face where injected, causing wrinkles to disappear and lasts from three to four months. With repeated use, the procedure can cause a permanent atrophy of facial muscles leading to a loss of **facial expression**. Other procedures that are increasingly used to smooth wrinkles or to replace lost fat in the face include collagen injections, dermal fillers, and fat injections.

Cosmetic surgery, typically, is not covered by health insurance, so beauty is becoming increasingly a sign of upper-class status, as only the wealthy can afford to undergo these procedures. Furthermore, as beauty is becoming a commodity that can be purchased by the wealthy, men and women whose faces and bodies are not naturally beautiful, but who cannot afford to change their appearance, find themselves at a disadvantage, given the preferential treatment that the genetically and surgically endowed receive in most every aspect of social and economic life.

And while it was, at one time, the case that only older women underwent facelifts and other procedures to make them appear younger, young women are now getting Botox injections as well as lip plumping procedures at very early ages, in order to prevent aging (in 2009, 20 percent of all patients were under 34). Indeed, the prevalence of cosmetic surgery in the United States today indicates an increasing need to deny the inevitable; as the physical signs of aging are being pushed further and further into the future, the wealthy can pretend that the biological rules do not apply to them.

Voluntary cosmetic surgery was initially, primarily, performed in the United States among white clients, but that has been changing in recent years. Cosmetic surgery rates in the United States have tripled for Hispanics in the last decade of the 20th century, and quadrupled for Asians and **African American**s. Part of the rise in cosmetic surgery numbers among ethnic groups in the United States can be attributed to women trying to attain Caucasian standards of beauty such as a thin nose for African Americans and Caucasian-looking eyes for Asian Americans. Because ethnicity is most easily detected in the face, plastic surgery has become a way in which we can conceal our ethnicity.

Because of these pressures, rhinoplasty (known as westernization rhinoplasty) is one of the most common procedures among African Americans and people of Middle Eastern descent, and blepharoplasty, a cosmetic surgery procedure to insert a crease into the **epicanthic fold,** is the most popular procedure among East Asian Americans. On the other hand, many minorities want to retain their ethnic features, but want to look younger or more beautiful as well. Because of this, some cosmetic surgeons have been working to preserve ethnicity during cosmetic surgery procedures, and have been researching ideal beauty among other cultures. These doctors are also working to create procedures that are appropriate for different skin types—some African Americans, for instance, scar more easily than Caucasians.

In Eastern nations as in the West, beauty is linked to finding a good partner and a competitive job, especially in the business world, so cosmetic surgery rates in **Korea**, **China**, and other Asian countries are skyrocketing. In Korea, where the standard of beauty means round eyes, pale skin, a sharp nose, and long legs, blepharoplasty is so popular that 1 in 10 adults have received it. In addition, many Asians are now having surgery to make their noses longer and more pronounced, and to reduce the size of the cheekbones.

Brazil is another country in which cosmetic surgery is increasingly common. In fact, Brazil is second only to the United States in the number of licensed cosmetic surgeons, and Brazilian women received more than 600,000 procedures in 2004 alone. The popularity of cosmetic procedures in Brazil may have to do with the fact that Brazilians expose their bodies much more than do people from other

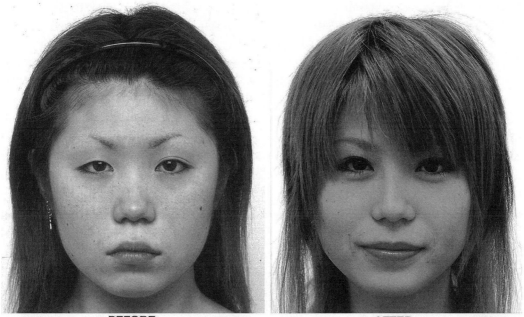

BEFORE   AFTER

Risa Arato is shown in this set of photos before (left) and after (right) her cosmetic surgery. Facing less social stigma and encouraged by new no-scalpel procedures, more Japanese women than ever before are walking into cosmetic surgery clinics and walking out with rounder eyes, bigger noses, and fewer wrinkles. Critics suggest that surgeries like this are a way for Asians to Westernize their features in order to conform to Western standards of beauty. (AP/Wide World Photos)

cultures; liposuction and butt implants are the most popular procedures (unlike facial procedures in the United States). Brazilian women talk openly about their plastic surgery (known as *plástica*), and while it was once only available to the rich, new, less invasive techniques are making the procedures less expensive, and more middle-class and even lower-class women (and men) are getting them as well. In the last few decades, Brazil has become the center of medical tourism in the Western Hemisphere; today, many American women travel to Brazil for inexpensive but safe procedures—a practice known as lipotourism.

See also Beauty; Gender

Further Reading

Balsamo, Anne. "On the Cutting Edge: Cosmetic Surgery and the Technological Production of the Gendered Body." *Camera Obscura* 28 (1992): 206–37.

Brush, Pippa. "Metaphors of Inscription: Discipline, Plasticity and the Rhetoric of Choice." *Feminist Review* 58 (1998): 22–43.

Davis, Kathy. *Reshaping the Female Body: The Dilemma of Cosmetic Surgery.* London: Routledge, 1995.

Gilman, Sander. "Imagined Ugliness." In *The Body Aesthetic: From Fine Art to Body Modification,* edited by Tobin Siebers, 199–216. Ann Arbor: University of Michigan Press, 2000.

Rose, Christine. "The Democratization of Beauty." *The New Atlantis* 5 (Spring 2004): 19–35.

Stark, Richard B. *Aesthetic Plastic Surgery.* Boston: Little, Brown and Company, 1992.

Cosmetic Tattooing. *See* Permanent Makeup

Cosmetics

Cosmetics, or makeup, refers to the application of temporary dyes and powders to the skin, usually the face, for decorative purposes. As with so many body adornments, makeup is used differently in different cultures, depending on that society's standards of **beauty**. Because unlike men, women are judged around the world by their appearance, it is not surprising that most cosmetics are worn by women. Makeup, in fact, is one way in which men and women are differentiated, making women appear more feminine and men, by comparison, more masculine.

Skin is the primary focus of cosmetics around the world, but hair, eyelashes, lips, fingernails, and teeth are also areas for which cosmetics have been developed. Cosmetics include products to color, shape, and enhance the lips; foundation, concealers, powders, and blush to even out and brighten the skin; eye liners, eye shadow, mascara, and eyebrow liners to enhance and define the eyes; and nail polish and nail art to decorate the fingernails and toenails.

The appearance of the skin is a common focus in societies around the world. Clear, clean, healthy skin is considered beautiful in many cultures, but many other cultures use body paint to make people more beautiful, powerful, or to convey important social information about the person. In England during the 16th century, it was common to wear heavy makeup, or even decorative patches made out of leather, to cover small pox **scars**. Artificially lightened skin is considered attractive in cultures around the world, especially where light skin is associated with the upper classes, and dark skin with working people. Lighter skin is especially desired for women. For that reason, one of the earliest forms of makeup found in many stratified societies is white face powder. The ancient Greeks, Egyptians, and Romans used lead-based makeup to lighten their faces, and Europeans in the Middle Ages used both lead and arsenic to lighten the skin, and even painted blue lines on their foreheads to make their skin appear translucent, a practice borrowed from Roman women. Japanese **Geisha**s use a heavy white rice powder to whiten their skin, because, again, white skin is associated with beauty and social status. In **China**, too, light skin was highly coveted. Skin whitening creams and powders remain popular throughout the world today, wherever white skin is associated with status and beauty.

On the other hand, rouges and powders have been used for centuries in order to add a sun-kissed or flushed appearance to the face. While products to darken the skin such as artificial bronzers did not become popular until the 20th century, when suntanned skin became fashionable, powders and creams to provide color to certain parts of the skin—usually the cheeks— have long been popular. Rosy cheeks are associated with youth and also with sexual arousal, making red cheeks on women very desirable—especially when contrasted with powdered white skin, as in the case of the Geishas and European women during the Renaissance. Ancient products were made out of red plants, such as strawberries, beets, and mulberries. Later rouges were made from red ochre and other red minerals.

Many cultures are also concerned with keeping the skin moist, and a range of oils, fats, and other products have been used in order to combat dryness, which is associated with aging. Many Sub-Saharan African cultures, such as the Nuba of Sudan, rub oil or fat onto their skin to keep it moist and shiny, and women will not go out if they do not have oil for their skin. The ancient Egyptians, too, used oils to keep their skin soft, and oils also served as the basis for a number of other important products like perfume and eye makeup. Cosmetics of all kinds have been used throughout the Middle East, but today, in areas controlled by fundamentalist Muslims, makeup is often prohibited.

The lips are another area of the face on which cosmetics have been focused. Because plump lips are associated with youth and high levels of estrogen, and because lips swell and color when a woman is sexually aroused, women have often worn products aimed at accentuating the lips, usually by coloring them red or pink, and by enlarging them, either through lip liners, or through various types of lip plumpers. Other cultures, on the other hand, favored small lips; the ideal lip in Japan was a tiny plump bow shape. Dyes were derived from plants like henna, berries, and even insects, and were often mixed with fat or beeswax to make a balm: Cleopatra used crushed beetles and ants in her lip stain.

The eyes are the other major area of the face that is addressed by makeup. Egyptians lined the eyes with **kohl** and other nat-

ural materials, both for decorative purposes and for protective and religious purposes—eye makeup was thought to protect the eyes from the glare of the sun and from the **evil eye.** It was worn by men, women, and children. In addition, darkening eyes makes the eyes look like they do when a woman is about to orgasm—darkened eyes are bedroom eyes. While many cultures associate large eyes with beauty and youth, developing mascaras, lip liners, and eye shadows that make the eyes seem bigger, many East Asian cultures at one time saw large eyes as barbaric, and found the less open eyes common among Eastern and Northern Asian cultures more beautiful. Today, however, Western-looking eyes are sought after in **Japan**, China, and **Korea**, and many women now undergo **cosmetic surgery** to make their eyes look more round. The ancient Egyptians were known for their heavy use of eye makeup, using kohl to line their eyes, and green malachite to shadow them, creating the distinctive cat eye seen in Egyptian art.

White teeth are seen as normative in much of the world today, but this has not always been the case. For centuries, both Indian and Japanese women blackened their teeth because black teeth were thought to be beautiful (or, in Japan, were not to be seen), as did women in Renaissance Europe, as a way to simulate the appearance of rotted teeth (which were a sign of status because only those who could afford sugar would typically have rotten teeth).

Makeup has often been used to distinguish the classes in stratified societies. In Medieval Europe, only the upper classes wore make up, for example, although by the modern period, women of all class

Harrod's Makeup Policy

In July 2011, a Harrod's sales assistant, Melanie Stark, was forced to quit her job at the venerable London retailer for not abiding by the company's dress code, which mandates that women wear full makeup at all times, including foundation, lipstick, lip liner, eyeliner, eye shadow, mascara, and blush. While Stark had worked for Harrod's for five years without being reminded of the policy, she was recently seen by a supervisor and told to put on makeup or go home. At the time of this writing, it's unknown whether Stark will attempt to sue Harrod's or whether the company will change its policy, but it has brought up a lively public debate about women's appearance and whether or not women's appearance must always be "improved" via cosmetics.

groups could afford to wear makeup. Even so, makeup can only go so far in terms of making a woman beautiful, and where makeup fails, cosmetic surgery is available to the wealthy to achieve results that working-class and poor women could never achieve.

In Europe, makeup began to change in the 19th century. It went from more obvious and pronounced to more subtle, and, as some saw it, deceptive. Very heavy makeup began to be associated only with the **theater**, while women (and some men) used makeup slyly, and in secrecy, partly because the Victorians saw obvious makeup as a sign of vanity. Today, while it is morally acceptable to wear makeup, many women still use makeup in secrecy—to accentuate their good features, to cover up their (supposed) flaws, and yet to pretend as if their appearance is natural.

The professional makeup industry began in the west at the turn of the 20th century, with Elizabeth Arden opening the first professional beauty salon in 1909, and Max Factor opening a similar operation in Hollywood that same year. Some of the biggest names in makeup like L'Oreal and Maybelline began in the first decade or two of the 20th century. With the opening of cosmetic chain stores, inexpensive cosmetics were made available to all Americans for the first time.

See also Beauty; Cosmetic Surgery

Further Reading

Wykes-Joyce, Max. *Cosmetics and Adornment: Ancient and Contemporary Usage.* New York: Philosophical Library, 1961.

Crowns and Headdresses

In cultures around the world, the head of the king, chief, or other royal figure was seen as the site of that person's power, both political and spiritual. Because of this, in many cultures, heads of state, chiefs, and sometimes heads of church have worn special headgear, including crowns, tiaras, and diadems. These special headdresses signify the power and legitimacy of the ruler. In the most general sense, crowns could be made of leaves, cloth, metal, or flowers. They are functionally related to the **halo**, or circle of light surrounding the head of gods or sacred figures, in religious art around the world.

Two types of crowns were worn by the pharaohs of ancient **Egypt**. Before the kingdoms of Upper and Lower Egypt were unified by the first pharaoh around 3150 BCE, the leaders of both kingdoms wore different crowns; the white crown, or *hedjet*, in Upper Egypt, which looked somewhat like a bowling pin, and the Red Crown or *deshret* in Lower Egypt, which was conical-shaped with a curlicue on it. These may have been worn as early as 6,000 years BCE. After unification, the double crown, called the *pschent*, combined both crowns into one. It wasn't just the rulers who wore these crowns; because Egyptian kings and later pharaohs saw themselves as descendents of the deities, both the gods and the kings wore these same crowns, signifying their power and authority over the land. For instance, the gods Horus and Nekhebet both wore the white crown, while Geb and Wadjet wore the red crown. No actual crown has survived history, so it is unknown what materials these items were made of, although they are well represented in surviving art.

Alexander the Great originated the practice of wearing a diadem, which then spread to Hellenic Rome and Egypt. The diadem was originally a ribbon worn around the head like a headband, and tied below the head. In Egypt, they were both of ribbon and metal. Caesar refused to wear it, however, when Antony offered it to him, and the practiced became discontinued for Roman

leaders. In Imperial Rome, Romans had a wide variety of crowns and wreaths, called *corona*, which could be made of anything from laurel leaves to gold, and were worn by military leaders, those honored for special accomplishments, priests, and brides at their weddings. The *corona radiata* was to be worn by gods and emperors alone. After the rise of Christianity in the Roman Empire, and the shift in imperial power from Rome to Byzantium, Constantine and future emperors once again adopted the diadem to represent their power. Sometime in the sixth century, the diadem began to give way to the closed crown.

In ancient Israel, the Jewish priests wore a turban-like headdress known as a *mitznefet*. Christian priests, too, wore headgear from the earliest days, perhaps the diadem. The *camelaucum*, a white linen cap once worn by Byzantine aristocrats, was adopted as a formal headdress by the Popes, by at least the sixth or seventh century. By the ninth century, the cap worn by the pope lengthened into an elongated helmet shape and by the 10th century, a tiara was affixed to the bottom of it; it was then called the Papal tiara, and was used exclusively for ceremonial purposes. Eventually, other Popes added additional tiaras with Pope Benedict XII wearing such a headdress in the 14th century. The last Pope to wear the ceremonial tiara was Pope Paul VI, who was crowned in 1963. Subsequent Popes from that time have neglected to wear it, because of its association with luxury and political authority. Popes and other high-level Catholic officials have also worn a different item for ritual purposes. This is the *mitre*, which also derives from the Byzantine camelaucum, and is a tall folding cap made of white linen or silk. Greek Orthodox officials, on the other hand, continue to wear gold crowns, derived from those worn by the later Byzantine emperors.

In Medieval Europe, crowns were worn by some of the ancient kings as well as the Holy Roman Emperors. Kings and queens were crowned by religious officials who placed the crown on their heads, signifying God's sanction, and many traveled to Rome to be crowned and anointed by the Pope himself. Today, most monarchies no longer carry on this tradition.

Crowns are worn today by kings and queens throughout the monarchies of Europe. Made of gold and decorated with precious stones, European monarchs have different crowns to choose from, depending on the occasion, including the crown to be worn during their coronation and the crown to be worn on state occasions. Other royalty wear other types of royal headgear. For example, in England, the wife of the King wears a special crown called a consort crown, while other royalty wear small, simple crowns called coronets. Tiaras are smaller, often only encircle part of the head, and are worn by royalty on ceremonial occasions when crowns would be too formal.

Other cultures had ceremonial headdresses as well for their kings and chiefs. For instance, Plains Indian tribes had royal headdresses; warbonnets made of eagle tail feathers and decorated with fur or beading were worn by chiefs who had earned each of the feathers by acts of bravery. Aztec nobility also wore headdresses made of feathers (from the parrots, macaws, and other indigenous birds), which were adorned with jade, gold, and jewels.

Queen Elizabeth of the United Kingdom is shown wearing the King George IV Diadem, which was made in 1820 for the coronation of King George IV. This is just one of many headdresses worn by the Queen. (AFP/Getty Images)

A variety of chiefdoms in **Sub-Saharan Africa** had special headgear made for their chiefs. Among the Pende, Yaka, and Suku tribes of the Democratic Republic of the Congo and Angola, chiefs once wore elaborately beaded horned crowns called *misango*, which were worn at public ceremonies and rituals. The Yoruba of Nigeria also have a variety of beaded crowns that were once worn by kings who trace their lineage to the god Oduduwa; these men alone can be called *Oba*. These may be decorated with symbolic designs, including the face of Oduduwa, the royal bird called *oka*, geometric designs, and included beaded veils called *iboju* to keep normal people from gazing into the king's eyes (which could be deadly). In addition, by **veiling** his face, the king's individual identity is suppressed and replaced by the power of the dynasty; this transforms him into the brother of the gods. Like many cultures in Africa and elsewhere, the Yoruba believe that a person's power, or *ori*, is located in the head, so the craftsmen who make the king's crowns must follow a great deal of precautions when making the crown. When the crown is placed on the ruler's head, it must be put in place from the back or from the side so that the king cannot see inside it, as its power is such that it could cause blindness or death.

See also Egypt; Greco-Roman Cultures; Native North America; Sub-Saharan Africa

Further Reading

Gardiner, Alan H. *Egypt of the Pharaohs: An Introduction*. New York: Oxford University Press, 1966.

Sebesta, Judith L., and Larissa Bonfante. *The World of Roman Costume*. Madison: University of Wisconsin Press, 1994.

Starkey, David. *Monarchy: From the Middle Ages to Modernity*. London: HarperPress, 2006.

D

Day of the Dead

The Day of the Dead, known as All Souls Day in Europe and Dia de los Muertos in **Central America**, is a Catholic holiday that falls on November 2, directly following All Saints Day. The holiday is celebrated to honor the departed and to make offerings to, and remember, the ancestors. In Mexico, it is believed that on October 31, the spirits of children return to the world and can spend 24 hours with their families; this is followed by the release of the spirits of the adults on November 2; celebrations can last for all three days in many regions.

For Catholics, as with members of other religions, praying for the dead can help them to move from the transitional state (for Catholics, this is Purgatory, and is reserved for those souls who are not pure enough to go directly to Heaven) to one's final resting place (Heaven, for Catholics). In addition, the day is associated with what anthropologists call ancestral cults—forms of religious belief and practice in which ancestors are believed to play a role in the lives of the living; and rituals are performed in order to make the ancestors look happily on their descendents. In Mexican Day of the Dead celebrations, celebrants attend mass, make offerings and say prayers to assist the recently departed on their journey from Purgatory to Heaven. They also visit and decorate the graves of their ancestors at the cemetery; bringing food, toys for the children, and liquor for the adults; and create home altars, decorated with candles, photos, and flowers, through which they make offerings, called *ofrenda*, to the dead (usually of food). These offerings help make the dead feel welcome on their annual return, and help secure their blessings in the future. Finally, people participate in public celebrations.

The Day of the Dead, as it is celebrated in Central America today, has aspects borrowed from the European All Souls Day tradition, but may have begun with the religious practice of the pre-Columbian cultures of Central America. The Aztecs, for example, believed that the dead go through nine different levels of underworld until they reach Mictlan, the place of the dead, a journey that took four years. The Aztecs devoted two months of each year to rituals for the dead; one month for adults and one for infants. The goddess Mictecacihuatl, who was said to have died during childbirth, presides over the celebrations. During these rituals, known as the Feast of the Little Dead Ones, and the Feast of the Adult Dead, skulls were used to honor the dead, who were thought to come back to earth during this period, and offerings of chocolate, candles, seeds, and meat were made to the dead. The Spanish tried to ban these rituals, thinking them to be sacrilegious, but when they were unsuccessful, they moved them to November 2 to coincide with All

Soul's Day. (In Mexico today, many people use November 1 to commemorate dead children and November 2 for adults.)

Celebrations throughout Latin America feature skeletons and, especially, skulls. Skulls made of sugar, papier-mâché, wood, and clay are used to decorate homes and public spaces, and represent both death and rebirth. Sugar skulls, for example, have the names of the dead painted on the forehead, and are eaten by relatives or friends of the dead. Celebrants sometimes paint their faces to look like skulls, or wear **masks** that, once again, represent the dead symbolically. One of the elements of the Aztec tradition that the Spanish found so unusual was the fact that celebrants see the dead as happy and not sad. This is reflected in the skull imagery used in the celebrations today, which universally feature smiling skulls. Celebrants often wear wooden masks of smiling skulls, known as *calacas*, or devil masks, and dance to honor the dead. In Veracruz, masked dancers known as *xantolo* dancers or *cuadrillos*, wear masks depicting skulls, devils, men, and women, which both celebrate and mock death.

See also Central America; Masks

Further Reading

Anocona, George. *Pablo Remembers: The Fiesta of The Day of the Dead*. New York: Lothrop, Lee, and Shepard Books, 1993.

Dia de Los Muertos celebrations have their roots in pre-Columbian Aztec and other native festivals memorializing departed loved ones. During the holiday, departed friends and family return from the land of the dead to visit with the living, who paint their faces to resemble skulls, or wear skull masks, to connect with the world of the dead. (Zepherwind/Dreamstime.com)

Brandes, Stanley H. *Skulls to the Living, Bread to the Dead: The Day of the Dead in Mexico and Beyond.* Malden, MA: Blackwell, 2006.

Carmichael, Elizabeth, and Chole Sayer. *The Skeleton at the Feast: The Day of the Dead in Mexico.* Austin: University of Texas Press, 1992.

Death Masks

A death mask is a mask, usually made of plaster or wax, of a person's face after he has died. The term is also used to refer to a representation of the dead that is not made from the dead person's face, which is placed on the face for burial. Because death masks are such a perfect representation of the face (and usually don't obviously appear to be of the dead), they are a lifelike reminder of the person who once was.

Many cultures throughout history have represented loved ones or famous or elite people after death. For instance, the Mycenean people created burial masks out of gold as early as 4,000 years ago, to be placed over the face of the dead as a way to magically preserve the body. Scholars once thought that the Homeric hero Agamemnon was buried with such a mask, and that that mask had been found; today it appears to be of a different period in time.

In ancient **Egypt**, royalty were mummified after death and placed into a coffin, and often a sarcophagus, for eternity. Within the decorated coffin, on top of the wrapped face, was placed a sculpted mask—of wood, clay, plaster, or even beaten from gold and other precious metals—to represent the face of the deceased, to protect the face and head during burial, and to guard against evil spirits. The mask also allowed the deceased's spirit to recognize the body

in the afterlife, and because the facial features of the mask were correlated to those of important gods, the wearer could travel safely to the afterlife. Most masks were probably not made by using the dead person's face as a model, but at least one such mold has been found, indicating that this may have been practiced. Often, however, the mask was made by molding clay or plaster onto a generic facial model, and then sculpting specific features onto the clay. Tutankhamen's mask was made out of solid gold. The masks were then painted and decorated; both men's and women's masks featured large eyes and painted and sculpted wigs. Later, during Roman-occupied Egypt, funeral masks gave way to the painted wooden portraits known as mummy portraits or Fayoum portraits. These portraits, placed over the face of the deceased, probably served the same functions as the earlier sculpted masks, although some may have been displayed on the wall of a home prior to death.

The Greeks also used burial masks, made of copper or gold, and all with closed eyes. All Greek burial masks depicted men. Romans, too, used burial masks, which were either placed over the face of the dead, or may have been worn by members of the funeral party. Roman masks may have been cast in wax directly from the face of the dead.

Among Inuits and other native peoples from the Pacific Northwest and the Arctic, burial masks were also common, and were especially used for deceased shamans. With bone eyes inserted into the eyeholes, and decorated with feathers, hair, and other items, these **masks** were placed on the face of the dead to prevent spirits from entering the body and reanimating it. Covering

Mask of the pharaoh Tutankhamun. Masks like these were worn over the faces of the dead in many cultures to help the dead to be recognized in the afterworld. (Michal Janošek/Dreamstime.com)

Burial masks of gold were also used in ancient **China** to cover the faces of dead royalty. This practice was found in the ancient kingdoms of Cambodia and Siam (now Thailand) as well.

Among the ancient Maya, burial masks made of jade and other precious stones were used, which would protect the deceased and ensure his survival into the afterlife. Death masks were also used on the faces of rulers at Teotihuacan and among the Olmec. The Quimbaya, an ancient Columbian civilization, used burial masks made of hammered gold. These masks were adorned as a human would be, with filed teeth and **nose piercing**s, and **jewelry**. Some had moveable parts, like moveable ears. As with the masks of other cultures, the eyes of the Quimbaya masks are closed, perhaps to represent seeing into the spiritual realm. Similar masks were also used in funerary complexes in the Chimú culture of northern Peru a thousand years ago; some were sized to fit over the face of the dead, and others much larger, to be interred with the deceased along with a wealth of treasure.

the eyeholes was thought to be especially important, both to keep out the spirits and also, perhaps, to let the deceased see. Similar masks have been found in Siberia, and may date back more than 2,000 years.

A very different kind of burial mask was used by the Vikings about a thousand years ago. These masks were used to cover the

Faces of Death

Faces of Death is a 1980 film, written and directed by John Alan Schwartz, which depicts graphic scenes of human and animal deaths. Not a typical Hollywood movie, the film has no plot, nor is it a true documentary. Instead, it's a sensationalistic look at real and faked deaths, filmed mockumentary-style, including those taken from news footage and stock footage. Very few scenes in the film were shot by the filmmakers; one exception is the footage of animals being killed at a slaughterhouse. The film has had a number of sequels made, and it and its sequels have been banned in dozens of countries.

faces of warriors and were made of the bones of animals such as wolves and goats. They were intended to signify his strength and virility and protect the wearer from demons after death.

Masks made directly from the face of the dead have also been found around the world. For instance, the Yenesei people of Central Asia made plaster burial masks at least 1,500 years ago from the deceased's face; in addition, dummy bodies were also made. The body would then be cremated with the ashes placed in a pouch affixed with a leather face mask, decorated to appear like the person, which signified that the person was truly dead. Lastly, the plaster mask was affixed to the dummy.

European death masks probably emerged out of the medieval practice of carrying wooden or wax representations of the dead on the funeral bier instead of the corpse. The newer death mask was created by oiling the dead person's face, ears, and neck and pouring plaster over the face to create a mold. The hardened mold would then be filled with plaster, which creates a three-dimensional portrayal of the dead in final repose. These masks were displayed at the funerals of the dead, and, unlike in ancient civilizations, were not interred with the dead. In addition, such masks can be used to later make sculptures or paintings of the deceased.

After the mold is made, the original mold is kept, so that new masks can be created over and over; in fact, many people own death masks of such luminaries as Beethoven, Napoleon Bonaparte, and Abraham Lincoln. Infamous people, too, like John Dillinger, Sacco and Vanzetti, and other famous killers have been immortalized in death masks after their executions. Madame Tussaud, whose eponymous wax museums display the wax likenesses of the famous and infamous alike, once used the heads of those decapitated in the French Revolution to make death masks. As the sciences of **physiognomy and phrenology** developed in the 19th century, sciences began studying the death masks of the criminal dead in order to try to detect the physical features associated with criminality. Before the rise of photography in the 19th century, death masks were also used to identify the dead.

Cultures that did not use death masks to bury the dead did often have times of the year at which the dead were honored. Those festivals, found in Africa, Europe, New Guinea, and in Native America, involved participants wearing masks that represented the spirits of the dead.

See also Central America; Egypt; Masks; Physiognomy and Phrenology

Further Reading

Fagen, Brian M. *Kingdoms of Gold, Kingdoms of Jade: The Americas before Columbus.* New York: Thames and Hudson, 1991.

Nunley, John, and Cara McCarty. *Masks: Faces of Culture.* New York: Harry N. Abrams, n Association with the Saint Louis Art Museum, 1999.

Quigley, Christine. *The Corpse: A History.* Jefferson, NC: McFarland, 1996.

Vadetskaya, E. "Painting on Tashtyk Burial Masks." *Archaeology, Ethnology and Anthropology of Eurasia* 29, no. 1 (2007): 46–56.

Dental Care

How people take care of their teeth, and standards of dental care and hygiene, differs around the world. In addition, the health of teeth is correlated with cultural features like diet, environment, and other cultural characteristics.

In the modern world, dental care is governed by the professional field of dentistry, which diagnoses and treats dental disorders. Dentists and other dental professionals like dental hygienists provide preventative information and care, as well as surgery and other forms of treatment for disease. Patients are instructed to brush their teeth regularly, usually with toothpaste containing fluoride, and to floss, to prevent tooth decay and bone loss. Tooth decay, or cavities, is treated with fillings, and when surgery is needed, oral surgeons and orthodontists can perform root canals, tooth extractions, and a variety of other surgeries. The professional field of dentistry dates to the mid-19th century, with the first school of dentistry, The Baltimore College of Dental Surgery, opening in 1840. However, the practice of treating tooth problems may date back 9,000 years, with the Indus Civilization in **India**, and other ancient cultures probably practiced dentistry as well, such as the Sumerians, Greeks, Etruscans, Romans, Egyptians, Japanese, and Chinese, many of whom thought that worms caused cavities. Tooth extractions were a common treatment for a variety of illnesses and have also been used as punishment.

Attitudes toward and use of teeth differ cross-culturally. For example, extreme degrees of tooth wear or dental attrition have been found in a number of populations and are related to the diet, food preparation techniques, and use of the teeth as tools. For instance, among a number of Native American and Arctic cultures, women are responsible for tanning leather, and use their teeth to soften the leather, which results in a particular pattern of tooth wear. In addition, nomadic cultures living in harsh desert environments, such as Bedouins, show more wear on their teeth because of the presence of sand in the diet.

On the other hand, Westerners have significantly more tooth decay, as well as malocclusion, than tribal peoples. The Western diet of high calorie, highly processed, low fiber foods may be correlated with malocclusion, because traditional cultures that rely on a healthier diet, lower in carbohydrate and higher in fiber, tend to have more aligned teeth. Whereas a low fiber diet results in less chewing stress during childhood, which may result in insufficient alveolar bone mass of the jaws, which itself results in malocclusion.

Altering the teeth for aesthetic reasons is a practice that has been found in cultures around the world. Some Australian Aboriginals practice tooth avulsion in which one or both of the front incisors are chipped out, a practice also found among some Vietnamese tribes, as well as among the Nuer of Sudan. Some cultures, such as the Masai and Waarusha peoples of Tanzania, remove the lower incisors of adolescents, and the Masai and the Shilluk of Sudan also remove the baby canine teeth of children. These practices are related to cultural beliefs that suggest that the presence of the teeth can cause, or exacerbate, illnesses. Other cultures file their teeth into sharp points, such as the Mentawai of Sumatra, the Efe of the Congo, or the Dinka of Sudan. In Bali, teeth are filed not for decorative reasons but because teeth symbolize negative emotions like anger, jealousy, and greed, which can be controlled through filing the teeth. In addition, canine teeth are associated with dogs, so filling down the canines makes a person less animalistic. For the Balinese, **teeth filing** is also an important rite of passage for adolescents and helps to ease their transition into adulthood. Upper-class Mayans also filed their teeth, sometimes etched designs onto the surface of the teeth, and also drilled holes into the teeth for the purposes of inserting jewels, a practice that would have also been limited to the elites. Some cultures also stained the teeth to make them more beautiful; in Vietnam, for example, black teeth were preferred to white, and the Iban of Borneo not only blackened their teeth, but filed them and inserted a brass stud into a drilled hole. In the Philippines, teeth were stained black, filed into points, and had holes drilled into them in which gold was inserted.

Today, much of dentistry is focused around cosmetic dentistry, an informal term that includes tooth whitening, tooth reshaping, bonding, and veneers, and other procedures that are done primarily for cosmetic purposes to improve the appearance of the teeth. Boys and girls with crooked teeth often wear **braces** for a period of months or years in order to straighten their teeth, and some adults in recent years have taken to wearing braces as well, especially since invisible braces were developed. Other common treatments include tooth whitening (which can be done at a dentist's office or at home using home whitening kits), tooth bonding and veneers, both of which cover one's natural teeth with an artificial surface, and dental implants and bridges that replace missing teeth with artificial teeth. Teeth can also be reshaped in order to achieve a more pleasing appearance, and gums can also be operated on in order to change the shape and appearance of the gums and teeth.

Many African Americans, especially those involved in the hip-hop culture, wear gold crowns over a tooth, typically an incisor, as a sign of status. More popular in recent years is the practice of having diamonds and other jewels inserted into the incisors. For those who do not want to make the permanent commitment, some dentists offer removable appliances that offer the look of gold teeth with or without implants.

In a recent survey, almost half of all American adults reported that they get a negative impression from people with crooked teeth, and most people agreed that those with healthy and straight teeth are treated better than those without good teeth. Indeed, for the nation's poor, many of whom cannot afford dental care at all, unsightly and missing teeth have become the most visible sign of poverty. And because Americans judge others on the basis of their teeth, those who are missing teeth find it even harder to get jobs, as missing teeth are often thought to be signs of poor parenting, limited intelligence, and low class status.

The desire for straight teeth and aligned jaws is not culturally universal, however. For instance, in **Japan**, crooked teeth, known as *yaeba*, are considered to be cute, especially for girls and young women. Older women, however, do not share in this fascination, and many Japanese women are electing to get braces or other treatments for their crooked teeth. In

This young Japanese woman shows off her *yaeba*, or crooked teeth, in this photo. Crooked teeth are seen as cute, especially for girls and young women, throughout Japan today. (Mettus/Dreamstime.com)

Japan, skin whitening has long been popular, and now tooth whitening is becoming increasingly popular as well. In Great Britain, too, crooked teeth are common, in part because the national health insurance only covers braces when teeth protrude a minimum of 5 millimeters from the mouth, and in part because of the traditional English diet. According to the World Health Organization, the British have the worst oral hygiene in the world, and visit the dentist far less than people in other nations.

White teeth have not been universally popular. While it's true that the people from the ancient Greeks on have attempted to whiten their teeth, other cultures have preferred black teeth over white. Some Native American tribes prior to colonization, such as the Natchez, stained their teeth black with tobacco and wood ash. In Heian-era Japan, women also intentionally blackened their teeth, as did men and women in South Asia, and women in Renaissance Europe did so to simulate the effect of rotten teeth from eating too much sugar.

See also Beauty; Braces; Central America; Gender; Teeth Filing; Teeth Whitening

Further Reading

Alt, K., and S. Pichler. "Artificial Modifications of Human Teeth." In *Dental Anthropology Fundamentals, Limits and Prospects,* edited by K. Alt, F. Rosing, and M. Teschler-Nicola. New York: SpringerWien, 1998.

Hillson, S. *Dental Anthropology.* New York: Cambridge University Press, 1996.

Price, Weston A. *Nutrition and Physical Degeneration. A Comparison of Primitive and Modern Diets and Their Effects, Etc.* New York: P. B. Hoeber, 1939.

Proffit, William R., and Henry W. Fields. *Contemporary Orthodontics.* St. Louis, MO: Mosby, 2000.

Rose, Jerome C., and Richard D. Roblee. "Origins of Dental Crowding and Malocclusions: An Anthropological Perspective." *Compendium of Continuing Education in Dentistry* 30, no.5 (2009): 292–300.

Diprosopus

Diprosopus refers to an extremely rare condition in which a person or nonhuman animal is born with two faces on the head. The term is from the Greek, meaning two-faced.

Diprosopus is generally thought to be a form of conjoined twins in which two twin embryos do not separate completely; rather than resulting in two bodies attached, it results in a single body with two faces. On the other hand, some think that diprosopus occurs due to an excess of the SHH protein, which controls the development of limbs as well as facial features in embryos. Too little of the protein has been found to result in infants born with facial features that are incomplete; another result can be a condition called cyclopia, which results in both eyes being found in a single socket in the middle of the face. Too much would result in diprosopus.

Diprosopus can be as minimal as two noses on one face, to as major as having two complete faces on one head. It is also associated with other disorders, generally of the brain, but also of the heart. Most in-fants with this condition are stillborn, al-though a few animals have survived for at least a few years and for some reason, a number of kittens have been born (and died) with the condition.

The most famous person with the con-dition was Lali Singh, who was born in March 2008 in a small village outside of New Delhi, **India**. Singh was born with a single set of ears but two noses, two mouths, and two pairs of eyes. Her birth was met with awe in her village, and in India as a whole, and villagers saw her as the reincarnation of the Hindu goddess of valor, Durga, who was traditionally repre-sented with three eyes and multiple arms. Other people saw her as the reincarna-

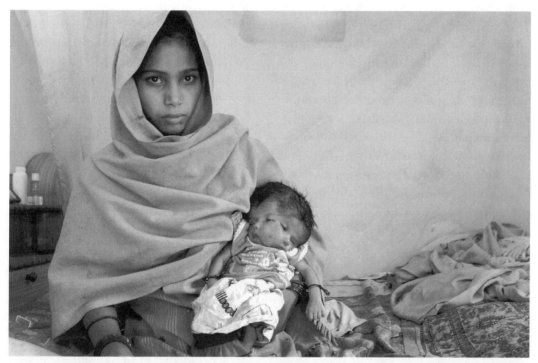

Mother Sushma holds her daughter Lali at their residence in Saini Sunpura, 50 kilometers (31 miles) east of New Delhi, India, on April 8, 2008. The baby with two faces, a condition known as diprosopus, was born on March 11 in a northern Indian village, where she was worshipped as the reincarnation of a Hindu goddess until her death at two months. (AP/Wide World Photos)

tion of Ganesh, the Hindu half elephant/ half human deity. After Singh's birth, thousands of people visited her home to make offerings to her. Because her parents did not accept that there was something wrong with her, they didn't visit a hospital after she was born to get the child tested or treated, and ultimately she died at two months old from a heart attack possibly caused by dehydration and an infection. Besides diprosopus, Singh also had opaque corneas and a cleft palate, which made feeding her difficult.

Terra cotta figurines with two faces known as the pretty ladies of Tlatilco have been found in Tlatilco, a pre-Columbian Mexican city. The sculptures have been dated from about 1200 BCE to the seventh century BCE. Some of the figures have two heads but others have two faces on a single head. Art historians have long thought the sculptures represented deities, but a doctor who studied them has made the claim that they are representations of diprosopus, and that the artists must have seen and studied the condition firsthand. It would not be until the 16th century until more modern representations of the condition would appear in the medical literature.

See also Disorders of the Face

Further Reading

Bendersky, Gordon. "Tlatilco Sculptures, Diprosopus, and the Emergence of Medical Illustrations." *Perspectives in Biology and Medicine* 43, no. 4 (2000): 477–501.

Rodriguez-Morales, Edda L., Maria S. Correa-Rivas, and Lillian E. Colon-Castillo. "Monocephalus Diprosopus, a Rare Form of Conjoined Twins, and Associated Congenital Anomalies." *Puerto Rico Health Sciences Journal* 21, no. 3 (2002): 237–40.

Disorders of the Face

There are a number of genetic disorders of the face that cause the facial features to deviate from the norm, and which cause the sufferers considerable social discomfort.

For example, Mobius Syndrome is a congenital disease that impairs the ability of people to make **facial expressions**— they cannot smile with happiness, raise their eyebrows in surprise, or furrow their brow in anger. Even closing one's eyes is impossible with Mobius Syndrome. It is caused by the nerves that control facial expression, as well as eye movement developing improperly during gestation. While Mobius Syndrome does not affect intellectual development, patients with this condition have been diagnosed with mental disorders, which demonstrates the importance of facial expression—without it, people can be labeled stupid, slow, or retarded, or at the very least, unfriendly and uninterested in others. In addition, lacking the ability to make facial expressions makes it appear as if the sufferer cannot empathize with other people—they cannot laugh, smile, or make a sad face in appropriate social situations. While there is no cure for Mobius Syndrome, those with the disease can elect to have surgery that, by relocating muscles into the face, allows them to form a simple smile, which itself can be invaluable in fitting into society.

Other disorders do not directly impact the patient's ability to make facial expressions, but because they so mar the appearance of the face, social interaction is still limited. For instance, Cherubism is a genetic disorder that causes the shape and structure of the face to radically change; in particular, the lower half of the face swells to three times normal size, and the eyes protrude as well. It is caused by a missing bone in the jaw that has been replaced by large amounts of fibrous tissue, causing the chin to grow throughout childhood. Surgery can treat the condition, reducing the appearance of the chin and solving some of the associated dental problems, but cannot cure it. People with Cherubism, like those with other facial disorders, have a much harder time making friends and fitting in socially than people with normal faces, making it a very stigmatizing condition to have.

Cleft palate and cleft lip are congenital disorders that result in a gap in the face, usually between the mouth and the nose, caused by an incomplete closure of the bones and tissues of the face during gestation. It is often caused by one of a number of syndromes, such as Apert Syndrome, Van der Woude Syndrome, Miller Syndrome, or Nager Syndrome, all of which cause abnormal growth of the skull and face. Cleft palate may be accompanied by either bulging eyes, downward slanting eyes, or other disfigurements. Cleft lip and cleft palate are both relatively easy conditions to treat with surgery, and, when performed early in life, the patients generally can have normal social lives. But as with the other facial conditions noted here, having a condition like this untreated can lead to enormous problems with other people, as well as psychosocial problems like depression and self-loathing.

Some conditions are caused by the abnormal or premature closure of skull su-

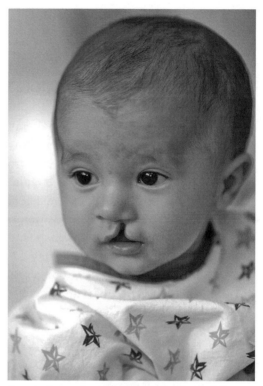

Angel, 4 months old, waits for his cleft lip operation by the doctors of the "Operation Smile" team at the Institute for Reconstructive Plastic Surgery in Guadalajara, Mexico, on September 22, 2009. Cleft lip is a congenital disorder that affects one in every 500–750 babies. (AP/ Wide World Photos)

tures, which results in the head growing abnormally, and sometimes bulging eyes or other distorted features. This is called Craniosynostosis, can result from any number of causes, and can be associated with a number of syndromes, including Crouzon Syndrome, Apert Syndrome, and Pfeiffer Syndrome. Surgery can be performed to make the face and skull look more cosmetically normal.

All of the above conditions can be devastating to those who suffer from them, even though very few of them cause pain.

But because the face is our badge of identity, and is seen as the outward expression of our internal selves, having a face that is deformed or abnormal brands someone as having a self that is abnormal. A facial disorder is not just a physical problem— it marks its bearer in the most visual way possible as being different. Studies show that those with facial defects are more likely, than any other part of the population, to be ignored, harassed, or rejected. They are judged by others to be less intelligent and less valuable, and this can result in high levels of social anxiety. They acquire what sociologists call an embattled identity, where the sense of who and what they are is not determined by social attributes but by physical defects. And just as their faces are permanently impaired, so are their self-esteem and social standings.

See also Facial Features; Hypertrichosis and Hirsutism; Identity

Further Reading

Greenwald, Laura. *Heroes with a Thousand Faces: True Stories of People with Facial Deformities and Their Quest for Acceptance.* Cleveland, OH: Cleveland Clinic Press, 2007.

Wright, Edward F. *Manual of Temporomandibular Disorders.* Ames, IA: Blackwell Munksgaard, 2005.

E

Ear Piercing

Ear piercing refers to putting a hole in the ear, usually the lobe, in order to wear **jewelry** through it. It is one of the most popular ways of adorning the head and face. In the West, the piercing of the earlobe has long been the most acceptable form of ear piercing, but today, many people have the upper and outer cartilage parts of the ear pierced as well. And while pierced ears are associated primarily with women in the modern West, men and women have both worn earrings in cultures around the world, as well as in European and Western history.

Pierced ears have been found on every inhabited continent throughout history. Evidence from the earliest civilizations in the **Middle East** show that pierced ears wore worn at least 6,000 years ago, but given the popularity of pierced ears in traditional societies today, they certainly must predate the archaeological record. Multiple ear piercings were used in some cultures, such as ancient Mesopotamia, pre-Colombian **Central America**, and in **Greco-Roman cultures**. Many cultures have also stretched the ear holes and worn ear plugs. Ancient Egyptians, Mayans, Aztecs, the Chinese, and traditional cultures around the world wore them.

Pierced ears have primarily been used as a form of adornment, and, for cultures that carry wealth in the form of jewelry, as a form of displaying wealth, such as among nomadic tribes like the Fulani of West Africa, the Tuareg of the Sahara, and the Bedouins of the Sinai Peninsula. The types of earrings worn in many cultures have been an indication of rank and status, and some societies pierce the ears for religious or magical purposes as well. In some societies, spirits are thought to enter the body through the ear, but the wearing of earrings repels them. Finally, among many Northwest Coast Indians, such as the Tlingit, ear piercing is used to mark individual rank. Because paying for an ear piercing was costly, the number of holes in one's ear showed the amount of wealth in one's family.

In many cultures young girls have their ears pierced a short time after birth; in some communities in **India**, Hindus pierce a girl's ears and nose 12 days after birth when she is given her name. The Tchikrin of central Brazil pierced boys' and girls' ears at birth, and immediately inserted wooden earplugs, which would be exchanged as the ear holes grew larger.

In other societies, ears are pierced as part of a rite of passage, usually at adolescence, or just prior to marriage. In Borneo, for example, parents pierce a child's ears to represent the child's dependence on the parents. The Fulani also use ear piercing to mark the life stages of their members.

The Bible mentions pierced ears and earrings in a number of places. From those references, it is known that the Hebrews

This Fulani woman of Mali demonstrates the very large earrings worn by women in this culture. (Dreamstime.com)

wore earrings as a form of adornment, and that gold earrings represented wealth, but also that slaves' ears were pierced as a mark of servitude. Exodus 21:5–6 tells that freed slaves who want to continue to serve their master could have their ears pierced in court as a sign of permanent service. Just as Roman Christians chose to use the stigma of tattooing to mark themselves as slaves of God, other Christians use pierced ears as a way to show this same commitment.

Elsewhere in the Middle East, Romans, Greeks, and Egyptians all wore earrings as a sign of beauty and wealth, and both men and women wore earrings. The finer the materials and the more elaborate the design, the wealthier the wearer. In Europe, the Middle Ages saw a decline in the wear-

ing of earrings, but jewelry of all kinds became popular again in the Renaissance, when elite men and women wore earrings to demonstrate their status and wealth.

In the United States, ear piercing began to lose popularity in the 1920s with the advent of clip-on earrings, but became popular again beginning in the 1960s, primarily with women and girls. Most ear piercings at that time were done at home, generally by sticking a sterilized or heated sewing needle through the ear into a piece of cork or other object, followed by the earring itself. This is very similar to how ears are pierced around the world. Also available since the 1960s were spring-loaded earrings in the shape of a ring with the ends sharpened to a point. By placing the earring around the earlobe, and squeezing, over a period of days or weeks the ear will eventually be pierced through.

By the 1970s, one could get one's ears pierced in a doctor's office or at department stores, which were sponsored by earring manufacturers. Ear piercing guns were developed in 1970, and quickly became the most popular way to get one's ears pierced, at mall, jewelry, or accessory stores.

While it has primarily been women in the United States to wear pierced ears, men in some groups have worn them as well. Sailors, for instance, used a pierced earlobe to indicate that the sailor had sailed around the world or had crossed the equator; another legend says that a pierced ear would improve a sailor's eyesight, and that if a sailor was found washed up on a shore, his gold earring would pay for his burial.

In the late 1960s, men began to wear earrings due to the influence of the gay community and the hippies. In the 1970s, punks began piercing their own ears and later, other male musicians began wearing earrings, leading to a fashion among rock stars, rappers, and basketball players. For a time in the 1980s and 1990s, it was thought that when a man pierced just one of his ears, it meant he was gay, although this is no longer recognized.

Earring types include stud earrings, in which a stud made of either metal or stone sits on the front part of the earlobe that is connected through the lobe to a back piece holding the earring in place. Hoop earrings generally pierce through the ear with a wire or post and then encircle the bottom of the earlobe. And dangling earrings attach to the earlobe with a post or a hook and include a longer portion of metal, beads, and/or stones that flow from the bottom of the earlobe. In the West, when men wear earrings, it is usually a stud or a small hoop.

In the end of the 20th century, newer ways of wearing earrings developed. First, multiple holes in the earlobe and, later the cartilage, developed. And while the earlobe is still by far the most common place historically and cross-culturally to find a piercing, in the modern body modification scene, a variety of specialized cartilage piercings have since become popular. These include the tragus, antitragus, rook, industrial, helix, orbital, daith, and conch piercings.

The inner conch piercing is a piercing that goes through the inner part of the ear, near the ear canal. Piercings through the outer part are called outer conch piercings. The tragus piercing pierces the small piece of cartilage that projects immediately in front of the ear canal. The antitragus piercing is a piercing on the small piece of cartilage in the inner ear, directly opposite the tragus. A daith piercing passes through the ear's innermost cartilage fold, above the ear canal.

A helix piercing is a piercing of the upper ear cartilage. A rook or anti-helix piercing is a piercing on the outer portion of the inner ear. A helix piercing together with an anti-helix piercing can be connected with a single straight piece of jewelry, usually an extended barbell, and is called an industrial piercing; in this piercing, the straight bar of the jewelry extends from the top of the ear to the outer edge. An orbital piercing is defined as any two piercings that are connected by a hoop, usually in the ear.

See also Ear Shaping; Ear Spools and Plugs; Earlobe Stretching; Jewelry

Further Reading

Mascetti, Daniela, and Amanda Triossi. *Earrings: From Antiquity to the Present*. London: Thames and Hudson, 1999.

McNab, Nan. *Body Bizarre Body Beautiful*. New York: Fireside, 2001.

Ostier, Marianne. *Jewels and Women: The Romance, Magic and Art of Feminine Adornment*. New York: Horizon Press, 1958.

Van Cutsem, Anne. *A World of Earrings: Africa, Asia, America*. New York: Skira International, 2001.

Ear Shaping

Humans have shaped dogs' ears for centuries. Certain breeds of dogs require, in order to conform to breed standards, cropped ears such as Great Danes, American Pit Bull Terriers, Boxers, Doberman Pincers, Miniature Pincers, and Schnauzers. A veterinarian normally crops the ears a few weeks after the puppy's birth. Although veterinarians did not provide pain medication for years, and some still do not, it is much more common today, and some veterinarians refuse to crop ears altogether, because of the pain it can cause dogs and the loss of communication methods it entails. Some breeders and dog owners continue to perform these surgeries themselves, without anesthesia, which can result in infection and blood loss, not to mention considerable pain. Because of these concerns, a number of localities have now banned or restricted the procedure.

In the contemporary body modification scene, human ears are also the focus of shaping and modification. For instance, ear cropping or ear pointing refers to the reshaping of the ear via the removal of part of the cartilage (and sometimes the sewing up of the resultant ear), in order to create a specific ear shape such as the Vulcan ears on *Star Trek*, or an elfin ear. Some people also choose to have their earlobes removed for aesthetic reasons or to remove a stretched earlobe. Because most surgeons will not crop human ears, most people who seek to have their ears shaped turn to cutters, piercers, and sometimes will do the procedure themselves.

On the other hand, ear shaping surgery, or otoplasty, is a relatively new form of **cosmetic surgery**, and is used to reshape ears that are deformed, large, mismatched, or that protrude too far from the head. It can also repair ears that were stretched or torn—either intentionally or inadvertently. *See also* Ear Piercing; Ear Spools and Plugs; Earlobe Stretching

Further Reading

Angel, Elayne. *The Piercing Bible: The Definitive Guide to Safe Body Piercing*. Berkeley, CA: Celestial Arts, 2009.

Camphausen, Rufus C. *Return of the Tribal: A Celebration of Body Adornment: Piercing, Tattooing, Scarification, Body Painting*. Rochester, VT: Park Street Press, 1997.

Ear Spools and Plugs

Ear spools and earplugs refer to the **jewelry** worn in stretched ear holes. Ear spools and plugs were commonly used throughout much of pre-Columbian America, and are still worn by some tribes today.

An earplug is a cylindrical piece of jewelry that fits into a large hole in the ear, and is sometimes flared at both ends to keep it in place. These are one of the most common forms of jewelry worn by modern body modification advocates with stretched ears. Earplugs can be made of wood, bone, stone, or even glass.

Ear spool is the term used to describe the jewelry worn in the ears in many **Central American** cultures. A spool is a large cylinder that fits through the ears with a large disk or decorative sheet on the front side. It is thought that ear spools were inserted into the ear by first slicing the ear open, inserting the spool, and as the wound heals, the spool is sealed into place. Other theories hold that the ears were pierced and then stretched to accommodate the jewelry.

Ancient Mesoamericans not only wore earrings but also stretched their earlobes and wore gold, jade, shell, and obsidian earplugs and ear spools. Archaeologists have unearthed masks from the Olmec civilization that show large holes in stretched earlobes for ear spools; ancient ear spools themselves have also been found. The Maya were also well known for wearing ear spools; only elites could wear the larger and more elaborately decorated spools. In fact, throughout the Americas, large and decorated ear spools and earplugs were used as a sign of high status. The ancient Incans wore engraved ear spools of gold, silver, copper, sometimes inset with stone or shells, and these were most likely reserved for the elites. Ear spools have been found in Guatemala and Panama as well.

Ear spools and plugs were once worn in a number of Native American and Meso-American cultures and have become popular among many young men and women in the West today. (iStockPhoto.com)

Mississippian Indians also wore earplugs made of clay, shell, stone, feldspar, and wood covered with copper. The earplugs found by archaeologists measure a half inch or so in diameter and up to 5 inches in length, which means that they emerged from the ears for quite a distance. Earplugs were most likely worn by both commoners and elites. The Indians most likely inserted feathers into their ears as well. Ear spools made of stone, wood, or shell were also found among tribes in Oklahoma, Ohio, and other eastern Native American sites. These were between 1.5 and 3 inches in diameter and were made up of two discs connected by a short spool, with the outer face of the disc decorated.

Today, earplugs are becoming relatively common body modifications, although they are not yet mainstream. Flesh tunnels are a modern form of earplugs and ear spools. They are a hollowed out version of a plug, and resemble an empty spool of thread, and can be worn with another decorative item running through the middle.

See also Central America; Ear Piercing; Earlobe Stretching

Further Reading

Bray, Warwick. *Everyday Life of the Aztecs.* New York: Dorset Press, 1968.

Foster, Lynn V. *Handbook to Life in the Ancient Maya World.* New York: Facts on File, 2002.

Earlobe Stretching

Earlobe stretching has been around for thousands of years, but only in the last few years has it become widespread in the United States. Ears are typically stretched so that the person can wear **jewelry**, but sometimes stretched ear holes are worn by themselves.

From statues, mummies, and other evidence, we know that stretched ears have been worn in major civilizations around the world, including **Egypt**, **China**, and by the Olmecs, Mayans, Aztecs, and Incans. Tutankhamen, for example, had a stretched ear piercing. Traditional societies, too, have practiced ear stretching. The men of the Marshall Islands, for example, used to stretch their earlobes and wear large gauge earrings through the holes. In Borneo, both men and women pierced their ears and wore multiple brass earrings on them, stretching the holes well beneath the shoulders.

In all cases, stretched ears, and the elaborate jewelry worn in them, seem to be associated with elite or elevated status. In many cases, we know that the ears were stretched intentionally to wear earplugs, ear spools, and the like, or simply to signify age, as the older the person was, the longer the ears were stretched. But in other cases, as in China, the ears may have been inadvertently stretched through the wearing of heavy hanging earrings in regular pierced ears. Today, stretched ears are still worn among some South American and African tribes, and often serves as a rite of passage and a mark of cultural identity for young boys or girls. However, the practice is dying as stretched ears are not only not viewed the same in the modern urban environment, but are often a hindrance in modern lifestyles.

In the West, the most common way to stretch an ear hole is to begin with a con-

A Dayak woman wears heavy earrings, which pull down on her earlobes, in a village near Mahakan River, Borneo, Indonesia, 1991. (Corbis)

ventional pierced hole in the ear. Once the piercing has healed, there are a number of ways of stretching the hole, which usually involve stretching it a little bit at a time in order to minimize tissue damage and pain. Tapering is the most common technique used for stretching, and involves the use of a conical metal rod known as a taper, which is pushed through the hole until the widest part of the taper is even with the skin; larger jewelry is then pushed through, parallel to the back of the taper. Larger tapers, and then jewelry, will be substituted over time as the hole gets bigger. Dead stretching is the practice of simply stretching a hole in the skin until it is big enough to accommodate the desired jewelry. A piercing can also be stretched via the hanging of weights onto the jewelry. This is a common way that people in traditional societies stretched ears in the past, although the practice can result in tissue tearing and thinning. A more modern way of stretching is via scalpeling, or using a scalpel to cut a large hole around a piercing, removing a piece of flesh.

Stretched piercings allow for a wider variety of jewelry than can be worn in many more conventional piercings, although the most commonly worn jewelry is known as an earplug, which is a cylindrical piece of jewelry that fits into a large hole and is sometimes flared at both ends to keep it in place. Flesh tunnels are a hollowed-out version of a plug, and resemble an empty spool of thread. They can be worn with another decorative item, like a feather, running through the middle. Ear spirals are another option, which are spiral-shaped coils that are inserted into the ear. Ear spools were worn in the ears in many **Central American** cultures, and are large cylinders that fit through the ears with a large disk or decorative sheet on the front side.

In the early 21st century, due to the modern primitive movement, stretched ears have become popular for many young people, who both like the way that stretched earlobes look, appreciate the variety of jewelry that can be worn in them, and in some cases, want to mimic the practices of so-called primitive people around the world. *See also* Ear Piercing; Ear Spools and Plugs

Further Reading

Angel, Elayne. *The Piercing Bible: The Definitive Guide to Safe Body Piercing*. Berkeley, CA: Celestial Arts, 2009.

McNab, Nan. *Body Bizarre Body Beautiful*. New York: Fireside, 2001.

Easter Island

Easter Island, known as Rapanui to its inhabitants, is a Polynesian island controlled by the country of Chile. The island was mostly settled between 300 and 600 CE by people who may have arrived from the Marquesas Islands. The first European explorer to arrive on the island was Dutch navigator Jacob Roggeveen, who landed in 1772, followed by Captain James Cook, who landed in 1774. From 1860 to the late 19th century, the island's population was decimated, largely due to the export of the native people to **South America**'s Peruvian slave traders. Those few hundred remaining islanders were forced, after slavery, to live on a reservation until the 1960s, because the island was rented to a sheep company that grazed its sheep over the island. Since that time, the people have been rebuilding their traditional culture.

Easter Island is famous for the giant stone statues, or *moai*, that cover the island—887 in all. These statues, which represent deceased and perhaps living chiefs (almost entirely male), were carved between the 13th and 16th centuries. The moai may have also acted as a form of communication with the gods, since they were so huge and positioned between the earth and the sky. The moai are thought by scholars to mediate between the different realms of sky and earth, and between people, chiefs, and gods. The statues were probably not just simple representations, however, but were likely embodiments of *mana*, or spiritual power, that would have been found in the chiefs as well. Finally, besides their sacred meaning, they almost certainly represented clan status, with different statues embodying different clan leaders. Ultimately, the moai most likely represented both religious and social authority.

From the late 18th century to 1868, only about a hundred years after the moai construction period ended, all of the moai were pushed over, face forward, most likely because of civil war between the clans, which left the island almost depopulated by the time the Europeans returned in the 1860s.

Moai at Ranu Raraku. Moai monoliths, which represented the bodies but especially the heads of ancestors and gods, were created, transported, and erected by the people of Easter Island, a small, remote Pacific island. (Shutterstock)

The statues are dominated by the heads, which make up the bulk of the size of the statues, but also include torsos, and in one instance, legs. The heads are dominant because, like other Polynesian cultures, the head—especially the head of the chief—was considered more powerful than the rest of the body, and was especially infused with mana, or spiritual power. Many of the statues were buried up to their heads, so the rest of the body could not be seen without excavation. The moai ranged from almost 4 feet high to more than 70 feet high, and weighed from 5 tons to 165 tons, with an average height of 13 feet and an average weight of 14 tons.

They were constructed by carvers, perhaps representing individual clans, who carved the statues out of volcanic ash, or tuff, taken from a volcanic crater on the island of Rano Raraku, although some were carved from other materials. Stone tools that would have been used for the carving have been located at Rano Raraku. Once the statues were completed, they were moved to ceremonial sites, mostly along the southeast coast of the island, and erected on flat stone pedestals known as *ahu*. Archaeological research shows that some of these ahu were dismantled and reassembled periodically, with newer and larger moai.

They were probably transported using sleds or rollers made from wood, as well as ropes and other materials. The islanders eventually overconsumed their resources and ultimately deforested the island; once the trees were gone, it was likely that they could no longer move the statues, and this probably marked the end of statue construction. In fact, archaeological analysis shows that the island was deforested by 1650, which is when the islanders stopped making the statues. Almost half of the statues were never moved, however, and were left standing where they were originally constructed, while others were probably dropped off in transport on the way to the coast. In addition, a large number of the statues were never completed at all.

The faces of the moai are highly stylized, with flat angles demarcating the heavy foreheads, large noses, long ears, and pronounced cheeks, lips, and chins. Eyes are represented with deep slits, which originally held pieces of white coral with pupils of obsidian or other materials, and many had red head coverings known as *pukao*, which may have represented individual clans.

The moai were carved with patterns representing the tattooing that was once practiced on the island. The detailed designs were primarily on the backs, and include tattoo motifs of stripes, circles, squares, triangles and other abstract designs. Some moai were also painted. Prior to colonization, men and women on the island wore tattoos, and tattoos were done on the face and head, which were considered to be the most sacred part of the body, but also included shoulders, upper backs, arms, buttocks, and thighs. **Facial tattoos** for both men and women generally consisted of very heavy curved and straight lines combined with dots, which appear somewhat like Maori **moko**. Some of the facial markings on women may have been related to fertility, and facial tattoo marks are also seen on the barkcloth figures made by the native peoples.

As with other Polynesian cultures, tattoos demonstrated kinship and rank, and the chiefly and warrior classes wore tattoos most commonly. Tattooing was done in the classic Polynesian style, with a tool known as *ta kona* carved out of bird bone and connected to a longer handled wooden implement, then dipped it into pigment and tapped into the skin with a mallet.

See also Facial Tattoos; Moko

Further Reading

Flenley, John, and Paul G. Bahn. *The Enigmas of Easter Island: Island on the Edge*. Oxford: Oxford University Press, 2003.

Métraux, Alfred. "Ethnology of Easter Island." *Bernice Bishop Museum Bulletin* (Honolulu) 160 (1940).

Van Tilburg, JoAnne. *Easter Island: Archaeology, Ecology, and Culture*. Washington, DC: Smithsonian Institution Press, 1994.

Egypt

Ancient Egyptian art is an excellent resource for trying to understand not only what the Egyptian face looked like but also how it was represented at the time. In addition, the ancient Egyptians, and especially the elites, devoted a great deal of time and energy to the adornment of the face and hair. Because the Egyptians left such a wealth of artwork, statuary, funerary materials, and mummies, we know a tremendous amount of how they treated their faces and what the standards of **beauty** were.

Much of what we have in terms of Egyptian art comes from the tombs in which the pharaohs and other powerful Egyptians were interred. Because Egyptians believed that the body must be preserved after death, in order for the soul to live on in the afterlife, Egyptians perfected a number of techniques for mummifying the body, as well as storing it. And because Egyptians believed that the body needed to be protected, and identified in the afterlife, they created elaborate sculpted and painted **masks** to represent the face of the deceased, which were placed over the wrapped body. Egyptian priests also wore masks of Anubis during the 70 days of embalming—both to call on Anubis to prepare the spirit of the dead, and to protect the priest from toxic embalming materials.

After the Middle Kingdom, anthropoid, or mummiform, coffins began to be used, which were coffins shaped and decorated to appear as the person in repose. Later, during Roman-occupied Egypt, **death masks** gave way to the painted wooden portraits known as mummy portraits or Fayoum portraits. Placed over the face of the deceased, they served the same functions as the earlier sculpted masks. Other representations—carved, sculpted, and painted—of the deceased were placed in his or her tomb, which were another way of ensuring that the person continued to exist; in fact, a word for sculptor in Egyptian was he who keeps alive. And finally, other reliefs, paintings, and sculptures, sometimes of servants, were included in the tomb as well, which were not intended to be seen by humans, but only by the dead person's soul, since the tomb would be his home for eternity. (The visual representations replaced the earlier practice, known as retainer sacrifice, of entombing the king's servants with him after his death, a practice that was discontinued by the end of the predynastic period.)

Those masks and portraits that survived the centuries provide a good example of how the Egyptians represented the human face. Portraits of kings and other royalty were more stylized, simpler, and less detailed than Western portraits. It was very rare to portray a ruler or commoner with gray hair or wrinkles, demonstrating the high value that Egyptians placed on youth. Symmetry was also highly valued; both bodies and faces were represented as symmetrical.

Egyptian artists represented bodies and eyes in frontal view, but legs, heads, and faces in profile view. (In fact, the funerary masks were some of the only forms of Egyptian art in which faces were represented in full frontal view. This is because the earlier Egyptian masks were sculpted to fit over the face, while the later Roman-era masks were painted in the Roman, rather than the Egyptian, style.) Men were painted with darker skin colors than women, and the heads of the gods were represented using long-standing conventions. For instance, Anubis was always shown with a jackal's head and Horus with a falcon's head.

What did the ancient Egyptians truly look like? This question, even with the large amounts of funerary art that has been discovered, is difficult to answer, given the stylized forms of art that the Egyptians practiced. Even the skin color of ancient Egyptians is difficult to discern from artwork, because the colors that were used to paint skin color were not based on true skin color, and the mummification process itself turns skin very dark. For example, Nubians were painted in very dark colors, but this choice of colors probably isn't about what they looked like as much as certain colors were used for specific nationalities, and women were depicted with lighter skin than men. Some scholars today feel that ancient Egyptians probably look like modern Egyptians, but others feel that they probably share more similarities with some Northern and Eastern African populations, such as Northern Sudan. Still others feel that Egypt was a melting pot of civilizations and that there was probably a wide variety of ethnic diversity within the kingdom. In recent years, scholars have been performing forensic analysis on Egyptian mummies, and most recently, using radiological techniques such as spiral CT scanning, scientists have been able to model and reconstruct three-dimensional faces of some mummies virtually. Even with this evidence, though, reconstructing the ancient Egyptian face to see what they really looked like is not yet fully possible.

In terms of adornment, Egyptians spent a great deal of time, energy, and money on hair. Egyptian hairstyles varied with age, gender, and social status, with elites being able to hire professional hairdressers, afford the most expensive wigs, and use the richest oils, dyes, and scents for their hair. Boys and girls until puberty wore their hair shaved except for a sidelock left on the side of their head. Many adults—both men and women—also shaved their hair as a way

Women offering a necklace and cup, from the tomb of Jeserkareseneb, Egyptian, XVIII Dynasty. This tomb painting illustrates the classic Egyptian way of representing the face, in profile, with the eye facing the viewer. (Corel)

of coping with the heat and lice. However, adults did not go bald, and instead wore wigs in public and in private. Slaves and servants wore their hair simply, often tied back from the face.

Men who did wear their own hair generally wore it short, with the ears exposed. Women, on the other hand, wore a variety of hairstyles (and wig styles) from long to short, but generally favored waves or curls. Many women used **henna** to dye their hair or cover their gray hair. Women also decorated their hair and wigs with flowers, ribbons, and jewels, with wealthier women being able to afford more elaborate decorations. Wigs were initially only worn by the elites, but later were worn by women of all classes, although those who could not afford quality wigs made of human hair wore cheaper wigs, made of vegetable fibers or wool, or hair extensions. Even certain wig styles were limited to the wealthy, and the wealthy could afford the oils needed to properly maintain wigs.

Egyptians also used makeup from a very early period, with evidence dating back 5,000 or 6,000 years. Scented oils and fats were used to soften and perfume the skin and hair, henna and other natural dyes were used to color the hair, fingernails, and lips, the scents of plants like rose or peppermint were used to perfume the hair and body, and minerals like ochre and malachite were ground up to create face and eye makeup. Men, women, and children lined their eyes and darkened their brows with **kohl**, malachite, or crushed insects, and elites, again, had a wide variety of products to use to enhance their appearance. Eye makeup was used for adornment, to protect against the glare of the sun, and to ward off the **evil eye**. Like so many other cultures, light skin for women was highly prized, and women washed their faces with egg whites and used lead-based makeup to whiten their skin further. Egyptians had also developed formulas to remove wrinkles, **acne**, and other blemishes on the skin.

Jewelry, too, was used by all classes to adorn the body and face. The wealthy wore elaborate necklaces and earrings made of fine metals, ivory, and precious stones as both adornment and status indicators. Some mummies and artwork show evidence of stretched ears, which may have been caused by the wearing of heavy jewelry. Tutankhamen, for example, had stretched ears. In addition, **head binding** was practiced by Egyptians during the Amarna period, which lasted through Tutankhamen's time.

See also Cosmetics; Death Masks; Head Binding; Henna

Further Reading

Picton, Janet, Stephen Quirke, and Paul C. Roberts. *Living Images: Egyptian Funerary Portraits in the Petrie Museum.* Walnut Creek, CA: Left Coast Press, 2007.

Schulz, Regine, Matthias Seidel, Betsy Morrell Bryan, and Christianne Henry. *Egyptian Art.* Baltimore: Walters Art Museum, 2009.

Strouhal, Eugen. *Life of the Ancient Egyptians.* Norman: University of Oklahoma Press, 1992.

Emoticon

An emoticon is a computer keyboard-generated sign that represents **facial expressions**. Used in computer-mediated communication, emoticons provide an emotional quality to e-mails, texts, instant messaging, and other Internet communication.

With the rise of the Internet in the 1990s as a new tool for communication came new concerns about how Internet communication is impacting real-life relationships. One result of the preponderance of Internet activity, especially the rise of social media sites like MySpace and Facebook, is that social networks have become larger, while at the same time, more shallow. People have more relationships with more people today than in the past, but those relationships are often more superficial. On the other hand, the Internet allows people to maintain relationships with family and friends from whom they are geographically separated, allowing for those relationships to thrive. Indeed, studies show that more than 50 percent of the time that is spent on the Internet, is spent communicating with others.

But how people communicate on the Internet is a different question. It is clear that Internet communication is different from face-to-face communication, and one of the major reasons for this difference is that without face time, people are unable to see the facial expressions or **eye contact** that are so critical to human interaction. Emoticons substitute for the presence of a real facial expression, and are intended to convey to the reader of an email or text the emotional qualities of the message.

Kevin Mackenzie may have proposed the first computer-based emoticon—-) to represent tongue in cheek—on ARPANET (which predated the Internet) in 1979, and a simple smiley face may have existed prior to that. But the shorthand use of letters,

punctuation, and numbers to convey meaning dates back to at least the 19th century. But it wasn't until the age of the Internet that the concept took off, as non-face-to-face communication became the norm in the West. Computer scientist Scott Fahlman was the first person to suggest using smiley and sad faces, :-) and :-(, as a way to convey emotion in digital communication, in a post on a university bulletin board in 1982.

For the first few years, emoticons were created by typing punctuation marks like colons, semicolons, dashes, and parentheses into a pattern that, when viewed from the side, reading left to right, look like simple facial expressions. While emoticons are still typically generated using a series of punctuation marks, many software programs and online forums now convert the individual symbols, :-), to a more graphic representation of the desired expression: ☺. In addition, there are now discussion forums, social networking sites, online games, and mobile applications that provide for a variety of emoticons, some animated, well beyond the original emoticons that could be created with a handful of keystrokes. These include alien faces, Frankenstein's monster, two-headed creatures, and animal faces.

The most popular emoticons are the smiley face and the sad face. The smiley face, like a real smile, has multiple uses and goes far beyond conveying the writer's happy state. Smiley faces are used to soften a message that might otherwise seem harsh, to indicate a joke, to show amusement, to caution the reader to not take the message too seriously, or to cheer up the reader. Sad faces are used both to indicate that something the writer is saying is unhappy, or that the writer is unhappy, but also to empathize with another writer over something that person has said.

Other emoticons are used to convey other emotional states like laughter or anger, and more subtle emotions like sarcasm, contempt, surprise, or perplexity, while other emoticons are primarily ornamental, or used to express nonemotional issues, like dancing or music.

While many emoticons are used around the world, some are culture specific, sometimes because the layouts of the computer keyboards in some countries differs from those used in the United States. But there are more important cultural differences behind some of these images.

In the 1980s, Japanese computer users created text-based emoticons (known as *kaomoji*) that are viewed vertically, rather than from the side; one version of a Japa-

nese smiley face looks like this: (^_^), while the emoticon for "ouch" looks like this: (>_<), and a sad face looks like this (T_T). As with Western emoticons, Japanese emoticons are now rendered more graphically via mobile phone applications, which provide hundreds of graphical emoticons (or *emoji*) for users to choose. In addition, because the Japanese alphabet includes Chinese phonogram characters, these are used in Japanese emoticons as well. For this reason, many Japanese emoticons cannot be interpreted by Westerners. Finally, Japanese emoticons are influenced by Japanese comic books, known as *manga*, which have multiple ways to express feelings. Some Japanese emoticons express emotions and situations not known in the West. For instance, m(__)m refers to *dogeza*, or kneeling and bowing to show regret or politeness. (It literally shows two hands on either side of the face, while the person is kneeling with their head on the floor.)

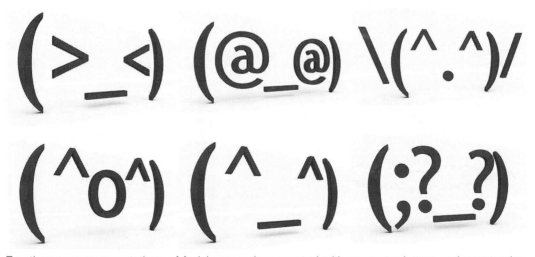

Emoticons are representations of facial expressions created with computer letters and punctuation marks. Japanese emoticons differ from American emoticons and demonstrate the differences in the importance of various facial expressions to each culture. (Dreamstime.com)

Interestingly, while the Japanese, like the Chinese, are very good at controlling emotions and facial expressions in face-to-face encounters, there is a huge variety of Japanese emoticons. In addition, Japanese emoticons (and the interpretations of them) are more focused on the shape of the eyes, while Western emoticons are more focused on the shape of the mouth. This is because Americans, even while we favor eye contact, tend to look at our conversational partners' mouths to understand their emotions, while the Japanese look more at the eyes for emotional cues, perhaps because the Japanese are more easily able to control the appearance of their mouths (when controlling their emotions) than their eyes.

Recent research has shown that the use of emoticons not only improves computer-based communication, by adding the emotional quality that had been absent, but that it speeds up communication as well, allowing the symbols to substitute for words in many cases. Finally, while women and girls tend to use more emoticons than men and boys, paralleling the gender-based use or control of emotions in real-world communication, when men and women communicate in mixed-gender forums, men tend to use more emoticons when communicating.

See also Eye Contact; Facial Expressions; Japan

Further Reading

Huang, A., D. Yen, and X. Zhang. "Exploring the Potential Effects of Emoticons." *Information and Management* 45, no. 7 (2008): 466–73.

Krohn, F. "A Generational Approach to Using Emoticons as Nonverbal Communication." *Journal of Technical Writing and Communication* 34, no. 4 (2004): 321–28.

England

England is the site of a number of popular events related to the face, including **gurning**, **blackface**, and **mummery**.

Gurning refers to making awkward and ugly **facial expressions**, usually in a competitive sense. It is most well known through the gurning competitions held in rural English villages going back to the Middle Ages. The most popular of these events is the Egremont Crab Fair, a 13th-century fair held annually in September that features the World Gurning Championship.

Blackface refers to the wearing of black makeup, usually by white performers, in order to impersonate and mock black people in comedy and musical performances. While blackface usually refers to the American tradition, which began during slavery and lasted through the Jim Crow era, it has been practiced in England as well, and in fact predates the American tradition by at least 300 years. Blackface was employed by white actors in Shakespeare's plays, most famously by actors portraying Othello, a Moorish soldier in the play *Othello*. While it is unknown exactly what Shakespeare intended Othello to look like, it is known that from the early 17th century, he was played by white men in blackface, and only in recent years has he been played by black actors. At that same time, England's Queen Anne, wife of King James I, and her court blackened their faces and arms to play black characters in a play written for them. Blackface in England predates African slavery as well, and has its roots in the relationship between Christians and Moors in Medieval Europe. (It is also worth pointing out that during the

16th and 17th centuries when blackfaced actors were performing in England, elite English women were whitening their own faces with lead-based makeup, in order to achieve the lightest, and thus most beautiful, appearance.)

An English clogging troupe called the Britannia Coco-Nut Dancers also performs in blackface. Clogging is a dance that uses wooden-soled shoes to stomp on the ground to the downbeat of the music. Practiced throughout Northern Europe from the 18th to the 20th centuries, clogging was said to have been started by factory workers who tapped their wooden clogs on the floor while working. In the case of the Coco-Nut Dancers, one history says that the performers' faces are blackened to protect the dancers from being seen by evil spirits, while another history suggests that the dance originated with Moorish pirates. Perhaps the most likely theory relates the black faces to the darkened faces of the Cornish miners who were the earliest performers, and who brought the dance to Lancashire.

Mummery refers to a British tradition that dates back to the Middle Ages in which costumed acting troupes perform in public, often by visiting private homes or public houses. The performances focused on the killing and resurrection of one of the characters, and usually featured performers wearing **masks** or other types of headgear to conceal their faces; sometimes the actors wore blackface, although in mummery the use of blackface was a form of concealment (and could be red as well) rather than a way to imitate or mock Africans. On the other hand, Mummer's Day celebrations were often called Darkie Day,

indicating that at least at some point, racial connotations were associated with the performances.

See also Blackface; Gurning; Mummery

Further Reading

Hobson, Jeremy. *Curious Country Customs.* Newton Abbot: David & Charles, 2007.

Epicanthic Fold

The epicanthic fold is a web of skin creating the upper eyelid of many people of Asian descent; in some people, it overlaps the inner corner of the eye. It is often associated with what is called a single eyelid, or an upper eyelid with no crease. The epicanthic fold is most commonly found among the populations of Central, North, East, and **Southeast Asia**, as well as some Native Americans, some Arctic peoples, and some Oceanic peoples. People living in Europe, **Central America**, and the southern continents lack the epicanthic fold, and have a double eyelid, or creased lid, although there are a handful of populations in Africa and the far northern reaches of Europe with the epicanthic fold. It can also be associated with a number of developmental disorders such as Down Syndrome, and is present in many children during development.

The epicanthic fold may be an adaptive feature found in environments where harsh sunlight reflects off of light surfaces, which can harm the eyes; the fold may be a protection against such the ultraviolet rays in these conditions, as well as against strong winds, cold, or sand, especially when combined with a minimal brow ridge (as brow ridges can also protect the eyes).

Since the 1950s, but especially in recent years, surgery to modify the epicanthic fold has grown increasingly common in Asian countries like **China**, **Korea**, and **Japan**, as well as among people of Asian descent in the United States. While the epicanthic fold, which overlaps the inner eye, can technically be removed through a surgery called epicanthoplasty, it is very rare. The most common surgical procedure to modify the appearance of the epicanthic fold is the blepharoplasty, in which a crease is created in the upper eyelid. The surgery involves stitching the levator muscle, which controls the opening of the eyelid, to the eyelid, as well as removing excess skin and fat pads in order to create the crease.

As this procedure becomes more common, it has grown increasingly controversial, with charges of racism and internal racism being hurled between supporters and opponents of the procedure. Blepharoplasty surgery is the most frequently performed **cosmetic surgery** in all of Asia, and among Asians living in America, with 500,000 procedures performed per year in

The epicanthic fold is a tiny fold of the upper eyelid that is found among some Asian populations. It is a focus of a surgical procedure known as epicanthoplasty, in which the fold is removed to make the eye appear more Western. Another popular procedure among many Asians today is the double eyelid surgery, which creates a crease in the upper eyelid, again, to make the eye appear more Western. (Dreamstime.com)

South Korea alone, and an increasing number of untrained and unlicensed doctors offering the procedure as well. In the United States in 2005, 437,000 Asian Americans had the procedure.

While up to half of all Asians with the epicanthic fold have the single eyelid, the double eyelid has become the standard of **beauty** among Asians. Women (and some men like action star Jackie Chan) who receive the surgery say that they want to have eyes that look larger, less sleepy, and that are easier to apply makeup on. Opponents of the procedure, however, charge that its popularity is a direct result of the globalization of Western standards of **beauty**, which demand light skin and Caucasian facial features, and that women who undergo blepharoplasty are, at least subconsciously, trying to look white. At the very least, say critics, Asians are emulating a standard of beauty found in Asian celebrities or Japanese anime, but in both cases, the beauty being emulated is not found among the majority of the population and seems to echo the big eyes (often green or blue) seen on Caucasians. It also helps to remember that the surgery emerged after the end of World War II, when Asian Americans who could afford it would have their eyelids surgically modified; those who could not would often use tape to try to approximate a crease in the lid.

Perhaps as a response to the controversy, some doctors are refining the blepharoplasty techniques to remove less fat and create a less pronounced crease, leaving the patients still looking Asian but less so than before. This ethnic correctness has not resulted in fewer surgical procedures, but simply less obvious procedures. Still, especially when blepharoplasty is combined with rhinoplasty, colored contact lenses, and breast augmentation (not to mention jaw bone and cheekbone surgeries) it is difficult to ignore the idea that the goal is to look non-Asian, or at the very least, to fit in better to Caucasian society. It is also difficult to continue to maintain that these surgeries are solely personal decisions, and have no wider cultural or political meaning.

Today, as the surgery becomes more commonplace (even as some women, particularly in America, are resisting it), pressures to get the surgery are often intense, especially within the family. Many parents pressure their children to undergo the procedure, and as peers leave surgery with their new round eyes, it becomes harder to resist. Those who are born with a natural double eyelid are seen as special, and are thanked for saving their parents money. One result is that in some areas like Korea, it is difficult to find young women who have not had the surgery.

See also Beauty; China; Cosmetic Surgery; Gender

Further Reading

Kaw, E. "Opening Faces: The Politics of Cosmetic Surgery and Asian American Women." In *In Our Own Words: Readings on the Psychology of Women and Gender*, edited by M. Crawford and R. Under, 55–73. New York: McGraw-Hill, 1997.

Scranton, Philip. *Beauty and Business: Commerce, Gender, and Culture in Modern America*. New York: Routledge, 2001.

Evil Eye

The evil eye is a belief, found in cultures around the world, that certain individuals can cause sudden harm to others through a look, which is often unintentional. A person with an evil eye has the ability to cause illness, misfortune, death, or property damage to another person by looking at or praising him, and the action is usually caused by envy. In Indo-European and Arabic folklore, evil eye references are common. For instance, the following are folklore motifs catalogued by folklorists Stith Thompson and Antti Aarne: "Evil eye" (D2064.4—this refers to a particular motif as categorized by Thompson and Aarne), "Magic paralysis by evil eye" (D2072.1), "Magic sickness because of evil eye" (D2176.3), "Evil eye covered with seven veils" (D2071.0.1), "Avoiding display of one's assets averts evil eye" (D2071), "Black as guard against evil eye" (D2071.1.4), and "Simulated change of sex to baffle evil eye" (D2071.1.3).

The evil eye belief has been found in cultures around the world, and probably derives from Indo-European, Mediterranean, and Middle Eastern cultures; its roots go back to the ancient civilizations of those regions. It may have started in Sumeria, and then spread through the Greco-Roman world to **India**, Spain and Portugal, northern Europe, and **North Africa**, and later, the Spanish colonies of the New World. It has not been found in the traditional folklore of Asia, Native America, or **Sub-Saharan Africa**. The evil eye is known as *ayin harsha* in Arabic, *bla band* in Farsi, *ayin horeh* in Hebrew, *droch shuil* in Scotland, *mauvais oeil* in France, *bösen blick* in Germany, *mal occhio* in Italy, *mal ojo* in Spain, *nazar* in India, *olho gordo* in Brazil, and *oculus malus* in ancient Rome.

There are numerous references to the evil eye in the Old Testament, and a few in the New Testament. As in other places with evil eye beliefs, those who are jealous or covetous possess the evil eye. The Bible notes how mothers protected their children from the evil eye, by dressing them in rags or making it appear as if they were unloved. Indeed, the term evil eye is used in the Bible as a synonym for covetousness as in, "He that hasteth to be rich hath an evil eye, and considereth not that poverty shall come upon him" (Prov. 28:22). In the New Testament, Jesus asks, "Is it not lawful for me to do what I will with mine own? Is thine eye evil, because I am good? So the last shall be first, and the first last: for many be called, but few chosen" (Matt. 20:15–16).

Jewish tradition is filled with practices associated with protecting against, or warding off, the evil eye. For example, the practice of having father and son read the Torah separately at synagogue is rooted in the fear of displaying one's large family in public, and arousing jealousy among those without a large family. Because children are so vulnerable to the evil eye, placing a red thread around the wrist of children has been a common practice, and is still practiced today by believers of Kabbalah.

These beliefs predate the ancient Hebrews and were found in other cultures of the Middle and Near East as well. They are probably also related to the concept of the all-powerful, all seeing eye, found in a number of cultures. Eyes are also used as protective amulets in these same cultures. For instance, the Eye of Horus served as protection against evil in ancient Egypt, and eyes were used on amulets in Mesopotamia, as in the hundreds of eye talismans found in Tell Brak in Syria. Indeed, in the ancient world, seeing is itself a concept that is infused with power and could be used as both a curse and a form of divination.

Beliefs about the evil eye are found associated with beliefs that too much praise and too much pride are dangerous, especially to the young. For instance, the ancient Greek gods would become jealous when humans were too beautiful or powerful, and could cause them great misfortune as a punishment. In many cultures with evil eye beliefs, not praising people is one way to make sure that they are not harmed by the evil eye. For example, Ugly and Disagreeable were once common names given to children in ancient Greece and North Africa; by calling their children ugly, parents ensure that their children remain safe from the evil eye.

Alternatively, giving praise to someone, or praising yourself, is tantamount to inviting the evil eye, and praise of infants is especially dangerous because they are extra vulnerable. In some cases, compliments are dangerous because they will invite outside scrutiny on the person, but in other cases, the compliment itself is simply a disguise, and the person making the compliment wants to possess what the other person has.

Folklorist Alan Dundes explained the evil eye as a phenomenon that could dry up or wither living creatures: crops, fruit trees, breast milk, cows, semen, and the like. Unlike a normal eye, which emits liquid, he saw the evil eye as absorbing liquid, from literally looking at someone too long. It is interesting to note that fish are apparently immune from the evil eye, perhaps because they are surrounded by water.

Like witches, people with the evil eye often do not know that they have it, and they are not easily detected. But as with witchcraft beliefs, people who are outsiders or marginalized in the community are often suspected of having the evil eye. Likewise, someone with deformed eyes is often a suspect. Greek and Roman beliefs hold that a baby who begins to nurse after having been weaned will grow up with the evil eye. Blue-or green-eyed people in Mediterranean countries are often suspect as well.

Evil eye beliefs may also serve as leveling mechanisms, in the way of witchcraft beliefs. Because they are found in communities in which health, wealth, and happiness are considered to be a limited resource, then both witchcraft and evil eye beliefs help to keep some people from gaining too much at the expense of others. Those who have an unusual amount of wealth, happiness, or beauty are subject to either witchcraft accusations or the evil eye. Too much good will always bring bad.

Why is it the evil eye, and not, for example, the evil mouth? It is thought that the eye is the source of the evil because it watches; it is intrusive. It is the way to look *into* a person, and as such, can harm him subtly. In addition, people fear being not only watched but being caught doing something that they should not be doing. And while most often, the evil eye is thought to be unconscious, it can also be done consciously, by overlooking, or looking to long at something or someone, out of envy. Because witches were generally thought to possess the evil eye, dealing with a known witch involved keeping his or her face away from the person, to protect himself from their harm. Finally, Plutarch, writing in the first century, thought that deadly rays could emanate from the eyes of certain people.

Every culture with an evil eye belief has a corresponding set of practices to avert it, known as apotropaic devices. Resisting praise is one, and in some cultures, if one does praise someone, following the praise by spitting can counteract the effect. Another method is to touch a person, or attach a stone (often blue) onto a person, to take off the eye after the praise is given. Still another method is to recite a short phrase after the compliment, to undo the damage done, such as *kein ayin horah* (without the evil eye) in Yiddish or *inshallah* (if God wills it or God willing) or *mashallah* (God has willed it) in Arabic. The Arabic expression indicates that one can only be harmed by the evil eye if Allah wills it so, so saying God willing after a compliment ensures that God will not let the eye do harm. In Mexico, if a person admires a child, he must touch the child and invoke God's protection so that the child will not be harmed.

Amulets are also common methods to avert the evil eye, and can be worn on a person, or hung over the doorway to a house to protect the home. One such amulet is a lemon pierced with nine nails; amulets made of liquid, like fruit, are especially effective. A doorknocker that makes the *mano fico* gesture (an Italian term that represents a penis in a vagina) is another way to protect oneself, and this gesture can be made with the hands, by inserting the thumb between the index and middle finger. The use of phallic imagery to protect against the evil eye dates back to Roman times, and even today, in Italy men will cover their testicles when in the presence of someone they suspect has the evil eye.

Children can be dressed poorly or can have some dirt rubbed on their face, to reduce their beauty and thus reduce the envy that might be aimed at them. In ancient times, newborns and mothers were sometimes confined to the home for 40 days to protect them from the evil eye. It is said that the modern practice of tipping a wait person started as a way of ensuring that the waiter is not jealous of you because you enjoyed your food.

Applying makeup around the eyes was another form of protection; ancient Egyptians used **kohl** to draw lines around their eyes to protect themselves, and in modern India, women do as well, both to protect themselves, and to ensure that they do not inflict harm on others. Indian women will also put kohl on their children's faces to ward off the eye, by making the child imperfect.

Using mirrors to reflect the evil eye back on the perpetrator, is also a common strategy, leading to the development of small mirror charms worn on people or kept in houses or cars; for example, in India and in the **Middle East**, it is still common to find clothing, scarves, and decorative textiles made with mirrors crocheted into cloth.

Amulets are often in the form of an eye, and often blue or black, both colors that were thought to repel the evil eye. For example, in Mexico, the *ojo de venado* is a seed that looks like an eye, and is used as an amulet, usually with a photo of a saint. In Turkey and Greece, brooches made of blue glass in the shape of an eye are worn as protection, and in the Middle East, blue glass eye beads called *Nazar Boncugu* are popular amulets. In Tibet, stone *dzi* beads, which look like eyes, are made into jewelry and worn as protection. In the English world, cat's eye beads were strung together to make protective charms. The *hamesh* hand in Hebrew (also known as the Hand of Miriam), or *hamsa* hand in Arabic (also known as the Hand of Fatima), is a charm made in the shape of a hand with an eye in the palm, and is a protective device in both the Arab and Jewish world. The eye in hand charm combines the hamsa hand with the blue glass beads of the Turkey and Greece, and is popular in the Christian world.

Once someone has indeed been affected by the evil eye, as indicated by the loss of fertility or, in a child, fever or vomiting, there are cures available. In the Middle East, burning the seeds of the espand plant while reciting a prayer can cure the child; this is also done as a preventative. Prayers are found in other cultures as well, as in Greece, where a prayer to the Virgin Mary is uttered. In other cultures, passing a raw egg over the victim, and then disposing of the egg, is another cure. This practice derives from the Mediterranean and is still found in Mexico today. In India, passing a flame across the face of the afflicted can cure the victim. In other cultures, holy water or olive oil can serve as a cure—either through drinking, immersion, or splashing.

See also Christianity; India; Middle East

A cluster of Turkish evil eyes, a traditional item used to protect against bad spirits. Charms like this have long been used to protect against the evil eye, a prominent belief in many cultures around the world. (Allen Lindblad/Dreamstime.com)

Further Reading

Aarne, Antti, and Stith Thompson. *The Types of the Folktale: A Classification and Bibliography.* Helsinki: Academia Scientiarum Fennica, 1961.

Dundes, Alan. *The Evil Eye: A Folklore Casebook.* Garland Folklore Casebooks, vol. 2. New York: Garland, 1981.

Evolution of the Face

The human face is the result of millions of years of evolution.

The origins of the human face are owed to a worm-like creature called pikaia, which evolved 500 million years ago during the Cambrian period. Prior to the pikaia, all of earth's creatures lived in the water and had no facial features, and thus, no faces. All of the major facial features, the mouth, nose, eyes, and ears, evolved to help their owners to hunt and eat, or to avoid being eaten by detecting predators.

The pikaia were the first animals to develop a primitive mouth, allowing them to take in food through a hole, rather than through absorption, like a sponge. The first eyes appeared 450 million years ago with the conodont, an eel-like creature that also had primitive teeth-like structures. The sacambaspsis, a fish from the late Ordovician period, had the first nostril-like features, or gills, which allowed it to take in oxygen. These little holes would later evolve into the first true noses, with the acanthostega, the first land animal, about 365 million years ago. Before that time, though, the acanthodian, another fish, developed the first hinging jaw, allowing the creature to open and close his mouth, rather than passively letting food rush in.

As the first mammals emerged, 150 million years later, the muscles of the face changed because of adaptations to living on earth, breathing air, and eating and swallowing food differently. The first mammal, the megazostrodon, had not just fur (rather than scales) covering the skin, but it had external ears that could move, a twitchy nose with whiskers (controlled by more developed musculature), and a mouth that was flexible enough (thanks again to new facial muscles) to allow for nursing. Those movements would become critical for communication with other animals.

As the primate order emerged 65 to 80 million years ago, the skull and face shape began to change further, with early primates like the plesiadapis. Snouts became shorter and the eyes, which on many mammals sit on the sides of the head, began to rotate forward, ultimately ending up on the front of the face and providing overlapping fields of vision, which allows binocular vision (and cuts down on peripheral vision). Primates developed new muscles, too, which allowed for the movement of small parts of the face like the lips or the eyebrows, increasing the ways in which primates could communicate with each other. As sight became more important, and smell and hearing less important to primates, the muscles associated with hearing (and controlling the ears) and smelling reduced, and the muscles associated with moving the middle face increased in size and complexity.

As the primate order diversified into suborders, infraorders, parvaorders, superfamilies, families, and subfamilies, faces continued to change at all of these levels. The snouts of anthropoids, to which humans belong, are shorter than the faces of prosimians, and sight is much more important to anthropoids than prosimians. The noses and dental patterns of cattarhines, to which humans belong, are different from those of plattyrhines. Humans (along with old world monkeys and apes) have a dental pattern of 2-1-2-3, which means two incisors, one canine, two premolars, and three molars, on each side of the mouth, as well as a nose with downward projecting nostrils separated by a narrow septum. Hominoids, which includes humans and apes, have flatter faces again than monkeys, and the dentition differs significantly from monkeys: the molars have the Y-5 pattern, or bunodont pattern, while monkeys have bilophodont molars. Hominoids also not only have a flatter face than other primates, but wider jaws and a brow ridge over the eyes.

As the hominin line separated from the apes, about 8 million years ago, and various genera and species began to emerge (some of which are ancestral to modern humans, but most of which are not), the faces of our hominin relatives began to change further. Bipedalism, which first emerged among our ancestors 4 to 5 million years ago, led to a decline of importance of the sense of smell and a rise in importance of sight. In general, as we move from Australopithecus, a genus that we know is ancestral to our own genus, Homo, the faces become flatter: snouts shorten until they are almost imperceptible, and foreheads rise as brains expand. On the lower face, canines shorten, molar size increases, the diastema—the gap between the canines and premolars—disappears, jaw size increases, and the chin emerges from the jaw. Those

are just overall trends, however, and different species exhibit different facial features during evolution. For example, *Homo habilus*, the first species in the genus Homo, had an extremely pronounced brow ridge, which reduces considerably by the time *Homo sapiens* emerges. With anatomically modern *Homo sapiens sapiens*, which first appeared about 200,000 years ago, the face looks as it does today: large, forward-facing eyes covered by a minimal brow ridge; a large, round cranium with high flat forehead; short snout; small canines and incisors; and a pronounced jaw and chin. Modern human jaws, however, while trending larger during the course of evolution, are a little smaller than they once were (both through changes in diet and because tools now do the work that teeth once did), and consequently, all human teeth can no longer fit comfortably in the mouth. This is why so many people have their wisdom teeth, or third molar teeth, removed.

Why are modern human faces so much flatter than both living nonhuman primates and human ancestors? Scientists consider the human face to be a product of juvenilization or paedomorphy, because the adult human face resembles, at least in part, the juvenile faces of some nonhuman primates, especially as it relates to shorter snouts. Some scientists posit that having relatively juvenile looking faces may discourage aggression within the species and encourage collaboration and cooperation, while others suggest that baby faces are linked to breeding, because they signal youth and fertility to potential mates (and studies have shown that men, in particular, prefer a more baby-faced female face in terms of mating). A third hypothesis suggests that modern

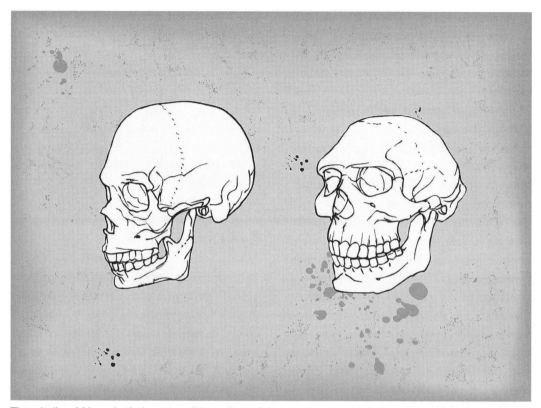

The skulls of Neanderthals, a hominin species living contemporaneously with modern humans until about 30,000 years ago, have much more robust features than do modern humans and have the largest noses of any hominin species, living or extinct. (iStockPhoto.com)

human faces are simply the result of the expansion of the brain, and have no specific function relative to the species. And finally, without the emphasis on smell associated with a large snout, humans have a much more finely developed sense of sight, and they use that sight, in part, to read the facial expressions of others of their own kind. Thus humans have the most well developed facial muscles of all animals, and the most experience with reading those facial expressions.

Not only have the physical structure and appearance of the human face evolved, but **facial expressions** have as well. Facial ex-

pressions are formed due to the interplay between the 14 bones of the face and the 52 muscles that control the face, and those muscles and bones, as explained, are the products of a lengthy history of evolution. Humans can more easily perceive facial expressions than other animal species due to their lack of facial hair; expressions are much easier to detect on a hairless face.

Darwin himself posited that the facial expressions of humans and other animals all have a functional basis: they show happiness by lifting the face and tightening the upper lip, which derives from preparing for a play bite, while they show anger through tightening the facial and mouth muscles, in preparation for an aggressive bite. Affection is expressed through the lips, whether through kissing, lip smacking, or sucking, and derives from the suckling of an infant to the mother's breast, and surprise is expressed through widening the eyes and the mouth, and rearing back in a protective stance. Darwin called these actions intention movements, or the incomplete or preparatory phase of noncommunicative activities like attack, play, or protection. Over time, these intention movements evolved into facial expressions, used for communication only.

Of the facial expressions that are now thought to be universal in humans—those expressing sadness, happiness, fear, surprise, anger, and disgust—Darwin thought that only smiling, laughing, and crying were innate, because they were the first expressions formed by infants, and because blind babies, who cannot see others forming those expressions, make them as well. It is probably true that all of these expressions are innate, but that some are more primitive than others, and that socialization and verbal cues help to reinforce them as a baby develops.

See also Animal Facial Expressions; Facial Expressions; Facial Features

Further Reading

Chevalier-Skolnikoff, Suzanne. "Facial Expression of Emotion in Nonhuman Primates." In *Darwin and Facial Expression: A Century of Research in Review*, edited by Paul Ekman, 11–89. Cambridge, MA: Malor Books, 2006.

Coss, Richard G., and Brian T. Schowengerdt. "Evolution of the Modern Human Face: Aesthetic and Attributive Judgments of a Female Profile Warped Along a Continuum of Paedomorphic to Late Archaic Craniofacial Structure." *Ecological Psychology* 10, no. 1 (1998): 1–24.

Darwin, Charles. *The Expression of the Emotions in Man and Animals*. Chicago: University of Chicago Press, 1965.

Fridlund, Alan J. *Human Facial Expression: An Evolutionary View*. San Diego: Academic Press, 1994.

Eye Contact

Eye contact is an important form of nonverbal communication. It shows interest in one's conversational partner, regulates communication, and establishes connections with others. Understanding and reacting to eye contact begins quite early; infants as young as two days old understand that a person is looking at them. Babies smile more at people who make eye contact with them, and can better recognize faces when eye contact is made. Even instantaneous eye contact can be an important form of communication. Eye contact is so important as a form of communication and as a communicator of social information that its absence in babies (who instinctively respond to a stare) is an early indication of autism. Humans are rare in the way that babies maintain eye contact with their mothers when nursing; this may be one sign of the importance of eye contact for human communication.

Whether or not a person looks another person in the eye, and for how long that look is sustained, carries important cultural meaning—meanings that are often contradictory. For example, in some cultures, looking someone in the eye is considered to be a sign of honesty, whereas looking away may indicate that the person is lying. This is the case in the United States. In the United States, not only is eye contact a sign that a person is trustworthy and sincere (whereas looking away signals dishonest intent), it is also a sign that a person is interested in the person they are talking to; looking away demonstrates a lack of interest. Along these lines, eye contact is also used as a form of flirtation in the United States, whereby interested parties switch back and forth between looking at the person of interest, and quickly looking away, as a way to signal sexual interest. Finally, in the United States, making eye contact is also a sign of confidence, as is a strong handshake. On the other hand, Americans generally avoid eye contact with strangers, especially in crowded spaces as on the subway, because eye contact in that context is seen as too intrusive, or can invite unwelcome attention. Prolonged eye contact, in particular, is generally seen either as an invitation to a fight or a sign that someone is in love.

In other cultures, looking someone in the eye, especially for an extended period of time, is considered pushy, aggressive, and is often interpreted as an invasion of privacy or a sign of social superiority. In **China**, for example, direct eye contact is interpreted as a challenge, so the Chinese will often look downward when they speak, especially when meeting someone new or speaking to a social superior. Native Americans also perceive direct eye contact as a form of aggression. This is also the case in **Japan**, where a lack of eye contact demonstrates politeness and respect.

Japanese women are more likely to refrain from eye contact, because cultural conventions demand more respect and submission from women than from men. And in general, in many Asian countries, younger people should not maintain eye contact with older people as a sign of deference. This is also the case in Africa, where traditionally young people and lower-class people did not initiate eye contact with older or higher status people. In recent years, these customs have been changing, however. And in **India**, people of different caste positions will avoid eye contact with each other entirely.

> The countenance is the portrait of the soul, and the eyes mark its intentions.—*Cicero*

Sustained eye contact can be an effective controlling mechanism. One recent study demonstrated that police who used sustained eye contact (known as holding gaze) could calm down, and control, members of the public better than police who only used verbal commands. Dogs and chimpanzees both use eye contact the same way—to demonstrate authority over a subordinate animal, or to initiate aggression. And while many nonhuman animals view eye contact the way that many cultures do—as a sign of aggression and higher social status—humans can use sustained eye contact as a way to demonstrate authority over dogs when training them.

In Muslim cultures, men and unrelated women are expected to refrain from eye contact, and women especially are expected to look away when in the presence of men, as a sign of modesty and deference. Women in purdah—those who are either veiled or confined to the home—especially must avoid eye contact with men. Middle Eastern men maintain more intense eye contact when speaking to other men, and the same is the case with women.

Avoiding eye contact with social superiors as a sign of respect is common in stratified societies around the world. In fact, we often hear reports of famous actors or singers demanding that their staff refrain from looking them in the face. But, interestingly, the opposite is also true: some people of high status instinctively avoid eye contact with social inferiors. For example, a 2009 study showed that when talking to strangers, people from upper-class backgrounds did not make eye contact with other people, and paid less attention to them. However, those from lower classes were attentive and maintained eye contact when speaking to others from their class. In addition, study participants can tell a person's social class from how much, or how little, eye contact they make with strangers. The study concludes that while the rich are disengaged from the people around them, the poor turn to social connections, in part as a survival mechanism.

Even in cultures where eye contact is more acceptable, too much looking is always cause for concern. For example, beliefs about the **evil eye** stem, in part, from a concern about people who look too intensely at another person. Such a look is deemed not only intrusive, but is often interpreted as malevolent, or at the very least, covetous. The result is that cultures with an evil eye belief—European, Asian, North African and Latin American cultures—

tend to avoid overlooking, especially at strangers. And people who are stared at generally feel threatened by the intrusiveness of the stare.

Psychological studies have also shown that where people look may be linked to more than simple communication strategies. For instance, scientists maintain that looking up and to the right when speaking may indicate lying, while looking up and to the left indicates remembering. In addition, looking at a person's face makes completing cognitive tasks harder than when not looking at a face, because looking at faces requires too much mental processing to allow for other work to be done at the same time.

See also Evil Eye; India; Middle East

Further Reading

Kraus, Michael, and Dacher Keltner. "Signs of Socioeconomic Status: A Thin-slicing Approach." *Psychological Science* 20, no. 1 (2009): 99–106.

Samovar, Larry A., and Richard Porter. *Communication between Cultures*. Belmont, CA: Wadsworth, 2009.

Eyebrow Grooming

Because the eyes are often seen as the window to the soul, the cultural elaboration of the eye is common around the world. Since eyebrows frame the eye, it makes sense that so many cultures have developed specific grooming practices focused on the eyebrow. The Chinese, for instance, felt that the eyebrows form the first line of defense for the face, and as such, must be carefully tended. Eyebrow grooming refers to methods used to shape and color the eyebrows. Shaping can be done by plucking, waxing, sugaring, shaving, or threading, and coloring can be done with pencils, powders, bleaches, and dyes. On the other hand, eyebrows perform important functions as well, such as protecting the eye from debris, rain, and sweat, acting as an identifying feature, and serving as an important vehicle for communication through **facial expressions**.

Whether eyebrows should be thick or thin, or natural or artificially groomed, depends on cultural standards, and have changed over time. In humans, women's eyebrows are typically thinner than men's, just as men's bodies are hairier than women's. Because of this natural difference,

cultural practices that exaggerate that difference may have developed. Thinning or removing the eyebrows tends to be much more common among women than among men, and is one way that **gender** differences between the sexes are enforced. According to anthropologist Desmond Morris, the roots of eyebrow grooming may also be found in folk beliefs; trimming the eyebrows may protect against evil, disease, or blindness. It could also be that minimizing the eyebrows was a way to ensure that one did not harm other people with the **evil eye**.

Women in ancient Greece used soot to darken their eyebrows, but Roman women, influenced by Cleopatra who had very thin eyebrows, plucked their eyebrows off entirely. In fact, through much of European

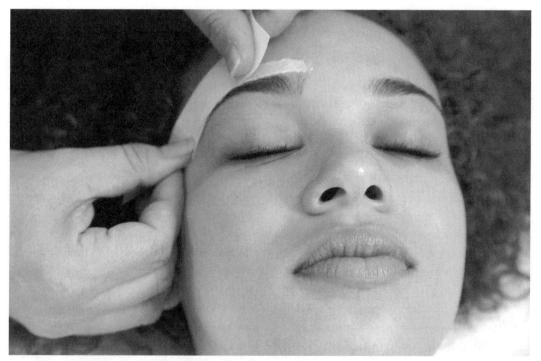

The eyebrows are, in many cultures, a focus of grooming. Many cultures expect women to have carefully groomed eyebrows, while men are often allowed to have unmaintained brows. (iStockPhoto.com)

history, elite women plucked their eyebrows into very thin lines or shaved them off altogether—through the Middle Ages and into Renaissance Europe. Some of the most famous representations of European women, like the *Mona Lisa*, or Queen Elizabeth, showed them with no eyebrows. (In 18th-century England, women sometimes wore artificial eyebrows made of mouse skin to replace the brows that they shaved off.) Often men serving in a priestly role shave their eyebrows as well: Egyptian priests were required to shave their faces, bodies, and heads, and Thai monks shave their eyebrows, too.

Shaved or plucked eyebrows were fashionable in Asia. In Heian-era **Japan**, elite women and men both shaved off their eyebrows and penciled or painted them back in a few centimeters above their original location. Beggars and outcasts, on the other hand, were forbidden from shaving their eyebrows or blackening them. (At other times in Japan, as in the Meji era, women preferred natural brows.) The attraction to eyebrows high on the face may have something to do with the term high brow, which means to be cultured and intelligent, while those with low brows, or heavy brow ridges, like apes, were considered to be the opposite. On the other hand, Islamic cultures have traditionally not shaved or plucked their eyebrows, and Mohammad once said, "Allah has cursed women who tattoo their bodies, wear false hair, those who pluck their eyebrows, and those who artificially widen gaps between their teeth." Today, there is ongoing debate in Muslim cultures about whether women (or men) can trim their eyebrows to keep them tidier.

In most cultures, it is expected that, at least for women, eyebrows should be separated, and should not come together to form a **unibrow** between the eyes. While there is much more latitude on this for men, for women, the hairier the brow the more masculine, and animal-like, the woman appears. In ancient **China**, very long eyebrows on seniors were called longevity brows and were a symbol of longevity. One reason, at least in Asian cultures, for keeping the space between the eyebrows clear was the ancient practice of **face reading**. In order to tell a person's fortune, face readers would look first at the space between the eyebrows, known as the *yin tang*, which is the primary area for a person's energy. The wider the space between the eyebrows, the more open and accepting the person is; the narrower the space, the more stubborn.

The shape of the brows is also subject to cultural standards. During the Tang dynasty, the ideal shape of the eyebrows was a mountain and Chinese women spent a great deal of time learning the techniques of drawing them in. Today, the ideal eyebrow shape in China is the crescent moon.

Today, the ideal eyebrow shape in the West is the high arch, perhaps because it signifies youth. In fact, one of the more common cosmetic procedures today is the eyebrow lift, which lifts the eyebrows in an attempt to make the face appear younger. In many women (and some men) who receive it, however, the result is a perpetually surprised look on the face. This should come as no surprise, since one of the functions of the eyebrow is to act as a form of communication; many of our facial expressions are expressed through the subtle movements of the brows. When the eyebrows are surgically modified or have been paralyzed through injections of Botox, the facial expressions so fundamental to our species are altered.

Today, eyebrows go from thick to thin with the passing of the fashion seasons. During the 1930s in Hollywood, actresses like Marlene Dietrich often shaved off their eyebrows and penciled them back in, while in the 1980s, the popularity of model Brooke Shields led to the popularity of natural brows. Some subcultures have their own eyebrow preferences as well. In the United States, the *cholas*, urban Latinas who are often associated with gang culture, favor very thin, penciled in (or tattooed on) eyebrows.

Eyebrows can be groomed with scissors, a razor, tweezers, wax, sugar, or threading. The most common approach is using a set of tweezers to pluck out individual hairs one at a time. Tweezing is one of the most ancient ways of eliminating hair, and dates back to at least ancient **Egypt**, but was probably used long before then. There are a variety of tools that are often used in conjunction with the tweezers, such as an eyebrow comb to comb the brows, a small pair of manicure scissors to trim excess length, an eyebrow pencil to fill in the gaps between the hairs and make the brow look more defined, and an eyebrow stencil to create the shape of the brows.

Waxing is another old technique for hair removal, and utilizes hot wax that is placed over the hair and pulled off with a cloth. It is related to sugaring, in which a mix of sugar, water, lemon juice, and honey is mixed into a paste, and, like waxing, is removed with a cloth. Either sugaring

or waxing was used by ancient Egyptian women (as well as ancient Greek women), who used a mixture of oil and honey to remove the hair from their entire bodies. It remained a common practice throughout the **Middle East** and North and East Africa for centuries. Waxing involves first measuring and marking where the brows should be, which could involve using a stencil, and then applying hot wax to the areas with unwanted hair, and pulling the hair off with a cotton or muslin strip. Generally, only the hair beneath the brow line is removed with waxing. Sugaring works the same way, but without heating.

Another ancient technique for eyebrow hair removal is threading. It was practiced in ancient **India**, the Middle East, and China, and is still the most common method for eyebrow grooming in India today, and is increasingly becoming popular in the West. It is also used to remove other types of facial hair, including chin hair, cheek hair, and upper lip hair. In threading, a cotton thread is twisted and held tightly between the fingers, and it is then rolled over the surface of the skin, entwining small hairs in the thread and removing them from the skin. Like tweezing and waxing, the hair is removed by the follicle, but unlike waxing, it is more precise, because it removes hairs a row at a time rather than in one big section. On the other hand, it is faster than tweezing, which removes hairs one at a time. It is performed by professionally trained practitioners.

Finally, men or women who have little to no eyebrows from conditions like alopecia or cancer treatments are often stigmatized because while this look was once fashionable, it is rare to see it today. Traditionally, the solution has been to paint or draw on new eyebrows, but today, there is a surgical procedure known as eyebrow restoration, which involves transplanting hair follicles from the head to the eyebrow.

See also Evil Eye; Facial Expressions; Facial Hair and Removal; Unibrow

Further Reading

Morris, Desmond. *The Naked Woman: A Study of the Female Body*. New York: Thomas Dunne Books, 2005.

Eyeglasses and Contacts

The wearing of eyewear—whether eyeglasses, colored contact lenses, or sunglasses—for either medical or cosmetic purposes can transform the appearance of the face.

The earliest corrective lenses were an evolution of the magnifying glass, and were used to help those with far-sightedness to read better. In ancient Rome, those who had trouble reading often improvised magnifying glasses through the use of bowls of water, or clear precious stones. The first true magnifying glass was developed by an Arab inventor in the ninth century, and was a section of a glass sphere that would be rested on a text to magnify the letters to allow for easier reading. These reading stones evolved by the 13th century into a lens, initially made of quartz, that could be inserted into a bone or metal frame and held in front of the eyes. By this time, it was recognized that keeping the convex side of the glass on the side of the eye, and the concave side on the side of the reading material, magnified the letters. It wasn't until the 16th century that the near-sighted were able to wear corrective lenses; prior to this time, all glasses were made for people who needed assistance with reading or writing.

True spectacles, to be worn on the face, rather than held in front of it, were developed in Italy at the turn of the 14th century, and the first known painting of a person wearing glasses was in 1352, in a fresco by Tommaso da Modena of Cardinal Hugh of Provence. These early eyeglasses did not have stems that rested over the ears; instead, they had a nosepiece that rested over the nose, and as such, were not made to be worn while walking or moving. In the 17th century, glasses makers began attaching ribbon to the frames and looping the ribbon over the years, a device that the Chinese improved upon by attaching weights to the ribbons to hang behind the ears. Finally, in about 1730, an English optician created the first rigid temple arms to rest over the ears, and in 1752, the hinged arms were invented, allowing the frames to be opened and closed.

Attitudes toward the wearing of glasses varied by society; in France, the wealthy only wore glasses in private, while in Spain they were considered to be a sign of status. For centuries, in fact, only the wealthy could afford glasses, which cost up to $200 in 18th century America, and everyone else—many of whom were illiterate anyway—went without.

One of the first truly fashionable eyeglasses was the monocle—a single framed lens, worn over a single eye—introduced in the early 19th century in England. While in some ways this device was a step backward to a time when eyeglasses were not worn on the face, they became extremely popular among wealthy Germans and Russians. A related device was the lorgnette, which was two framed lenses that the user held with a handle, and which was invented in the 18th century and stayed popular for about a hundred years. Another throwback device was the pince-nez (which actually dated back 200 years), a set of spectacles with no earpieces that were held on the face by pinching the nose. These were most popular in the late 19th century, 200 years after the development of hinged eyeglasses, demonstrating that fashion dominated practicality when it came to eyeglasses.

Eyeglass shapes during this era varied, with round, oval, and square shapes, wire frames, no frames, and, starting in the 20th century, tortoiseshell frames being available. Different color lenses were also options. Today, there is a huge variety of shapes, sizes, and colors—both of lenses and of frames—that are both driven by fashion and shape other fashion trends.

Contact lenses made out of blown glass were first developed in the late 19th century, and in the 1930s, plastic lenses were created for the first time, but it wasn't until the 1960s that soft contact lenses were developed that were comfortable enough to wear for long periods at a time. As contacts became more popular, the majority of wearers were soon women, as wearing glasses has often been seen as unfeminine. Even today, eyeglasses are often seen as a sign of intelligence, nerdiness, or bookishness, and are the simplest way to make a movie or television character appear nebbish. Since women have long been expected to be beautiful and sexy, rather than intelligent, the wearing of glasses is seen as unfeminine, as in the expression, "men don't make passes at girls who wear glasses."

Sunglasses, which are nonprescription lenses (although they can be prescriptive as well) worn to protect the eyes from ultraviolet light, are about as old as eyeglasses, and their precursors are even older. The Inuits, for example, wore snow goggles made of walrus bone with a slit in the lens that cut down the amount of sunlight to reach the eyes, which was important in an environment with sunlight refracting off of white snow and ice, and flat panes of quartz tinted with smoke helped keep out the sun in **China** as early as the 12th century. It is said that Chinese judges used these same lenses to conceal their emotions during court. In the 18th century, different tints became available for prescriptive lenses, but it wasn't until the early 20th century that people began wearing glasses specifically to avoid the sun, with actors as one of the earliest groups to begin wearing them, in order to conceal the redness in their eyes from the lights used during filming. By the 1930s, sunglasses became a common sight in beach towns in America beginning with Atlantic City, and later, around the world. They became even more popular during the 1960s due to Foster Grant's ad campaign, which featured celebrities wearing Foster Grant sunglasses and the caption, "who's that behind those Foster Grants?"

The earliest glasses were essentially reading glasses—used to treat far-sightedness and eyes that were weakened due to aging or disease. Today, reading glasses, which can be cheaply purchased without a prescription at drug stores, are still a visible symbol of aging, especially when worn attached to a cord worn around the neck.

Celebrities, politicians, and other famous people who wear a specific type of eyeglass over a long period of time tend to become associated with that look. For instance, John Lennon wore small round wire Windsor glasses, which not only became an obvious sign of the singer and songwriter, but also became associated with hippies. Buddy Holly wore thick, black horn rimmed glasses until his death, and they have since been associated with a type of nerdy cool for men, and also some women. Jackie Onassis popularized oversized sunglasses, perhaps as a way to achieve some privacy for herself when out in public, and was rarely seen without

them. Dame Edna Everage, an Australian cross dressing performer, always wears spectacularly adorned cat eye glasses, which, along with her lilac wig, have become her trademark look.

Glasses can indeed become an important part of a wearer's identity. Long after the popularization of contact lenses, and even now, when laser eye surgery is a safe and effective way to treat many vision problems, many people—both celebrity and regular folk—continue to wear glasses because they have become a part of who they are.

Glasses can also be seen as a form of disguise; celebrities who wear dark sunglasses, even when indoors, are perhaps trying to conceal their identities, as they

Australian actor Barry Humphries, dressed as Dame Edna Everage, appears at a press conference in San Francisco on August 25, 2004. One of the most prominent and easily recognizable features of the Dame Edna persona are the elaborate cat eyeglasses. (AP/Wide World Photos)

do when wearing baseball caps, although it's likely that the sunglasses draw more attention to them than would otherwise be the case. The idea that a pair of glasses can disguise one's identity is found in the Superman and Wonder Woman comics, in which the heroes are disguised when in regular clothing and glasses. Many blind people wear sunglasses as well to hide their eyes from the public. In addition, sunglasses ensure that the wearer cannot have **eye contact** with other people, which can discourage conversation and protect privacy. This is a simple way for celebrities to ensure that the public doesn't communicate with them. In recent years, sunglasses are also a way for people— again, especially celebrities, who are so often in the media spotlight—to hide their emotions, or to conceal the fact that they have gotten **cosmetic surgery** on their eyes. Sunglasses can also come in handy when trying hide evidence of drug use or domestic violence.

Glasses, and especially sunglasses, have long been considered a form of fashion, and today, they are often worn when there is no function to them whatsoever. The wearing of sunglasses indoors became popular in the 1980s and was considered to be a sign that the wearer was cool. Today, there are fashion glasses, which look like regular eyeglasses but that have no protective lens.

Contact lenses, too, are a fashion accessory when purchased in colors. Known as cosmetic contact lenses, they can be corrective, but are often simply worn to change the color of the eye. Lenses can even be worn to make the eye appear cat like or unusual; singer Marilyn Manson's unique appearance is defined in part by the contact lenses that he wears, which are white with a black circle around the outer edge. A popular new trend among girls and young women in **Japan** and South **Korea** is the circle contact lens, which makes the iris appear larger, and ultimately, the entire eye appears bigger. In fact, it is South Korea that is also leading the way in fashion eyeglasses, or ulzzang glasses, which are inexpensive fake eyeglasses that are thought to be cute, and are worn to accentuate the eyes.

Even though eyeglasses are no longer worn by the wealthy, they are still not widely available in many developing nations, and are out of reach for the very poor, both because of the cost of glasses and also the lack of optometrists in the Third World. Because of this, there are a number of organizations, such as the Lions Club, which collect used eyeglasses in the West and distribute them to the needy in other nations. Another development is the creation of self-refraction glasses that can eliminate the need for an optometrist. Created by the Center for Vision in the Developing World, these glasses can be manually adjusted by the wearer to fit their own vision problems, without ever seeing a doctor. The organization has been testing the glasses around the world, and hopes, ultimately, to solve a problem that leaves as many as a billion people without good vision around the world.

See also Eye Contact; Korea

Further Reading

Corson, Richard. *Fashions in Eyeglasses from the 14th Century to the Present Day*. London: Peter Owen, 1980.

F

Face Folklore

Every culture has folk beliefs—customs, practices, remedies, and ideas about the natural world, people, and animals. Beliefs about the face primarily deal with the relationship between one's **facial features** and personality, one's facial features and the future, and remedies to fix problems like **warts**. Beliefs about the **evil eye** are another type of folk belief about the face.

In the American folk tradition, as in other cultures, one's facial features are often thought to indicate one's personal character. This belief, known more formally as physiognomy, is indicated by hundreds of statements about the relationship between one's face and one's personality or temperament. For example, having a large head may mean that one is intelligent, or that one is stupid; having a long head means one is calculating or long-sighted. A flat area at the back of the head means one is stupid, and a broad forehead means one is broad minded. A prominent temple means one is determined, and defined eye ridges mean one is stupid or mean. Having a square chin indicates determination, but having a dimple in the chin means one is mischievous. Having black eyes means one can't be trusted, grey eyes indicate greed, blue eyes indicate faithfulness, and brown eyes indicate luck. And having one brown and one blue eye means one will have bad luck. Large ears mean that one is generous, may

be rich, and is attentive, while short thick ears means that one is thoughtless. Having a **unibrow** means that one will make a lot of money; on the other hand, won't live very long. People with unibrows are also stingy, deceitful, and may be thieves. Thick eyebrows mean someone has a bad temper, and cross-eyed people are definitely unlucky to all who cross their path.

> His dress told her nothing, but his face told her things which she was glad to know.—A.A. Milne, Once on a Time

If one's face itches, eyes water, or ears burn, that's a sure sign that something is soon to happen. For instance, an itchy head means that someone is speaking poorly of you; it may also mean that you will wear a strange hat, or that danger is on its way. An itchy neck on the other hand means that you might receive a shock or that you will fail in something. Burning ears means that someone is talking about you; depending on the ear, this may be good or bad. Eyes that throb, itch, or tear indicate good or bad luck, while encountering a person with crossed-eyes will always experience bad luck. And finally, warts may be an indication that one has been cursed by a witch, or one has touched a toad. But the good news is that according to folk beliefs, there are as many ways to give away, throw away, or sell the wart as there was to receive it in the first place.

The evil eye is perhaps the most important folk belief regarding the face, and beliefs about this span cultures throughout the **Middle East**, South Asia, the Mediterranean region, **North Africa**, and Latin America. The evil eye is a belief that certain people can cause sudden harm to others through simply a look or stare, or by giving them praise. The evil eye is thought to be caused by jealousy. Protecting oneself, or one's child (who are often victims of the evil eye) from harm can be as simple as carrying an amulet (which usually contains an image of the eye or a mirror to reverse the damage of the eye), deflecting praise, or preventing praise by ensuring that one's child appears ugly or worthless. If the evil eye has already caused harm, there are also remedies available, which include prayer, and often involve the use of a raw egg that can trap the evil inside it. *See also* Evil Eye; Warts

Further Reading

Brunvand, Jan H. *American Folklore: An Encyclopedia*. New York: Garland, 1996.

Face Painting

Face painting uses nontoxic paints, clay, chalk, **henna**, or dye to decorate the face, usually for ritual or performative purposes. Face paint acts like wearing a **mask** in that it can radically transform the appearance of the wearer, but unlike masks, painted faces allow the **facial expressions** to be seen (and often exaggerated), which is especially important in dramatic performances. Face painting is probably the original form of makeup, evolving from ritual and hunting practice to simple adornment.

Face painting has been practiced around the world, as evidence from Paleolithic burial sites have revealed. In traditional societies, face painting is used typically during the performance of certain rituals or ceremonies, during important hunts, and at other important times. The patterns used often demonstrated group affiliation in that each tribe or group uses different colors and designs, but they are not primarily used to mark social position or group membership. In this sense, face painting is used to make the wearer different from his or her normal appearance, rather than to permanently mark his social position on the body, as in practices like tattooing or **scarification**. Face painting is also a way to capture and to convey emotions, and as such it is an important part of the symbolic communication in many rituals.

Face painting is commonly used in rites of passage, such as initiation rituals marking the passage of boyhood to manhood in traditional societies. In these rituals, boys are often painted to demonstrate their liminal status, and sometimes are painted (and decorated) to resemble animals, or spirits; the paint is often seen as a form of temporary protection until the initiate completes the ritual and re-emerges as a man.

The dead are also often painted as a way to help them transition from the world of the living into the afterworld.

Face paints are typically made from clay and pigments found in leaves, fruits, and berries, sometimes mixed with oils, fats, or other liquids. They could also be made from minerals such as chalk. The most common colors include white, red, and black, but can include any color found in the natural world. The colors used are often symbolic: red is typically used to symbolize blood, death, or fertility, for example, and others are seen to have protective qualities. The types of patterns drawn have symbolic meaning as well—they may represent a mask; they may represent animals; or they may represent gods or ancestors.

Today, face (and body) painting is practiced among the indigenous people of Australia, Polynesia, Melanesia, and parts of Africa, and many Native American tribes once practiced it as well. It is also used by Japanese **geisha**, who use heavy, white pancake makeup on the face and neck, which is accented by dark red lips and black-

accented eyes. Mehndi, which uses dyes made from the leaves of the henna plant, is a form of decorative face and body painting used in **India** and the **Middle East**, especially on brides and bridal guests.

In Papua New Guinea, most tribes use face painting for ceremonial purposes. During bridewealth ceremonies prior to a marriage, the bride and relatives of both the bride and the groom often paint themselves to celebrate the occasion, and to signify good fortune. Papuans use body painting at other ceremonies as well as a means of reinforcing group membership.

Many Australian Aboriginal communities have been painting their faces and bodies for thousands of years, as a way of demonstrating important social positions such as one's totem and clan. It is also a

Face painting is used in cultures around the world to represent temporary changes in status, and is often worn during rituals, as in the case of this Huli Wigman native from New Guinea. (Corel)

means of communication, and when used in traditional dances, can tell a story. Because traditional paints were made out of earth, and aboriginal religion centers on the earth, using paint in this way was a sacred activity. Designs on the face mirror design motifs found in other forms of Aboriginal art, including spirals, stripes, and circles.

Face painting has also been practiced in India. Here faces were painted with natural colors and patterns to act as camouflage during hunting, and face painting has been common in rituals and in performances for hundreds of years. Even today, performers paint their faces to represent gods or demons during folk dances or temple festivals. For example, Kathakali is a classical Indian dramatic performance involving dancers who use costume and face paint to evoke the stories of mythological characters taken from important collections like the Mahabharata. The face paint exaggerates the elaborate facial expressions of the performers, and, combined with the music, dance, and hand gestures, conveys the story without words.

China, too, has a tradition of using face painting during performances. Chinese opera performers have long painted their faces with colors that symbolize different emotions and character traits and that represent gods and mythological heroes. For instance, red was used to represent courage and loyalty, yellow ambition and fierceness, green violence and lack of restraint, black fierceness and rough character, purple nobility and justice, and white treachery and craftiness. Gold and silver are used to represent the gods and spirits.

Young men of the Nuba and the Massai tribes, both pastoral groups in **Sub-Saharan Africa**, use face painting at ceremonies and rituals to demonstrate their strength and attractiveness. For instance, Massai men use chalk to paint their faces during the final initiation ritual where they transition from warriors into elders. Boys in the Xhosa tribe of South Africa paint their faces and bodies with white clay during their initiation rituals; after the white clay is washed off, signifying that their boyhood has ended, they are then painted with red ochre signifying their transition to manhood. Among the Pondo, another South African people, diviners wear white face and body paint to link themselves to their ancestors. Among the Bororo, a pastoral tribe living in Nigeria, Cameroon, and Chad, face painting is used during a festival known as *Gerewol*, in which male dancers dressed in traditional costume with elaborately painted faces dance and sing in front of women, who then choose their favorite performer, based on his appearance, dance moves, and facial expressions.

Many Northwest Indians used face painting, again primarily for ceremonial activities, such as attending potlatches, as well as during warfare and hunting. Some groups used stamps, which were dipped into paint and then stamped onto the face, to mark clan emblems. Paints were made of powders made from clay, minerals, roots, berries, and tree bark mixed with water, and were applied using either fingers or brushes made of sticks. The use of face paint during warfare was intended to make the warriors look frightening, in patterns ranging from stripes to dots to solid sections of the face. For instance, Plains Indians painted their faces red, brown, black, white, yellow, green, and blue, and, as new dyes became available through trading with Euro-Americans, new colors were used as well. As in other cultures, colors had symbolic significance, with red signifying violence and war and used during and in preparation for war, yellow indicating death and worn during mourning (or to signify that a warrior is ready to die), green symbolizing power, and white symbolizing peace, to be worn when engaging in peace talks.

Many Native American dancers traditionally painted their bodies and faces for dance performances with designs such as arrows, lightning, stars, and lines. Some tribes used body paint in conjunction with permanent tattoos. It is speculated that the term redskin may have derived from the practices of certain Native communities to cover much of their bodies with red pigment. Face painting is still used by Native American tribes today during ceremonial dances and rituals.

In the West today, face painting is practiced by artists who specialize in it, as well as makeup artists and fine artists. These artists display their work on models at festivals and competitions around the world, and in magazines such as the *Face and Body Art Magazine*.

Actors and clowns around the world have painted their faces for centuries, and continue to do so today. Face painting is also used as camouflage in the military and among hunters. Face painting is popular at secular festivals, theme parks, and carnivals, especially for children, and is used by some sports fans to demonstrate their allegiance to their home team. More subdued forms of face paints for everyday occasions evolved into the **cosmetics** we know today.

See also Australia and New Zealand; Cosmetics; Geisha; Henna; Mimes and Clowns

Further Reading

Kupka, Karel. *Dawn of Art: Painting and Sculpture of Australian Aborigines.* Sydney: Angus and Robertson, 1965.

Thevóz, Michel. *The Painted Body.* New York: Rizzoli International, 1984.

Face Perception

Humans and other animals have brains that are specially designed to perceive the face, as distinct from other images or parts of the body. In fact, half of the human brain is devoted to sight, and much of that is devoted to recognizing faces. On the other hand, the part of the brain that *identifies* an individual face, the fusiform gyrus, is also used to distinguish between other similar objects, indicating that the ability to identify faces may derive from the ability to categorize objects in general.

Identifying faces is critical in social animals like humans. They look at faces in order to detect emotions, to communicate with each other, and to identify each other, because the face is the most identifiable feature of a person or other animal, and the part of the body that varies the most between individuals within a species. Animals recognize the faces of their family and friends—it's a critical survival skill.

> Sometimes when you stand face to face with someone, you cannot see his face.—*Mikhail Gorbachev*

Being able to perceive faces means not only understanding that one is looking at a face, but also being able to identify the individual face, as well as a number of details about the person such as age, sex, ethnicity, and one's relationship with that person. In addition, in order to recognize a person truly, the part of the brain that attaches emotions to images must be working as well. Without the emotional attachment to a face, recognize the face is not possible. For example, people with **prosopagnosia** cannot recognize faces because the fusiform gyrus has been somehow impaired.

Having the ability to identify other individuals is critical; social animals need to be able to detect quickly whether another individual is a stranger or someone who is known to them. Infants and the young of any species in particular need to be able to identify faces that are friendly; without that skill, they are especially vulnerable. And finally, without the ability to identify the faces of others, humans would lose the ability to communicate with and interact with those who are important to them.

Infants, who have very poor eyesight, are not born with the ability to identify individual faces. But within just a few days, babies are able to identify the faces of the people who are closest to them—generally their parents. Tests show that by two and a half months, when looking at faces of people they know, the temporal lobe of the brain (and specifically the fusiform gyrus) is activated in babies, demonstrating recognition.

Faces within a species are more similar to each other than they are different, thus identifying individual faces involves quite a bit of subconscious cognitive effort. The more a face departs from the average, the more recognizable it is. **Caricatures** are more easily recognized than other kinds of representations because they highlight the differences from the norm; the more different and exaggerated, the more easily recognizable. In fact, people may store memories of others as caricatures.

When looking at the face, human minds are able to capture quickly the individual features of the face and the spatial relationships between those features, and use that information to create a structural model of the face. It is then placed into the memory (and associated with information about that person's identity), so that it can be called upon when that face is seen again, even if seen from a different angle. The brain may store millions of faces in its memory, in fact. Recognizing faces involves not just the facial features and the relationship between them, but also the bumps and contours of the face.

How well people are able to recognize faces depends upon the relationship to the individuals, and other characteristics such as the ethnicity or gender of the person. For example, the cross-race effect refers to the fact that people are more easily able to distinguish between faces within their own ethnicity and less able to distinguish between faces from outside it. Not only can people more easily distinguish between individuals of our their ethnicity but they are better able to read and interpret the **facial expressions** of those in their own ethnic group, a finding that has important implications for inter-ethnic interactions. (In fact, studies show that when racist people are taught how to differentiate between the faces of people of another ethnicity, their racism lessens.) Other studies have shown that men recognize fewer female faces than women do, while women recognize as many male faces as men do. In addition, certain features are critical to facial perception and recognition. Facial recognition software, for example, does not work when the eyes of the subject are concealed.

Nonhuman social animals must also recognize faces, for the same reasons as humans. Without the ability to recognize other faces, animals like dogs or monkeys could not identify friends and family, detect emotions in other animals, or communicate with each other. (The great apes, on the other hand, are the only animals who share with humans the ability to recognize their own faces in a mirror.) While it's true that nonhuman animals rely more on smell for identification purposes, facial features are another important way that animals identify each other. And just as members of one ethnic group can more easily identify the faces of members of the same ethnic group, members of one species can more easily distinguish between faces of the same species. Humans, for example, cannot easily detect differences in the faces of monkeys, and monkeys can more easily detect differences in other monkey faces than in human faces. Ultimately, studies show that the faces that people can most easily recognize and distinguish are those faces to which they have been exposed.

How humans develop the ability to distinguish between faces has long been a subject of study. Research indicates that infant primates—both human and monkey—are able to distinguish between faces, and seem to show a distinct preference for faces and for face-like objects, as opposed to non-face-like objects, even when they have not been exposed to faces previously.

See also Facial Expressions; Prosopagnosia

Further Reading

Bruce, V., and A. Young. *In the Eye of the Beholder: The Science of Face Perception.* Oxford: Oxford University Press, 2000.

Face Reading

Face reading refers to the Chinese practice of reading facial features and shapes in order to determine personality and health characteristics. It also can be used to refer to the way in which people read other people's faces in order to gauge their emotions, or what they are thinking.

Chinese face reading, or *Mian Xiang*, is a form of physiognomy that is based on the idea that facial characteristics reveal emotional and intellectual traits, as well as the overall character of a person. For instance, the Greeks felt that the appearance of the forehead—high or low, wrinkled or smooth, rounded or flat—indicated whether the bearer was confident, intelligent, bold, fickle, weak, honest, or spirited.

According to practitioners, Chinese face reading is at least 3,000 years old (dating back to a thousand years before Aristotle), and unlike the physiognomy theories of the ancient Greeks (which were themselves resurrected multiple times throughout Western history), Chinese face reading had numerous practical applications. Chinese medical practitioners, for example, have long relied on face reading to help understand the psychological, physical, and emotional state of a patient, while Chinese parents have called in face readers to help them to evaluate potential mates for their sons or daughters.

Face reading is based on some of the same principles on which **acupuncture** is based. Chinese medicine is a holistic approach that focuses not on disease or pathology but on wellness and balance. It sees the body as divided into several systems of function that correspond to physical organs, and illness is a result of systems being out of balance or harmony. The diagnosis of illness, then, is not associated with a certain organ or part being diseased, but of a systemic disorder, which must be treated on that basis. Meaning one acupuncture point in the foot, for example, corresponds to the liver, so stimulating that point on the foot will stimulate the liver pathway and could help with problems associated with the liver, such as genital or digestive problems.

In face reading, the face is divided into left and right halves, with the right side of the face corresponding to the male, or yang aspect, and the left side corresponding to the female, or yin aspect. Men, and one's male relatives, are represented by the right side of the face, while women and female relatives by the left side. In addition, men's faces are read from the left to the right and women's from the right to the left. The face can also be split into upper and lower, with the upper half of the face corresponding to spiritual leanings and the lower half of the face demonstrating earthly and practical concerns.

The facial features, too, are thought to correspond to both personal characteristics and how a person deals with the world. For

A soothsayer in a small Chinese village, telling fortunes by a person's facial features, 1947. Chinese face reading has long been used in China to tell information about a person's personality or even their future. (Getty Images)

instance, the nose represents wealth, so the shape of the nose can indicate whether or not the bearer will be wealthy, will be able to hold onto wealth, and how the bearer will spend money. In face reading, the eyes tell about the character of the person. The shape of the eyes, whether they are clear or cloudy, and the shape of the eyebrows can tell what kind of a person the bearer is— trustworthy, honest, powerful, or successful. People with a great amount of white (or sclera) visible in the eyes are said to be prone to accidents, for example. The lips indicate how a person communicates and what type of personality he may have, while the ears also indicate personality, intelligence and how well a person listens. In addition, the relationship between the features is of import; people with wide set eyes are considered slow, while those with close set eyes are said to be detail oriented.

Each feature has an ideal shape or appearance—the best nose has a rounded tip, high arch, and wide top, while the best mouth is large with upward sloping corners. The best ears are flat, thick, and round, which indicates good relationships and health, while good chins jut out, indicating ambition.

> A face is like the outside of a house, and most faces, like most houses, give us an idea of what we can expect to find inside.—*Loretta Young*

The shape of the face is important as well, and each major face shape corresponds to an element. Square faces correspond to the earth element, triangle to fire, narrow to wood, long to metal, and round to water. These elements, in turn correspond, again, to personality traits. People with narrow or wood faces are philosophical and love to learn, while people with wide faces (a combination of earth and water) have a quick intellect and are good moneymakers.

Face reading, unlike physiognomy, was also a form of divination, in that a trained reader could see in the face, as with palm reading, the course that a person's life may take. For instance, having a square chin indicates that one will live into old age.

Related to face reading is a form of divination known as moleomancy or molesophy, in which facial moles are read in order to ascertain if. Moles can be advantageous if they are located on a part of the face associated with luck or wealth, and hidden moles are often thought to be more advantageous than easily seen moles. In Chinese mole reading, moles can also be seen as warning signs—different colors can indicate trouble in relationships, for example, while other moles may suggest a propensity toward food allergies or a short life.

While most Chinese knew the basic principles of face reading, specialists are trained in the intricacies of the practice. Bringing in a trained face reader was especially important when making important decisions such as choosing a wife for a son, or when trying to understand one's destiny. Will I be prosperous? Will my son be wealthy? Will my potential daughter in law bear an heir? These are all questions that could be put to a face reader.

Face reading began in **China**, but spread starting in the 14th century to **Japan**, **Korea**, and **Southeast Asia** with the spread of Chinese culture. The use of face reading became critical in Japan and Korea and, as in China, people used it in business, politics, and arranging marriages. In World War II, the Japanese Air Force used face reading experts to help it choose the recruits who would serve as pilots; those whose faces indicated that they would not be successful were instead trained as mechanics, drivers, and other positions.

Today, Japanese scientists are further refining the ancient practice, using face-sensing technology to analyze the photos of thousands of faces in order to detect their **facial expressions**—and their underlying meaning. The technology may ultimately lead to a photo-based lie detector, which can more accurately detect whether or not a person is telling the truth, and can perhaps lead to a mind-reading device. Japanese scientists have also created a robot called Kansei that can not only simulate up to 36 human facial expressions, but can use them in the appropriate situation, based on the words played to the robot. For instance, when the robot hears words like war, it creates a facial expression of fear and disgust. *See also* Physiognomy and Phrenology

Further Reading

Bridges, Lillian. *Face Reading in Chinese Medicine*. St. Louis, MO: Churchill Livingstone, 2004.

Yang, Henning H. L. *Mian Xiang: The Chinese Art of Face Reading*. London: Vega, 2001.

Zebrowitz, Leslie A. *Reading Faces: Window to the Soul?* Boulder, CO: Westview Press, 1997.

Face Saving and Losing Face

Face is a sociological concept that refers to the need to maintain dignity, self-respect and status in social situations. Losing face means being publically insulted and having one's dignity and good name maligned, while saving face means preserving one's dignity and self-respect.

In dramaturgical theory, sociologists discuss the ways in which humans are actors on a stage, displaying an impression of themselves that is consistent with their own sense of self and that is intended to be favorably received by one's audience. The actors, or people, wear **masks**, which are carefully constructed and show one's self in the best possible light. This mask can slip and the actor, or person, can find that their sense of self is damaged through loss of face.

Sociologists say that in all cultures, people are concerned about, and take actions toward, maintaining and enhancing face, and that because most people share this concern, they work together to preserve other people's dignity as well as their own. For instance, the sociological term studied nonobservance refers to a way in which people willingly overlook another person's flaws or lies to prevent that person from being embarrassed. Face-saving techniques like this are common in society because everyone in a social group benefits from it—"if I save you from embarrassment, at a future point in time, you will save me from embarrassment." Ultimately, all people are vulnerable to being shamed and to losing dignity, and thus most cultures have developed strategies for saving face, restoring face, and for avoiding face-threatening interactions.

Furthermore, countries and cultures, too, have face, and can lose or regain face in the public eye. Some scholars have demonstrated that much of international diplomacy comes down to the question of face—with each of the countries involved in a negotiation attempting to save their own face. The country that gives up too much, or makes too many concessions, can be seen on the international stage as having lost face. Often, then, international negotiations between two parties often involve a third, neutral party, whose intercession can sometimes help each country save face.

A related concept is positive face and negative face. Positive face refers to one's positive self-image, while negative face refers to a person's desire to not be imposed upon by others. In a recent study, threats to one's negative face were deemed to be more important to Americans while threats to one's positive face were deemed to be more devastating to Chinese subjects.

Some cultures are much more concerned about saving and losing face than other cultures, and in particular, Asian cultures are most likely to be concerned about face. Western cultures that are more individual-oriented (what are known as low-context cultures) tend to be less concerned about face, while cultures that focus more on groups (high-context cultures) than individuals tend to be more face-conscious. People in low-context cultures engage in more direct communication, and think less of other people's feelings, while people in high-context cultures such as in Asia and the **Middle East** care more about group harmony and tend to favor indirect communication techniques like evasion.

Indeed, the term face first arose in **China**, where there are dozens of Chinese terms that refer to face such as "selling face," which means to gain popularity, or "ripping up face," which means to stomp on someone else's feelings. Having no face, on the other hand, means being without shame. In China, faces can be lost, but can also be borrowed, given (to show respect), stolen, or fought for through competition with others. Chinese languages have multiple words for face, including *mian*, *lian*, and *yan*. All of these terms essentially refer to a person's social face, and include respect, honor, prestige, and social standing, although *lian* refers more toward the bearer's moral character and trustworthiness, while *mian* is more closely related to social standing and prestige. Interestingly, in Chinese, faces cannot easily be saved when the bearer is seen to have lost his or her moral decency, although regaining status, or avoiding damage to one's status, is easier to do. For example, *liu-mian-zi* means that one can retain face by showing wisdom and avoiding mistakes and *jiang-mian-zi* refers to increasing face when someone complements a person to a third person.

Japan, which inherited many of China's cultural traditions, also has a strong focus on face. Like the Chinese, the Japanese are heavily concerned with the shame of losing face, perhaps because it is a small country with a large population that has to live cooperatively together. For centuries, suicide has been used as an honorable way to avoid or overcome shame. In addition, Japanese people, like the Chinese, work hard to control their emotions in order to create or maintain a peaceful atmosphere, even when that means that many Japanese are not able to express their emotions.

See also China; Facial Expressions; Japan

Further Reading

Korzenny, Felipe, and Stella Ting-Toomey. "Cross-cultural Interpersonal Communication." *International and Intercultural Communication Annual* 15. Newbury Park, CA: Sage, 1991.

Littlejohn, Stephen W., and Kathy Domenici. *Facework: Bridging Theory and Practice.* Thousand Oaks, CA: Sage, 2006.

Rosenberg, Sarah. "Face." Beyond Intractability Knowledge Base Project, Conflict Research Consortium, University of Colorado, 2004, http://www.beyondintractability.org/essay/face/.

Face Transplant

Face transplant surgery involves attaching either a full or partial face from a deceased donor onto a patient whose face has been disfigured by accident or, sometimes, by a congenital condition.

Because the face is such a critical component of **identity**, and the primary way in which people interact with each other, losing one's face, or having one's face disfigured through accident or disease, can be a devastating blow to a person. Human sense of self is impacted through the loss of the part of the body that presents public image, and with four of the five senses located on the face, when the face is destroyed, the ability to communicate with others is almost totally destroyed. For these reasons, doctors have been working for years to develop and perfect face transplant surgery, in order to give a new face to patients who have lost theirs.

The technology to transplant a face from a donor to a recipient was developed in the last decade, but prior surgeries paved the way for its development. In 1994, an Indian girl had her face and scalp torn off in a farming accident. Surgeons in **India** were able to re-attach her face, which had never been done before. Prior to this time, skin grafts were the only option when people lost part of their face, but the grafts did not allow the patient to look or function normally. The patient, Sandeep Kaur, made a remarkable recovery and while she does not have full mobility in her face, she looks normal and has gone on to lead a normal life. Over the next few years, a handful of similar reattachment surgeries were performed, giving doctors the hope that they might one day be able to transplant a new face from one person to another.

The technology to transplant human faces was first developed by doctors who experimented with animals and human cadavers. For example, Chinese surgeons worked on 50 rabbits and 10 human corpses before performing the first transplant surgery in **China** in 2006.

The first partial face transplant was performed in France in November 2005 on a woman named Isabelle Dinoire whose lower face had been chewed off by her dog while she was asleep. Dinoire received a lower face, including a nose, mouth, and chin, from a woman who had just died. The second partial face transplant surgery was conducted in 2006 on a farmer named Li Guoxing who had the right side of his face torn off by a bear. Doctors there replaced his face with a new one that included a new nose, upper lip, cheek, and eyebrow. It wasn't until 2008 that the first partial face transplant was done in the United States, on a woman named Connie Culp, who had been shot in the face by her husband. Culp received lower eyelids, cheekbones, a nose, and an upper jaw.

Like recipients of organ transplants, face transplant patients must take immunosuppressant drugs to prevent the body from rejecting the new face for the rest of their lives. Li, however, died in 2008 after allegedly taking herbal medicine rather than the medicine prescribed to him. Besides taking anti-rejection medicines, patients must undergo months of physical therapy and healing until their faces begin to look normal. Initially, the transplanted face looks like an ill-fitting mask. Perhaps more importantly, patients must learn to make **facial expressions** once again; therapy trains patients to smile, frown, and make other expressions, since they are no longer automatically generated by the emotions.

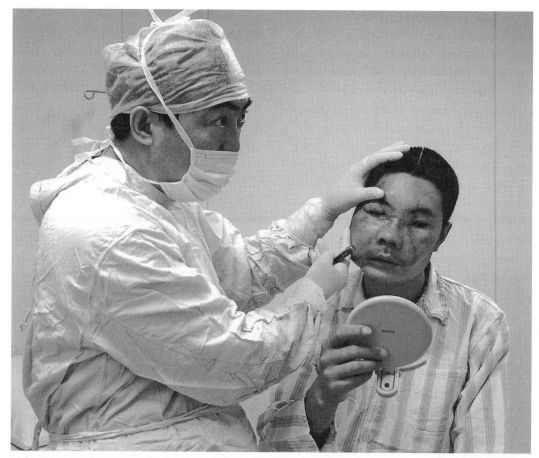

Li Guoxing received the world's second partial face transplant in 2006 after having been mauled by a black bear. He died two years later, after he stopped taking his immunosuppressant drugs. (AP/Wide World Photos)

The first facial transplant surgery performed on a patient whose face was disfigured by disease rather than accident was in 2007 on a French man named Pascal whose face was covered by tumors caused by neurofibromatosis (or elephant man disease). He received a new nose, mouth, cheeks, and chin in the procedure.

The first full face transplant was performed in March 2010 in Spain on a Spanish farmer named Oscar. The recipient, whose face had been damaged from an accidental shotgun blast, received an entire face from a donor, including mouth (with lips, teeth, and palate), nose, jaw, cheeks, and cheekbones. At the time of this writing, four months after the surgery, the patient has regained some function and feeling in his face, but he has a long way to go in terms of regaining function and a more normal appearance. Since the Spanish procedure, doctors have now performed the second full facial transplant, on a French man named Jerome, who suffers from neurofibromatosis. He received a full face including, for the first time, both eyelids and working tear ducts, as well as new hands. And in 2011, the first American full face transplant surgery was undertaken on a man named Dallas Wiens, who had his lips, nose, eyes, and eyebrows burned off in an accident. Two months after his surgery, the patient made his first public appearance at a press conference, and told the press that his new face, which has allowed him to smell again, feels natural. Doctors are hoping to start using the procedure performed on Wiens, which was paid for by the military, to assist some of the injured soldiers who have returned from Iraq and Afghanistan, many of whom have badly burned faces from improvised explosive devices.

Face transplant surgery involves slicing away the skin and generally the fat, muscles, arteries, veins, and nerves of the donor's face. In some cases, bone is removed along with tissue. The recipient is prepared by having the damaged skin, fat, and muscles cut away. The nerves, muscles, veins, and arteries are then sewn to the recipient's nerves, muscles, veins, and arteries, and the skin is then sewn to the edge of the recipient's skin. If bone is transplanted, the new bone is attached to the old bone via titanium screws and plates.

As with organ transplants, donors and recipients must be matched with blood type, antigens and antibodies through a process called HLA typing. In addition, the recipient must be healthy enough to survive the surgery, while the donor is kept on life support until the organ is removed. With face transplants, the donor and recipient must have approximately the same skin coloring and similar bone structure as well, so that the new face fits the bone structure of the recipient and matches cosmetically as well. When parts of the bony structure are transplanted, the fit is even more important—patients who receive teeth or part of a mandible from a donor must have those bones align perfectly. The recipient, once the healing is completed, no longer looks like the person once did, but does not look entirely like the donor either, because of the difference in bone structure between the individuals. Instead, the recipient looks like a combination of the donor's face and the person's own face.

Face Off

Face Off is a 1997 action movie directed by Hong Kong director John Woo and starring Nicolas Cage and John Travolta. The premise of the film is that scientists have developed a surgical procedure that allows doctors to graft the face of the terrorist played by Cage onto the FBI agent played by Travolta, so that the FBI agent can go undercover and find out about an upcoming bombing. Meanwhile Cage's character forces the doctor to graft the face of the FBI agent onto his own face, resulting in Cage's character deceiving people into thinking that he is Travolta's character. This film anticipated real face transplant surgeries that would not be performed for another eight years, and that even today do not come anywhere close to the surgeries performed in the film.

Besides the surgical risks and the risks of rejection following the surgery, face transplant patients face additional problems. Many organ recipients report strange feelings and new behaviors after their surgeries; a theory known as cellular memory suggests that the donated organs contain memorie" of the donor, and that recipients inherit those memories in the form of musical taste, food preferences, or even shifts in personality. For recipients of a face transplant, because the face is so fundamental to our identity, there is a risk of depression and other psychological problems as patients may no longer feel like themselves. Face transplant patients have reported feeling that their new face was foreign and that they couldn't see themselves when looking in the mirror. Family and friends of patients also have to adjust to the fact that their loved one no longer looks like themselves.

Some medical ethicists also worry about the ethical implications of major surgery like face transplant surgery being performed on people whose lives are not at risk. Some worry, for example, that as the techniques are perfected, people may choose to have their faces replaced with more attractive faces. But as Dinoire, the first face transplant recipient has said, "It's medical reasons, not cosmetic reasons. One is nothing without a face."

See also Facial Expressions; Facial Features; Identity

Further Reading

Barker, John H., Niki Stamos, Allen Furr, et al. "Research and Events Leading to Facial Transplantation." *Clinical Plastic Surgery* 34 (2007): 233–50.

Brown, C. S., B. Gander, M. Cunningham, A. Furr, D. Vasilic, O. Wiggins, J. C. Banis, M. Vossen, C. Maldonado, G. Perez-Abadia, and J. H. Barker. "Ethical Considerations in Face Transplantation." *International Journal of Surgery* 5 (2007): 353–64.

Tilney, Nicholas L. *Transplant: From Myth to Reality.* New Haven, CT: Yale University Press, 2003.

Facebook

Facebook is a social networking Web site, created in 2004 by Harvard student Mark Zuckerberg, which today is the most popular social networking site in the world with 600 million members as of June 2011.

Social networking sites, also known as connector Web sites, allow people to create personal profiles, network with others, and create a form of virtual community. Social networking sites are used for friendship (e.g., MySpace, Facebook), professional networking (Linked-In), dating (Match.com, OKCupid), and for shared passions (Flickr). There are even social networking sites for animals, like Catster, Dogster, and Bunspace. Facebook combines many of these features, by allowing users to create personal profiles, find friends, look for relationships, and share their passions by uploading videos and photos, live chatting, linking to news stories, donating to nonprofits, playing games, and giving each other gifts, "pokes," and the like.

Facebook, like other social networking sites, heavily relies on photos posted by users. Each user has a profile photo as well as an area where he can post other photos as well. But the profile photo, which many users change frequently, is the first representation of the person behind the profile that users will see. Some people use cartoon avatars instead of photos, and there are now Web sites that can turn one's own photo, generally of one's face, into a cartoon avatar.

Facebook's predecessor was a site called Facemash, created by Zuckerberg for (male) Harvard undergrads to rate female students. While Facebook no longer has a rating component, photos of users are still extremely important. For example, users can tag a photo that they upload to the site with the names of their Facebook friends who are in it; those people who are tagged in the photo are then notified of the photo.

One of the most common criticisms leveled at Facebook is that users' privacy is not well controlled. Facebook stalking is now a commonly used term to refer to the ways that people can cyberstalk other people on Facebook, viewing their photos and watching their activities covertly. Another danger is that employers are increasingly using Facebook to spy on the profiles of both employees, and hiring managers routinely look up potential employees on both Google and Facebook. Employees have been fired or reprimanded for posting negative or unflattering comments on Facebook that their bosses have seen, and others have found that photos of themselves partying or engaging in unprofessional behavior has caused them public

Facebook is a popular social networking website that allows individuals with different interests to connect and socialize. Since its founding in 2004, more than 800 million people use Facebook to connect with friends, family, and acquaintances; to post photos of themselves and others; and to update the world on their interests and activities. (Lucian Milasan/Dreamstime.com)

embarrassment or worse. Young people are now being warned by experts to treat all of their Facebook photos—including those showing them engaged in underage drinking—as potential parts of their future job applications.

In 2011 Facebook unveiled facial recognition software that would automatically tag users' photos with the names of the people in them. The software compares the photo to the Facebook database of billions of users' photos, and urges the user to tag the photos when it finds a match. Other users can set up their privacy settings so that they can opt out of being so tagged, but most users have not done this. Users must also visit photos of themselves that friends have tagged and must manually un-tag themselves, if they don't want others to know their identity in the photos. In addition, opting out still won't stop Facebook from gathering data based on users' photos and posts, so those concerned about a large corporation gathering so much personal information about its users have not been reassured by the opt out feature. Many people also wonder what Facebook may ultimately do with a facial recognition database containing millions of identified faces. Finally, for those people who would like to look up a former classmate, boyfriend, or potential date, online, they must do so using their name, email address, or other identifying feature. Someday soon we may be able to search for someone with just a photo, which for some critics, means the end of our personal privacy.

See also Artistic Representation; Emoticon

Further Reading

Kirkpatrick, David. *The Facebook Effect: The Inside Story of the Company That Is Changing the World.* New York: Simon and Schuster, 2011.

Facial Care

Facial care refers to the methods used by men and women—but primarily women—to care for their skin. Different cultures have different facial care methods and these have changed over the past few thousand years.

Today, in the West, skin care involves a different set of steps depending on the age of the person. For the most part, however, modern skin care regimes involve washing the face to remove oil and dirt, exfoliating to slough off old skin and rejuvenate the appearance, moisturizing with lotions or creams, and applying sunscreen to protect against sun damage. Teenagers and young men and women also usually apply acne-controlling products to the face, while older women apply wrinkle-control products. Today, prescription and nonprescription retinoids are used for both purposes. On top of these skin care products, **cosmetics** and **cosmetic surgery** are both commonly used to make the face appear more youthful and beautiful.

In the past, skin care regimes tended to focus on essentially the same issues that today's methods do: cleansing, moisturizing, and, instead of protecting against sun damage, people in the past attempted to make their skin appear lighter than it really was.

Skin care in the ancient classical civilizations focused heavily on moisturizers, perhaps because of the heat in the Mediterranean region. Soap was used when bathing, often followed by olive oil to moisturize. Olive oil itself was also used as a cleanser in ancient Rome, and honey was used throughout the Mediterranean region to both exfoliate and moisturize the skin. The Romans used flour and butter on acne, while the Greeks used lead to clear blemishes. Cleopatra was said to bathe in sour milk, which both moisturized and exfoliated her skin. Roman women, too, indulged in facials of milk, wine, and bread, which were thought to keep skin smooth, soft, and young. Skin care products were made of oils like sesame and olive mixed with herbs like chamomile, marjoram, lavender, peppermint, rosemary, and lily. Other herbs like myrrh, frankincense, cinnamon, cardamom, saffron, nutmeg, and narcissus arrived in the region from the Persian Empire and were added to skin care recipes. **Kohl**, **henna**, ground charcoal, iron oxide, red ochre, malachite, and bees wax were mixed with other substances to act as eye shadow, rouge, and lipstick. Both kohl and henna arrived from Africa where they were already popular cosmetics on that continent.

Light skin was preferred in Greece, Rome, and **Egypt**, because having light skin indicated that one did not work outside. Egyptians washed their faces in egg whites, and Greeks and Romans used lead-based makeup to lighten their faces—upper-class men and women both indulged in the practice. It continued through the Middle Ages and Renaissance in Europe, with skin lightening products made of lead, chalk, and arsenic all being used. Lead-based creams were also used to remove freckles and to exfoliate the skin. These toxic products often caused facial disfigurements and even death.

Men in Rome, Greece, and Egypt all removed facial hair by shaving, plucking, and the use of creams. Men in those cultures cared about their grooming and appearance, and used, like the women of the period, scented oils to keep their skin moist and sweet smelling. Some men of the period wore makeup on their eyes and lips as well. Men in the Middle East, too, wore makeup, including lining the eyes with kohl as did Roman and Egyptian men. This was both a form of adornment as well as protection against the **evil eye** and sun damage to the eyes.

Skin care was important in ancient **China**, and herbal remedies, skin care products, and aromatherapy were used to maintain clear skin. Facial creams were made of egg whites and vermillion—this left the skin soft, smooth, and created a lighter appearance. Facial masks were made of motherwort, talcum, and the bodies of insects called kermes. Another recipe for a facial mask called for peach blossoms and the blood of a black chicken; this mask nourished the skin and left it lighter in appearance.

Because the Chinese believe that the health of the skin is affected by the amount of heat in the blood, certain foods are blamed for causing acne or dried skin, such as spicy or fatty foods. Other foods, on the other hand, are beneficial to the skin. Elite women ate special foods that were thought to be good for the face, like *Tremella fuciformis*—a jelly fungus—which was said to stimulate the complexion and discourage freckles. **Beauty** practices found in other areas of the world were popular in China such as creams made of almond oil and honey or bathing with milk. Powdered pearl was also an expensive, but highly desired skin care product. It was supposed to be spread on the face to smooth the skin and nourish the complexion.

The Japanese, like the Chinese, both applied a variety of products to their faces to make their skin appear smoother, whiter, and more beautiful, and ate certain foods that were thought to result in more attractive skin. For example, wakame, derived from sea algae, is both eaten and added to skin care products in order to make the skin more youthful looking. Exfoliants were made of natural products such as the ground adzuki bean, rice bran, clay, and powdered sea vegetables. Moisturizers were made from camellia oil, rose hips, and jojoba oil. Herbal teas and extracts were applied to the skin or used in masks.

Ancient Indians used a number of herbs and plants to create skin care products, including coconut, almond, jojoba, grape seed and emu oils, honey, shea butter, witch hazel, and ground cornmeal, turmeric, and almond and walnut shells. These could be combined to make exfoliants, moisturizers, and other skin care products.

The Mayans, too, had a number of skin care remedies, including using avocado in face **masks**, rose hip seed oil for acne, cliffrose bark tea for skin rashes, and acacia mixed with honey as an astringent. Today, a number of the herbs that these cultures used are still found in skin care products, like witch hazel, avocado, rose hips, olive oil, honey, bees wax, aloe vera, and chamomile.

See also Beauty; China; Cosmetics; Egypt; Greco-Roman Cultures; Japan

Further Reading

Mogilner, Victoria. *Ancient Secrets of Facial Rejuvenation: A Holistic, Nonsurgical Approach to Youth and Well-Being*. Novato, CA: New World Library, 2006.

Sherrow, Victoria. *For Appearance' Sake: The Historical Encyclopedia of Good Looks, Beauty, and Grooming*. Phoenix, AZ: Oryx Press, 2001.

Facial Expressions

Facial expressions are the movements of the face. They express the emotional state of the person or animal and are an important form of nonverbal communication. In Darwin's words, facial expressions are a "language of emotion."

Facial expressions in humans are formed due to the interplay between the 14 bones of the face and the 52 muscles that control the face, and those muscles and bones are the products of a lengthy history of evolution. Those muscles originally evolved in primitive aquatic creatures in the Cambrian era, and allowed these creatures to take in food, oxygen, and water. As land animals evolved, the muscles of the face changed because of adaptations to breathing air and eating and swallowing food differently. As mammals and, later, primates evolved, the muscles changed further, allowing for the ears, mouth, nose, and eyes to be controlled by different muscles. With further evolution, the muscles changed and allowed for muscular movements that had nothing to do with eating, smelling, or hearing, but that could convey emotional states and would allow animals to communicate with other animals.

Primates, and especially hominoids (which includes apes and humans), can create a huge number of facial expressions, due to the large number of muscles in the face. But humans have more facial muscles than nonhuman primates, giving them more and more subtle expressions—up to 7,000 different expressions—and because humans have no hair on their faces, it is much easier to see the expressions that they do make. The eyebrows, the large area of white in the eyes (known as sclera), and the pronounced lips all contribute to the variety of facial expressions that humans are capable of. And finally, without the emphasis on smell associated with a large snout, humans have a much more finely developed sense of sight, and use that sight, in part, to read the facial expressions of others of their own kinds. What humans lack in smell and body language is more than made up for in facial expressions.

As a communicative system, facial expressions predate human language by millions of years. Today, even with language, facial expressions are faster and both more obvious and more subtle than words. For instance, a subtle, unconscious, wrinkling of the forehead can indicate lying, rapid eye blinking indicates nervousness, and dilation of the pupils of the eyes indicates excitement.

Today, human facial muscles, which control facial expressions, are highly specialized, and are focused around the eyes, the nose, and the mouth. (The ears in humans and other primates are not as flexible as they are in other animals, and thus have much less in the way of facial muscles.) For example, there are three different muscles in the forehead that control the movement of the eyes: the Occipitofrontalis muscles, which raise the eyebrows; the Corrugator supercilii muscles, which lower the edges of the eyebrows, and the Procerus muscles, which lower the centers of the eyebrows. Ekman and Friesen's Facial Action Coding System measures facial movements and calculates which muscle(s) are used for every single facial expression that a human can make. This system has been used to count all of the movements possible in the human face (hundreds of thousands), most of which are never used by humans. In addition, the vast majority of the facial expressions possible in humans do *not* reflect emotions—many, instead, are gestures or signals (such as a wink) used to convey information, but not necessarily emotional information. The system has also been used to show which muscles are used for which emotional expressions, and which require the involvement of multiple muscles.

Charles Darwin posited that the facial expressions of humans and other animals all have a functional basis: they show happiness by lifting the face and tightening the upper lip, which derives from preparing for a play bite, while they show anger through tightening the facial and mouth muscles, in preparation for an aggressive bite. Affection is expressed through the lips, whether through kissing, lip smacking, or sucking, and derives from the suckling of an infant to the mother's breast, and surprise is expressed through widening the eyes and the mouth, and rearing back in a protective stance. Darwin called these actions intention movements, or the incomplete or preparatory phase of noncommunicative activities like attack, play, or protection. Over time, these intention movements evolved into facial expressions used for communication only.

Darwin, like many thinkers before him, claimed that facial expressions, or a handful of them, are universal—not only found in every culture but recognized in every culture. While scholars discussed this idea for centuries, Darwin was the first to attempt to prove that the universality of facial expressions means that they are inherited from prehuman ancestors and are still shared today with many nonhuman animals. In other words, Darwin's contribution was to show the evolutionary basis of shared emotions and expressions: those ancestors who best used their facial muscles for communication were probably more reproductively successful, passing on those traits to their offspring. Some of Darwin's predecessors, on the other hand, thought that they were created that way by God.

In fact, many facial expressions, such as anger, sadness, or joy, are easily recognizable by animals with whom humans share a close bond, like dogs, or those to whom humans are closely related, like great apes. Yet it was not until the work of psychologist Paul Ekman in the 1960s that modern scientists were able to prove the universality of facial expressions. After Darwin's time, the scientific consensus was that facial expressions were culturally specific. Ekman traveled to New Guinea to test his proposition that even a culturally isolated people like those in the highland tribes of Papua New Guinea would recognize the facial expressions of other cultures. Participants in Ekman's research were able to not only recognize the facial expressions of other people, but were able to match those expressions to the proper emotion being expressed.

Of the facial expressions that are now thought to be universal in humans, Darwin thought that only smiling, laughing, and crying were innate, because they were the first expressions formed by infants, and because blind babies, who cannot see others forming those expressions, make them as well. We now know that babies are born with fully formed facial muscles, and can perform facial expressions without first seeing others do them. It is probably true that all of our expressions are innate, but that some are more primitive than others, and that socialization and verbal cues help to reinforce them as a baby develops. It appears that distress, disgust, and sadness are among the earliest expressions used by babies, and by four weeks, smiling develops. It is thought, however, that smiling to express true happiness only develops after about six weeks, indicating that perhaps the facial expressions come first and are only linked to the emotions later. Fear comes much later, at five to nine months. But while creating facial expressions is innate in babies, babies begin mimicking the expressions that they see around them within their first week of life.

If facial expressions are universal, that means of course that the emotions underlying them are universal, and for some scholars, that means that human nature might be a concept worth revisiting.

On the other hand, some modern scholars have challenged the notion that all facial expressions, and all emotions, are universally formed and recognized. Beyond the most basic expressions—happiness, surprise, fear, anger, contempt, disgust, and sadness—there are thousands of other more subtle and complex expressions, many of

Charles Darwin once suggested that there are universal facial features, shared by all humans and by our closest relatives, the great apes, and this hypothesis has now been proven. This Peruvian baby's expression demonstrates happiness. (Corel)

which may indeed be culturally specific. Just as cultural categories are linguistic terms to refer to concepts that are found in specific cultures, it would be unusual to expect that such cultural categories do not extend to emotional states, or that cultural categories are not linguistically variable.

Do facial expressions simply reflect emotions unconsciously, or do they, at least in part, create them? For some scientists, human emotions *are* facial expressions, in that the neuromuscular activity that creates them is indistinguishable from the emotions that underlie them. Some scholars argue that not only do expressions correspond to emotions, but that the intensity of such expressions corresponds to the intensity of the feeling. Furthermore, the lack of a facial expression would indicate the lack of an emotion, so what might be considered emotional states that are not expressed facially are, according to this train of thought, not emotions at all. Other scholars, on the other hand, maintain that emotional feelings can be generated in the absence of facial expressions, if the person has access to memories that can generate the feeling.

While many of facial expressions are involuntary expressions of emotions, humans are also adept at masking their emotions with facial expressions that are not tied to an emotion, or that are used to convey a false feeling. Even then, it is often able to detect artificial facial expressions. For example, a true pleasure smile involves the movement of not only the lips and cheeks (the zygomatic major) but also the eyes (the orbicular oculi); a false smile generally just involves the mouth, and thus looks (and feels) very different. (Artificial smiles are also thought to be asymmetrical.)

On the other hand, scholars have shown that facial expressions can reinforce the emotions underlying them; smiling, for example, can make people feel happier. Even when the smile is fake, it can sometimes cause feelings of happiness in a person who is engaged in it. One hypothesis is that feedback from the facial muscles and skin–say, when creating a smile—then triggers an emotional response: a happy feeling. In fact, studies done on patients injected with muscle-freezing toxins have demonstrated

Laughter

Laughter is a form of emotional expression found in humans and some nonhuman animals such as apes or even rats, which may express deep happiness, joy, or amusement. Visually, laughter appears to be an extension of the smile, one of the most universal of all facial expressions (in both humans and many mammals). Like smiling, laughter is contagious, creating laughter in others. Like the smile and other facial expressions, laughter serves as a basic form of communication, expressing the emotion of one individual and helping to bond him or her into the social group. Scientists have found that laughter is about more than just humor. People laugh when something incongruous happens, to release tension, and they laugh at inconsistency and the resolution of inconsistency. And finally, they laugh because other people are laughing. In fact, laughter very rarely occurs when someone is alone; most people only laugh when in the company of others. Laughter is said to be good, because it releases endorphins and increases blood flow, but regardless of the physical health benefits of laughter, the social benefits are critical.

that when the patients could not form a facial expression, the part of the brain that processes emotions, the amygdala, was quieter than in patients who could form the facial expression.

If facial expressions evolved among social species, and their primary function is to allow them to live in social communities, then reading, and responding to, the facial expressions of others is as important a skill as making them. Some expressions trigger an instant response; fear, anger, happiness, contempt, and so on all trigger a similar, or compatible, response in a viewer. This of course serves an important evolutionary purpose. If human ancestors saw fear in another person's face, and did not respond to it, then they may not be able to escape the threat. In general, facial expressions promote facial expressions in other people, and promote, perhaps more importantly, feelings of empathy. Seeing

how other people feel, and then mimicking that expression, makes the viewer feel something too.

Smiling is one of the most interesting of the facial expressions, because of the multiple emotions that can underlie a smile, and the multiple ways that people can use and interpret smiles. People (and some animals) smile for happiness, for hiding feelings, for deference and submission, for placating others, to hide embarrassment, or to smooth social interaction. Understanding the meaning behind these different types of smiles is an important social skill.

Recognizing facial expressions in other people is relatively easy when it comes to some of the more common expressions such as anger or happiness; some expressions, however, like disgust or contempt, are sometimes harder to discern, in part because they differ from other expressions in very small ways. Interpreting facial expressions gets harder when the parties involved do not know each other, or when the person making the expression is of a different ethnicity or culture than the person looking at them. For instance, in Ekman's research on the universality of facial expressions in the 1960s, Papuan tribesmen often confused the facial expressions for fear and surprise.

Not only can humans more easily distinguish between individuals of their own ethnicity, but they are better able to read and interpret the facial expressions of those in their own ethnic group, a finding that has important implications for inter-ethnic interactions. (In fact, studies show that when racist people are taught how to differentiate between the faces of people of another ethnicity, their racism lessens.)

To complicate matters further, facial expressions, even when universal, are not displayed in the same contexts in all cultures. Cultural display rules govern whether smiling or laughing is appropriate in one context, and some cultures are much more guarded with respect to using facial expressions in front of other people. The English stiff upper lip, for example, refers to the way that the English (especially the upper classes) maintain control over their emotions in the face of adversity. In addition, in many cultures men are socialized to display (and feel) less emotions, thus their use of facial expressions is often more limited than among women.

Face-to-face communication allows for the use of facial expressions; without it, communicating is often much more difficult. Face-to-face communication allows people to do more than communicate and understand others, but also to fit into society socially. (People with Aspergers Syndrome,

a form of autism, often cannot recognize or interpret facial expressions, and subsequently have a hard time interacting socially with others.) But today, we have less face-to-face contact than ever before. Phone calls must rely entirely on what a person is saying, and how he or she is saying it, while Internet communication—emailing, texting, instant messaging—relies only on the written word, as well as on **emoticons**, which have been developed in the last few years to substitute for the lack of facial expressions. Flaming, in which Internet newsgroup and listserv users post angry comments about other people, is extremely common today because of both the anonymity of the Web, but also because of miscommunications due to the lack of facial expressions in Internet communication.

In some social circles, communication via the face has become even more difficult. A recent study showed that Botox could harm friendships because Botox users cannot create the full range of facial expressions, leading to misunderstandings when one friend does not react as expected to emotional issues. On the other hand, a different study suggests that Botox users are less vulnerable to negative emotions, since they often cannot make the facial expressions associated with anger or sadness. In addition, they will be less likely to make other people sad or angry since they can't use those expressions.

See also Animal Facial Expressions; Evolution of the Face

Further Reading

Darwin, C. *The Expression of the Emotions in Man and Animals*. London: Murray, 1872.

Social X-Ray Specs

Social X-Ray specs are prototype glasses that have a small camera inserted into them. The cameras record the facial expressions of other people and, through software, analyze them, giving the wearer audio feedback as to what the expressions indicate. They have been tested on people with autism who often have a hard time interpreting the facial expressions, and emotions behind them, of other people. Created by scientists Rana el Kaliouby, Simon Baron-Cohen, and Rosalind Picard, their company Affectiva is in talks to sell the technology to companies who see its value. For instance, the technology can be used to help marketers interpret the facial expressions of people watching commercials or movies.

Ekman, P. "Cross-cultural Studies of Facial Expression." In *Darwin and Facial Expression: A Century of Research in Review,* edited by P. Ekman, 1–83. New York: Academic, 1973.

Ekman, P., W. V. Friesen, and P. Ellsworth. *Emotion in the Human Face.* New York: Pergamon Press, 1972.

Izard, C. E. *The Face of Emotion.* New York: Appleton-Century-Crofts, 1971.

Russell, James A. "Is There Universal Recognition of Emotion From Facial Expression? A Review of the Cross-Cultural Studies." *Psychological Bulletin* 115, no. 1 (1994): 102–41.

Facial Features

The features of human faces are the result of millions of years of evolution, and because of this evolutionary history, their faces look different from other animal species. The snouts are shorter; the eyes are set in the front of the face; mouths come equipped with lips; they have a prominent white portion to the eyes (the sclera); and they have eyebrows and a chin. In addition, because their faces are not covered with hair, their facial features stand out more than they do in hairy animals.

Before about 500 million years ago, distant ancestors to humans, who lived in the sea, had no facial features at all. The first facial feature, a primitive mouth, developed in order to help its owner, a worm called a pikaia, to get food more efficiently. In fact, all of the major facial features evolved to help animals hunt and eat, or to avoid being eaten.

Mouths first evolved to eat food, and within the mouth, specialized teeth tear, rip, and chew food, allowing it to be consumed easily; later, mouths became useful for communication as well. Noses are used primarily to smell food, but later evolved to help find mates as well. Eyes first evolved to detect food, and to escape predators, but now are used to see and navigate throughout the world, and to read the **facial expressions** of others. And ears evolved last, and were probably most useful in helping to hear prey as well as to hear, and avoid, predators.

As humans develop in the womb during gestation, this evolutionary history is repeated. A four-week-old embryo looks like a fish or reptile embryo with just a hint of the eyes and mouth beginning to develop. At five weeks, rudimentary gills appear that disappear later. Then the eyes move from the side of the head toward the front of the face, and finally, a three-month-old fetus has a fully formed face, and can swallow, frown, and suck.

Humans' facial features derive most directly from those of their primate ancestors. Primates have flatter faces than most other mammals, sacrificing a longer nose and the sense of smell for greater vision. Because the eyes our located on the front of the face, rather than on the side, they have binocular vision rather than the peripheral vision in other mammals. As sight became more important to ancestral primates, and smell and hearing less important, the muscles associated with hearing (and controlling the ears) and smell reduced, and the muscles associated with moving the middle face increased in size and complexity. As the human line evolved, and their brains expanded, the faces of their ancestors changed further, resulting in the high forehead they have today. And as teeth and jaws reduced in size, because of the use of fire and tools to prepare food, humans developed a chin—the only one in the animal kingdom.

The most distinctive feature, and arguably the most important, of human faces are the eyes. The eyes not only allow humans, like most other animals, to see food sources and avoid predators, but to interpret the communicative signs of other humans. They also allow communication: how they open, close, and squint their eyes, how often they blink, the ways they use **eye contact**, how their eyes wrinkle when smiling or laughing—all of these are important ways that they communicate with others.

In addition, the appearance of the eyes is an important signifier of beauty and an important part of human identity. Facial recognition software, for example, cannot recognize a person if the eyes are covered. How the eyes look has to do with their size and shape, the color of the iris, how much white is visible in the eye, the shape of the eyelid, and the features of the eyelashes and eyebrows.

Eye color is a polygenetic trait that is inherited and caused by melanin, which also controls skin color; the more melanin in the iris, the darker the eyes. The original human eye color was brown, as humans evolved in Africa, and dark eyes, skin, and hair would have protected them against harsh equatorial sunlight. Brown remains the dominant color around the world today. As humans moved out of Africa beginning about 150,000 years ago, other eye colors developed due to mutations, and in some populations, those eye colors would be more highly valued than brown, and thus selected through differential mating patterns. Blue eyes may be very recent in origin, having developed only about 10,000 years ago in the Baltic region of Europe. Eyes can be light or dark brown, amber, hazel, gray, blue, green, and violet, and a combination of those colors. People with albinism have red eyes, which lack melanin, and people with heterochromia have eyes that are two different colors.

In northern cultures in which light skin and hair predominate, light eyes tend to be culturally preferred—particularly blue eyes. In fact, studies have shown that blue eyes, perhaps because they are so rare, are heavily preferred in cultures around the world. One reason may be that when the pupils dilate, it is easier to see in light colored eyes, making blue-eyed people appear more attractive. Some scientists also think that men with blue eyes desire blue-eyed mates, because it ensures that their own genes will be passed on to their offspring. But as more and more people are marrying outside of their ethnic group, blue eyes (and other eye colors that are created by a pair of recessive genes) will become even rarer, and perhaps even more valued.

The length and color of the eyelashes, and the shape, color, and thickness of the eyebrows also plays a role in the appearance of the eye. While eyelashes are found in nonhuman animals—they protect the eyes from debris—eyebrows are unique to humans, and both enhance and exaggerate the eyes. Their primary function, however, is to keep sweat and rain from dripping into the eyes. Eyebrows also play a major role in facial expressions—raising the eyebrows indicates surprise while furrowing them can indicate anger, frustration, or concentration. In most cultures, heavy or bushy eyebrows are associated with masculinity while thinner, more refined eyebrows are a sign of femininity. Extremely prominent eyebrows are an important identifying mark—Mexican artist Frida Kahlo was well known for her prominent eyebrows and exaggerated them in her self-portraits.

Human eyes are already large compared to those of other animals, but large eyes are associated with youth and fertility and are often prized in women. The more estrogen a woman has, for example, the larger her eyes. For this reason, women have been using **cosmetics** to exaggerate the appearance of the eyes for thousands of years, and in recent years, eyelid lift surgeries and face-lifts are a new way to give the eyes a larger, more youthful appearance. The shape of the eyelid, too, can make the eyes appear larger or smaller. The primary function of eyelids is to protect the eyes from debris; blinking keeps the eyes moist. Because many people of Asian descent have what is called the **epicanthic fold**—an extra web of skin covering the inner eyelid—and an upper eyelid with no crease, many Asians, due to the dominance of Western standards of beauty, elect to have their eyelids surgically altered. Blepharoplasty is a surgical technique aimed at making the eyes appear bigger by creating a crease in the eyelid, and is now the most popular **cosmetic surgery** among East Asians around the world.

The nose is also a distinctive facial feature, although it doesn't play a large role in communication, as humans do not greatly rely on the sense of smell. The nose's primary function is to warm air before it enters the lungs, which is why people who evolved in cold climates and high latitudes tend to have longer noses than those who live in warm climates. But the nose itself may have evolved in humans as a side effect of other changes to the face—most notably the reduction in size of the upper and lower jaws—through the course of our evolution.

Noses, like eyes, are also subject to cultural preference. For example, the ideal Greek nose was a long, straight nose, while the ideal Roman nose was hooked. From an evolutionary perspective, men should have large, strong noses, while women's should be small and childlike. It's not surprising that short, upturned noses have been most popular among northern European cultures in which those noses have been most common. In addition, as Western beauty standards became normative around the world, cosmetic surgery to create an upturned nose quickly became the single most popular form of cosmetic surgery next to breast augmentation surgery. For clients from Mediterranean regions, that meant nasal reduction surgery, in which the longer and often hooked nose common in those regions was reduced to create the northern European ideal. For clients from Africa, on the other hand, reconstructive techniques have now been developed that allow doctors to reduce such noses in width while at the same time building up the cartilage.

The downside to rhinoplasty, however, is the danger in making a person no longer look like himself. The actress Jennifer Grey had nose reduction surgery and found that she no longer looked like Jennifer Grey; subsequently, she was offered far fewer acting jobs and her career suffered as a result. Other famous people, like Barbra Streisand, are primarily distinguished by their noses; without that feature, they would look very different indeed.

The mouth is an incredibly important facial feature. It allows people to eat food as well as to communicate both verbally—through speech—and nonverbally, through facial expressions. Like the eyes,

Barbra Streisand, shown here in 1956, is a celebrity who is well known for her distinctive facial features—in particular, her nose. (AP/Wide World Photos)

the mouth plays a huge role in the physical appearance and attractiveness of a person, and in addition, plays a direct role in social and sexual behavior through kissing and other sexual activities.

The size and shape of the mouth and the appearance of the lips play a major role in physical attractiveness. As with the other facial features, women's desirability is based on having features that indicate youth and fertility. In this case, lips that are large and red (the red coloring comes from the fact that blood can be seen beneath the surface) indicate the presence of estrogen and also can be a sign of sexual arousal. As women get older, the lips reduce in size, and women are judged less attractive. As with eye makeup, lipstick and lipgloss provide an artificial way of enhancing the lips and making them appear darker and larger.

The chin evolved as the result of the changes to the face during evolution; in particular, as human ancestors' jaws reduced in size, the chin emerged as the last remnant of the jutting jaw. The muscles of the chin play a major role in chewing and in communication. Chin size is a result of sexual selection; men in general have larger chins and jaws, while women tend to have smaller chins and jaws, and these traits are then preferred when men and women select mates. Large jaws indicate the presence of testosterone, while small chins indicate estrogen. A recent study has demonstrated that women with larger chins have more testosterone than other women, and are consequently more sexually active. Very large chins can be obvious signs of identity; comedian Jay Leno is well known for the size of his chin.

The cheeks do not serve a function; they are simply the area of the face between the eyes, nose, and ears. The upper part of the cheeks, or the cheekbones, is bony while the lower part of the cheeks is fleshy. Women having color in the cheeks is an indication of youth and fertility. Consequently, forms of makeup were developed thousands of years ago that artificially color the cheeks.

The forehead, like the cheeks, lacks a direct function. Instead, it formed in humans as the frontal region of the brain expanded, pushing the upper part of the face foreword, and creating a forehead. The muscles on the forehead play a major role in creating facial expressions, by lifting up the eyes or pushing them down, either individually, together, and from the center or the sides. The forehead is not an area of the face that is typically adorned with makeup or **jewelry**, although certain hairstyles like bangs and head coverings like veils take advantage of the forehead. An exception to this is the **bindi**, which is the dot worn on the forehead of Hindu women in South Asia. It can be made of powder, makeup, can be adhered with a plastic or felt sticker, or can be a form of jewelry. Another Indian adornment is the forehead tiara.

Finally, the ears are an important feature of the face because it is through the ears that humans are able to hear; for that reason, it plays a critical role in communication. In other animals, however, ears played a greater communicative role than they do in humans, because animals use their ears not only to hear other animals, but many mammals have highly developed muscles that allow them to move their ears. Dogs, cats, rabbits, horses, and other animals thus use the movement of their ears to communicate important information to other animals, an ability that humans have lost. While human ears are small and unremarkable compared to the ears of animals like elephants or bats, some people's ears are bigger and more obvious than others. Otoplasty, or ear-reducing surgery, is used by people who find that their ears are so big as to cause them social anxiety. Ears are one of the most adorned features of the face, subject to the most popular form of piercing in the world: the **ear piercing**. Women, and in some cultures men, have been piercing their ears for thousands of years, in order to wear jewelry in them.

Facial features differ to some extent among ethnic populations. For instance,

Europeans tend to have smaller facial features than non-Europeans. In particular, Middle Eastern and Southern European populations tend to have longer noses; Africans and East Asians tend to have wider noses; East Asians and Africans tend to have broader faces; and northern Europeans tend to have more prominent chins.

See also Beauty; Cosmetic Surgery; Cosmetics; Facial Expressions

Further Reading

Rhodes, Gillian, and Leslie Zebrowitz, eds. *Facial Attractiveness: Evolutionary, Cognitive, and Social Perspectives*. Westport, CT: Ablex Publishing, 2002.

Zebrowitz, Leslie. *Reading Faces: Window to the Soul?* Boulder, CO: Westview Press, 1997.

Facial Hair and Removal

Facial hair refers to both the light hair found on the bodies and faces of men and women, and also the androgenic hair—the hair that develops after puberty—found on men's faces. Women tend to have very light and fine hair on the face, but genetic makeup will influence the color and thickness of facial hair in women. In addition, postmenopausal women will often develop thicker facial hair. Eyebrows and eyelashes, on the other hand, represent the areas of the face in which darker and thicker hair grows on both sexes of any age. Men and women have been coloring, cutting, styling, and removing the hair on the face for thousands of years.

Because women naturally do not have a great deal of hair on their faces, it is considered a sign of femininity to have as little facial hair (except for eyebrows and eyelashes) as possible. Because of this, most women in Western cultures shave or wax and sometimes bleach the hair that grows on their upper lip, chin, and elsewhere on the face, and carefully tweeze the hair on their eyebrows in order to keep the eyebrows controlled and to conform to current style. On the other hand, eyelashes are considered a sign of femininity, because they make the eyes appear larger, and are encouraged, via makeup and other products like false eyelashes, to appear as long and thick as possible.

Because of the social stigma associated with facial hair in women, women who do have what is considered excess facial hair are generally considered to lack femininity or to appear mannish. Excessive hairiness on a woman is known as hirsutism, and bearded ladies who had this condition were once common attractions at circus and carnival freak shows.

For men, the presence or lack of facial hair can represent high or low status, conformity or rebellion, and youth or age, depending on the culture. Facial hair, or the ability to grow facial hair, most commonly represents masculinity, however, and men who cannot grow a mustache or a beard are often seen as less masculine than other men. Wearing a beard is often also associated with wisdom and virility, and it is common in some cultures for older men to allow their beards to grow quite long. Some cultures dictated that during mourning, facial hair be removed, as with the Greeks, while the Romans would grow their hair and beards when mourning.

Romans and Egyptians preferred a clean-shaven face for men, and men began shaving

Cultures around the world have norms regarding facial hair. In some cultures, men should be free of facial hair, while in other cultures, men should be encouraged to wear facial hair. In most cultures, women are expected to have largely hair-free faces. (Dreamstime.com)

at 21. Well-to-do men had their slaves shave their faces, but beginning in the fourth century BCE, professional barbers arrived in Rome. Other cultures embraced beards for men. The Greeks, for example, grew beards, as do men in many Arab and West Asian countries. Beginning about the fourth century BCE, however, Greek men adopted the practice of shaving their faces, which was popularized by Alexander the Great, while by the first century CE, Roman men began wearing beards, thanks to a trend started by the Emperor Hadrian.

Some professions and social statuses require men to be either clean-shaven or to wear facial hair. For example, Egyptian priests were required to shave their faces, bodies, and heads, and many countries' military branches require their soldiers to be clean-shaven. Roman slaves, philosophers, and soldiers were able to wear beards, even when the norm in Roman society was to be clean-shaven. In some cultures, moustaches are commonly worn by men in the military, with higher ranked officers wearing larger moustaches; the British Army has mandated moustaches for years. Many religions also either mandate the wearing of a beard or prohibit shaving, either for priests or for all of the faithful. For example, Sikhs do not cut their beards, Orthodox Christian priests were expected to grow beards, some Muslims feel that growing a beard is mandatory, and many Hasidic Jews also do not shave.

In Western culture, however, most men do not wear facial hair. It fell out of fashion during the 17th century, but became fashionable again in the 19th century, and, since the 20th century is associated with old men and hippies, who popularized the beard again in the 1960s.

Women in ancient Rome used razors, tweezers, pumice stones, and depilatory creams to rid their faces of unwanted hair, and women in the West have continued, since that time, to control the hair on their faces. For instance, beginning in the Middle Ages, European women of means shaved, pumiced, or plucked their eyebrows, and often shaved some of their hairline as well, in order to achieve the beauty standard of a wide, high forehead. Sometimes eyelashes were plucked out as well. These practices continued well into the Renaissance, and by the 18th century, both men and women were shaving their eyebrows and wearing artificial eyebrows made of the skin of dead mice in their place. The practice of women shaving off—and redrawing—eyebrows became popular again briefly in the 1920s and 1930s as a number of Hollywood actresses began the trend.

Removing the hair via shaving with a razor is the most common form of hair removal today, and is used by most men in the West to control their hair growth. Most men who shave do so every day, in order to appear clean-shaven, as it generally takes only a day for stubble to appear through the skin after shaving. On the other hand, wearing a beard, moustache, goatee, or other form of facial hair is often a stylistic choice, and some men go back and forth between being clean-shaven and wearing facial hair.

Plucking is probably the oldest style of hair removal, and is a form of epilation, which means removing the entire hair shaft from the skin. Shaving would have been the next method, using first flint or obsidian razors and then copper and ultimately iron and steel razors. Shaving is a form of depilation, which refers to removing the hair above the skin, usually with a razor blade, and is a temporary method of hair removal. The first razors were found in **Egypt** and **India** around 3,000 BCE, when copper tools were developed. Today, shaving can be done with an electric razor or a manual razor, and with or without lubricants. **African American** men have traditionally removed their facial hair with depilatory powders that remove the hair without a razor, and that prevent razor bumps and ingrown hairs, which are common among African Americans.

Today, other forms of hair removal include epilation methods that remove the entire hair shaft, such as waxing, plucking, and threading, all of which are temporary but last longer than shaving, and electrolysis and lasers, which is a permanent form of hair removal. Transgendered people and male to female transexuals will often opt for permanent hair removal methods for their face and bodies. Most men, however, still overwhelmingly favor shaving, although a few men in the West now use waxing and other methods to groom their eyebrows.

See also Gender; Greco-Roman Cultures; Hypertrichosis and Hirsutism

Further Reading

Peterkin, Allan. *One Thousand Beards: A Cultural History of Facial Hair.* Vancouver: Arsenal Pulp Press, 2001.

Reynolds, Reginald. *Beards: Their Social Standing, Religious Involvements, Decorative Possibilities, and Value in Offence and Defence through the Ages.* New York: Doubleday, 1949.

Facial Piercing

Facial piercings are a form of body piercing that are done on the face. Today, facial piercings are decorative, but they have been used for ritual purposes as well.

The most common facial piercings around the world are **oral piercings**, or piercings of the mouth and lips, and **nose piercings**. Today, however, there is a wide range of facial piercings that do not involve the nose or the mouth.

The most common forms of nose piercing are the nostril piercing and the septum piercing. In a nostril piercing, the wearer has one side of his nostrils pierced. The practice of piercing the nostril in order to wear **jewelry** has been found in the **Middle East**, Europe, and Asia. Nostril piercing is extremely common in **India** as both a marker of beauty and social standing for Indian girls. Nostril piercing was also practiced among the nomadic Berber and Beja tribes of **North Africa** and the Bedouins of the Middle East. In these cases, the size of the ring represents the wealth of the family. As jewelry, it is given by the husband to his wife at marriage, and is her security if she is divorced.

In the United States, nostril piercing did not become popular until it was introduced by hippies in the late 1960s and 1970s. Afterward punks and other youth subcultures in the 1980s and 1990s adopted the nostril piercing, and today it is common with young people from a variety of backgrounds. Next to the earlobe piercing, it is the most popular form of piercing today. While some men have their nostrils pierced, it is far more common among women.

A nasal septum piercing, which is a piercing through the flesh that divides the nostrils, is less common in the West than nostril piercings. Septum piercings were worn by a number of traditional societies, but especially among men in warrior societies, probably because wearing a large bone or horn through the nose makes a person look very fierce. The use of septum tusks is common, for example on Borneo, New Guinea, and the Solomon Islands, as well as among some Australian Aboriginal groups. Typically, septums were pierced in these cultures as part of initiation rituals for boys. Ancient Mesoamericans like the Aztecs and the Mayans as well as the Incans also had their septums pierced, and wore elaborate jade and gold jewelry.

Septum piercing was popular among some Native American tribes such as the Shawnee and many tribes of the Pacific Northwest Coast. Bones were often worn through the piercings, and sometimes beads were strung through the hole and hung in front of the mouth.

The second most common facial piercing is the oral piercing, or piercings in and around the mouth. Historically, the most common oral piercing is the lip and labret piercing, although today in the West, a huge number of other piercings are practiced. Lip piercings are either labrets, in which a stud or a spike is attached below the lower lip, above the chin, or are piercings anywhere around the lip in which a ring encircles the lip. Labrets were commonly worn among a number of Northwest Native American tribes, as well as ancient Mesoamericans like the Maya and the Aztecs. A number of African tribes also wear lip plates in large stretched lip holes. The Dogon of Mali and the Nuba of Ethiopia were two tribes that practiced lip piercing and wore rings, rather than labrets or lip plates.

Other than the nose and the mouth, facial piercings can now be done in a wide variety of locations. The area of the eye is one popular new location. Eyebrow piercings are generally vertical or angled piercings through the ridge of the eyebrow, and are typically found on the outer edge of the eyebrow. Jewelry for eyebrow piercings is usually a barbell or ring, both of which go through the eyebrow from bottom to top or top to bottom. An alternative to the vertical eyebrow piercing is the horizontal eyebrow piercing, which pierces horizontally along the upper brow ridge. Because this piercing goes through the surface of the skin, rather than using the extra flesh on the eyebrow as in the traditional eyebrow piercing, it is a surface piercing and thus uses a surface bar rather than a barbell or ring. A much rarer piercing is the eyelid piercing, which is a piercing done on the eyelid itself, generally with a ring.

Outside of the eye, there are a number of piercing choices. The temple piercing is a surface piercing to the area outside of the eye, on the temple of the face, and usually uses a surface bar. The anti eye-

brow is a facial surface piercing through the upper cheek just below the eye. They are sometimes known as tears because of the location of the jewelry. The jewelry, usually a specifically bent surface bar or sometimes a curved barbell, has two beads that sit on the surface of the skin, the top of which generally sits closer to the eye, with the bottom angled away from the eye.

Cheek piercings are done on the fleshy part of the cheek, usually where a dimple would be found. It is not a surface piercing because the jewelry goes through the skin and emerges on the other side—inside of the mouth. Jewelry is usually a labret stud, so that just the stud of the jewelry appears on the surface of the cheek. People who are attempting to look like an animal

Facial piercing is becoming increasingly common in the West, as this woman's multiple piercings indicate. (Anthony Gillilan/iStockPhoto.com)

often have multiple cheek piercings in the form of steel whiskers that emerge from the skin.

The nick piercing is another cheek piercing, but one that uses the highest point on the inside of the mouth, and then travels straight up under the skin and muscles of the mouth and exits underneath the eye, usually with a single stud appearing on the surface of the skin; it is not a surface piercing. The end of the jewelry sits inside of the mouth, against the gums.

A chin piercing is a rare piercing that at first looks like a labret, with a stud sitting beneath the lower lip, but with additional studs emerging under the chin. It is a surface piercing in which the bar travels through flesh of the chin, and does not use the inside of the mouth at all. A horizontal philtrum is another rare piercing that uses the upper lip divet, just below the nose, to pass a barbell through. It does not go inside the mouth, yet is not a surface piercing, because it uses the flesh above the lip to pass through. The two beads of the jewelry sit on either side of the divet, below each nostril.

The forehead is a relatively recent spot for surface piercings. Forehead piercings are sometimes worn by people with loose skin, although they are difficult to heal without much excess skin. Sideburn piercings, done where a man's sideburns would grow, is another surface piercing on the face. Finally, a **bindi** piercing uses a vertical barbell above the bridge of the nose, in the spot where Hindu bindis are painted onto the skin.

See also Labrets, Lip Plugs, and Lip Plates; Nose Piercing; Oral Piercing

Further Reading

DeMello, Margo. *Encyclopedia of Body Adornment*. Westport, CT: Greenwood Press, 2007.

Facial Portraits in Tattoos

Since the 1970s, when professional tattooists began to borrow new tattoo styles from other cultural groups, portrait tattooing has become popular in America.

Prior to the 1970s, American tattooists worked with technology developed at the turn of the century—an electric tattoo machine invented by Samuel O'Reilly, which allowed the artist to use a number of needles at once for outlining as well as for shading and coloring. This technology was responsible for the American tattoo style: strong black lines, typically made with five (or more) needles, heavy black shading, and color.

In the 1960s, a new style of tattooing developed; influenced by American bikers, Chicano gang members, and American convicts, this new style was created originally by hand, using a single needle and exclusively black ink. Once bikers and Chicanos began using tattoo machines, they continued to favor this style, which allowed for much finer lines and details than could be created using the multi-needle style of professional tattooists. It was this style that allowed for the development of portrait tattoos. Freddy Negrete and Jack Rudy, two East Los Angeles tattooists, were possibly the first professional tattooists working in this style in the late 1970s. They, along with tattooist Charlie Cartwright, perfected this technically difficult style, bringing it to mainstream prominence. Because of the use of single needles, this type of work was more finely detailed than traditional American tattoos, allowing the creation of finely shaded, photorealistic portraits on the skin. Tattooist Ed Hardy was impressed by the work that these men were doing, and helped promote the style further.

Today, many professional tattooists do portrait tattoos, although, because it is technically difficult, it is not found at every studio. Portrait tattoos only include the face, or face and upper body, as in photographic or painted portraits. They are created from a photograph brought in by a client, and attempt to capture the personality and essence of the subject.

Portrait tattoos are generally made of clients' loved ones. Mothers, children, pets, and other family members are the most common subject, and often clients choose to get a portrait tattoo after a loved one has died. Some people, however, choose to get portraits of celebrities or other famous people. Britney Spears, Kurt Cobain, Jack Nicholson, Marilyn Monroe, and Albert Einstein are all people who have been represented numerous times in portrait tattoos.

Portrait tattoos are usually made with exclusively black ink (although more artists are using color today), and they are as realistic as possible given the technical abilities of the artist and the technical constraints of the medium. Because the body is not flat like a canvas, there is often some distortion to the face of the subject. But many artists can create remarkably realistic portraits, and clients whose loved ones have died are gratified to have such a close representation of them on their bodies.

This tattoo of Captain Jack Sparrow from the Disney film *Pirates of the Caribbean* is an example of photorealistic portrait tattoos. (Tattoo and photo by Jeff Hayes, Rival Art Studios, Albuquerque, New Mexico)

Portrait tattoos are much more meaningful to many people than carrying a photo of a person; because they are permanently on the body (in a process that is quite painful). The client feels a greater connection to the subject than is possible through print or digital images.

See also Facial Tattoos

Further Reading

Fulbeck, Kip. *Permanence: Tattoo Portraits.* San Francisco: Chronicle Books, 2008.

Facial Proverbs, Idioms, and Metaphors

There are a number of English proverbs, metaphors, and idioms regarding the face, and most of these have to do with how central the face is to human appearance, human identity, and the expression of our selves. It is the part of the body that is presented to the world.

In English, the most common use of the term face, other than as the front of the head, is to refer to the outward appearance of a person or thing. Buildings have faces, cities have faces, and playing cards have faces.

> To love another person is to see the face of God.—*Victor Hugo*

Of all of the parts of the body, the face alone can stand in for the entire person and represent him to the world. When women say they are putting on their faces, they both mean that they are putting on their makeup, and that their face needs to be presentable, because it's that face that the world will use to judge them.

The face can also represent people (a sea of faces), or **facial expressions** and emotional states—one can have an angry face or a brave face; a long face is a sad face. For instance, one can pull a face or make a face, which means to adopt a negative facial expression. A poker face, on the other hand, is a face that lacks all facial expression. The term comes from the game of poker, in which players need to maintain impassive facial expressions so they don't let

other players know what is in their hands. A straight face is similar to poker face, but implies more directly controlling one's laughter. The African proverb, "sometimes the face can tell what the lips can't say," indicates that emotions and thoughts can be read on the face.

Another common use of the term refers to confronting an issue, person, or problem—one can face his or her enemy metaphorically, and one can face his or her partner literally. Looking someone in the face could mean literally looking at a person, but it could also mean facing him or her metaphorically—dealing with him or her directly, and facing one's responsibilities. Getting in someone's face can mean both being right in front of him or her, but it can also mean getting involved in his or her business. In your face means that something is very forward or aggressive, as in "in your face pornography." Setting one's face means to oppose something, while saying something to one's face means to directly challenge him or her.

Faces also imply trust—we may trust one person because he or she appears to have a trustworthy face. The Italians say, "he who speaks to your face is not a traitor," which implies that people who don't speak directly to someone, or who talk behind his or her back, cannot be trusted. Taking something or someone at face value means that he or she is trusted based on what he or she says; there is no need to investigate the matter further. On the other hand, flying in the face means that something contradicts something else, and often implies a breach of trust as well. Doing an about face means to change one's mind, and go in an entirely different direction.

Two-faced means not being trustworthy; telling someone one thing but then doing something different.

The face also represents the ego, and how we are seen by the world. Losing face means being publically insulted and having one's dignity and good name maligned, while saving face means preserving one's dignity and self-respect. Showing one's face means to come out in public after doing something shameful, or being publically shamed, while hiding one's face means to avoid public scrutiny because of an embarrassment. Throwing something in someone's face means that one confronts another person with something shameful that he has done, and publically airs it. Having egg on one's face means being publically embarrassed, and a slap in the face means that one was publically insulted. Red in the face is a more literal phrase—it means to be publically embarrassed, and literally refers to the fact that when one is embarrassed, he or she often blushes, which means that the face becomes red as the blood vessels in the face fill with blood. (Blue in the face, on the other hand, means that the face has been depleted of oxygen because of talking too much, and implies that one's conversational partner has not heard a thing that was said.) The Chinese, who are more concerned with this concept than other cultures, have multiple expressions related to this issue. For example, selling face means to gain popularity, ripping up face, means to stomp on someone else's feelings, and having no face means being without shame. The Chinese proverb "a person needs a face; a tree needs bark" is related to this idea, and means that a person needs a good reputation to survive in the world.

The idea that the face represents the true self is reflected in a number of proverbs. For example, the Swedish proverb, "a nice face is the best letter of recommendation," indicates that having a nice face tells the world that one is a nice person. On the other hand, a number of proverbs caution against reading too much into a nice face. The English proverb "the face is no index to the heart" and the Japanese proverb "a gilt-edged visiting card often hides an ugly face" both warn that what is on the face may not necessarily represent the true person. The Japanese say, "kind hearts are better than fair faces," and the Chinese say, it is "easy to know men's faces, not their hearts" and "many a good face is under a ragged hat." Here, judging a person by his or her face may not always be smart.

A number of expressions about the face in the West derive from the Old Testament, which often uses face to refer to God. For example, "to seek the face" (Ps. 24:6, 27:8, 105:4; Prov. 7:15; Hosea 5:15) is to seek an audience or favor with God, when God "hides His face" (Deut. 32:20; Job 34:29; Ps. 13:1, 30:7, 143:7; Isa. 54:8; Jer. 33:5; Ezek. 39:23,14; Mic. 3:4), he withdraws his protection and favor from man, while "the upright shall dwell in thy presence" (Ps. 140:13) means that the upright shall be awarded God's grace and protection.

See also Face Saving and Losing Face; Facial Expressions

Further Reading

Ammer, Christine. *The American Heritage Dictionary of Idioms*. Boston: Houghton Mifflin, 1997.

Beck, Emily M., and John Bartlett. *Familiar Quotations: A Collection of Passages,*

Phrases, and Proverbs Traced to Their Sources in Ancient and Modern Literature. Boston: Little Brown, 1980.

Mieder, Wolfgang, Stewart A. Kingsbury, and Kelsie B. Harder. *A Dictionary of American Proverbs.* New York: Oxford University Press, 1992.

Facial Reflexology

Reflexology is a holistic health practice by which pressure is placed on the feet and hands in order to promote health and well-being. In particular, reflexology is used to diagnose and treat illness and reduce stress. It is related to the practice of **acupuncture**, because it is based on the idea that the body is broken into zones, which correspond to points on the hands and feet, similar to the acupoints of acupuncture. These zones and points are linked by the energy meridians of the body, known as *chi* or *qi*. However, reflexology was developed by an American doctor in 1913.

According to proponents, placing pressure on specific areas of the hands and feet will affect the corresponding body parts and result in better blood flow to the affected regions (in acupuncture, acupoints correspond to areas of the body, and by inserting a needle into a particular point, healing will occur).

Facial reflexology is an even newer approach than reflexology, developed in the 1980s by Dutch reflexologist Lone Sorensen. While some consider it to simply be a New Age pseudo-science, proponents say that the face, too, is divided into a number of zones, based not on the Chinese acupuncture zones but on South American body maps. Within those zones are 12 stimulation or meridian points that are correlated with other parts of the body, and that when stimulated, this will result in better circulation, a better complexion, and better overall health. For instance, the point just above the lips corresponds to the sexual organs while the point just below the lips corresponds to the pancreas. Practitioners claim that because of the closeness of the face to the brain, by manipulating the facial points with one's fingers, information has much less distance to travel to reach the brain.

Facial reflexology is also based on the principles behind physiognomy, which claims that the personality and character traits of a person can be gleaned from studying his or her face. In facial reflexology, for example, having lines between the eyebrows indicates that one is an active thinker, and that this results in neck tension and a difficulty to fall asleep. Proponents claim that the head of a person corresponds to the forehead of the face, the hands correspond to the ears, the torso corresponds to the nose, the shoulders to the eyes, the genitals and the lower digestive tract to the mouth and finally, the feet to the chin. For this reason, a red nose would be suggestive of a problem with the heart or lungs, while a constrictive mouth might indicate constipation. By reading the facial features, practitioners are able to diagnose the underlying health problem, and then, through specific massage techniques, are able to help cure them.

See also Acupuncture

Further Reading

Lopez Sorensen, Lone. *Facial Reflexology.* Paharganj, New Delhi: Health Harmony, 2008.

Facial Symmetry

The human face, like the body, is symmetrical in form, with each side of the face approximating the other side in size, shape, and appearance.

From an evolutionary perspective, symmetrical faces indicate good genes and overall health, and should be selected for via mating patterns. Perfectly symmetrical faces are thus beautiful faces. In addition, research shows that athletes are more symmetrical in both face and body than most people (their bodily symmetry is what allows them to exceed athletically); it is thought that this is why top athletes tend to be more attractive than the norm. Studies have shown that babies will gaze longer at faces that are symmetrical, and adults, when given the choice between photos of beautiful people, will predictably choose those with more symmetrical features than those with less symmetrical features. These preferences are not only cross-cultural, but are found in nonhuman animals as well.

The ancient Greeks especially valued faces that were symmetrical, in harmony, and in proportion. The ideal Greek face, for example, was two-thirds as wide as it was high, and it could be divided into thirds vertically, from chin to upper lip, from upper lip to eyes, and from eyes to hairline. In the Renaissance, a mathematical concept called the Golden Ratio, Golden Mean, or Golden Section was developed to provide the mathematical model for the most beautiful face, and the most perfect items. Pythagorus was the original proponent of this theory, and in the Renaissance, Leonardo da Vinci and others continued to work with it.

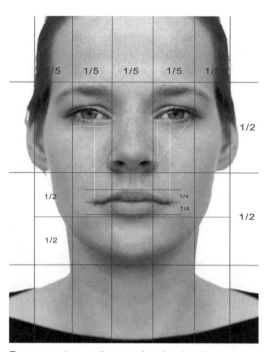

For centuries, artists and scientists have suggested that the most beautiful and healthy face is a face that is symmetrical. (Dreamstime.com)

The Golden Mean, also known as the Divine Proportion, is still used today, and is based on a mathematical concept called *phi*, which translates to 1.618033. Phi is derived from the Fibonacci sequence, which is a sequence of numbers that derives from summing up the previous two numbers in the sequence, as follows: 0, 1, 1, 2, 3, 5, 8, 13, 21, and so on, where 0 plus 1 equals 1, 1 plus 1 equals 2, 1 plus 2 equals 3, 2 plus 3 equals 5, and so on. Artists and scholars have found that this sequence of numbers is found in a number of places in nature (such as in sunflowers or artichokes) and plays a role in human facial symmetry as well. Phi is derived from dividing the numbers in the Fibonacci sequence by the one directly preceding it; this gives the ratio of each number, and ultimately equals a

Golden Ratio

The Golden Ratio (or Golden Section or Golden Mean) is a mathematical number, known as phi (which equals 1.618 . . .), derived from taking the ratio of distances in geometric figures. Specifically, it can be found by dividing a line into two parts and calculating the number that can be found when the long part is divided by the smaller part, which is equal to the length of the line divided by the long part. A Golden Rectangle, for example, is a rectangle whose side lengths each conform to the Golden Ratio, and, when a square is removed from it, the remaining rectangle continues to be a Golden Rectangle. The number is said to be found in both the pyramids at Giza and in the Parthenon in Athens. Besides architecture, proponents suggest that the Golden Ratio is found in the ideal human face. Perfect faces are faces that can be divided into a number of Golden Rectangles, all of which conform to the Golden Ratio. Everything from the distance between the eyes, the shape of the nose and teeth, and the relationship between all of the features, is taken into account.

number approximating 1.618033. It is this number that is considered to be the ideal ratio for objects of **beauty**, whether natural or human-produced.

To figure out whether the proportions of an object meet the Golden Ratio, measurements are taken of the object. If the length of the total measurement is to the length of segment 1 as the length of segment 1 is to the length of segment 2, then it meets the standards of the Golden Ratio.

Using this mathematical concept, the ideal human face can be divided into three equal rectangles that themselves have the proportions of phi; in other words these rectangles are 1.618 as high as they are wide. In the bottom half are four sections— the mouth, chin, and nose bisect the two middle sections, and the insides of the eyes begin at the outer edges of the two middle sections. The face can be subdivided further; a perfect square should be formed

by the points marked by the midpoint of the irises and the outer corners of the lips, while an additional rectangle is formed by the width of the nose and the inner edges of the eyebrows. These squares and rectangles are further divided into golden sections, which are ideal dimensions between the facial features. Each of these sections, lengths, and proportions should conform to phi. Even the dimensions of the teeth are said to be based on this divine proportion— the front two incisors should form a rectangle with the width 1.6 as wide as the height.

Today, many plastic surgeons utilize these concepts when evaluating a patient's face and deciding upon the dimensions of the **facial features**, and the relationship between them. *See also* Beauty; Facial Features

Further Reading

Moller, A.P., and R. Thornhill. "Bilateral Symmetry and Sexual Selection: A

Meta-analysis." *American Naturalist* 151 (1998): 174–92.

Rhodes, Gillian, and Leslie Zebrowitz, eds. *Facial Attractiveness: Evolutionary, Cognitive, and Social Perspectives.* Westport, CT: Ablex Publishing, 2002.

Facial Tattoos

Facial tattooing refers to the practice of tattooing permanent marks on the face. Facial tattoos are most well known among Pacific Island cultures such as New Zealand, the Marshall Islands, Tahiti, and Hawaii, as well as some tribes in New Guinea. A great many Native American tribes also practiced facial tattooing. In most of these cultures, the practice of facial tattooing was largely eliminated through colonization and missionary activity, although in recent years it has made a comeback in some areas.

Indigenous tribes from the Arctic, across Canada, and across much of North America used facial tattoos as signs of status, affiliation, achievements, and often marriageability. Women were far more likely to have facial tattoos than men. Chin tattoos were extremely popular tattoos for women in many Plains Indian tribes, such as among the Cree, the Ojibwa, and the Chipewyan, as well as among a number of California tribes such as the Mojave, and up the Pacific Northwest Coast. For instance, at the time of European contact, Inuit women wore facial tattoos that partially covered the forehead, cheeks, and especially the chin, and that were made up of lines and geometric patterns. As with other tribes, chin tattoos, which were received after puberty, were used to show that a woman was marriageable, and were also thought to protect women from enemies. Among many Pacific Northwest tribes, women were marked with facial tattoos consisting of lines that radiated from the mouth to the jaw, as well as those that extended from the nose to the ears. Among all the groups, the chin tattoo was the most common, received when a girl reached puberty.

In Oceania, facial tattoos were extremely popular until colonization, beginning in the 18th century. On Easter Island, for example, both men and women wore facial and head tattoos—the head was considered to be the most sacred part of the body. The tattoos generally consisted of very heavy curved and straight lines combined with dots. Some of the facial markings on women may have been related to fertility, and facial tattoo marks are also seen on the barkcloth figures made by the native peoples. In Hawaii, too, men wore facial tattoos, which were made up of a combination of straight lines, but the chiefs did not wear facial tattoos.

The most well known and classic of all facial tattoos is the **moko**, the black curvilinear tattoo worn by the indigenous tribe of New Zealand, the Maori, as a sign of status as well as affiliation. Women's tattoos were originally limited to the lips and sometimes other parts of the body or forehead; in the 19th century, the spiral chin tattoo was developed. A woman's moko, which covered the chin and lips, could take one or two days to complete. A man's moko, which covered the whole face, was done in stages over several years and was an important rite of passage for a Maori

The Hangover Part II Tattoo Lawsuit

In 2011 Warner Brothers released the film *The Hangover Part II*, a sequel to the 2009 film *The Hangover*, starring Zach Galifianakis, Justin Bartha, Bradley Cooper, and Ed Helms. In the sequel, Helms's character wakes up during his bachelor party in Thailand to find that his face has been tattooed. The tattoo is a replica of boxer Mike Tyson's tribal tattoo, created by tattooist Victor Whitmill. Before the release of the film, Whitmill sued Warner Brothers, alleging that because the work was copyrighted (he copyrighted Tyson's tattoo in 2003), Warner Brothers could not use it. While a judge in the case ruled that the film could be released, there was still a concern that filmmakers would have to digitally alter every frame of the film to alter the tattoo. In June 2011, however, the case was settled out of court, with Warner Brothers paying Whitmill an unknown settlement.

man; without the moko, a man was said to not be a complete person.

Some Eastern cultures practiced tattooing as well. Among the Naga of Northeast India, men wore facial tattoos that demonstrated their achievements in warfare and **head hunting**. Facial tattooing was also once practiced by Hindus, who tattooed women on the forehead as a means of identification and a sign of marriageability. In **Japan**, a country well known for its full body tattoo style known as *irezumi*, the original tattoo form was most likely facial tattooing. Archaeological evidence shows that the ancient peoples of Japan tattooed their faces with dots around the eyes, cheeks, forehead, and lips. In addition, the women of the Ainu, an ethnic group living on an island at the northernmost end of Japan, have worn upper lip tattoos for hundreds and perhaps thousands of years. And in Myanmar, the indigenous Chin tribe has been tattooing girls on the face for hundreds of years, ostensibly to keep them from being captured as slaves by other tribes.

In the **Middle East**, too, facial tattooing has been practiced. In some Bedouin tribes, for example, women wear facial tattoos made up of lines, crosses, and geometric designs, as a sign of **beauty**.

In the West, due to the tradition dating back to the Greeks and Romans of tattooing criminals on the face with a mark of their crime, facial tattoos are traditionally the mark of a convict. Even without that explicit connection, facial tattoos are extremely stigmatizing in the non-tattooed world. Most American and European tattooists do not want to contribute to marking an individual for life as an outcast, thus many tattooists will not tattoo on someone's face. Perhaps the most powerful prison tattoo in the United States is the tear, tattooed just below the outside corner of the eye. The tear immediately identifies an individual as a convict or ex-convict (each tear signifies a prison term served, or a man may wear a tear for each person he killed), and thus serves as a kind of self-inflicted brand, not unlike the marks that were forcibly tattooed on prisoners at one time in Japan, England, and Germany. The tear may also be seen as a symbolic expression of the convict's suffering at the hands of justice.

However, in recent years, facial tattoos have experienced a surge in popularity among the body modification community, especially among those who embrace modern primitivism, partly because of their extreme appearance, and partly because of their connection to primitive cultures.

Besides the primitivist connection, though, modern wearers of facial tattoos often use their tattoos as a sign of rebellion against society, because of the continuing taboo against them. Another reason for the increasing popularity of facial tattoos has to do with the mainstreaming of tattooing in general. As tattoos (as well as piercings) become more popular and thus more acceptable, those within the body modification community feel that they need to use more extreme versions of tattoos and piercings, in order to stay ahead of the rest of society.

Facial tattoos are also popular with the small population of those who transform their bodies into animals, such as Eric

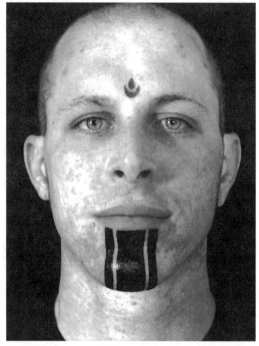

Facial tattoos are still relatively rare in the United States, although they are common in other cultures. This chin tattoo is reminiscent of the chin tattoos worn by women in many Native American cultures. (Tattoo and photo by Jeff Hayes, Rival Art Studios, Albuquerque, New Mexico)

Sprague (the Lizardman), the Great Omi, Stalking Cat, or Katzen.

See also Famous Faces; Moko

"Rapest" Tattoo Case

On April 14, 2011, an 18-year-old man named Stetson Johnson met a woman through MySpace and woke up a few days later having been beaten with a baseball bat, tasered in his genitals, and tattooed on both his chest and face: on his chest were the words "I like little boys" and on his forehead, "rapest." Two men and two women were arrested for the crime; the women allege that Johnson tried to rape them. Johnson, whom his mother describes as having a diminished mental capacity, then had his brother tattoo a bar code on his forehead to cover up the misspelled word. In June, three of the suspects pleaded guilty to kidnapping and assault, while one pleaded no contest, and were sentenced to 5 to 10 years in prison.

Further Reading

DeMello, Margo. *Bodies of Inscription: A Cultural History of the Modern Tattoo Community*. Durham, NC: Duke University Press, 2000.

Famous Faces

While we live in an age of celebrity in which we recognize hundreds and perhaps thousands of faces of people we don't personally know, not all famous people have famous faces. Famous faces are, ultimately, very distinctive faces.

What makes a face distinctive? Generally, faces are distinctive when they have a feature, or set of features, that is out of the ordinary—extra large features make a face distinctive. The proportions of the face, if unusual, may make a face distinctive as well. Facial disorders or injuries that have left a person's face highly unusual, obviously make a face distinctive, as would excessive **cosmetic surgery** that has left a person looking abnormal. Studies have shown that the more a face deviates from the average, the greater the level of distinctiveness in that person's face. Furthermore, the more distinctive the face, the more memorable it is.

Even relatively average faces can be made more distinctive through the use of **caricatures**. Caricatures emphasize or exaggerate a facial feature or features, in a way to make even a relatively normal-size nose appear huge. Caricatures make people more recognizable than do photos or representational drawings.

Facial features that are extra large make faces distinctive. People with exception-

ally big noses have been well known for their noses. Jimmy Durante (1893–1980) and W.C. Fields were both actors with very large noses. Durante was a Vaudeville actor and a comedian who used his nose as part of his act, naming it Schnozzola; Durante himself was also known by that nickname. Fields (1880–1946) was another Vaudeville performer who was known in part for his nose—unlike Durante's, which was long and hooked, Fields's nose was bulbous and red, due in part to rosacea, which caused the redness, and rhinophyma, which caused its abnormal growth.

In fiction, the two most famous large-nosed characters are Pinocchio and Cyrano de Bergerac. De Bergerac was the lead character in the 1897 play *Cyrano de Bergerac* by Edmond Rostand, which was inspired by the 17th-century French dramatist Savinien de Cyrano de Bergerac. The de Bergerac character was a poet who was in love with his cousin Roxanne, but because of the enormity of his nose, he was unable to approach her directly to express his love to her. Pinocchio was a character in an 1883 children's book, the *Adventures of Pinocchio*, written by Carlo Collodi. Pinocchio was a talking wooden puppet who wanted to be a boy; when he lied or was under stress, his wooden nose would grow. Since the popularity of Pinocchio, primarily through the 1940 Disney movie, Pinocchio has become a common appellation for someone who is either a liar, or who has a long nose.

> There was a time when people said, "Jim, if you keep on making faces, your face will freeze like that." Now they just say, "Pay him!"—*Jim Carrey*

While human eyes do not differ radically in size, the appearance of larger eyes can make someone distinctive. Marty Feldman (1934–1982), for example, was an English actor and comedian known for his large eyes that appeared to bug out of his head. His unusual appearance was caused by Graves' disease, a condition marked by an overactive thyroid, which can cause receding eyelids and bulging eyes. Eyes that are unusually colored are also distinctive. Actress Elizabeth Taylor, for example, is well known for her violet eyes. Sharbat Gula is not a name that is known to most people, but a 1984 photo taken of Gula, then a 12-year-old Afghan girl by Steve McCurry, is one of the most well-known images of the 20th century. Gula was living in a refugee camp in Pakistan as a result of the Soviet attacks on Afghanistan when McCurry photographed her for *National Geographic* magazine. After the image was featured on the cover of the magazine, Gula's face achieved instant fame, although she was not identified until a *National Geographic* team located her in 2002. One of the main reasons for the photo's success was Gula's eyes—a piercing green. Another person known for the appearance of his eyes is industrial metal singer Marilyn Manson. Born Brian Hugh Warner, Manson has cultivated a shocking appearance, and wears a white contact lens with a black circle around the outer edge.

Distinctive eyebrows have also been a source of fame. Mexican artist Frida Kahlo (1907–1954) was well known for her dark, bushy eyebrows; she often painted images of herself with a **unibrow**, and those paintings have helped shape the public's perception of her since her death. Comedian Groucho Marx (1890–1977) was also known for his dark eyebrows, even though they were painted on with grease paint to match a moustache that he painted on before one of his early Vaudeville shows.

When either the ears, the chin, or the mouth is extra large, these characteristics will also make a person more notable. Talk show host Jay Leno is known for his very large chin, a result of mandibular prognathism, a condition in which the lower jaw protrudes beyond the norm. Those with big ears, like England's Prince Charles or actor Will Smith, also stand out from the crowd, although a simple surgical procedure to pin down protruding ears to the head is an easy way to deal with the embarrassment of having large ears. Large mouths and lips, while often considered sexy (especially when found on women) are also distinctive. Rock stars Steven Tyler and Mick Jagger have naturally large mouths, and actress Angelina Jolie is known for her large, bee-stung lips. In the past decade or so, large lips have gotten more popular and lip augmentation procedures like collagen or Restylane injections have become more common. As a result, not only have Hollywood actresses' lips gotten bigger, but the unnatural-looking duck lips that often result are becoming more normal in Hollywood.

Facial hair, too, is a way to make a person notable. Perhaps the most famous moustache in history belonged to Adolf Hitler; while during Hitler's time the toothbrush moustache was commonly worn in both Germany and the United States, since the end of World War II, it has been so intractably linked with Hitler, with Nazism, and with the Holocaust, that it has essentially gone extinct.

Celebrity Faces

Celebrities often derive their fame from their unique appearance. Celebrities are generally more handsome or beautiful than most people, but many celebrities have distinctive physical traits that make them stand out even more. For example, model Cindy Crawford, popular during the 1980s and 1990s, was most known for the mole above her lip. Other celebrities with distinctive facial moles include Madonna, Marilyn Monroe, Rod Stewart, Sarah Jessica Parker, and Enrique Iglesias. While in Crawford's case, her mole emphasized her **beauty**, in other cases, the moles have been seen as a distraction, leading Parker and Iglesias to have them removed. Having a gap between one's top incisors is another distinctive facial feature seen in some celebrities, most notably model and actress Lauren Hutton. Most models and actresses with gapped teeth were encouraged to have the gap fixed, but since Hutton's fame, other women have felt free to show their gap in public, like Madonna and actress Anna Paquin. Large noses are generally seen as a less attractive feature, but some celebrities have resisted having their noses surgically altered, such as, most famously, Barbra Streisand. Finally, having a facial scar is generally not seen as positive for celebrities, especially women, but there are a handful of celebrities whose scars have helped make them who they are, like Tina Fey, Harrison Ford, Joaquin Phoenix, Seal, and Danny Trejo.

Extreme cosmetic surgery is another ticket to fame—wanted or unwanted—for people today. One of the most well known cosmetic surgery patients is Jocelyn Wildenstein, a wealthy American socialite who underwent a series of plastic surgery procedures that have left her looking somewhat like a cat. She has allegedly spent millions of dollars on plastic surgery over the years, and is known by the tabloids both as Cat Woman and Bride of Wildenstein. The story detailing Wildenstein's surgeries explains that as a young wife and mother married to a billionaire art dealer, in the 1970s she caught him in bed with a 21-year-old Russian model. Hoping to keep him—he is also said to love large cats—she began a series of surgical procedures to make herself look more like a cat. She is known to have received several silicone injections to the lips, cheek, and chin along with a face-lift and eye reconstruction, all of which have resulted in a strangely misshapen face. The story continues that her husband was horrified and immediately filed for divorce, leaving her for the other woman, with the divorce having been finalized in 1999.

Born Dennis Avner, Stalking Cat is another person whose fame derives from his multiple surgeries. He has spent much of his life transforming himself into a tiger through a series of radical body modification procedures. Avner, who is part Native American, says that he was told by an Indian chief to follow the ways of the tiger, and decided to transform himself into his totem animal, like whom he already behaves, occasionally hunting his own food and eating raw meat.

He began his transformation in 1981 at the age of 23, and now has tiger stripes and fish scales tattooed on his body and face; a modified hairline; surgically pointed ears; surgically flattened nose; silicone injections in his lips, cheeks, and chin; 6 subdermal implants inserted into his brow; 18 transdermal implants that act as whiskers above his lips; a bisected upper lip; and a full set of fangs. He also wears green contact lenses with slits as irises, and detachable bionic ears, but hopes to get another set of transdermal implants, in his head, to act as permanent cat ears. He also plans to attach a permanent pelt to his skin.

Michael Jackson (1958–2009) is the most famous plastic surgery recipient of all. While originally famous for his music— Jackson was one of the most well-known and well-respected musicians of the 20th century, producing the best-selling album in history and receiving more number one singles and more musical awards than any other artist—in his later years, Jackson's musical fame was largely overshadowed by his eccentric lifestyle and his surgically altered appearance. Since the 1980s, when Jackson was in his 20s, he began getting a number of plastic surgery procedures to alter his nose, chin, and cheeks. Plastic surgeons and members of the public have speculated about the number and extent of Jackson's surgeries; he has probably received multiple nose jobs, had his lips thinned, had his cheeks and chin sculpted, had permanent eyeliner tattooed around his eyes, and probably some eye and forehead lifts as well, although during his life, Jackson only admitted to having his nose

altered. Jackson discussed in media interviews the way that his father criticized him for having a large nose, and this was probably a factor in his quest to alter his face. His skin also became significantly lighter through the course of his life; while he was accused of using skin whitening products, he was suffering from vitiligo, which causes depigmentation of the skin, and his treatment for that condition may have been the cause of his light skin. Jackson's surgeries, especially to his nose, were so extensive that it is reported that in 2004 he had his nose reconstructed with cartilage taken from his ear in an attempt to mitigate the damage he had done.

Michael Jackson was a pop star famous for his extensive cosmetic surgeries. (AP/Wide World Photos)

Finally, facial disorders that leave the face disfigured are an unhappy way to achieve fame. Perhaps the most disturbing facial disorder was seen in Englishman Joseph Merrick (1862–1890), who was called the Elephant Man. No one knows today the exact disease that Merrick suffered from, but scientists speculate that it may have been neurofibromatosis, which causes tumors and warty growths, or Proteus syndrome, which causes the abnormal growth of the head, thickened skin, subcutaneous masses, the growth of the bones, and the abnormal growth of tissues.

While Merrick was born looking normal, as he grew up, he began to develop thickened skin, bony protrusions and his appendages swelled to abnormal size. His head developed a huge protrusion that grew so big that he could not lay his head down, and because of the growths on his mouth, he could not speak intelligibly. The folk explanation for his condition was that his mother was frightened by an elephant when pregnant with him, an example of the then-popular belief in maternal impression theory. Because of his frightening appearance, he became a dime museum freak, and was displayed throughout Europe as a half man/half elephant, until he was abandoned in Belgium and returned to England in 1886 where he spent the rest of his life as a patient in London Hospital thanks to the kindness of a doctor there. During the last years of his life, Merrick's facial deformities and head continued to grow, and played a part in his ultimate death, which was caused when he attempted to lay down and most likely the weight of his head broke his neck.

Joseph Cary Merrick, Victorian England's famous "Elephant Man," is shown in a photo from the Radiological Society of North America. In the century following Merrick's death in 1890, the most widely held theory was that he suffered from neurofibromatosis, often referred to as "Elephant Man disease." But recent radiologic exams performed by Amita Sharma, MD, and her colleagues at the Royal London Hospital where Merrick lived and where his skeletal remains have been kept indicate that the disease that caused Merrick's disfigurement was Proteus Syndrome, a rare disorder unrecognized in Merrick's day. (AP/Wide World Photos)

See also Caricatures; Disorders of the Face; Facial Features

Further Reading

Cahlon, Baruch, and Sam S. Rakover. "Face Recognition: Cognitive and Computational

Processes." *Advances in Consciousness Research* 31. Amsterdam: John Benjamins Publishing Company, 2001.

Fawkes, Guy

Guy Fawkes was a 16th-century Englishman who, along with a group of co-conspirators, attempted to blow up the English Parliament and kill King James in 1605. Fawkes was a Catholic activist who had seen the persecution of Catholics under Queen Elizabeth, and now, under King James, thought that they could only get freedom through violent action.

Led by Robert Catesby, a group of 13 men placed 36 barrels of gunpowder in the cellar under the House of Lords. It is thought that one of the group had second thoughts and sent a letter to Lord Monteagle, a Catholic, warning him of the plan; the letter eventually reached King James, whose men found Fawkes in the cellar with the gunpowder and arrested him. (Others think that the King already knew of the plot, known as the Gunpowder Plot, and fabricated the letter in order to implicate the conspirators.) Fawkes was tortured for four days in the Tower of London and was hanged two months later. His co-conspirators were partially hanged, drawn,

The Guy Fawkes mask represents the man implicated in the plot to assassinate King James I of England in 1605. It was popularized in the 2006 movie *V for Vendetta*, when it was worn by an anonymous revolutionary. Today, it is common for protestors to wear the mask during their demonstrations. (Sandrogauci/Dreamstime.com)

and quartered; Fawkes only avoided the second part of his execution by jumping from the gallows and breaking his own neck, although his lifeless body was quartered anyway. November 5, the night the plot was discovered, is now known as Bonfire Night, because bonfires were set throughout London that evening to celebrate the safety of the king. Bonfire Night, also known as Guy Fawkes Night, is typically celebrated by setting off fireworks and burning effigies of Guy Fawkes, who continues to be the conspirator most associated with the plot.

> There is a face beneath this mask, but it isn't me. I'm no more that face than I am the muscles beneath it, or the bones beneath that.—*Steve Moore, V for Vendetta*

In the 2006 film adaptation of the graphic novel *V for Vendetta*, the main character, known as V, wears a Guy Fawkes mask in honor of Fawkes and blows up Parliament, and today, online activists who call themselves Anonymous have worn the same Guy Fawkes mask from the film when staging protests against the Church of Scientology. The **masks** are used to conceal the protesters' anonymity, and to protect them from the wrath of the church. The Guy Fawkes mask has now been associated with a number of protests, both because of its ability to render the protesters anonymous, but also because Fawkes himself has become somewhat of an antigovernment, anti-authority folk hero.

See also Masks

Further Reading

Fraser, Antonia. *Faith and Treason: The Story of the Gunpowder Plot*. New York: Doubleday, 1996.

Freckles, Moles, and Birthmarks

Freckles and moles are both marks on the skin that can be either inherited from one's parents and thus present at birth, or that can develop during one's lifetime, generally due to sunlight exposure. Freckles are more commonly found among light-skinned people, and are essentially small spots of melanin. Moles are a form of benign lesion, usually colored brown or black, which is also caused by melanin—specifically they contain melanin cells or melanocytes.

Freckles and moles are found on both the face and the body, although freckles are more common on the face. Most moles are benign but some moles can become cancerous during the course of one's lifetime. While freckles are flat, moles can be either flat or raised, and can sometimes have a hair follicle inside. Beauty mark is the term for a small mole that, due its placement in a particular spot on a woman's face, is considered to be a mark of **beauty**. In the West, moles found just outside of the eye, or above and to the outside of the lips, are called "beauty marks." Marilyn Monroe, Cindy Crawford, and Madonna all had the latter type of beauty mark. Beauty marks can also be drawn on with makeup or can be applied with cosmetic tattooing.

In some cultures, freckles and moles are seen negatively and are thought to be caused by magic or some other evil. However, sometimes freckles or moles are seen as a sign of beauty or luck. Marilyn Monroe had a mole just above her upper lip, which was widely seen as a mark of beauty. (AP/Wide World Photos)

Birthmarks are, like freckles and moles, found at birth or in the first few weeks after birth, but are not caused by melanin production, and are not hereditary. Instead, they are a form of lesion that forms due to either an overgrowth of blood vessels in the skin in the case of vascular birthmarks, or an abnormal development of pigment cells in pigmented birthmarks. Birthmarks are found on approximately 80 percent of all babies, but most disappear after a few months or years. Some are flat and some are raised, and can be colored brown, tan,

blue, or red. Port wine birthmarks are bright red marks, often quite large, which often appear on the face and cause considerable discomfort to the person with it. Vascular birthmarks are most commonly found on the face and head.

Moles, freckles, and birthmarks have long been subject to folklore regarding their causes, how to get rid of them, and what they indicate about the wearer.

For instance, in many cultures, moles were signs of ugliness, associated with witches and toads. The witches' teat, for example, was thought in Medieval and Renaissance Europe to be a corporeal sign of witchcraft, and indicated the devil's mark on his subject. In addition, the witches' teat is the spot where the witch suckles either the devil himself, or one of her animal familiars. Suspected witches were stripped and their bodies shaved and then searched for such a mark, and, because most people have at least one mole or other lesion, it was very often located, and the witch condemned.

Moles are often used in physiognomy, the science that uses facial characteristics to read a person's character. Moleomancy or molesophy is a form of physiognomy in which facial moles are read in order to ascertain if the bearer will be lucky or unlucky. Moles can be advantageous if they are located on a part of the face associated with luck or wealth, and hidden moles are often thought to be more advantageous than easily-seen moles. In Chinese mole reading, moles can be used as a form of divination or reading the future. Here, moles can also be seen as warning signs— different colors can indicate trouble in relationships, for example, while other moles may suggest a propensity toward food allergies or a short life.

Beliefs about moles include the following: moles are lucky, but hairy moles are unlucky; a mole on the forehead indicates ambition while a mole on the chin indicates a long life, and those with moles on the lip are fond of delicate things. Moles on the eye mean one is farsighted, and moles on the nose means they will have success. A mole on the right eyebrow indicates a happy marriage, but on the left eyebrow it means a life of sorrow, and having a mole on the neck means that one will die by strangulation. Some English sayings regarding moles include "a mole on the face, you'll suffer disgrace," "a mole on the lip, you're a little too flip," and "a mole on the ear, you'll have money by the year."

Freckles are also subject to folklore, and in particular, there is a large number of folk cures for freckles. Freckles can be removed through rubbing cow manure or urine on the face, but a nicer approach suggests washing the face with dew in a wheat field before a March sunrise. An alternative approach says that washing one's face with dew in May, and then rubbing one's hands on another part of the body will transfer the freckles from the face. Freckles can also be removed by rubbing one's face with a penny and throwing the penny away, while a German method is to wash one's face with rainwater taken from a tomb. Freckles can also be caused in a number of ways: washing one's face in water that boiled eggs will cause freckles, as will popping the seed pods of the maple tree into one's face.

Birthmarks are subject to the greatest number of folk tales. In particular, cul-

tures around the world have come up with thousands of explanations for the presence of birthmarks on babies, most of which have to do with something that the mother did while pregnant. In German, the word for birthmark is *muttermal*, or mother's mark. Pregnant mothers especially knew that placing one's hands on one's body during certain events would transfer the trauma to the place on the baby's body where the mother placed her hands. Another extremely common belief is that if a mother's desires are not fulfilled when she is pregnant, that wish will be transferred to the baby in the form of a birthmark. This is why the Italian word for birthmark is *voglia,* which means wish; the French word is *envie,* or desire; and the Spanish word is *antojo,* or craving.

For example, if a woman desired a certain kind of food when she was pregnant, and was unable to get what she wanted and then touched her forehead, she would give birth to a child with a birthmark in the shape of the food on the baby's forehead. Similarly, a trauma to the mother during pregnancy can be transferred to the unborn child—traumas involving blood resulted in a baby born with a bloody red birthmark. An African belief says that women should not look at hideous or disfigured people when pregnant, lest their baby be born with such a disfigurement. Death in particular seems to result in birthmarks—pregnant women knew to not touch their bodies when at a funeral; if they did, an image of the coffin would be transferred to the baby on the spot where the mother touched her body. All of these beliefs are examples of sympathetic magic, and what anthropologists call the law of contagion—objects or persons that were once in contact will remain in contact even after separation. So a woman can mark her unborn baby by touching her body at the same time that she experiences something traumatic, emotional, or unusual. It is also an example of the theory of maternal impression—the idea that what a pregnant woman does while pregnant will be transferred to her unborn child.

There are a number of folk remedies for the removal of birthmarks, although some cultures believe that it is unlucky to remove a birthmark. One common folk cure is to rub the birthmark with the inside-out afterbirth, and then to bury it. Rubbing the mark with the item that caused it—if the birthmark was caused by the mother's unfulfilled desire—and then throwing that item away will also result in the disap-

pearance of the mark. A German remedy is to kill a black chicken and rub the birthmark with the blood of the chicken, while an English remedy is to rub the hand of a dead person (often a stillborn baby is preferred) over the birthmark. Sometimes it is recommended that the following is recited, "What I have, take with you, in the name of the Father, Son, and Holy Ghost." This causes the birthmark to leave with the dead body.

See also Face Folklore; Face Reading; Physiognomy and Phrenology

Further Reading

Daniels, Cora L. M. *Encyclopedia of Superstitions, Folklore, and the Occult Sciences of the World: A Comprehensive Library of Human Belief.* Detroit: Gale Research, 1971.

G

Geisha

Geisha are female Japanese entertainers with very distinctive makeup, fashion, and hairstyle fashions.

Geisha emerged out of an ancient Japanese custom of having female serving girls who entertained customers and sometimes sold sexual services. In the 16th and 17th centuries, walled pleasure quarters were built in Kyoto, then the capital of Imperial **Japan**, in which courtesans would entertain men with sex and theatrical performances.

Starting in the 18th century, true geisha emerged—women who specialized in a variety of forms of performance, and were highly trained in the arts of pleasing their male customers. Geisha are apprenticed as young girls called *maiko*, who work for a geisha house called an *okiya*, and who learn art (such as calligraphy and poetry), entertaining (including dance, musical instruments, and singing), and social skills. They also learn how to create the complicated appearance of the geisha, involving hair, makeup, and dress.

The geisha's makeup was based upon the ideal standard of female beauty in Japan, which mandated very light skin, which contrasted with dark eyes and red lips. Maiko traditionally wore and continue to wear today the most iconic form of geisha makeup, while older geisha wear a more subtle form. The process begins with an application of wax over the face, neck,

and chest (with a region on the nape of the neck left unpainted), followed by a paste of white powder (once made of lead); the wax allows the powder to adhere to the skin. The white base is accented by very red lips, in the shape of a flower bud or cupid's bow surrounded by white, and very dark eyebrows (older geisha wear longer eyebrows while younger geisha's are shorter) and eyes, drawn on with charcoal or, today, modern cosmetic pencils. In the past, Japanese women in general, including geisha, blackened their teeth, which helped to make them disappear into the mouth.

The geisha's white face is emphasized by the darkness and gloss of her hair. The traditional hairstyle of the geisha is known as the *shimada* hairstyle, a form of chignon that differs according to the age and level of training of the geisha. As with the makeup, the hairstyles worn by the maiko are more elaborate than those of the mature geisha, and include a number of different styles to be worn on different occasions, including the split peach or *momware* style of shimada, called the *ofuku*. Geisha both young and old must have very long hair in order to allow for the creation of the hairstyles. Once the hair has been combed and woven into the style, it is adorned with a variety of combs, hairpins, and other decorations. In order to preserve these elaborate styles, geisha once slept with their heads supported by wooden pillars attached to their tatami mat beds. The pillar, known

A geisha on an evening stroll in Fukagawa, woodcut by Toyokuni Utagawa. Geishas wear a very distinct form of makeup and hairstyle, which is intended to draw attention to the most ideal features of a woman's appearance in Japan: small red lips, pure white skin, well-defined black eyes, and shiny black hair. (Library of Congress)

as *takamakura*, kept the geisha's hair from touching the bed, preserving the style for about a week. Today, many geisha wear wigs instead of undergoing these elaborate rituals.

Finally, geisha are known for the beautiful kimonos that they wear. Maiko, again, wear more colorful and extravagant kimonos than do mature geisha, and they are further distinguished from other geisha by the color and appearance of the obi, or tie, of their kimono.

Geisha still exist today, although their heyday is long over, and their roles are often very different. Many still live in geisha houses, but some live independently and young girls no longer apprentice with a geisha house. Instead, older girls and women may train to be a geisha after attending regular school. Many geisha today only exist to perform for paying tourists, and legitimate geisha do not have sex with customers.

See also Cosmetics; Face Painting; Japan

Further Reading

Aihara, Kyoko. *Geisha: A Living Tradition.* London: Carlton Books, 2000.

Downer, Lesley. *Women of the Pleasure Quarters: The Secret History of the Geisha.* New York: Broadway Books, 2001.

Scott, A. C. *The Flower and Willow World: The Story of the Geisha.* New York: Orion Press, 1960.

Gender

The human face is shaped by both the biological constraints of sex, but also the social and cultural assumptions and stereotypes of gender.

Faces are critical in the human species because we use them primarily to communicate. We communicate to others our emotions, our fertility, and our health. In many cultures around the world, men are expected to control the feeling, and display, of their emotions. Men in most (but not all) cultures are expected to be stoic, rational, and unemotional, while women are socialized to feel, to nurture, and to empathize. Because of these cultural demands, women are more likely to use more **facial expressions** than men, while men are taught to control their faces, so as not to betray their emotions.

The face is the product of millions of years of evolution by natural selection, in which the traits most helpful for survival and reproduction become selected for over the generations. But Darwin, who popularized the theory of evolution by natural selection, also gave us a second theory to account for the evolution of physical traits. Sexual selection states that males and females of a species develop different traits that help them to become more reproductively successful. These traits develop through competition for mates—generally by males for females. While usually this results in the male of the species having more ornaments (colorful plumage, big tusks or antlers, big manes) to attract a female, it can also result in females developing characteristics that show off her fertility and reproductive status.

> A man's face is his autobiography. A woman's face is her work of fiction.—*Oscar Wilde*

In the human face, sexual selection has resulted in men with bigger heads, bigger jaws, bigger noses, and a bigger brow ridge than women, and women with smaller, more childlike features. In addition, the difference in sex hormones leads to different features, with women having fuller lips, lighter skin, and more fat on the cheeks due to the greater quantity of estrogen, and men having thicker eyebrows and facial hair due to the greater quantities of androgens. Women's eyes, while approximately the same size as men's, ap-

pear larger than men's due to the higher placement of the eyebrows on the woman. All of these features emerge after adolescence, and make it easy for humans to identify potential mates. In women, these secondary sex characteristics decline after menopause.

Because of the importance in signaling to a potential mate one's fertility, especially for women, a variety of cultural practices has emerged that emphasize the natural differences just outlined. Since according to evolutionary psychologists, men are attracted to women with the outward signs of youth and fertility—large eyes, full lips, narrow jaws—women have long used artificial means to highlight those features.

Eyes, for example, are a major focus of **cosmetics** around the world, with the goal being to make the eyes seem as large and youthful as possible. During the 16th and 17th centuries, European women put eye drops from the belladonna plant into their eyes to make their retinas appear larger; today, it is popular in **Korea** to wear big eye contacts to make the eyes appear larger. And it was popular in Greece, Persia, and Rome to use the powdered form of the metal antimony in the eyes to make the whites sparkle. For thousands of years, women have been darkening their eyelids with **kohl** and other products to make them stand out more. Also for thousands of years, women have been dying their lips with a variety of berries, leaves, and other dyes to make them seem larger and redder; flushed and full lips indicate sexual arousal and fertility. Those same products are also used on the cheeks, to make the wearer seem young and sexually aroused. Because unlike men, women are judged around the world by their appearance, it is not surprising that most cosmetics are worn by women. Makeup, in fact, is one way in which men and women are differentiated, making women appear more feminine and men, by comparison, more masculine.

Even today, women spend enormous amounts of money, time, and energy on maintaining a youthful and fertile appearance, while men are much less burdened by this requirement. Because the standard of **beauty** in Western society demands youth as the feminine ideal, it is not surprising that cosmetic surgery procedures are most popular with women, with more than 9 million cosmetic procedures performed on women in 2009 in the United States alone. And while it was at one time the case that only older women underwent facelifts and other procedures to make them appear younger, young women are now getting Botox injections as well as lip plumping procedures at very early ages, in order to prevent aging (in 2008, 20 percent of all patients were younger than 34).

As women age, they must work harder, not only employing makeup and **cosmetic surgery** to reverse the signs of aging, but other methods as well. For example, after menopause, women develop more facial hair, and because facial hair is one of the most obvious signs of masculinity, this must be removed at all costs, through a variety of techniques like depilatory creams, tweezers, and laser hair removal.

The one area of the face that both men and women have hair is the eyebrows. In general, women's eyebrows are thinner than men's, just as men's bodies are hairier than women's. Because of this natural difference, cultural practices that exagger-ate that difference may have developed. Thinning or removing the eyebrows tends to be much more common among women than among men, and is another way that gender differences between the sexes are enforced.

Because men (for the most part) do not wear makeup or otherwise attempt to make themselves seem young, fertile, or feminine, their faces naturally signal masculinity. Large jaws, large brow ridges, rugged features, and ungroomed facial hair are obvious signs of masculinity, but can, when taken to an extreme, be seen as threatening as well. A recent study demonstrated that successful African American businessmen tend to have baby faces, or faces with smaller facial features, and that those features made their wearers seem warmer and less threatening, which led to their success. (The opposite was found to be true for white businessmen.)

Another way in which the cultural representation of faces differs by gender has to do with the wearing of **masks**. Masking in traditional cultures around the world is found associated with **shamanism**, hunting rituals, and adolescent initiation rituals—all of which are more strongly associated with men than with women. In these rituals, one or more figures, usually men, wear animal masks in order to draw on the spirit of the animal, and either appease it or take its power. Theatrical performances most likely grew out of these ancient rituals, and again, in cultures around the world, we find that theater performers were often exclusively men, associated masking with men. Even today, there are still performative traditions in which men **masquerade** as women—most notably in drag. On the other

Veiled Men of Tuareg

While in most cultures in which veiling is practiced, the women are veiled; there are a handful of cultures in which men wear veils or scarves over their faces. The men of the nomadic Tuareg tribe, for example, who travel the Saharan desert on camel, wear a blue scarf called the *alasho* or *tagelmust* over their heads and lower faces to protect them from the desert wind and sand. They are known to observers as the veiled men of Tuareg, and to the Tuareg themselves as the people of the veil. While the Tuareg adopted Islam beginning in the seventh century, their use of the veil predates the introduction of Islam into their culture. Instead, it has both the practical benefit of protecting the face from the harsh desert conditions, and it is also thought to ward off evil spirits. Young men begin wearing the veil during a rite of passage marking their transition to adulthood, and never take it off except in the company of family.

hand, the use of makeup by women is perhaps the female equivalent of a thousand-year long tradition of men covering their faces and becoming something or someone different.

See also Beauty; Cosmetic Surgery; Cosmetics; Masks

Further Reading

Jackson, Linda A. *Physical Appearance and Gender: Sociobiological and Sociocultural Perspectives.* Albany: State University of New York Press, 1992.

Perrett, D.I., and E. Brown. "What Gives a Face Its Gender?" *Perception* 22, no. 7 (1993): 829–40.

Greco-Roman Cultures

People who lived in the classical civilizations of Greece and Rome had a number of beauty and punitive practices associated with the face, many of which were shared with neighboring cultures.

The Greeks and the Romans both had high standards of beauty. Greek and Roman art represents an idealized standard, with facial angles and bodily measurements that could not be approximated in real life, such as the long, straight nose featured in so much of Greek art. We do know that the Greeks and the Romans both valued symmetry in faces. The ideal Greek face, for example, was two-thirds as wide as it was high, and it could be divided into thirds vertically, from chin to upper lip, from upper lip to eyes, and from eyes to hairline.

While the Greeks and the Romans borrowed some of their beauty values from each other, they also had distinctive ideas about what constituted a beautiful face. For instance, the ideal Greek nose was a perfectly straight nose, while the ideal Roman nose was hook shaped.

Both Greek and Roman women also used a variety of cosmetic techniques to make themselves more beautiful. The ancient Greeks and Romans used lead-based

This statue found in the Museum of the Acropolis in Athens demonstrates the Greek ideal of female beauty. (Corel)

makeup to lighten their faces, because light skin was associated with beauty and status in those cultures. It was also popular in Greece and Rome to use the powdered form of the metal antimony in the eyes to make the whites sparkle. Women in ancient Greece used honey and olive oil to moisturize and protect the skin and a variety of natural materials such as ground charcoal, iron oxide, and bees wax mixed with other substances to act as eye shadow, rouge, and lipstick. Greek women, however, used less makeup than did Roman women or other women from this period, such as Egyptians. Greek women tended to look more natural in terms of their makeup and clothing choices. They did, however, take very good care of their skin, and whitened their teeth.

Roman women, too, took care of their skin, indulging in facials of milk, wine, and bread. Roman women used antimony and lampblack to line their eyebrows, and colored their eyelids with saffron, malachite, or azurite. They used mulberry, cinnabar, red plaster, and miniate to redden their lips and cheeks, and lead and chalk to whiten their skin. Romans used volcanic rock powder, baking soda, pumice stone, and other ingredients to clean and whiten their teeth. Female slaves in Rome called *cosmetae* spent much of their time mixing the ingredients that went into makeup. Greek and Roman women both kept their cosmetics in cosmetic cases made of wood and glass or in ceramic jars.

Roman men favored clean-shaven faces, while Greek men originally wore beards. Most Roman men shaved (or sometimes had the hair plucked from their faces), while slaves, soldiers, and philosophers could wear beards. Starting in about the fifth century BCE, however, Greek men, too, began shaving their faces, while Roman men began wearing beards in the second century CE.

The Greeks picked up the practice of tattooing faces in the fifth century BCE, but did not use it as a form of adornment. The Greeks followed the Persian practice of using tattoo marks for punitive purposes. The Greeks tattooed both prisoners and runaway slaves on the forehead, usually with a mark demonstrating their crime. The term stigmata was used to describe these marks by the Greeks and later the Romans.

The Romans inherited punitive facial tattooing from the Greeks, and later began marking soldiers. Because Christians were widely persecuted by the Romans, Christians were commonly marked with tattoos on their foreheads signifying the crime of being Christians, or, again, the punishment given to them. When the Roman Empire later converted to **Christianity** under Constantine, he banned facial tattooing, but allowed it on the hands and calves of criminals, although it was no longer forced upon Christians.

The Greeks were perhaps the first culture to develop the philosophy of physiognomy—the idea that facial characteristics are outward indications of internal character. For instance, the Greeks felt that the appearance of the forehead—high or low, wrinkled or smooth, rounded or flat—indicated whether the bearer was confident, intelligent, bold, fickle, weak, honest, or spirited.

Both Greeks and Romans believed in the **evil eye**, known as *oculus malus* in Ancient Rome. Greek beliefs held that a baby who begianto nurse after having been weaned would grow up with the evil eye. Blue-or green-eyed people in Mediterranean countries were often suspect as well.

See also Christianity; Evil Eye; Facial Tattoos

Further Reading

D'Ambrosio, Antonio. *Women and Beauty in Pompeii*. Los Angeles: J. Paul Getty Museum, 2001.

Pontynen, Arthur. *For the Love of Beauty: Art, History, and the Moral Foundations of Aesthetic Judgment*. New Brunswick, NJ: Transaction Publishers, 2006.

Gurning

Gurning refers to making awkward and ugly **facial expressions**, usually in a competitive sense. The word most likely derives from the Scottish word *girn*, which may derive from the word "grin" and means to snarl or show the teeth in rage or pain.

Gurning is most well known through the gurning competitions held in rural English villages going back to the Middle Ages, as well in Australian competitions. The most popular of these events is the Egremont Crab Apple Fair, a 13th-century fair held annually in September, which features events like pony leaping, fancy dress wheelbarrow racing, a pipe smoking contest, an egg throwing competition, and, the main attraction, the World Gurning Championship, featuring a variety of gurning events. This event features contestants pulling their best, most distorted faces while wearing a horse collar. Pulling a gurn is the colloquial term for gurning, and many champions give their best faces a name, like Quasimodo, Popeye, or the Bela Lugosi.

While the term gurning is usually used to refer to the practices outlined above, it also can be used to refer to the faces that some guitarists make when performing guitar solos, as well as the faces made by

Britain's Queen Elizabeth II watches the antics of Tommy Mattinson, the world Gurning champion, during a visit to Whitehaven, England, June 5, 2008. Gurning is the art of making grotesque faces while sticking the head through a horse's collar, with the winner being the person receiving the largest amount of applause from the audience. The world champion is selected annually during the Egremont crab apple fair, in an event said to date back to 1267. (AP/Wide World Photos)

users of methamphetamines or other drugs like ecstasy.

See also Facial Expressions

Further Reading

Hobson, Jeremy. *Curious Country Customs.* Newton Abbot, UK: David & Charles, 2007.

H

Halloween

Halloween is celebrated throughout the world on October 31. In the West, it is a day when children dress up in costumes and wear **masks**, traditionally representing demons and other frightening creatures, and go door to door asking for candy. It has its origins in both the Catholic holiday of All Hallow's Eve (the evening before All Saints Day) and the pre-Christian holiday of Samhain. Today, it is primarily a secular children's holiday.

Samhain was a Celtic festival held to commemorate the harvest in the fall, and to celebrate the end of the light part of the year and the onset of the dark half of the year. It dates to at least the Middle Ages in Ireland, when it may have been a sort of festival of the dead, similar to today's **Day of the Dead** celebrations. (Some also believe that it dates to much earlier, with the Druid belief that the night of October 31 meant that the door between the world of the dead and the world of the living opened.) With the introduction of Christianity throughout the islands of Great Britain, Catholic authorities may have tried to ban the celebrations, but in the seventh century, some scholars believe, All Saints Day was moved from May to the evening before November 1 to coincide with the existing celebrations. This was formalized by Pope Gregory III in the eighth century.

All Saints Day may itself derive from the Roman festival known as Lemuria, held in May, during which Romans made offerings to the spirits of the dead and attempted to remove them from their homes. After the rise of Christianity, Lemuria became All Saint's Day, held on May 13 (and in Ireland, in April). It may also have been related to another Roman holiday celebrating the dead called Feralia, held in February. All Saints Day became a day devoted not to the dead in general, but to the saints, while the next day, All Souls Day, was devoted to the dead. Today, many Christians remember all of the dead on November 1.

> False face must hide what the false heart doth know.—*William Shakespeare*

Today, Halloween is a combination of the ancient Roman, Catholic, and Irish festivals of the dead. The tradition of wearing frightening masks dates back to the Middle Ages when the Irish wore costumes and masks, or sometimes veiled faces, in order to mimic and placate the spirits of the dead, or to frighten them off. It may also have been that wearing masks would make the spirits mistake them for other spirits, thus leaving them alone. Trick-or-treating began as souling an English and Irish tradition in which the poor, wearing masks, would go door to door and beg for soul

Since the rise of Halloween as a holiday, children have worn masks and costumes in order to beg for candies, as with these youths in the Philippines. (AP/Wide World Photos)

cakes in exchange for praying for people's dead relatives. Souling replaced the ancient practice of leaving food out for the dead, in front of houses and on the side of the road. It was said that if the soulers were not given a cake or other treat, they would retaliate by pranking the person who rejected them. This tradition led to guising, in which children dress up in costume and go door to door to ask for food or other treats, which began in the late 19th century in Scotland.

The modern jack-o-lantern derives from a tradition of carving large hollowed turnips with faces, and filling them with candles, which was also intended to scare off the spirits.

Halloween became what it is today when it arrived in the United States with the Eu-

ropean colonists, and especially with the arrival of the Irish in the 19th century. Dressing up in costumes and masks and going house to house to beg for food or money developed in the United States at this time, which later became trick-or-treating. *See also* Day of the Dead; Masks

Further Reading

Macgregor, Alexander. *Highland Superstitions: Connected with the Druids, Fairies, Witch-craft, Second-Sight, Hallowe'en, Sacred Wells and Lochs, with Several Curious Instances of Highland Customs and Beliefs*. Stirling, UK: E. Mackay, 1922.

Rogers, Nicholas. *Halloween: From Pagan Ritual to Party Night*. Oxford: Oxford University Press, 2002.

Santino, Jack. *Halloween and Other Festivals of Death and Life*. Knoxville: University of Tennessee Press, 1994.

Halo

A halo is a circle of light that emanates from the head of sacred figures or gods in religious paintings and sculptures. Halo imagery is found in Christian, Buddhist, Greek, Roman, and Hindu art.

The head is seen, in cultures around the world, as the most sacred part of the body. In Polynesia, for example, where the head is considered to have more spiritual energy, or *mana*, than other parts of the body, it is considered to be *tapu*, or sacrosanct, and the heads of the kings are more tapu than other people's. This is one reason for the Maori tradition of keeping the preserved heads of dead leaders, as well as some enemies. Another result of this belief is that in many cultures, heads of state, chiefs, and sometimes heads of church wear special headgear, including crowns, tiaras, diadems, and war bonnets, which emphasize their sacred and secular power.

In art, another way of representing the spiritual power or blessed nature of people or deities is to depict them with a white, gold, or sometimes red ring of light around their heads. In Greek art, Perseus was depicted with rays of light emanating from his head while killing Medusa, demonstrating his spiritual power at that moment, and other heroes and deities were also portrayed with this type of imagery. This tradition, which may have been imported from Persia, was also seen in both Roman and Egyptian art. Roman frescoes

In religious art from the Christian, Buddhist, and Hindu traditions, holy figures are often represented with a circle of light surrounding their heads, indicating their spirituality, as in this painting of Saint George slaying the dragon. (Steve Allen/Dreamstime.com)

of gods with haloes around their heads still survive today, and in ancient Egypt, gods may be portrayed with a solar disc over or behind their heads.

In Asian art, deities are sometimes represented with a halo of flames rather than light surrounding their heads; this is seen in **China, India**, and Tibet, especially when associated with demons. In Islam, where the prophet Mohammed is rarely represented in art, he may sometimes be represented symbolically with a flaming halo. Buddhist art often depicts Buddha's head surrounded by a halo, and other Buddhas and saints are sometimes depicted with them as well. In Buddhism, haloes have different colors that are used for different entities—orange for monks, and green for Buddhas, for example. Emperors and kings have sometimes been represented with halos, demonstrating their spiritual power. Indian emperors, for example, were depicted in this fashion, and after about the second century CE, Roman emperors, too, began to be depicted this way; later this practice extended to the Byzantine emperors and Russian royalty.

After the rise of Christianity in both the West and the East, Jesus started to be shown in art with a halo, as was Mary, his mother, the saints, as well as other sacred creatures like angels. Only Jesus, however, is portrayed with a cross on his halo, a common convention in the Middle Ages. The use of haloes in Christian art began to decline in the Renaissance as artistic conventions changed, and realism became more important in art.

See also Artistic Representation; Buddhism; Christianity; Crowns and Headdresses; India

Further Reading

Didron, Adolphe N. *Christian Iconography: The History of Christian Art in the Middle Ages*. New York: F. Ungar, 1965.

Parani, Maria G. *Reconstructing the Reality of Images: Byzantine Material Culture and Religious Iconography (11th–15th Centuries)*. Leiden: Brill, 2003.

Vatsyayan, Kapila. *Buddhist Iconography*. New Delhi: Tibet House, 1989.

Head Binding

Head binding refers to the deliberate reshaping of the human skull in order to make it flatter or sometimes cone-shaped. Usually performed on infants, because the skull bones are not yet fused, it has been practiced by a number of cultural groups who associate a flattened or otherwise shaped head with beauty, intelligence, or status. Head binding does not appear to cause any neurological or other damage to those who practice it.

The earliest known examples of head binding are found among Neanderthal remains from about 45,000 BCE. The ancient Egyptians practiced head binding as early as 3,000 BCE, and it was practiced as well by the Huns at the end of the classical period, but the cultures most well known for the practice were those of pre-Columbian Mesoamerica and **South America**, as well as Native America.

For the Inca of Peru and the Maya of **Central America**, an artificially shaped head signified nobility. The Maya wrapped infants tightly with cloth to a cradleboard, a process that could last for years until the head reached the right shape. Head binding has also been found in Venezuela, Colombia, Ecuador, Chile, Argentina, and Guyana.

Some Native American tribes also flattened the heads of their babies, or bound them in such a way as to create a pointed head. The Choctaw used the cradleboard method to flatten their babies' heads, as did the Chinookans, who associated round heads with slavery and flat heads with wealth. The Coast Salish of British Columbia also bound their babies' heads in order to mark high status on them physically.

Head binding was also practiced in Papua **New Guinea**, using barkcloth bandages and a vine to tie the bandage tightly around the head. Bandages were continu-

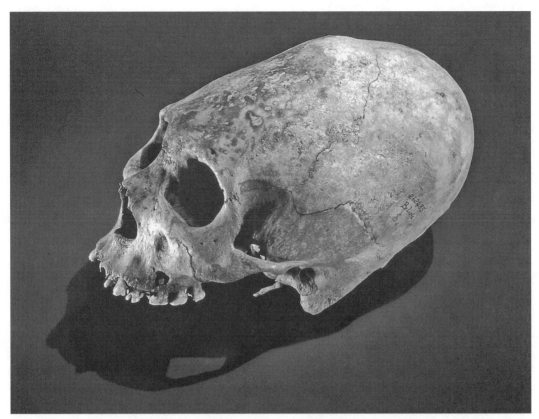

Skull that was bound, Lake Titicaca, Bolivia. Head binding refers to the deliberate reshaping of the human skull in order to make it flatter or sometimes cone-shaped. Usually performed on infants, because the skull bones are not yet fused, it has been practiced by a number of cultural groups who associate a flattened or otherwise shaped head with beauty, intelligence, or status. (National Museum of American Art, Smithsonian Institute, USA/Photo © Boltin Picture Library/The Bridgeman Art Library International)

ously reapplied but could be worn for a period of years until the head was elongated enough. Long heads were seen as attractive and girls' heads were generally longer than boys.' Aboriginal Australians also practiced head binding, who associated a long head with intelligence, spirituality, and high status. In Borneo, among some Dayak tribes, flat foreheads were a sign of beauty, and were created by strapping a cushion across the child's head, and gradually increasing the tightness of the straps. In Fiji, too, head binding was once practiced. Early European observers noted that the Malekulan shaped their infants' skulls into a conical shape so extreme that they wondered how their intellectual faculties could be retained.

Some African tribes such as the Mangbetu of the Congo also practiced head binding, using cloth to bind the head in order to create the desired long head, which was seen as beautiful, especially for women.

In the West, the French bound their babies' heads with bandages, replacing the bandage with a fitted basket, a practice that continued through the 19th century.

See also Central America

Further Reading

Grimshaw, Beatrice. *Fiji and Its Possibilities.* New York: Doubleday, Page, 1907.

Henshen, F. *The Human Skull: A Cultural History.* New York: Frederick A. Praeger, 1966.

Williams, Carol. *Framing the West: Race, Gender, and the Photographic Frontier in the Pacific Northwest.* New York: Oxford University Press, 2003.

Head Hunting

Head hunting refers to the practice of collecting human heads, generally after battle. It was long practiced in **New Guinea**, but has been found in a number of other cultures as well. In most cases, the heads that are kept are skulls, with the flesh, hair, and brains removed; only in a handful of cases are the actual heads preserved and kept for posterity.

One reason why the heads of the dead may have been collected is that in many cultures around the world, but especially in Polynesia, the head is seen as the location on the body where the spirit of the person resides. In Polynesia, that spirit is known as *mana*, but it could also be where the soul or the power of the person is thought to be located. By taking the head, the power or spirit of that person can remain with the person who holds onto the head.

Head hunting has been practiced in Melanesia, Africa, **Southeast Asia**, **China**, **India**, **Japan**, **South America**, New Zealand and in ancient and modern Europe. In New Guinea, until recent years, tribal warfare was common and clans collected the heads of vanquished warriors, keeping them in the men's long houses, or buried beneath them. The heads were thought to contain the spirit and the power of the dead men; keeping the skull meant that the spirit would help protect the clan. Decorated skulls were also sometimes hung on skull racks known as *agiba*, which were carved boards painted to resemble anthropomorphic spirits. The racks were painted anew before each new skull was hung on it in order to re-infuse the rack with power. Skull racks, which were owned by the clan, could contain hundreds of skulls.

Head hunting was also practiced by tribal peoples in Indonesia, Burma, Taiwan, India, and the Philippines. In Indonesia, head hunters typically collected just a single head at a time as part of what anthropologists explain as an expression of manhood and a way to end a period of mourning. In India, members of the Naga tribe received tattoos to commemorate each skull brought back from a successful trip; the skulls themselves were displayed in communal village skull houses.

Some pre-Columbian Central American cultures also practiced head hunting. For instance, the Zapotecs, the Toltecs, the Maya, the Aztecs, and the Mixtecs may have all collected human skulls from the victims of war and human sacrifice, and displayed them on public racks known as *tzompantli*, which could contain many thousands of skulls.

Tribal people in the Amazon region of South America have also practiced head hunting. For example, the Jivaro (also known as the Shuar), who live in Ecuador and Peru, not only collected human heads as part of their battles, but shrunk and preserved them. Shrinking the heads may have been a way of reducing the power within them, or allowing it to be harnessed by the person who shrunk it. According to a witness in the 1920s, after the heads were severed from the bodies, the warriors peeled the flesh from the skulls, and then sewed together the skin of the face, closing the holes of the eyes, mouth, ears, and nose. The skin heads are then filled with sand and placed into a pot filled with water, which is brought almost to a boil, at which point the heads are pulled out, having shrunk to a third their original size. The process of filling the heads with sand and shaping the face continues for another couple of days until the heads were said to look just like their former inhabitants.

In New Zealand, the Maori practiced head hunting, but also preserved the heads of their own friends and family members, rather than just enemies. The Maori, like other Polynesian peoples, believed that the spirit of the man was especially found in the head, so preserving the head of an enemy warrior or one's own chief was a way of keeping that spirit. Like the Jivaro, the Maori preserved the heads by removing the brain and soft tissue, closing the eyes and the mouth, and steaming or roasting it until dried. Unlike the Jivaro, these heads were not shrunk, but preserved in their original size, and the person's features were kept as if that person were still alive. Enemy heads were then displayed publically, while those of clan members were kept in private, and only brought out for ceremonial occasions.

While Europeans did not preserve or shrink heads (although the ancient Germanic and Celtic tribes did practice head hunting), they initiated trade relations with both South American and Maori peoples in order to get access to their heads. This resulted in increased head hunting and an increase in warfare in general, as Europeans introduced guns into traditional tribes, allowing them to kill more people. The Europeans traded guns for heads to both the Jivaro and the Maori, practices that

The Shuar

The Shuar are a tribe of native people who live in both the highlands of the Andes and the Amazonian lowlands of Ecuador and Peru. They have an economy based on horticulture and hunting, and are known around the world for their practice of shrinking heads. In particular, thanks to tribal warfare between the highland groups, known as Muraiya Shuar, and lowland groups, known as Achu Shuar, the Muraiya have collected the heads of the Achu peoples, which are thought to contain the souls of the dead. The heads, known as *tsantsa,* are shrunk and are said to allow the keepers of the heads to control their wives' labor. As with the trade in tattooed heads between the Maori and Europeans in the 18th century, Europeans began trading weapons for heads with the Shuar in the 19th century, which, as with the Maori, led to an increase in tribal warfare. Because of the notoriety of the practice of collecting and shrinking heads, the Shuar were never conquered by the Spanish.

continued until the governments of Ecuador, Peru, and New Zealand banned the trade. In New Zealand, the English trade for Maori heads was even more insidious than in South America. The Maori at the time tattooed their faces with the **moko**, the distinctive facial tattoo that was as unique to each person as a fingerprint. It was not just the dried heads but the fact that they were tattooed that was so interesting to the European traders, which had devastating results for the Maori. During the tribal wars of the 1820s, when European demand for the heads was at an all time high, war captives and slaves were most likely quickly tattooed, killed, and their decapitated heads sold to European traders. As the traffic in heads escalated, the Maori stopped preserving the heads of their friends, so that they wouldn't fall into the hands of the Europeans. Evidently, it also became dangerous to even wear a moko, as one could be killed at any time and have one's head sold to traders.

Head hunting has also been a part of modern societies and contemporary warfare. For instance, during World War II and the Vietnam War, American soldiers collected the heads (and other body parts) of Japanese and later Vietnamese soldiers, which was (and is) against government policy.

See also Central America; Moko; New Guinea; South America

Further Reading

Knauft, Bruce M. *South Coast New Guinea Cultures: History, Comparison, Dialectic*. Cambridge: Cambridge University Press, 1993.

Nicholas, Thomas, ed., *Tattoo: Bodies, Art and Exchange in the Pacific and the West*. Durham, NC: Duke University Press, 2005.

Simmons, D. R. *Ta Moko: The Art of Maori Tattoo*. Auckland, New Zealand: Reed Books, 1986.

Up de Graff, F. W. *Head Hunters of the Amazon: Seven Years of Exploration and Adventure*. New York: Duffield, 1923.

Henna

The leaves of the henna plant, when ground up and mixed with water, coffee, or tea and made into a paste, are used by cultures around the world to dye the skin and the hair. In the hair, henna acts as a semi-permanent hair dye, turning the hair a reddish color, and, when used on the skin, it is either used cosmetically, or as a type of temporary tattoo.

Henna has been used as a hair dye for thousands of years in North Africa, the **Middle East**, and the Indian subcontinent as well by ancient Egyptians, Greeks, and Romans. It has also been used to paint the nails, and served, and still serves, as a body decoration, known as *Mehndi*, in India, Pakistan, and Bangladesh, as well as other Muslim and North African countries. Henna was also a common remedy for a variety of medical complaints. While it is much more common today to see henna used as an adornment on feet and hands, it was once a used as makeup for the face. For instance, in ancient **Egypt**, women used henna paste to stain their lips, and today, henna is often used as a semi-permanent eye liner.

Henna has also been used as a prescription against the **evil eye**. The evil eye is a belief that certain individuals can cause sudden harm to others through an intentional or unintentional look. Looking at a person or praising them can cause damage, and the underlying cause of the evil eye is often envy. In Middle Eastern, North African, Arab, and Near Eastern cultures with a belief in the evil eye, a variety of techniques have been developed to either protect against the evil eye, or to undo the damage done when one has been harmed by the evil eye. One of those protective devices has been henna.

Throughout this region, henna was used to protect people thought especially vulnerable to the evil eye, such as beautiful children, who had henna applied to their bodies at birthdays and at babies' births. In addition, ceremonies in which children are publically displayed, such as at circumcisions, or when women are dressed up for the public to see (and envy) are events at which the evil eye is most possible, and during which henna should be applied as a preventative.

See also India

Further Reading

Dundes, Alan. "Wet and Dry: The Evil Eye: Am Essay in Indo-European and Semitic Worldview." In *Interpreting Folklore,* edited by Alan Dundes, 93–312. Bloomington: Indiana University Press, 1980.

Van den Beukel, Dorine. *Traditional Mehndi Designs: A Treasury of Henna Body Art.* Berkeley, CA: Shambhala Publications, 2000.

Holy Mandylion. *See* Image of Edessa

Henna is worn by brides in India and in the Middle East and is a popular form of adornment for the hair, face, hands, and feet. (Dreamstime.com)

Hypertrichosis and Hirsutism

Hypertrichosis is a very rare medical condition that causes excessive hair growth on the face and body. Because humans are a relatively hairless species—with hair only found on the top of the head, around the genitals and underarms, and in men, on a few other spots—having excessive hair growth causes people a great deal of psychological and social anxiety. Hypertrichosis can be a congenital condition or an acquired condition, and can cover either the entire body or one region of the body. While congenital hypertrichosis cannot be cured, other forms, which can be caused by cancer or drugs, can be managed with medication. Hirsutism, on the other hand, refers to the excessive growth of facial hair on women or children, and is caused by too much testosterone, resulting in a male pattern of hair growth. It is much more common than hypertrichosis and can be congenital or acquired, and can be treated with hormone injections. For both hypertrichosis and hirsutism, hair removal methods like shaving, waxing, and depilatory creams can temporarily control the condition and provide some social relief to the patient.

In the past, people with hypertrichosis were considered freaks, and many indeed made their living being displayed with traveling freak shows. Such people were considered *born freaks* because they had disfiguring diseases or disabilities, rather than *made freaks* (such as tattooed or heavily pierced people). Often known as monsters, or half men/half animals, hypertrichosis sufferers faced a huge amount of social stigma.

The original hairy lady, as female freaks with hypertrichosis or hirsutism were often called, was Julia Pastrana, an indigenous Mexican woman whose body was covered with long black hair and whose ears, nose, and teeth were abnormally shaped. Pastrana was purchased by a promoter named Theodore Lent (who later became her husband) who exhibited her throughout Europe and the United States in the mid-19th century, where she danced and sang to huge audiences. She died shortly after giving birth to a child who had inherited her own condition, who himself died within days. Lent sold both of their bodies to a doctor at Moscow University who dissected and mummified them, and then Lent retrieved the bodies and took them on tour. Amazingly, Lent later met another

woman with hypertrichosis whom he married and began exhibiting as Zenora Pastrana, while still exhibiting his wife's and baby's bodies.

The first documented person with hypertrichosis was Petrus Gonzales, who was born in the Canary Islands in the 16th century with the congenital form of the condition. After being educated in Paris, he married and sired two children with his condition, and the entire family traveled through Europe, becoming a popular attraction at many royal courts.

Other hypertrichosis or hirsutism sufferers who were part of freak shows include Stephan "Lionel the Lion-Faced Boy" Bibrowski, Percilla "Monkey-Faced" Be-

Portrait of JoJo, the "Dog-faced Boy." JoJo, born Fedor Jeftichew in Russia in 1868, had hypertrichosis, a condition that causes abnormal hair growth on the body. P. T. Barnum, who brought JoJo to the United States and encouraged him to bark and growl as part of his act, said that JoJo and his father (who also had hypertrichosis) were wild half-animal/half-men captured by a Russian hunter and brought to civilization. (Getty Images)

jano, Alice "Dog Faced Girl" Doherty, the "Missing Link" Krao Farini, Feodor "Jo Jo the Dog Faced Boy" Jeftichew, Grace "the Wolf Girl" Gilbert, Alice "the Bear Lady" Bounds, and the Burmese Hairy Family.

Human abnormalities like these were once understood to be primarily the result of maternal impression, the theory that if a pregnant woman was scared, her child may be born with an abnormality relating to what scared her. Lionel the Lion-Faced Boy, for instance, was said to be born with his condition because his mother was frightened by a lion when pregnant with him. In addition, pregnant women were warned from attending circus sideshows where freaks were displayed, lest they become frightened and the attributes of the freaks transfer to the fetus.

In the 18th century, the science of teratology developed, which was the scientific study of monsters, or those born with dis-abilities. This led to a new understanding of freaks that saw them as part of God's natural order, a belief that was later discarded in favor of the missing link theory that developed after Darwinism, which saw freaks as being a literal half-human, half-animal creature, which gave rise to the freak known as the wild man. But as modern genetic science developed, which explained in simple terms the transmission of characteristics, freaks no longer were objects of awe and fascination, and became objects of pity, leading to the eventual disappearance of the freak show.

See also Disorders of the Face

Further Reading

Bogdan, Robert. *Freak Show*. Chicago: University of Chicago Press, 1988.

Garland Thompson, Rosemary, ed. *Freakery: Cultural Spectacles of the Extraordinary Body*. New York: New York University Press, 1996.

Identity

The face is the primary badge of human identity, and is seen as the outward expression of our internal selves. It is how we present ourselves to the world, as well as how we see, hear, smell, and otherwise interact with the world. Faces are critical to the establishment of ourselves as individuals and as members of a collectivity. The face acts as our primary identity tag; it is a thumbprint, if you will, with no two faces in the world exactly the same.

This is why having a face that is deformed or abnormal makes a person not just look abnormal but also feel abnormal. A facial disorder is not simply a physical problem—it marks its bearer in the most visual way possible as being different. Those with facial defects acquire what sociologists call an embattled identity, where the sense of who and what they are is not determined by social attributes but by physical defects.

Of all of the parts of the body, the face alone can stand in for the entire person, and represent us to the world. When women say they are putting on their faces, they mean they are putting on their makeup, but they are also saying that their face needs to be presentable, because it is that face that the world will use to judge them.

Facial features—the eyes, nose, lips, chin, forehead, and cheeks—are key to our identity: to understanding, recognizing, and

> A man finds room in the few square inches of his face for the traits of all his ancestors, for the expression of all his history, and his wants.—*Ralph Waldo Emerson, Conduct of Life*

representing it to others. In particular, the appearance of our eyes is an important part of our identity. Without the eyes, we would not look like ourselves. Facial recognition software, for example, cannot recognize a person if the eyes are covered. Glasses, too, can indeed become an important part of a wearer's identity. Long after the popularization of contact lenses, and even now, when laser eye surgery is a safe and effective way to treat many vision problems, many people continue to wear glasses because they have become a part of who they are.

Children emphasize faces in their drawings, and in fact, children's earliest drawings tend to be of faces. In addition, kids' toys almost always have faces—even when those toys represent inanimate objects like airplanes. We are programmed to perceive and recognize human faces, and unless we have a disorder of the brain, our brain lights up when we see a person whom we recognize. Other social animals, too, recognize friends and family by their faces, and our dogs and cats know to paw us in the face when they want something. They recognize that the face is where we are.

The human face is the most obvious representation of a person's identity. The faces of four American presidents carved on Mount Rushmore are easily identifiable to any American. (PhotoDisc/Getty Images)

We think that faces tell us about the person inside. Not only do **facial expressions** communicate the emotions that we are feeling, but most cultures have some belief in the pseudo-science of physiognomy, which claims that the personal characteristics of a person can be detected in their facial features. Even without subscribing to this theory directly, most of us think that we can judge other people at least in part based on their face. People who are beautiful are judged to be smarter, more successful, happier, and more worthwhile people than those who are not considered beautiful.

The face is also thought to both absorb and reflect the life history of a person. Brandi Carlisle's song "The Story" opens with the following lines:

All of these lines across my face
Tell you a story of who I am.

She is talking about more than just the fact that as we age, our faces will develop wrinkles, age spots, and other signs of aging. We think that our faces show our wisdom or lack thereof, the collection of good and bad decisions we've made over the course of our lives, and that have made us, fundamentally, who we are.

Caricatures, too, demonstrate that a simple portrait of the face can succinctly capture the identity of the person being portrayed. That's why caricatures have so long been used in political commentary. Caricatures are a form of unmasking, whereby the artist, through highlighting a few key features of the subject, is able to make the internal character of the subject visible on the face. Through distortion of the face, the internal character is supposedly revealed.

The term face is used to refer to the forward or external part of any number of objects, from buildings to playing cards to cities, emphasizing the way in which we see the face as being the public side of the private person. Mount Rushmore and the moia of Easter Island are both examples of cultures displaying their most important cultural figures in a way that highlights the most important part of their identities—by featuring only the face. The modern head shot, the photo that actors and models use to advertise themselves for potential jobs, is a photo taken only of the face—the only part that really matters. Likewise, we keep photographs of the faces of our loved ones on our walls, in our wallets, and on our computer screens; it is the face that most represents the person, and the qualities of that person, whom we love.

See also Caricatures; Disorders of the Face; Facial Expressions

Further Reading

Cleese, John, and Brian Bates. *The Human Face.* New York: Dorling Kindersley, 2001.

Image of Edessa

The Image of Edessa was a piece of cloth said to bear the image of Jesus Christ, and was known from the 5th to the 13th centuries when it disappeared. It is known as the Holy Mandylion in the Greek Orthodox tradition, and while it disappeared eight centuries ago, it is considered by many to be the **Shroud of Turin**—the bloodstained burial shroud of Jesus found in the 14th century that currently is kept at Turin Cathedral. A few believers, however, feel that the Image of Edessa is still present today, and in fact is the **Veil of Veronica** held in Manoppello, Italy.

The Image of Edessa was referenced in a number of ancient Christian texts and letters beginning in the seventh century, many written by members of the Church who claimed to have seen it with their own eyes before it disappeared in the 13th century. Its presence was said to have aided the city of Edessa when it was attacked by Persians in 544. Medieval Christian art also shows images of the shroud when depicting the burial of Jesus, and believers claim that these works correspond to the appearance and features of the shroud itself.

The legend of Abgar tells the story of Abgar V Ouchama, king of Edessa, who was given the cloth by one of Jesus's disciplines in the first few years after his death. According to the first version of the story, told by Eusebius in the early fourth century, Abgar had written to Jesus via a messenger named Ananias to ask him to come to Edessa to cure him of his leprosy; Jesus responded by letter saying that after his death and ascension, he would send a disciple to cure him. After Jesus's death, the apostle Thomas sent an apostle named Thaddeus Jude who founded the church there and healed the king with the words of Jesus. While no image was mentioned in this account, it is said that Jesus's letter aids in the saving of Edessa from the Persians.

A later version of the story, by a European traveler named Egeria, mentions a messenger named Ananias traveling to Edessa with the letter from Jesus. A still later version was told at the turn of the fifth century by Ephram, a Syrian theologian who wrote in the *Doctrine of Addai* that Abgar sent a painter, also Ananias, from Edessa to Jerusalem with the letter. Ananias was instructed that if Jesus would not return with him, he should instead paint Jesus, and bring the portrait back to the king. This portrait was sealed inside a wall near a burning lamp, and the lamp miraculously burned the image of Jesus onto a tile; the oil from the lamp was then used to counter the Persians' sixth-century attack. A still later sixth-century account suggests that the city was saved by the Persians because of a wet cloth that the living Jesus pressed his face into, transferring his image; some accounts have him giving the cloth to the messenger Ananias, who brought it back to Abgar to cure his leprosy. The account specifically says that the city was saved thanks to a "divinely wrought portrait" sent to Abgar by Jesus.

These various accounts contradict each other in a number of ways—the key element in them differs. It might be a shroud bearing the miraculous image of Christ, a portrait of Christ, a letter from Christ, or a cloth on which Christ rubbed his face. In all of the cases, the words or image of Jesus helped to repel the Persians' 544 attack, but by the third version of the story, it was definitely a miraculous image of Christ that saved the city. So the cloth, if it was a cloth, was either formed by the miraculous transfer of Jesus's image after his death, was painted by a portrait artist, or was created when Jesus rubbed his face on a wet cloth.

The linen cloth, which according to legend had a faint image of Jesus's face, was found in 525 (or perhaps 544) behind the stones over the gate in the wall surrounding Edessa (now Urfa, Turkey), and was then housed in a church built especially for it. It disappeared in 609 when Edessa was conquered by the Sassanians of Persia. In 944, during a siege by the Byzantine army, it (and the letter from Jesus) was moved to Constantinople (now Istanbul, Turkey), as part of a trade for Muslim prisoners, where it was housed in the Great Palace. Ultimately, the Image was thought to be stolen along with a number of other relics when the city was looted by French or Venetian crusaders during the Crusades in 1204. It then was said to be acquired by Emperor Baldwin II in 1247 and given or sold to King Louis IX who installed it at La Sainte Chapelle in Paris. It disappeared again during the French Revolution and never reappeared. Another history has the image going from the convent of San Silvestro in Capito, Italy, to the Vatican in 1870 where it, now called the Mandylion of Edessa or Holy Face of San Silverstro, remains enclosed in a silver frame, to this day. A third claims that the image arrived at St. Bartholomew in Genoa in 1388 where it, now called the Holy Face of Genoa, remains today.

In 1996, the Vatican analyzed its icon, and found that the linen cloth had a positive (as opposed to the negative image of the Shroud of Turin) image of Christ painted on it—an image that had been altered over the years. Interestingly, the Genoan image is almost identical to the Vatican image— also painted on, as per one of the legends, but clearly created by man, and not Christ. In addition, the Genoan image was at one time probably encased in the same frame that holds the Vatican image, based on the rivet holes of each image that correspond to the silver Vatican frame. While images of Jesus were common in this period, the fact that both of these images were painted on linen (rather than wood, as would have been the tradition) implies that the artists were trying to make their paintings appear to be the legendary Image of Edessa.

If the Image of Edessa, however, is not one of the two (or more) existing paintings, then that means it disappeared, and may have reappeared as the Shroud of Turin. The shroud was discovered in the 14th century by a French knight named Geoffrey de Charny. The shroud definitely entered the historical record in the 16th century, when it was transferred to the Turin Cathedral in northern Italy in 1578. While the Shroud of Turin is a representation of the body of a man, and the Image of Edessa just the face, it is thought that the Image of Edessa did in fact contain the full image of Christ's body, but that it was folded in fourths, displaying only the image of Christ's face. In fact, an eighth century account of King Abgar's receiving the cloth shows him receiving a cloth with a full body image of Christ. Today, scholars and religious devotees are not in consensus about the relationship, if any, between the legendary Image of Edessa and the Shroud of Turin.

See also Christianity; Shroud of Turin; Veil of Veronica

Further Reading

Guscin, Mark. *The Image of Edessa.* Leiden: Brill, 2009.

Humber, Thomas. *The Sacred Shroud.* New York: Pocket Books, 1978.

Nickell, Joe. *Inquest on the Shroud of Turin: Latest Scientific Findings.* Amherst, NY: Prometheus Books, 1988.

Wilson, Ian. *Holy Faces, Secret Places: An Amazing Quest for the Face of Jesus.* New York: Doubleday, 1991.

Wilson, Ian. *The Shroud of Turin: The Burial Cloth of Jesus Christ?* rev. ed. Garden City, NY: Image Books, 1979.

India

Many Indian women adorn their faces with piercing, tattooing, and **jewelry. Facial tattooing, face painting, facial piercing**, and the use of **kohl** are widely practiced on the Indian subcontinent, among tribal peoples as well as among caste Hindus. Some of these practices are religious in origin, although many are used primarily for adornment today. In addition, India has a long tradition of mask making.

The **bindi** is the dot worn on the forehead of Hindu women in South Asia. It can be made of powder, makeup, can be adhered with a plastic or felt sticker, or can be a form of jewelry. It is related to the *tilaka,* which is worn by both men and women, and, unlike the bindi, is worn as a form of adornment and is used for religious purposes. Traditionally the bindi, like the tilaka, was most commonly red, but today it can be found in multiple colors. Originally, the bindi was worn exclusively for religious purposes as well as to mark status

A portrait of a bride. Namita is a 24-year-old Bengali woman from Calcutta, India. This photo shows many of the adornments that Indian brides wear, including a nostril piercing, face jewelry, a bindi, and henna. (Dreamstime.com)

strated their achievements in warfare and head-hunting. Among the Khond tribes of Andhra Pradesh, on the other hand, women wear facial tattoos made of lines, dots, and circles that cover much of the face. Tattoos are also used by some caste Hindus; this probably derives from Hinduism as both Krishna and Vishnu wore tattoos, and one theory explains women's **facial tattoos** as a way of identifying women who were captured by Muslims in the Middle Ages. In any case, tattoos for Hindus were certainly used to mark status, especially for women. Forehead tattoos were common, and higher caste women had fewer tattoos. Also, tattoos implied chastity and fidelity for a woman, and most women were tattooed prior to marriage, since tattoos were often a sign that she was marriageable. Facial tattoos in India have been declining in popularity, however, in recent years.

After 1797, criminals in some parts of India had their criminal status tattooed on them by the colonial authorities, a practice that was entirely new to India. The Hindi word for tattoo, *godna* (to prick, puncture, dot, or mark) came to mean the marking of criminals starting in the 19th century. Criminals were marked, often with the word thug on their forehead. Since the forehead mark was so prominent, it precluded them from re-joining society, so some criminals wore their hair long or their turbans low to cover the marks.

Face painting has a long history in dramatic performance in India; this probably dates back to when hunters painted their faces as camouflage. Today, performers paint their faces to represent gods or demons during folk dances or temple festivals. For example, Kathakali is a classical Indian

on the wearer. Married women once wore the bindi to signify their marital status, with red bringing good fortune. Widows must stop wearing the bindi after the death of their husbands, and many women stop wearing their bindis during mourning for a deceased relative. While wearing the bindi is optional in most of the Hindu world, in some locations it is mandatory for married women to continue to wear it.

People in India have practiced tattooing since at least the 15th century and probably before. Indigenous tribal groups use tattoos to mark tribal identity, individual identity, marriageability, and sometimes ritual status. Among the Naga of Northeast India, men wore facial tattoos that demon-

dramatic performance involving dancers who use costume and face paint to evoke the stories of mythological characters taken from important collections like the Mahabharata.

Nostril piercings are very commonly worn by Indian women, a practice that was brought to the region by Muslim invaders in the 16th century. The most common location is the left nostril, which is associated with the female reproductive organs; this is supposed to make childbirth easier or to lessen the pain associated with menstruation. Both studs and rings are worn in the nose, and sometimes the jewelry is joined to the ear by a chain. Occasionally, both nostrils are pierced. Nostril piercings are used to make a woman beautiful, to mark social status, and are still very popular in India, Pakistan, and Bangladesh. In some communities, nose piercings are associated with married women. Hindus traditionally pierce a girl's ears and nose 12 days after birth when she is given her name. Tribal peoples in Nepal, Tibet, and some parts of India also sometimes have their septums pierced.

Indian weddings are a major occasion to adorn the body and face of the bride. *Solah shringar* refers to the 16 adornments that a bride is expected to wear on her wedding day. One important element is a nose ring worn in the left nostril and adorned with precious stones, usually connected with a gold chain to the ear. Traditionally, the nostril ring, or *nath*, was given by the husband's parents to the wife, and signified her virginity. Another element is the bindi on the bride's forehead and a number of white and red dots painted around it and the bride's eyebrows. The dots probably recall the facial tattoos that were once more common in India. The eyes are lined with kohl, and a *maangtika*, a piece of jewelry worn over the middle part in the hair that drapes down over the forehead, is worn. She also wears earrings, necklaces, and other items of jewelry on her arms, hands, and feet. Light skin is highly prized in India, and Indian women will always wear skin lightening products on their wedding day.

An ancient belief associated with India has to do with the power of the eyes in Hinduism. The god Shiva has three eyes, and other gods like Indra have eyes all over their bodies. The **evil eye**, known as *nazar*, is a common belief in India, and stems from the idea that certain people have the power to injure others through the force of their stare. Indian women line their eyes with kohl, both to protect themselves, and to ensure that they do not inflict harm on others. Indian women will also put kohl on their children's faces to ward off the eye, by making the child imperfect. High caste men also should not be seen eating in front of low caste men, for fear of incurring the evil eye. Eyes here signify power and knowledge, and using eyes as a form of communication is an important aspect of Indian life. In India, if a person needs something from another person, the person will look up at the person in order to connect with him; looking up is a form of respect, and implies looking up at the gods. On the other hand, lower caste people will often look away from an upper caste person as a sign of respect, and often, people of different caste positions will avoid **eye contact** with each other entirely.

India has an ancient tradition of mask making for ritual performances. **Masks** were once worn during Hindu rituals but are now also worn during theatrical and classical dance performances. Masks can be made of wood, gourd, bamboo, or papier-mâché, and are elaborately painted and decorated with jewels, embroidery, glass, and beads. Facial features are dramatic and highly stylized. Animals, birds, gods, and historical and mythological characters are represented in masks, depending on the function of the performance. Masks carved with monstrous faces are intended to scare off evil spirits, just as carved sculptures found on temples do, while masks representing gods and goddesses are worn during rituals honoring those deities. For example, demonic masks are worn during the devil dances performed in Tibet and Darjeeling, while gods like Kali and Shiva predominate in the *chhou* masks worn in West Bengal. Rituals in which the stories of the major epics like the Ramayana or Mahabharata are told involve actors and dancers wearing masks denoting those characters. For instance, the goddess Chandi is represented with a mask made of bamboo strips; after the dance, the mask is cut up and thrown into the river so as not to dishonor the goddess. In Kerala, the history of the god Krishna is told in eight plays told on subsequent nights; performers wear huge masks and perform in Krishna's temple. Some masks used in Indian rituals are enormous; the masks used in the Satriya dance, also based on the life of Krishna, are 10 feet tall, while the masks used in the folk play Ankia Nat may be as tall as 15 feet, and must be carried by multiple actors.

See also Bindi; Chakras; Evil Eye; Eye Contact; Jewelry; Masks; Nose Piercing

Further Reading

Editors of *Hinduism Today* Magazine. *What Is Hinduism? Modern Adventures into a Profound Global Faith.* Kapaa, HI: Himalayan Academy, 2007.

Maheswaraiah, H.M. "Caste Mark." In *South Asian Folklore*, edited by Peter J. Claus, Sarah Diamond, and Margaret Ann Mills, 99–100. New York: Routledge, 2003.

Mohapatra, R.P. *Fashion Styles of Ancient India: A Study of Kalinga from Earliest Times to Sixteenth Century A.D.* Delhi: B.R. Publishing, 1992.

Inuit

Inuit refers to the indigenous peoples who live along the Arctic coasts of Siberia, Alaska, Greenland, and Canada. These people practiced **facial tattooing, facial piercing**, and used **masks** in **shamanism**.

Tattooing has been practiced among the Inuit for at least 3,500 years, according to archaeological evidence, and, as in the nearby Pacific Northwest, was primarily worn by women. Elderly women did the tattooing, using bone or ivory needles pulling threads blackened with soot. The women literally sewed the thread through the skin, leaving the black color in the skin, a skill that they developed through sewing clothing.

The first European descriptions and depictions of Inuit tattoos date to the mid-16th century, and describe women's facial tattooing, which partially covered the forehead, cheeks, and especially the chin, and was made up of lines and geometric patterns. As with other tribes, chin tattoos, which were received after puberty, were used to show that a woman was marriageable and were also thought to protect women from enemies. They also showed that she was able to endure pain, which was an attractive feature to look for in a wife. Women also sometimes received tattoos on the thighs, as a way to make childbirth easier and to show infants something of beauty when they emerged from the womb.

Chin tattoos were once very common for Inuit women, as in this 1903 photo of an Inuit mother with a baby on her back. (Library of Congress)

Men also wore tattoos, but, as with the tribes in the Pacific Northwest, they indicated success in hunting or warfare, with special tattoos for killing a man (such as two horizontal lines across the face) or killing a whale (a line extending from the mouth to each ear, or sometimes a simple dot on a joint). Also common were tattoos that were worn in the spots in which other Northern Native people wore labrets, such as between the lower lip and the chin, and on both sides of the mouth. These circular tattoos may have also acted as a form of spiritual protection.

As is found among many tribes of Pacific Northwest Coast Indians, the native peoples of Alaska and the Arctic region pierced their lips and inserted labrets into the holes. Made typically of bone, these wore worn in the lips of both men and women. Children would have their lips pierced at puberty and the holes were enlarged by inserted larger plugs until the final labret was inserted.

This region of the world has long been known by anthropologists for its shamanistic practices. In fact, the term shaman comes from the language of the Evenk, a northern Siberian people. Shamans here, as in other cultures, enter a trance state in order to communicate with spirits, who are then called upon to heal the sick. Inuit shamans often wear masks as part of their rituals. For example, the Koryak, Evenk, and Yukaghir tribes wear masks made of leather during funeral rituals, and the Chukchi of Siberia wear masks representing evil spirits to scare children. Other tribes living near the Bering Sea wore masks of animals like bears during hunting rituals.

See also Facial Tattoos; Masks; Shamanism

Further Reading

Griffin, Joy. "Labrets and Tattooing in Native Alaska." In *Marks of Civilization,* edited by Arnold Rubin, 181–90. Los Angeles: Museum of Cultural History, UCLA, 1988.

Van Stone, James W. *An Early Archaeological Example of Tattooing from Northwestern Alaska.* Chicago: Field Museum of Natural History, 1974.

J

Janus

Janus was a Roman god whose purview included openings such as gates and doors, as well as beginnings and endings.

Janus is most commonly depicted in statues and other representations as having two heads; one head faces toward the front, or toward the future, and the other faces the back, or the past. (Some images of Janus, however, have four faces.) For this reason, Janus symbolizes transitions, beginnings and endings, and change in general. In early representations of the god, he was often depicted with one shaved face, representing the sun and youth, and the other bearded, representing the moon and age. The month January is named after him, because January was considered by eighth-century Romans to be the doorway to the new year. (Prior to this time, the new year began in March, with the spring.) Janus was also worshipped at the beginning of every month, as well as at planting season and harvest, and his name was invoked at the beginning of each day. In addition, offering a prayer or sacrifice to Janus at the beginning of any new enterprise was a way of ensuring success. His most notable temple in Rome, the Ianus Geminus, had two gates—one facing the rising sun, and the other facing the setting sun.

Janus is a mythical representation of the condition **diprosopus**, in which a person or animal is born with two faces. The existence of people or animals with this condition may have served as the precursor for the Janus myth. According to Roman myth, however, Janus was given both faces, and the ability to see the past and the future, as a thank-you from the god Saturn after his deification. Unlike many Roman gods, this god did not come from the Greeks, but he may be related to the Etruscan god Ani. The name Janus comes from the Latin *ianua*, meaning gate.

Janus's two faces were seen as positive, and gave the god the ability to see both past and future. However, there was a darker side to his powers. The term double-edged is often used to refer to Janus, indicating that, like a sword with two faces, Janus's abilities could have both positive and negative implications. The notion of being two-faced (i.e., deceitful), was not associated with Janus, although today, the term Janus-faced has a similar connotation, although it could also mean that a person or thing has two meanings or aspects. A Janus-faced word is, similarly, a word with two opposing meanings.

See also Diprosopus

Further Reading

Cicero. *The Nature of the Gods,* trans. P.G. Walsh. New York: Clarendon Press, 1997.

Price, Ed Simon, and Emily Kearns. *The Oxford Dictionary of Classical Myth and Religion.* Oxford University Press: Oxford, 2003.

Japan

Japan is an island nation in the Pacific Ocean with one of the world's oldest cultures. Japan shares with many Asian cultures a set of beliefs about the face, and in particular, **facial expressions**.

Some cultures are much more concerned about the linked concepts of saving and losing face than other cultures. Japan, for example, is one culture in which honor and shame are deeply important, and thus, saving face is an important goal. One explanation for this may be that Japan is a small country with a large population that has to live cooperatively together. Working together without insulting other people (or causing them to lose face) is thus extremely important. So, for example, the Japanese do not like to reject people's requests or to criticize others; instead, when they are faced with a request that they cannot or do not want to fulfill, they will tell someone that they are thinking about it, rather than rejecting it outright.

In addition, Japanese people work hard to control their emotions in order to create or maintain a peaceful atmosphere, even when that means many Japanese are not able to express their emotions. In fact, because smiling, and showing one's teeth, is indicative of emotion, Japanese men traditionally do not smile, and it was once fashionable for Japanese women to blacken their teeth so that they would never be seen. The ancient **Geisha** practice of shaving one's eyebrows was another way that women could disguise their emotions. Today, some Japanese are adopting the Western mode of displaying emotions and smiling publically, although large smiles are still rare in Japan. Because of the complicated concerns around smiling, the Japanese have at least 10 different named smiles, all with different acceptable uses, from the happy smile (*bakushu*) to the embarrassed smile (*terawari*).

For centuries, suicide has been used as an honorable way to avoid or overcome shame in Japan. For the Japanese, people strive not only to not lose face for themselves, but for their families and companies as well. On the one hand, this can lead to a situation where representatives of Japanese companies do not admit their mistakes, but on the other hand, it can be lead to situations where Japanese businessmen have taken their own lives, to keep from bringing shame onto their companies.

Another example of face in Japan is found in the martial art Kendo. In Kendo, a martial art based on the use of traditional Japanese sword fighting, a combatant who flinches is seen as losing face.

Eye contact, too, is heavily controlled in Japan, as in other Asian cultures. In Japan, direct eye contact can be considered an invasion of privacy. It also can be used to demonstrate status: seniors and others with high status can use eye contact with lower status individuals, but juniors (in age and in status) should not attempt to stare at higher status people. On the other hand, because facial expressions are so tightly controlled in Japan, the Japanese are adept at interpreting the facial expressions of others, and tend to look to one's eyes for clues as to a person's feelings and intentions, while Westerners tend to focus on a person's mouth. Japanese **emoticons**, too, tend to focus more on the eyes, while American emoticons are more focused on the mouth. And finally, classical Japanese art featured faces that were inexpressive, at least compared to faces found in Western portraiture.

The Japanese have had a number of major makeup trends. **Geisha** are female entertainers who emerged in the 18th century, with a very distinctive appearance. Their makeup emphasizes the highest standards of Japanese beauty and involve heavy, white pancake makeup on the face and neck, dark red lips in the shape of a flower bud, black-accented eyes, and lacquered black hair. Sometimes geisha would also blacken their teeth so that they would not be seen when they open their mouths. Today, Japanese street fashion includes a number of styles involving hair and makeup that are worn by young Japanese women and girls. For example, *Ganguro* refers to a trend in which young women dye their hair blond or red and darken their skin with artificial tanners.

The Japanese, like many Eastern cultures, have long used **masks** in their dramatic performances. In the *Noh* musical dramas, the main performers wear one of 125 different masks to portray their characters from only five different types: old people, goblins, devils, gods, and goddesses. Like other classical performance forms, male actors play both male and female characters. Masks are made from clay, wood, papier-mâché, and cloth, and portray humans, animals, gods, and demons. Performers can convey emotions by slightly adjusting the mask or showing different angles to the audience.

A Japanese geisha. Geishas are female entertainers who have a very distinctive appearance. Their makeup emphasizes the highest standards of Japanese beauty, and involves heavy white pancake makeup on the face and neck, dark red lips in the shape of a flower bud, black-accented eyes, sometimes blackened teeth, and lacquered black hair. (Corel)

See also Emoticons; Eye Contact; Face Saving and Losing Face; Facial Expressions; Geisha

Further Reading

Louis, Frederic. *Daily Life in Japan at the Time of the Samurai, 1185–1603.* New York: Praeger, 1972.

McCormick, James P. "Japan: The Mask and the Mask-Like Face." *Journal of Aesthetics and Art Criticism* 15, no. 2 (1956): 198–204.

Vollmann, William T. *Kissing the Mask: Beauty, Understatement and Femininity in*

Ganguro

Ganguro refers to a trend popular in Japan in which young women dye their hair blond, orange, or pink, and color their skin with artificial tanners, with eyes and lips highlighted by white makeup or concealer. It was most popular at the turn of the 21st century, and is still seen today. Sometimes known as black face, ganguro girls also use white makeup on their eyes and lips, false eyelashes, and sometimes wear the circle contact lenses popularized in the Korean ulzzang culture. Ganguro is a radical challenge to traditional concepts of Japanese beauty, which value very light skin combined with very dark hair. Ganguro style also focuses on clothing, footwear (primarily platform shoes), and jewelry and features items and images found in the cute culture, like Hello Kitty, anime, and manga. Ganguro began in two fashionable districts in Tokyo—Shibuya and Ikebukoro—and spread from there to other urban areas.

Japanese Noh Theater: with Some Thoughts on Muses (especially Helga Testorf), Transgender Women, Kabuki Goddesses, Porn Queens, Poets, Housewives, Makeup Artists, Geishas, Valkyries, and Venus Figurines. New York: Ecco, 2010.

Jewelry

Jewelry refers to the use of metals, beads, glass, bone, wood, shells, or stones to adorn the body and face and has been worn by men or women (or both) in every known society throughout the world. Jewelry is typically created with a precious metal such as gold, platinum, silver, or bronze acting as the base and adding to that any number of stones, beads, or glass as further decoration. Other common bases include carved or molded wood, clay, and bone. Some jewelry does not use a base at all but instead is made from beads, shells, or stones strung together on a string or animal sinew.

Jewelry is both decorative and functional. In many societies, the wearing of precious stones and metals was a way of storing and displaying wealth, and jewelry itself often served as a form of currency as well as dowry for women.

Facial jewelry includes earrings, which are worn on the ear; nose rings, which are worn in pierced noses; rings, studs, and bones, which are worn in **facial piercings;** and forehead jewelry, which adorns the forehead. Many African cultures use jewelry to stretch the earlobes, or enlarge ear piercings, while some African and South American tribes as well as ancient Mesoamericans have used lip plates or plugs to stretch the lips. A number of Pacific Northwest Indian groups also used labrets in their lips. Both of these practices are used by some in the West today.

Earrings are the most common form of jewelry worn on the face or head and, historically, date back thousands of years. They have been both signs of wealth and, for women, beauty, but can signify other types of social status. Extremely expensive materials and intricate designs indicate wealth, while the number of earrings in an ear may also represent high status. Earrings are typically worn on pierced ear lobes, but clip-on earrings can be worn on nonpierced ears. Today, many people also have the upper and outer cartilage parts of the ear pierced, and earrings are worn there, too. While pierced ears are associated primarily with women in the modern West, men and women have both worn earrings in cultures around the world, as well as in European and Western history.

Earrings were once worn in the ancient civilizations of the **Middle East**, **China**, **Japan**, **India**, and Mesoamerica. They have also been worn in traditional cultures throughout Africa, Asia, America, and the Arctic. Besides earrings, which are generally worn inserted into small holes in the lower ear, ear plugs have been used in many cultures in which ear holes are large. For instance, the Tchikrin of central Brazil pierced boys' and girls' ears at birth and immediately inserted wooden earplugs, which would be exchanged as the ear holes grew larger.

Earring types include stud earrings in which a stud made of either metal or stone sits on the front part of the earlobe, which is connected through the lobe to a back piece holding the earring on behind the lobe. Hoop earrings generally pierce through the ear with a wire or post and then encircle the bottom of the earlobe. And dangling earrings attach to the earlobe with a post or a hook and include a longer portion of metal, beads, and/or stones that flow from the bottom of the earlobe. In the West, when men wear earrings, it is usually a stud or a small hoop.

Many cultures stretched their earlobes and either wore dangling earrings in the stretched holes, as in ancient China, or ear plugs or ear spools in the holes, as in Ancient Mesoamerica. In both cultures, stretched ears were a sign of status.

Forehead jewelry is another ancient form of facial jewelry. Most commonly seen in India and other South Asian cultures, it is worn by women as a form of adornment. This type of jewelry is made typically of gold or silver chain, often combined with gems, and is hung over the head or attached to the hair. Another Indian form of forehead jewelry is known as the **bindi** or tilaka. This is a dot traditionally made with makeup, but today often made from gold, silver, or gemstones, and worn by women in the middle of the forehead. The bindi is traditionally worn for adornment while the tilaka is traditionally worn for religious purposes. Both demonstrate social status, and both have their origins in the Hindu belief about the chakras. In the Hindu context, the bindi signifies the third eye or the sixth **chakra**, which is correlated with intuition, clear thinking, and psychic abilities, such as the ability to see into the future. Related to the bindi is the tikka, another form of forehead jewelry. The tikka is a jewel made of gold or silver with a large gemstone in the middle, which is suspended down the forehead and is attached to the hair with a hook. Forehead jewelry in general is assigned with status. Wealthy Chinese women once wore strips of gold decorated with gems on their foreheads, and of course the tiara, worn on the forehead or on top of the head, has long been used as a sign of status in the West.

Nose rings are a popular form of facial jewelry in some parts of the world. The practice of piercing the nostril in order to wear jewelry probably spread from the Middle East to Asia in the 16th century by Mogul emperors. Since that time, it has become extremely common in India as both a marker of beauty and social standing for Indian girls. Like forehead jewelry, nose rings and other forms of nose jewelry are extremely popular and can be extremely elaborate. Jewelry can be a ring, which encircles the nostril from the outside to the inside, or a stud, and in India, the nose ring or stud can be attached by a chain to the forehead adornment or earrings as well. As is the case with earrings, the size or materials used in nostril jewelry may represent wealth and status, as in some Middle Eastern tribes.

A less common form of nose jewelry is the septum ring, which is worn in a septum piercing, which is a piercing through the flesh that divides the nostrils. Septum piercings were worn by a number of traditional societies, but especially among men in warrior societies, probably because wearing a large bone or horn through the nose makes a person look very fierce.

Finally, many people today have other parts of their face pierced, including the eyebrows, tongue, lips, and cheeks, and specialized jewelry is made specifically to be used in facial and body piercing.

Outside of the face, there are two additional types of jewelry that are of interest here. The cameo is a pendant that is carved in the likeness of a person, and a locket is a hinged pendant made out of precious metals that opens and closes and usually includes a photo of a person. Both are

While facial piercings (and the jewelry worn in such piercings) are becoming more common in the West, it is still very rare to see someone with as many piercings as can be seen on Dennis Lang. (Paul Hakimata/Dreamstime.com)

worn on a chain around the neck, and are often used as memorials of the dead or as commemorations of a loved one. Cameos were worn in ancient Greece, Egypt, and Rome, and were originally carved from stone and usually featured gods and goddesses; Cleopatra had cameos carved with her likeness as well. They fell out of fashion during the Middle Ages, but became popularized again during the Renaissance by Queen Elizabeth, and were very popular during the Victorian era in England, when shell became the most common medium.

Lockets, on the other hand, probably began as amulets, and allowed the wearer to keep protective herbs or medicines on their person. One could also keep poison in a locket, or other substances intended to either harm or hurt someone. By the 19th century, a practice emerged in Europe in which people would have a tiny portrait painted of a loved one, and that portrait would be worn inside the locket. (For those who could not afford such an extravagance, the locket often contained instead a lock of hair from the beloved.) With the rise of photography in the 19th century, the painted portrait gave way to the photograph. As with cameos, lockets became extremely popular in the Victoria era, when improvements in technology allowed for lockets to be mass produced.

See also Ear Piercing; Ear Spools and Plugs; Facial Piercing; Labrets, Lip Plugs, and Lip Plates; Nose Piercing

Further Reading

Evans, J. *A History of Jewellery 1100–1870.* London: British Museum Publications, 1989.

Mascetti, Daniela, and Amanda Triossi. *Earrings: From Antiquity to the Present.* London: Thames and Hudson, 1999.

McNab, Nan. *Body Bizarre Body Beautiful.* New York: Fireside, 2001.

Ostier, Marianne. *Jewels and Women; The Romance, Magic and Art of Feminine Adornment.* New York: Horizon Press, 1958.

Tait, H. *Seven Thousand Years of Jewellery.* London: British Museum Publications, 1986.

Judaism

The Hebrew word face (*paniym*) in the Jewish Bible refers to both the physical face and the presence or wholeness of an individual, demonstrating the importance of the face in ancient Jewish belief.

In Esther 1:2, for example, the phrase "saw his face" meant that one had access to someone else, while "seek my face" from Psalms 27:8 meant "seek me," and "hide your face" from Psalms 102:2 meant that you refused to answer.

The concept of face was especially important to the ancient Hebrews when discussing God. The face of God was not the literal face of the creator; instead, the face of God refers to God's presence and, perhaps more importantly, his feelings about his worshippers. For example, 1 Chronicles 16:11 encourages worshippers to "seek the Lord and His strength, seek his face continually;" here, "seek His face" means to seek his presence. When the faithful have proven their faith, they "shall behold His face" (Ps. 11:7), and when those who have wronged God acknowledge their wrongdoing and "seek His face," it means that they look to God for forgiveness.

On the other hand, when God "hides His face," he literally turns his back on his followers because of their sins and no longer protects them. "Receiving the face of God," however, means that God has chosen an individual or a group to favor, while simultaneously turning His face from another group or individual.

In ancient Hebrew society, as in other cultures of the **Middle East**, the face is also associated with intimacy and privacy. This is one reason why **veiling** is so important in Middle Eastern cultures. It also explains why, even though numerous Biblical passages encourage the faithful to seek God's face (i.e., presence), no one is actually allowed to truly see God's face.

Many orthodox Jewish women cover their hair after they are married, with wigs, scarves, or other coverings. In conservative Judaism, women must cover their hair during religious services, but not at other times. (AP/Wide World Photos)

In Exodus 33:20, for example, God tells Moses "you cannot see my face, for no one may see me and live." Even so, Moses, in that conversation, experienced the glory of God to such an extent that he needed to veil his own face.

Veiling was also practiced by Jewish women; like other women in the Middle East, it was at one time considered unseemly for a Jewish woman to go out in public without her hair, and sometimes her face, covered, both as a sign of modesty as well as status. Today, it remains Jewish practice for married women to cover their hair while in the synagogue, and many Orthodox women continue to cover their hair in public (or even at home) with a scarf or a wig; some have even taken the practice of veiling their faces in public. In addition, the Christian practice of a woman wearing a veil during the wedding ceremony originated as a Jewish practice; the Jewish bridal veil is placed on the bride's face by the groom, a tradition known as *badeken* and covered in Genesis 24:65.

See also Middle East; Veiling

Further Reading

Baskin, Judith. *Jewish Women in Historical Perspective*. Detroit: Wayne State University Press, 1991.

Diamant, Anita. *The New Jewish Wedding*. New York: Simon and Schuster, 2001.

K

Kohl

Kohl is a mineral-based cosmetic, used primarily to line women's (and sometimes men's eyes). It is most commonly used today in **India**, where it is known as *kajal*, and the **Middle East**, where it is known as *surma*, and was widely used by the ancient Greeks and Romans, who themselves got it from **Egypt**.

Kohl has been used for thousands of years as both an eye adornment as well as protection against both heavy sunlight in hot climates, sand in desert regions, and infections (it may act as an antibacterial agent). It was also thought to protect one from the **evil eye**. Some also believe that lining one's eyes with kohl improves one's vision.

In Egypt, kohl was made from antimony or galena, mixed with almond or frankincense oil or fat into a paste. It could also be made from other minerals, producing other colors. For example, green malachite produced a green color, and lapis produced blue. Men and women both wore it, and mothers applied it to their children's eyes. It was so important that those preparing bodies for mummification outlined the dead's eyes with kohl.

Today, kohl is still widely used in India and the Middle East, and its traditional functions—protection and beautification—are still found. In the Middle East in particular, where so many women practice **veiling**, lining the eyes with kohl is often the only real way that a woman can adorn her face and express her personality. Bedouins, too, continue to use kohl to protect their eyes against fierce sunlight and sand. Even in Muslim cultures that discourage women from beautifying themselves in order to attract male attention, kohl is still widely used because of its other functions.

In India, kohl is made from burning cloth that has been dipped in sandalwood paste; the resulting soot is mixed with ghee (clarified butter) or oil to produce the paste. Indian women today use kohl, as in the past, both to protect themselves, and to ensure that they do not inflict harm on others. Indian women will also put kohl on their children's faces to ward off the evil eye, by making the child imperfect.

The minerals from which kohl was traditionally based—primarily antimony and galena—are now known to be dangerous. Both can lead to lead poisoning, which is common in the Middle East and is associated with long-term kohl use. Today, Westerners associate dark eyes lined with kohl with the exotic Middle East, and belly dancers and others inspired by this region use modern forms of kohl on their eyes. Western cosmetics that contain the name kohl are generally made from nontoxic ingredients and are not truly made of kohl.

See also Cosmetics; Egypt; Evil Eye; India; Middle East

Kohl is widely used to adorn the eyes, especially in India and the Middle East. It is also commonly used to protect children from evil eyes, as with this boy in India. (Dreamstime.com)

Further Reading

Parry, Carol, and Joseph Eaton. "Kohl: A Lead-Hazardous Eye Makeup from the Third World to the First World." *Environmental Health Perspectives* 94 (1991): 121–23.

Korea

Koreans, like many other Asians, are especially concerned with the concepts of losing and saving face. Losing face means being publically insulted and having one's dignity and good name maligned, while saving face, or *chae-myun*, means preserving one's dignity and self-respect. The Korean word for face, *kibun*, also means pride, and Koreans work hard to not cause insult to another's kibun. Because of this concern, Koreans will often work hard to conceal their emotions by controlling their **facial expressions** so as not to incur embarrassment.

Like many other Asian countries, Korea has long been very status conscious, and losing face is thus extremely dangerous to one's self-esteem and identity. As in **China** and **Japan**, directly criticizing someone, especially one's social superiors, is not done in Korea, because of the danger of losing face to the person being criticized, and many Koreans will not give bad news to others, for the same reason. In terms of international relations, diplomats who need to deal with the North Korean government must struggle with how to engage with North Korea on explosive issues like human rights or nuclear arms without insulting the country, and causing them to lose face.

Koreans, like members of other Asian countries, have long learned to control their facial expressions so as to ensure harmony and lack of conflict, and this social conformity extends to the popularity of **cosmetic surgery** in Korea today. In South Korea, where the modern standard of beauty means round eyes, pale skin, and a sharp nose (none of which are naturally found in Koreans), cosmetic procedures like blepharoplasty, in which a crease is created in the upper eyelid, are so popular that 1 in 10 adults have gone under the knife. Besides the eyelid surgery, other popular procedures in Korea include procedures to make noses longer and more pronounced, and to reduce the size of the cheekbones. One result is that in some areas in Korea, it is difficult to find young women who have not had cosmetic surgery.

A new trend in Korea illustrates both the Korean need to conform as well as the more recent fascination with large, Western eyes. A popular new trend among girls and young women here is the circle contact lens, which makes the iris appear larger, and ultimately, the entire eye appears bigger. In fact, South Korea is leading the way in fashion eyeglasses, or ulzzang glasses, which are inexpensive fake eyeglasses that are worn to accentuate the eyes. Ulzzang is a Korean term that means "best face" and emphasizes exaggerated eyes as well as other Western facial features like fair skin and a high nose bridge.

There is a long tradition of wearing **masks** in Korea, associated with ancient shamanistic practices as well as theatrical and religious practices brought over from China. Korean soldiers (and their horses) once wore masks; jade and bronze masks were worn during funerals and during shamanistic rituals to scare off evil spirits, and at one time, Koreans used **death masks** for burials of notable people. Korea also has a long theatrical tradition during which masks play a central role; in fact, it's likely that these folk dance performances originated in ancient shamanistic practices.

Ulzzang

Ulzzang or uljjang means best face in Korean, and is a phenomenon in Korea and in other parts of Asia (or Asian communities outside of Asia) that celebrates cuteness, fashion, and style. In particular, ulzzang emphasizes a specific kind of female beauty in which very large eyes are featured. An ulzzang is someone who has achieved popularity for her appearance, and a number of Web sites exist that allow users to post their photos and viewers to rank them.

The ulzzang look often takes work to achieve. It involves the wearing of cosmetic circle lenses, which are contact lenses that make the iris seem much larger; false eyelashes; and eye makeup, which further emphasizes the size of the eye, as well as pale foundation to lighten the skin. Many girls have had upper eyelid surgery to achieve the Western rounded eye, but those who have not achieve the look with eyelid glue or tape, which creates the appearance of a fold or double lid. Because of the emphasis on this kind of beauty in Korea, Korean pop stars and television stars all share these physical features and are considered to be ulzzang.

Ulzzang's characteristics are borrowed from Japanese anime, a form of animation popular since the 1960s, which itself borrowed from American animated characters like Betty Boop and Bambi. The large eyes and small facial features from these characters are now ubiquitous not only in anime, but in Japanese and Korean youth culture in general.

Because these performances involve appeasing ancestral spirits, the performers wear spirit masks during the dances. Other dance dramas involving masks were imported from China and influenced by Buddhism. Today, these performances can be broken into two types: village festival plays and performances that derive from the court, known as *sandae-guk*. For instance, the *Hahoe Byeolsin*, the most well known of the village festival performances, occurs every 10 years and traditionally involved 12 wooden masks that were kept in the village shrine between performances; today, 9 of those masks remain. Court performances were used to entertain visiting royalty, to exorcise evil spirits, and to welcome government officials, and virtually all involve masks made from gourds or rice paper.

See also Beauty; Buddhism; China; Cosmetic Surgery; Face Saving and Losing Face; Facial Expressions; Japan; Masks

Further Reading

Kaw, E. "Opening Faces: The Politics of Cosmetic Surgery and Asian American Women." In *In Our Own Words: Readings on the Psychology of Women and Gender*, edited by M. Crawford and R. Under, 55–73. New York: McGraw-Hill, 1997.

L

Labrets, Lip Plugs, and Lip Plates

A labret is a piercing that is made below the lower lip, above the chin. Lip plugs and lip plates are adornments to be worn inside of lip piercings and enlarged holes in the lips. Lip plugs and lip plates have been worn by traditional cultures in **South America,** in **North America**, in the Arctic and sub-Arctic regions, and in Africa. Labret piercings have become popular in recent years in the West, in particular within the Modern Primitivist community.

Labrets have been commonly worn by traditional cultures around the world, and in fact, the labret is one of the most commonly seen facial piercing in non-Western cultures. Traditional labrets were made of wood, ivory, metal, or quartz and other stones.

Labrets were worn, starting perhaps 3,000 to 4,000 years ago, among a number of Native American tribes, including many Northwest Coast Indians, such as the Tlingit, Haida, Chugach, Inuit, and Tsimshian, among whom the labret was often a sign of status. High status Tlingit girls and women, for example, wore labrets as both decoration and to mark rank. Labrets would be inserted into the skin after an excision was made, usually as part of a rite of passage for girls who have just experienced their first menstruation. (Some observers, on the other hand, noted that infants were pierced.)

In some groups, men also wore labrets, and men could wear single or double labrets, worn on either side of the mouth. (Different historical periods in the northwest are associated with either male or female wear, or both.) Like women, men received theirs as part of an initiation ritual. Labrets in this case, however, were not generally small studs inserted into a pierced opening below the lip, but were large plugs inserted below the lip, or sometimes in the lip itself, as with lip plates. Materials for labrets included walrus ivory, abalone shell, bone, obsidian, and wood.

Labrets were sometimes as wide as the lips, and were made of stone, bone, wood, and ivory. Beads were also sometimes strung from the labrets (into which holes had been drilled), creating the appearance of a beaded beard. The first labret was small, and would be replaced by increasingly larger labrets as the hole grew bigger. For that reason, labret size indicated both age and status. Holes sometimes grew so large that without jewelry, the lip would hang down, exposing the teeth and gums. While most labrets were worn below the lip, between the lip and the jaw, some tribes wore labrets, which were typically round plugs, on both sides of the lips.

Labrets were also commonly worn in pre-Columbian Mesoamerica. Among the ancient Aztecs and Mayans, labret piercings were only worn by elite men, who wore elaborately sculpted and jeweled labrets fashioned from pure gold in the shape of serpents, jaguars, and other animals.

In cultures in which the hole in the lip was enlarged, instead of studs, lip plates or lip plugs would be worn. Lip plates and lip plugs are items made of clay, wood, stone, bone, or metal inserted into a hole in the lower lip, or the area beneath the lip, above the chin. Small plates or plugs are generally inserted after slicing open a hole into the lower lip. After the hole heals around the plate, it is removed and larger ones are inserted, gradually stretching the hole. (In some cases, a plate is also inserted into the upper lip.) Lip plates are usually no larger than 3 centimeters in width, but the women of southern Chad wear extremely large plates, often as large as 24 centimeters.

Lip plates are generally worn by women as a form of decoration, status (with size serving as a marker of social or economical importance), and marriageability. Lip plugs are worn by men and women alike. Women with lip plates are seen as more beautiful than unadorned women.

Tribes that are known for their traditional lip plates include the Mursi and Surma of Ethiopia, the Suya of Brazil, the Makololo of Malawai, the Makonde of Tanzania, and the Sara and Djinja of Chad. Among the Djinja, it is the young girl's fiancé who will perform the procedure on her. Among the Makololo tribe, lip plates are called *pelele* and are used to arouse the men in the tribe. The Lobi women of Ghana and the Ivory Coast and the Kirdi of Cameroon wear lip plugs to protect the women from evil spirits who enter via the mouth. It is said that the lip plates worn by the Sara, who wear plates in both the upper and lower lips,

look like the beaks of sacred birds, such as the spoonbill or broadbill.

Lips are pierced with a thorn, and the opening is enlarged by inserting a stalk of grass or other implement into the hole. Larger and larger plugs or plates are inserted as the hole gets bigger, with the sizes of the plates reaching six inches or more. Women who wear lower lip plates often have two or four of their lower teeth removed as well. It has been suggested that women in Africa may have originally worn lip plates in order to deform their faces,

A Mursi (or Murzu) woman wearing a plate in her lower lip, Debub Omo Zone, Ethiopia, Africa. Lip plates like this have been worn by traditional cultures in South America, North America, the Arctic and sub-Arctic regions, and in Africa. (Uros Ravbar/Dreamstime.com)

to protect them from Arab slave traders. Whether that is true, the reason given today is that it beautifies a woman. In some tribes, however, men wore lip plates, too.

Today, labrets are commonly worn in the body modification community in the West, and especially among modern primitives and Goths. Labrets are received at piercing studios, either via a normal piercing technique, or, in the case of larger labrets or lip plugs, through slicing the skin underneath the lip with a scalpel.

Also known as the Mao (because it looks like the mole above Mao Zedong's chin), the jewelry used in the West today is usually a labret stud, which consists of a metal shaft with a simple round stud protruding from the face; it is attached inside of the lip with a flat piece of backing metal. Also popular is the labret spike, which is structurally similar to the labret stud but looks more like an arrowhead protruding from the face. Captive bead rings (in which a bead bisects the ring and is held in place by the spring pressure of the metal) can also be used in labret piercings, but when a ring is worn, the piercing is generally referred to as a lip piercing, rather than a labret, because the ring encircles the lip; a typical labret looks like a bead or stud emerging from underneath the lip.

While the single stud underneath the lip is the most traditional and common form of the labret, a number of newer forms are worn today. A lowbret is a piercing placed as low as possible on the chin, but still accessible through the inside of the mouth. A Medusa is the opposite of a labret piercing, with the stud emerging from above the upper lip, below the nose, rather than below the lower lip. A Madonna or Monroe is a Medusa labret placed above and to the outside of the lip area, in order to simulate a beauty mark of the kind worn by Madonna and Marilyn Monroe. The jewelry used for these piercings is typically a labret stud or a jeweled stud.

Whereas normally labrets only show a single bead or stud, the vertical labret piercing is a piercing in which two studs are visible, one beneath the lip in the area in which a normal labret would be positioned, with the second positioned directly on top of the lower lip. A jestrum is very similar, but is a vertical labret that pierces the upper lip and the area above the upper lip, with studs emerging from just below and just above the upper lip. Two labrets on each side of the lower lip are called snakebites or venom piercings, because the double holes look somewhat like snakebites. In the West, while lip plates are not yet popular even among the most dedicated of modern primitives, lip plugs are sometimes worn in stretched holes in the lips.

See also Central America; Oral Piercing

Further Reading

Fisher, Angela. *Africa Adorned: A Panorama of Jewelry, Dress, Body Decoration, and Hair.* New York: Henry Abrams, 2000.

Griffin, Joy. "Labrets and Tattooing in Native Alaska." In *Marks of Civilization,* edited by Arnold Rubin, 181–90. Los Angeles: Museum of Cultural History, UCLA, 1988.

Jonaitis, Aldona. "Women, Marriage, Mouths and Feasting: The Symbolism of Tlingit Labrets." In *Marks of Civilization,* edited by Arnold Rubin, 191–205. Los Angeles: Museum of Cultural History, UCLA, 1988.

M

Makeup. *See* **Cosmetics**

Makapansgat Pebble

The Makapansgat pebble or cobble is a reddish-brown rock made of jasperite found in South Africa in 1925, which looks like a face. It has what looks to be two eyes, a nose, and a mouth.

While the rock's appearance is entirely natural, it is thought by archaeologists and art historians to have been found and kept by ancient hominins due to its human-like appearance. A teacher named Wilfred Eizman found the rock in a cave near the remains of *Australopithecus africanus*, a predecessor (and perhaps ancestor) of humans living about 2.5 million years ago, and it may be that members of this species found and transported this rock from its original location, indicating an interest in art or perhaps even religion. Some scholars feel that the rock has as many as three faces: the primary face, a face produced by turning the rock upside down (which paleoanthropologist Raymond Dart suggest looks like an Australopithecus) and a third face found on the back. Because the rock did not originate in this cave (and probably came from a site some kilometers away), and because it was not a tool (*A. africanus*, in fact, did not create stone tools), the presence of the rock in a hominin encampment suggests that these creatures may have ap-

preciated the rock for its aesthetic, symbolic, or ritual value.

We know that humans are hardwired to recognize faces, and from an early age, are attracted to the human face. Many nonhuman mammals, as well, are attracted to the faces of others, and chimpanzees, like humans, recognize their own faces in the mirror. So the idea that Australopithecines—very primitive hominins with brains not much larger than chimpanzees—would be attracted to an object representing a face should not surprise us.

See also Facial Features

Further Reading

Dart, Raymond. "The Waterworn Australopithecine Pebble of Many Faces from Makapansgat." *South African Journal of Science* 70 (1974): 167–69.

Kleiner, Fred. *Gardner's Art through the Ages,* vol 1. Eastbourne, UK: Gardners Books, 2010.

Mardi Gras

Mardi Gras, French for Fat Tuesday, is a celebration in many parts of the world that takes place during the final week before Ash Wednesday, during which Catholics celebrate prior to the beginning of Lent, the 40-day period leading up to Easter when believers fast as a way of paying penance for their sins. In many countries, the celebrations are referred to as Carnival (which means the removal of meat, referencing the fasting that most Catholics due during Lent). These celebrations may derive from pre-Christian rites of inversion, when slaves and peasants would temporarily be allowed to engage in behaviors otherwise prohibited to them. Such rituals are seen by sociologists as important ways to release stress, but still maintain the social order in society.

Masking during parades and masquerade parties are among the most important elements of Mardi Gras or Carnival celebrations. One of the reasons that **masks** have long been an important part of such rituals is because they conceal one's identity; they allow revelers to safely celebrate, as well as mock their social superiors, without fear of reprisal. Because of this, Venice, home to one of Europe's most ancient Carnivals, has seen a number of laws passed over time that sought to restrict the wearing of masks. In other locations, the wearing of masks is prohibited throughout the year, with the one exception being during Carnival celebrations. The Carnival celebration of another Italian town, Viareggio, is known for the use of masks that caricature well-known local figures. In some celebrations, such as in French Guiana, women called *touloulous* use costumes and masks to conceal completely their identities; they then attend balls at which they pick men to dance with and later, perhaps, have sex with. This is somewhat similar to the southern German *Weiberfasnacht*, where women, not men, are in control.

The tradition of wearing masks during Carnival celebrations may date back to Greek and Roman **theater**, during which actors wore masks that allowed the audience to see them better. This tradition may have spread throughout the Roman Empire to Venice and other regions that later borrowed the use of the masks for their own celebrations. On the other hand, pre-Christian festivals in Europe may have also utilized masks, which could have gotten incorporated into the newer, Christian festivals.

Carnival masks differ with the region. In Germany, where **Fastnacht** is celebrated, people dress up as demons and witches, because the winter is the time when evil spirits reign; one of the goals of the celebration is to cast out those spirits and bring in the Spring. Many Latin American celebrations feature revelers dressed up as the devil as well. In some areas of Portugal, children wear tin masks, while other Portuguese celebrations feature revelers wearing large heads sculpted from papier-mâché. In Slovenia, carved, wooden masks are featured. Another European Carnival, celebrated in Malta, includes a grotesque mask competition. Many Carnivals include black-or white-tie masquerade balls during which all guests are masked. In the Cadiz region of Spain, on the other hand, revelers don't wear masks, but instead paint their faces with lipstick.

In Venice, which has been hosting Carnival celebrations since the 13th century, masks have long been a central component of the celebrations. Venetian masks either cover the full face—these are known as *Bauta* masks—or they cover just the eyes and nose; these are known as *Columbina* masks. In addition, until the 18th century when it was prohibited, full face masks were worn in Venice during times when

A couple wearing masks during Carnival in Venice, Italy. Carnival, also known as Mardi Gras, is a celebration held just before Ash Wednesday when celebrants wear masks and engage in behaviors that are otherwise frowned on in society. (Dreamstime.com)

members of different classes wanted to socialize with each other, or when individuals were engaging in illegal or illicit activities. They were also worn during political events when anonymity was required. Another Venetian mask is the *Medico della Peste*. This mask is characterized by the long nose or beak, and was once worn by doctors treating plague victims, in order to protect them from airborne diseases.

In North American Mardi Gras celebrations, as in Mobile or New Orleans, krewes or mystic societies are social organizations that operate year round and play a central role in the Mardi Gras festivities by creating Mardi Gras floats and throwing parties. During the parades, society or krewe members wear masks and throw beads or gifts,

and later, attend the balls wearing formal wear and masks, as in the European masquerade balls. Key colors to be found on Mardi Gras masks are green, gold, and purple, and like Venetian masks, these are often elaborately decorated with feathers, beads, and jewels.

See also Masks; Masquerade

Further Reading

Abrahams, Roger D. *Blues for New Orleans: Mardi Gras and America's Creole Soul.* Philadelphia: University of Pennsylvania Press, 2006.

Sands, Rosita M. "Carnival Celebrations in Africa and the New World: Junkanoo and the Black Indians of Mardi Gras." *Black Music Research Journal* 11 (1991): 75–92.

Masked Characters

Masked characters have long been featured in films, plays, and literature. In popular culture, **masks** are a way to disguise a person's identity, can conceal a disfigurement, and can make a character look dangerous.

Since *The Texas Chainsaw Massacre*, Tobe Hooper's 1974 film about a demented family of former slaughterhouse workers who trap, torture, and eat hapless travelers, horror films have utilized masked characters to great effect. In this film, the lead villain goes by the name of Leatherface, and wears a grotesque mask made from the skin of one of his victims. The image of Leatherface, in his mask and holding a chainsaw over his head, has now become one of the most iconic images in horror film history. In **Halloween**, John Carpenter's classic 1978 film, a boy named Michael

Myers brutally murdered his sister on Halloween while wearing a Halloween mask. After being committed to a psychiatric hospital and escaping, he returns to his hometown and, on Halloween, begins stalking and killing a series of teenagers, this time wearing a plain white mask. Two years later, the first *Friday the 13th* film came out, featuring a villain named Jason Voorhees who wore a hockey mask while hunting and killing a group of teenagers at a summer camp. Horror films since this time have continued to use the mask as an element, which makes the character and audience unable to identify the killer (or even understand why he is killing), and makes him that much more frightening. For instance, in *Saw*, released in 2004, a killer named Jigsaw kidnaps seemingly random strangers, locking them into a room together and forcing them to either kill each other, or cut off their own limbs, in order to escape. Jigsaw wears a mask of a pig's face throughout the *Saw* films. Here again, the mask conceals his identity from his victims and serves to frighten them (and us). Finally, *Scream*, released in 1996 and directed by Wes Craven, is a self-referential horror film that took the conventions of the genre and both expanded on them and made fun of them. For example, the characters in Scream watch horror movies throughout the film, and talk about the lessons they have learned from them (like never walking into a basement), although most of them die by the end of the film anyway. *Scream*'s antagonist, GhostFace, refers to what the viewers and victims thought was one killer (but was actually two) in the first *Scream* film; the character wears a black coat and a cheap-looking

ghost mask. After both killers are killed at the end of the first film, the disguise was re-used by subsequent killers in all of the sequels. Because the costume and mask are so simple, multiple characters (including, at one time, the heroine, Sidney) wear it during the films, making the identities of the killers that much harder to figure out.

Other films that were not strictly horror films have used masks in ways that are intended to frighten the viewers as well as conceal the identity of the wearer. For instance, Darth Vader, the supervillain of the *Star Wars* series of films, is introduced in the first film in 1977 as the mysterious Dark Lord of the Sith, and wears an ominous black helmet and face mask, which conceals his identity, covers his burns from a fight with Obi Wan Kenobi, and allows him to breathe through a ventilator and speak through a voice processor. In the second film, released in 1980, it is revealed that Darth Vader is actually Anakin Skywalker, the hero Luke's father. This makes the wearing of the mask all the more poignant, in that it allowed Luke and Vader to interact and fight without Luke knowing that it was his father, who had gone to the dark side.

Another film, *The Phantom of the Opera*, based on a book published in 1910 called *Le Gaulois* and a subsequent Broadway show, featured a masked antagonist named Erik in the book (the Phantom in the film). Erik secretly lives in the Paris Opera House, and wears a mask whenever he must be seen, to cover his horrifically disfigured face. While not a true horror film, the mask serves to make the Phantom's character more frightening and to make Christine, the object of his attentions, fear him.

Perhaps no medium has exploited the mask more than the comic book/graphic novel, and in particular, the superhero story. Because superheroes often lead double lives, the mask is an important element of their costume because it conceals their identity. Spiderman, Batman, the Green Lantern, Black Panther, Flash, Hawkman, Ms. Marvel, and Captain America are all comic book superheroes who wear masks to maintain their anonymity while fighting evil. A different kind of superhero is Stanley Ipkiss, the hero of the film and comic book, *The Mask*. Played by Jim Carrey in the film, Ipkiss is a reluctant superhero, who is only given superpowers after placing a wooden mask (which represents a Norse god named Loki) onto his face, which transforms him into The Mask. After spending much of the film fighting villains, Ipkiss finds love and throws away the mask, which has only caused him trouble.

Another character whose mask conceals his identity and other life is Zorro. While not a comic book character, Zorro (whose real name is Don Diego de la Vega) fights on behalf of the oppressed against both villains and authorities. Like some comic book superheroes, de la Vega falls in love with a woman who is not interested in him, but has fallen for Zorro. The trope of the mask and the double identity lies at the root of this conflict, and is seen in the Spiderman film, in which Peter Parker, Spiderman's straight ego, falls in love with Mary Jane, who is in love with Spiderman. In the film, Mary Jane pulls Spiderman's mask partway off in order to kiss him, but does not realize that Spiderman and Parker are the same person.

See also Famous Faces; Masks

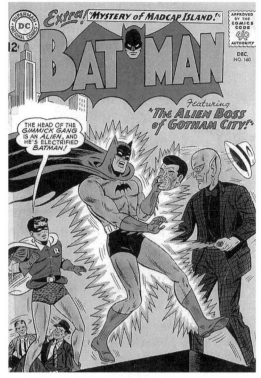

An issue of *Batman*, December 1963. Because one of the functions of masks is to conceal identity, masks are commonly worn by superheroes (and villains) in comic books and movies. (DC Comics/Photofest)

Further Reading

Packer, Sharon. *Superheroes and Superegos: Analyzing the Minds Behind the Masks*. Santa Barbara, CA: Praeger/ABC-CLIO, 2010.

Worland, Rick. *The Horror Film: An Introduction*. Malden, MA: Blackwell, 2007.

Masks

Masks are devices worn over the face, and sometimes the head, to conceal one's identity or to allow an individual to impersonate someone else. To mask means, literally, to conceal, and derives from the Arabic word *maskhara* or *mashara*, which means to falsify or transform into animal or monster. The Egyptian word *msk* means leather or second skin. Masks can also create identity, either individual or social, when worn as part of a social ritual. Masks are used as part of celebrations such as **Mardi Gras** or **Halloween**, are used during the commission of crimes to maintain anonymity, can be used to protect the face, such as with gas masks, and are used in some religious activities such as **shamanism**. Masks can be made of cloth, leather or animal skin, paper, plastic, wood, and a variety of other materials, and are found in almost every culture.

Humans have been wearing masks, most likely, for thousands of years. The cave paintings at Lascaux, France, which date to approximately 17,000 years ago show a human, perhaps a shaman, wearing the face of a bird, and the paintings at Trois Freres, another cave in France dating to about 14,000 years ago, may also show a shaman dressed as deer, with a deer mask and headdress. The modern interpretation of these images suggests that one of the earliest forms of **masquerade** was dressing up like an animal, most likely for ritual purposes. Africa, too, has rock art appearing to depict humans dressed up with animal heads, such as in the Tassili rock art in the Sahara Desert that dates to about 6,000 years ago. Modern Africans still use masks in many of their rituals. North American petroglyphs also appear to show humans dressed as animals, as in the petroglyphs found in Wyoming, New Mexico, Arizona, and Utah. In the case of the petroglyphs found in the Four Corners region as well

as in Wyoming, the modern Native tribes in this area, the Pueblo and Plains tribes, still use masks in their rituals. And finally, Australian rock art depicts people who appear to be wearing the masks of animals. Modern aboriginals, however, do not use masks in their rituals, although they do use body painting.

There is good evidence that humans may have been impersonating animals much earlier than the above examples. For example, at an archaeological site called Hortus in France, a leopard skin dating back perhaps 40,000 years is thought by some to have been a cape worn by a Neanderthal shaman. Similarly, in the Lonetal Valley in Germany, a 30,000 year old ivory sculpture was found in 1939 of a man wearing a lion costume, including the head of a lion. While these may not have involved the modern form of mask, they certainly would have been, if the interpretations are correct, pre-human forms of masquerade.

Perhaps a desire to change one's identity and assume a new persona may be a fundamentally human impulse. Because humans are identified so closely with their faces, and because their faces allow others to identify them, wearing a mask is the best way to change identities, indicating its central role in theater and in the commission of crime. But even outside the context of crime or theater, humans often have an urge to transform themselves into someone, or something, different. Making oneself look different may open the door to actually being different. In other words, by wearing a mask, one can actually change one's identity, and when masks are used by many members of a community, as part of a communal ritual, the community may reinvent itself, even temporarily, as well as strengthen its social bond.

The earliest uses of masks was most likely in shamanistic rituals, as seen in the Upper Paleolithic cave paintings and rock art mentioned earlier. Here, shamans may have worn the masks of animals as decoys or as protection from harm. Alternatively, shamans often channel spirits in order to heal the living; wearing an animal mask may be one way to mimic the behavior of the animal spirits. These masks would make the invisible animal spirits visible in this world. Another interpretation of the use of animal masks by shamans is that shamans are often called upon to ensure success in a hunt. By wearing animal masks during these rituals, the shaman may be negotiating with the animals for their sacrifice. (Humans dressed as animals appear quite frequently in hunting scenes in cave and rock art.) And finally, another explanation may be that the shaman is conducting a fertility ritual, and the spirit of the animal is needed for the shaman to participate. Another use of masks in order to heal is the use of the disease mask. Disease masks were once worn in **China**, Burma, and Sri Lanka, and were thought to be able to cure diseases like measles, cholera, and blindness. A healer puts on the frightening mask, and literally dances the illness out of the subject.

Masks are often worn during rites of passage, especially adolescent rituals, when initiates move from one life stage—adolescence—to another—adulthood. Masks are especially common during what anthropologists call the liminal phase of the ritual, when the initiates are stripped of their previous identity, as well as during the reincorporation stage, when they re-emerge into society with their new identities. Interestingly, masks are far more commonly found in male initiation rituals, which emphasize productive activities, rather than female rites, which emphasize reproductive abilities. Men tend to dominate in maskmaking around the world, in fact, which may be related to men's involvement in hunting or their greater historical role in performance. Another rite of passage, which involves masks, is the funeral ritual, during which the dead transition from this world into the next. In some rituals, the priest or other participants at the ritual wear masks to represent the spirits that will accompany the dead to the afterlife. Sometimes the masks had a practical function as well. For instance, Egyptian priests wore masks representing the god Anubis during the 70 days of embalming—both to call on Anubis to prepare the spirit of the dead, and to protect the priest from embalming materials. Masks have been worn by funeral participants in Polynesia, Indonesia, Melanesia, and Africa. In other cases, the dead themselves wear a death mask or burial mask, which serves a number of functions, including making the person recognizable in the afterworld, protecting the face from evil spirits, and ensuring the survival of the person in the afterlife.

Other types of rituals in which masks play a role are rituals of inversion. These rituals, best exemplified in the Carnival or modern Mardi Gras, involve participants who challenge—temporarily—the existing social order. Peasants may mock the elites, slave owners may serve their slaves dinner, and kings may dress as peasants.

Masks give participants a way to not just conceal their identities but take on the identities of others—those more or less powerful than themselves, those of a different gender, and even the Devil. These festivals are common during transitions between seasons—Carnival, for example, marks the transition from winter to spring.

Masks are also common in totemic cultures—cultures in which a tribe, lineage, or clan takes as its ancestor an animal like a bear or wolf. In such cultures, masks of the totem animal might be worn by a shaman or another holy person. Wearing the mask of the totem animal could allow the wearer to communicate directly with the spirit of the animal, to ask for assistance in hunting, for example.

African cultures commonly use masks in a variety of communal rituals, including rites of passage, harvest festivals, and protective rituals. Masks represent a variety of spirits, animals, people, and even stars. For instance, the Goli mask used by the Baule of the Ivory Coast represents the face of the sun combined with the horns of a buffalo, and is used during harvest ceremonies, ceremonial visits, and funerals. The Senufo of West Africa, on the other hand, create masks that have both human and animal features and are used in male adolescent rituals and to communicate with dead ancestors. The Kwele of Gabon and Cameroon create masks in the likeness of an antelope, and use these masks during rituals that protect the participants from witchcraft; an antelope is killed and consumed as part of the ritual. African masks are highly stylized and maskmakers are respected artists.

Many Native American cultures used, and still use, masks in their rituals. For instance, the Cherokee have long used masks for rituals and storytelling, and have a tradition called the Booger Dance, which may have evolved in the 19th century, and features masked dancers who scare off evil spirits or bogeymen. The masks are made from gourds and are painted with garish and exaggerated designs meant to represent enemy tribes and, later, Europeans.

The use of masks in the theater is most likely related to the use of masks in ritual.

This bear mask by artist Rick Bartow reflects the culture of the Mad River Band of Yurok in Oregon. The mask is one of the items in the 800,000-piece collection at the National Museum of the American Indian in Washington, D.C. At the museum, the masks are fed cornmeal or corn pollen to care for their spirits, in line with some native cultures' beliefs. Masks are used in many Native American religious rituals. (AP/Wide World Photos)

Religious rituals, after all, would have been the earliest performances in societies, so as those performances moved from strictly religious to entertainment, the use of the mask would have continued. The use of the mask to conceal or change one's identity is only possible when there are observers present, of course, so the presence of the audience is found in masking rituals as well as in theatrical performances.

In theatrical performances, masks not only make the wearer look like someone else, but these masks represent exaggerated facial expressions, which make it easy for the audience to interpret the emotions and thoughts of the characters from far away. The ancient Greeks, for example, used masks in the theatre as well as in rituals and other celebrations, such as during the worship of Dionysus. Greek masks were made of linen, leather, or cork, covered the entire head, and included human or animal hair. In Greek theater, as in other traditions, men performed as both men and women, and wearing the mask of a woman allowed the men to behave in ways that they otherwise would not be able to, and that, often, women were prohibited from. West African theatrical performances, which derived from religious rituals, involved masked performers, and featured actors wearing masks to portray both indigenous and modern characters. Indian theatre, too, derived from ancient Indian rituals, and still features masks. Masks can be made of papier-mâché or wood, are elaborately decorated, and represent gods, goddesses, and mythological and historical characters.

Because of the way that the mask conceals the face, and thus the identity of the wearer, masks have long been used to deceive others. For example, masks are commonly worn during the commission of crimes, especially bank robberies, and members of the white supremacist group the Ku Klux Klan conceal their faces by wearing conical hoods.. This protects their anonymity as well as incites fear in those who see them. The executioner's wearing of a mask performs the same functions. On a more subtle level, because facial expressions betray our emotions, masks allow us to conceal our emotions. Thus we can mask our emotions via false facial expressions.

Finally, the sociological term character mask refers to the way that humans may take on roles or behaviors that they may not desire. In this case, they are acting out a role and wearing an artificial or public face while doing so. The term mask then refers to the false identity taken on by a person, as well as the effects on the person.

See also Day of the Dead; Halloween; Mardi Gras; Masquerade; Mummery; Native North America; Sub-Saharan Africa

Further Reading

Nunley, John, and Cara McCarty. *Masks: Faces of Culture*. New York: Harry N. Abrams, in Association with the Saint Louis Art Museum, 1999.

Masquerade

To masquerade is to disguise oneself as someone or something else. Masquerading is most commonly seen at masquerade or costume balls and masquerade ceremonies, such as Carnival events, popular since the Middle Ages in Europe and throughout the European-influenced world, or New Year's fertility ceremonies, and are found from **China** to **Japan** and Mexico to Europe.

Masquerade balls are common settings in film and literature for dramatic occurrences, because the characters are disguised. This allows for mistaken cases of identity, murderers to conceal their identities, and criminals to hide in plain sight. In fact, some masquerade balls were intended to be a sort of game wherein participants must try to guess other people's identities.

"Masquerade Ball-Mi-Careme," 1908. *Mi Careme* is a mid-Lenten festival celebrated in Europe since the Middle Ages. Party-goers dress up, wear masks, and try to guess who each person is. The *Mi Careme* celebration was featured in Guy de Maupassant's short story "The Mask." (Library of Congress)

Alternatively, because the identities of the guests are secret, this allows participants to engage in behaviors that they would otherwise never engage in. For example, in French Guiana, women called *touloulous* use costumes and masks to completely conceal their identities; they then attend balls at which they pick men to dance with and later, perhaps, have sex with.

In Shakespeare's *Romeo and Juliet*, the star-crossed lovers fall in love at a masquerade ball, not realizing, because of their disguises, that they are members of long-dueling families. In *The Phantom of the Opera*, the Phantom, who wears a mask to conceal his deformed face, makes a dramatic appearance at a masquerade ball, presenting a new opera that he has written especially for Christine, the object of his love. And in "The Masque of the Red Death," a short story by Edgar Allen Poe, Prince Prospero throws a masquerade ball in the abbey in which he and other nobles are hiding from a deadly plague called the Red Death. During the ball, a guest wearing a mask resembling a corpse wanders through the abbey, and is angrily confronted by Prospero, who dies upon meeting him. The other guests pull the mask from the guest and find that he is in fact Red Death himself, upon which they too die. At least one actual murder has taken place at a masquerade ball: Gustav III, King of Sweden (1771–1792), was assassinated by a masked nobleman during a masquerade ball at the Royal Opera House in Stockholm. The killer, along with his co-conspirators, confronted the king at the ball with the words, "good day, fine mask," and shot him in the back.

See also Mardi Gras; Masks

Further Reading

Vuillier, Gaston. *A History of Dancing from the Earliest Age to Our Own Times.* Boston: Milford House, 1972.

Middle East

The Middle East refers to the region of the world that covers the Muslim countries in Western Asia and sometimes includes those in **North Africa**. The region is known for a number of decorative practices involving the face such as nostril piercing, the use of **henna**, and particularly for **veiling**. One practice that is very rare in the Middle East, because of the influence of Islam, is the use of **masks**.

Nostril piercing has been practiced throughout the Middle East as a form of decoration for women as well as a form of portable wealth, especially for nomadic peoples like the Bedouins. In these cases, the size of the ring represents the wealth of the family. As jewelry, it is given by the husband to his wife at the marriage, and is her security if she is divorced.

Henna, known as *Mehndi*, in much of the Middle East, is used to decorate the face, the hands, and to color the hair. While it is much more common today to see henna used as an adornment on feet and hands, it was once a used as makeup for the face. For instance, in ancient Egypt, women used henna paste to stain their lips, and today, henna is often used as a semipermanent eyeliner. Henna has also been used as a prescription against the **evil eye**. The evil eye is a belief that certain individuals can cause sudden harm to others through an intentional or unintentional look. Looking at a person or praising him can cause damage, and the underlying cause of the evil eye is often envy. In Middle Eastern cultures with a belief in the evil eye, a variety of techniques have been developed to either protect against the evil eye, or to undo the damage done when one has been harmed by the evil eye. One of those protective devices has been henna.

But the practice most strongly associated with the Middle East is certainly the veil. Veiling for women was a sign of prestige in many of the ancient cultures of the Middle East. In Assyria, Persia, and Greece, for example, elite women covered their hair or faces. Because veiling was a sign of status, many cultures prohibited the wearing of veils by prostitutes, although lower-class women often did wear veils in order to appear as if they were of a higher class. The practice may have traveled to Arab countries, before the time of Muhammad, via the Byzantine and Persian Empires. Eventually, Islam embraced the veil, and as Islam spread from Saudi Arabia to other cultures, the wearing of veils spread along with it, becoming common by the eighth century—first by elites, and later by lower-class women. By the 10th century, many countries began instituting laws restricting the behavior of women, and mandating veiling or seclusion.

In Muslim countries, women may cover their faces, a portion of their face, their hair, or, in the most extreme cases, their entire bodies. Veils can cover the entire face; they can cover the entire body, as in the burqa worn in Afghanistan and originating in Pakistan; or they can be worn around the head and under the chin, as in the hijab, the most popular form of head covering.

In cultures that have a strong honor-shame complex, as in the Middle East, a woman can bring shame onto her entire family by her personal conduct. If she were to be violated, her whole family, but especially the men, would be shamed. But veiling oneself when appearing in public protects a woman from the gaze of men, protecting her honor, and that honor is then extended to the members of her family. In addition, the veil represents wealth and status. The veil is one way to protect the wealth, status, and honor of well-to-do families by ensuring that the women in those families do not have sexual relations with lower-class men.

See also Veiling

Further Reading

Abu-Lughod, Lila. *Remaking Women: Feminism and Modernity in the Middle East.* Princeton, NJ: Princeton University Press, 1998.

Fernea, Elizabeth W., and Basima Q. Bezirgan. *Middle Eastern Muslim Women Speak.* Austin: University of Texas Press, 1977.

Shirazi, Faegheh. *The Veil Unveiled: The Hijab in Modern Culture.* Gainesville: University Press of Florida, 2001.

Mimes and Clowns

Mimes and clowns are two types of performers whose distinctive appearances are created through the use of makeup.

Mimes are performers who tell stories without speaking; instead, they act out, or mime, a story using their bodies, hand movements, and **facial expressions**. Miming is related to **mummery**, in that both are forms of street performance that date back hundreds of thousands of years. In the case of miming, clearly the use of gestures and hand signals to communicate predates human speech, and is thus hundreds of thousands of years old. Expressive movements without speech also led to the many forms of dance seen around the world; classical Indian and Thai dance, for example, both share many stylistic features with mime.

We know that mimes performed in ancient Greek theater; Telestes was a performer who interpreted, through gesture, the story that was sung or told by the chorus. True pantomime, though, in which no speech or singing takes place, and the action is depicted entirely through gestures, emerged with the performances of ancient Rome. Actors during this period performed short scenes of love, tragedy, comedy, and current events, as well as literary works.

Miming later continued after the fall of the Roman Empire with the traveling performers of Medieval Europe. Miming, singing, dancing, juggling, and performing acrobatics were some of the activities that these actors engaged in, entertaining commoners and royalty alike. At the end of the Middle Ages, a new form of improvisational performance emerged called commedia dell'arte. This new theatrical form involved actors, wearing **masks** with exaggerated facial features, who depicted stock characters and specific moods. It was derived from the tradition of masking during Carnival in northern Italy. Stock characters include servants, lovers, masters, and clowns. Commedia dell'arte was unusual in that female performers acted alongside men, and actors were highly physical, incorporating dancing, tumbling, and other activities into their performances. Miming also played a role in what were called dumb shows, plays or pieces of plays performed without dialogue in both the Middle Ages and the Renaissance.

During the 19th century, some of the conventions of the modern mime emerged: a silent figure wearing heavy, white face makeup, combined with a more refined, less slapstick form of performance. In the 20th century, Parisian mimes like Jacques Copeau, who trained mimes with masks, and Marcel Marceau took the art form much further, creating new styles of miming. Today, miming is largely a form of street performance, and mimes are easily recognized by their distinctive white makeup combined with black touches around the eyes and other facial features. Even though many mimes today spurn the traditional makeup, it is still the most distinctive identifying feature of a mime to many.

Clowns are other street performers known for their distinctive makeup. In general, the term clown refers to any comic performer such as court jesters, buffoons, mimes, or acrobats. These performers often used their comedy to criticize and satirize existing social conditions; even court performers could sometimes get away with subtly, or openly, criticizing the king. Comic performers like these were found in professional acting troupes as well, such as in the commedia dell'arte in Renaissance Italy, and in Shakespeare's plays in Elizabethan England.

Joseph Grimaldi was an English mime, who created a character called Clown at the turn of the 19th century and created the con-

ventions for clowns still used today: a white face, with colorful paint creating exaggerated eyes, cheeks, and mouth. His physical appearance and performances shaped clowns into the present day. On the other hand, not all clowns look like the classic white-faced, red-nosed, red-haired clown. A famous clown type is the auguste clown, whose face is painted a flesh tone, but who has large white areas drawn around his eyes and mouth (which is painted black). The auguste clown is one of the most buffoonish of all the clowns.

Rodeo clown, Homestead, Florida, 2009. Clowns and mimes both wear elaborate makeup on their faces in order to entertain the public and represent the character that they are portraying. (Dreamstime.com)

With the rise of the circus in the 18th century, clowns moved from the theater into this new venue. One of the most famous of all the circus clowns is the hobo or tramp. Dressed in rags, with the white face but a sad expression, he's one of the more widely recognized clowns today. Another famous American clown is the rodeo clown, who dresses like typical clowns but participates actively in rodeo events, but in a comic way.

Because of the exaggerated appearance and behavior of clowns, many people are afraid of them, and a number of horror movies have used the clown as a figure of fear.

See also Mummery; Theater

Further Reading

Janik, Vicki K. *Fools and Jesters in Literature, Art, and History: A Bio-Bibliographical Sourcebook.* Westport, CT: Greenwood Press, 1998.

Lust, Annette. *From the Greek Mimes to Marcel Marceau and Beyond: Mimes, Actors, Pierrots, and Clowns: A Chronicle of the Many Visages of Mime in the Theatre.* Lanham, MD: Scarecrow Press, 2000.

Robb, David. *Clowns, Fools and Picaros: Popular Forms in Theatre, Fiction and Film.* Amsterdam: Rodopi, 2007.

Moia. *See* Easter Island

Moko

The native people of New Zealand, called the Maori, are known around the world for their tattooing. Although their tattoos do not cover as much of the body as many South Pacific people such as the Samoans, the Maori developed their own unusual style of tattooing, covering the face and the buttocks. First described by Captain James Cook in 1769, Maori tattooing remains one of the most unique and beautiful of all tattoo traditions.

The moko is the curvilinear facial tattoo worn by Maori men and women as a sign of status as well as affiliation, and only high status Maori and warriors at one time were tattooed. Women's tattoos were originally limited to the lips and sometimes other parts of the body or forehead; in the 19th century, the spiral chin tattoo was developed. Men could wear the moko, or, if they had their bodies tattooed, the tattoo extended over the area between the waist and the knees, primarily covering the buttocks.

The tattoo design was first drawn onto the skin, and then carved into the skin with a tool known as *uhi whaka tataramoa*, which operated much like wood carving to which it can be related both in design and technique. The tattooist, who was always a man, literally carved the design into the skin. After cutting the skin, pigment was rubbed into the wound.

The procedure was said to be incredibly painful, and caused so much facial swelling that, after tattooing, the person could not eat normally, and had to be fed liquids through a funnel. During the lengthy tattoo, as well, the tattooed person could receive liquid food through the tunnel, thus keeping the contaminating food from the wounds. A woman's moko, which covered the chin and lips, could take one or two days to complete. A man's moko, which covered the whole face, was done in stages over several years and was an important rite of passage for a Maori man; without

Tawaiho, the Maori king of New Zealand, ca. 1900–1923. Tawaiho wore a *moko*, the traditional facial tattoo worn by the Maori until missionary activity almost wiped out the practice. (Library of Congress)

the moko, a man was said to not be a complete person.

Unlike tattoos in Polynesia and elsewhere, which have designs that are worn by everyone of the same tribe, clan, or rank, Maori tattoos were totally individual. While they did indicate a man's social and kinship position, marital status, and other information, each moko was like a fingerprint, and no two were alike. Maori chiefs even used drawings of their moko as their signature in the 19th century. Because the moko, in part, signified rank, different designs on both men and women could be read as relating to their family status, and each of the Maori social ranks carried different designs. In addition, some women

who, due to their genealogical connections, were extremely high status, could wear part of the male moko.

As in Marquesan tattooing, Maori facial designs were divided into four zones (left forehead, right forehead, left lower face, and right lower face) and these further divided, giving an overall symmetry to the design. The right side of the face conveyed information about the father's rank, tribal affiliations, and position. The left side of a face, on the other hand, gave information about the mother's rank, tribal affiliations, and position. Each side of the face is also sub-divided into eight sections, which contain information about rank, position in life, tribal identification, lineage, and more personal information, including occupation or skill.

Tattooing styles varied from tribe to tribe and region to region, as well as over time. Cook, for example, noted that the men on one side of an inlet were tattooed all over their faces, whereas the men on the other side of the inlet were only tattooed on the lips. He also noted that some moko did not include the forehead but only extended from the chin to the eyes. Also, Cook's men noted that there was at least one man at that time who had straight vertical lines tattooed on his face, combined with spirals, as well as two elderly men with horizontal lines across their face. Tattoos of this sort were never again seen on subsequent visits. And by the 19th century, different styles of moko were seen, including both the classic curvilinear style as well as vertical and horizontal parallel lines.

The Maori had a tradition of preserving the tattooed heads of deceased persons of nobility in order, it was presumed, to keep alive the memory of the dead. The heads were also held to be sacred, in that they continued to possess the deceased's *mana*, or magical quality. But in 1770, just a year after initial contact, Europeans became interested in these tattooed heads, and initiated a heads-for-weapons trade that lasted until 1831, when it was banned by the colonial authorities.

The first dried head to be possessed by a European was acquired on January 20, 1770. It was brought by Joseph Banks, who was with Cook's expedition as a naturalist, and was one of four brought on board the Endeavour for inspection. It was the head of a tattooed youth of 14 or 15, who had been killed by a blow to the head.

The trade became especially scandalous because during the tribal wars of the 1820s, when European demand for the heads was at an all time high, war captives and slaves were probably tattooed, killed, and their decapitated heads sold to European traders. As the traffic in heads escalated, the Maori stopped preserving the heads of their friends, so that they wouldn't fall into the hands of the Europeans. Evidently, it also became dangerous to even wear a moko, as one could be killed at any time and have one's head sold to traders. By the end of the head trade in the 1830s, the moko was dying out, due to missionary activity.

Like Hawaiian and Tahitian tattooing, Maori tattooing was also influenced by European contact. On Cook's first visit to New Zealand, the ship artist, Sydney Parkinson, drew pictures of the moko, exposing Europeans for the first time to the Maori and their art, and, inciting the interest in tattooed heads that would follow. Tattoo techniques changed as well as a result of contact. Originally, the Maori applied their wood carving techniques to tattooing, literally carving the skin and rubbing ink into the open wounds. After European contact, sailors brought metal to the Maori, enabling them to adopt the puncture method found in other parts of Polynesia.

After European contact, the moko became associated with Maori culture as a way for the native people of New Zealand to distinguish themselves from the Europeans who had settled there, but by 1840, due to missionary activity, the male moko was falling out of fashion. It was revived briefly during the wars against Europe from 1864 to 1868, but by the turn of the century, there were only a handful of tattooed Maori alive. Ironically, it was during the period in which the male moko was declining that the female chin moko was gaining in popularity as a symbol of identity.

Since the late 20th century, some Maori have begun wearing *ta moko* again as an assertion of their cultural identity. A few Maori tattoo artists are reviving traditional methods of applying ta moko, but most use electric machines.

See also Australia and New Zealand; Facial Tattoos

Further Reading

Friedlander, Marti, and Michael King. *Moko: Maori Tattooing in the Twentieth Century.* Auckland, New Zealand: David Bateman, 1999.

Gathercole, Peter. "Contexts of Maori Moko." In *Marks of Civilization*, edited by Arnold Rubin, 171–78. Los Angeles: Museum of Cultural History, UCLA, 1988.

Nicholas, Thomas, ed. *Tattoo: Bodies, Art and Exchange in the Pacific and the West.* Durham, NC: Duke University Press, 2005.

Simmons, D. R. *Ta Moko: The Art of Maori Tattoo*. Auckland, New Zealand: Reed Books, 1986.

Mongolia

Mongolia is an Asian country surrounded by Russia and **China**. It was once the seat of the Mongol Empire, ruled by Genghis Khan, which at one time covered much of what is now Eastern Europe, Russia, China, South and **Southeast Asia**, and the **Middle East**. Until 1921, Mongolia was a part of China, and only since that time has it been an independent nation. Mongolia has a great many cultural influences from China, Russia, and Tibet.

Shamanism has long been practiced in Mongolia, as it has been among other nomadic peoples in Siberia and in the Arctic regions of the world. Because of this long history of shamanism, known as *tengerism*, Mongolia has a unique masking tradition.

As in other cultures that practice shamanism, shamans, known as *boge*, are able to connect with the spirit world, generally via trance, in order to answer questions, see the future, or provide healing in this world. Mongolian shamans, who could be male or female, once wore (and often still do) a traditional kaftan ornamented with pieces of metal, which symbolize armor; bells, which scare off evil spirits; and circular mirrors, called *toli*, which are used to scare away evil spirits, and shamans use a goatskin drum called a *tuur*, whose sound drives away the evil spirits. These items are often inherited from other shamans. And finally, traditional shamans wear **masks**, although many now wear helmets or other forms of headgear instead, or along with the mask. Masks and headgear are often chosen to represent the animal spirits that are necessary for the shaman's journey. Wearing antlers or eagle feathers may bring swiftness to the shaman's journey, or strength, while wearing owl feathers could give the shaman the wisdom of the owl. The shaman may visit the sky spirits, the ancestors, the spirits of animals, and other beings on their journeys.

As with shamanism in other cultures, in Mongolia, one is chosen by the spirits, often after surviving a serious illness, which is interpreted as spirit possession. If the person overcomes his or her illness, he or she can train with a senior shaman and learn to help others. The primary way to invite the spirits to possess one is to enter a trance. Shamans may use drumming, dance, alcohol, or intoxicating drugs, such as juniper smoke or the muscaria mushroom, to help achieve a trance state. Because the shaman often travels through the spirit world on the back of a deer or other animal, masks representing those animals are often worn. Another common mask is the bear mask, used for the *ominan* ritual that initiates new shamans.

Masks are also worn in Buddhist rituals. The form of **Buddhism** practiced in Mongolia, introduced through Tibet, is known as Lamaism, and includes large festivals involving music, dance, and masks. *Tsam* festivals, for example, are New Year festivals, introduced in the 18th century, during which participants destroy the evil from the previous year. Buddhist monks perform the ceremonies and wear costumes and masks in which they depict Lamaist gods and spirits, as well as shamanistic spirits, many of whom have been absorbed into the Lamaist pantheon. Masks are often grotesque, as with the Citipati, characters wearing skeleton costumes and skull masks who represent the Lords of the Charnel Grounds, or the characters wearing demon masks who banish evil. Another important character is *Yama*, God of the Realm of Death, who wears a buffalo mask and catches souls with a lasso. Masks worn in Mongolian ceremonies have no holes for eyes, so performers must look through the mouth in order to see. Because of their importance as receptacles of spirits, they are treated as sacred objects and kept in monasteries.

While shamanism was largely replaced by Buddhism when it was introduced in the 16th century, it remained a popular religious practice for many, especially in Inner Mongolia. After the Communist Revolution in China, shamanism, as well as other forms of religious practice like Buddhism, was banned. After the ban on religious practice was lifted in 1992, shamanism and Buddhism both began to flourish again. Today, shamans offer their services for pay and provide healings, exorcisms, divi-

Tsam festivals involving masked dances were once held in many Buddhist countries to exorcise evil. This photo is of a shaman dressed as a fire god near Pailingmiao, Inner Mongolia, October 5, 1936. (AP/Wide World Photos)

nation, and good luck spells, but no longer wear masks.

See also Buddhism; China; Masks

Further Reading

Eliade, Mircea. *Shamanism: Archaic Techniques of Ecstasy.* Princeton, NJ: Princeton University Press, 2004.

Heissig, Walther. *The Religions of Mongolia.* Berkeley: University of California Press, 1980.

Sarangerel. *Riding Windhorses: A Journey into the Heart of Mongolian Shamanism.* Rochester, VT: Destiny Books, 2000.

Mug Shot

A mug shot is a photo of a person taken shortly after being arrested for a crime. The first mug shot was taken by 19th-century detective Allan Pinkerton, who used photos of criminals on wanted posters that were distributed throughout the western United States. The term itself derives from the slang term for face, mug.

Today, police and other law enforcement agencies use these photos, known more formally as booking photos, to track the appearance of arrestees and convicts (along with a detailed description of appearance including height, weight, race, hair color, hair style, and identifying features like tattoos or moles). Mug shots of previous arrestees are often shown to witnesses of crimes, who use the photos to identify the possible perpetrators of new crimes, and they are still used on wanted posters today, generally by the FBI. They are also used by the press when someone who already has a mug shot on file is wanted by the

police for a new crime. In addition, in recent years, celebrity mug shots are released to the tabloid media after celebrities have been arrested, and very high profile arrestees' mug shots are also released and publicized by the media. For instance, the mug shots of Hugh Grant (arrested in 1995 for engaging in lewd behavior with a prostitute), James Brown (arrested in 2004 for domestic violence), and O. J. Simpson (arrested in 1994 for two counts of murder) are among the most well-known celebrity mug shots. Mug shots are considered to be public domain.

This mug shot of O. J. Simpson is one of the most famous mug shots in U.S. history. Simpson, an actor and ex-NFL player, was charged with murdering his ex-wife Nicole Brown Simpson and her friend Ronald Goldman. (AP/Wide World Photos)

> I never forget a face, but in your case I'll be glad to make an exception.—*Groucho Marx*

Mug shots are taken by the arresting agency on the same day that a person has been taken into custody. At the same time, fingerprints are taken, and today, electronic copies of both the fingerprints and the mug shots are included in the arrestee's electronic record. Mug shots include only the face (and sometimes neck) of the person, and are generally taken in front and profile views. In the past, arrestees were made to hold a card with their identifying information on it, so that that information would be forever included with the photograph. A collection of mug shots is often referred to as a mug book, when compiled into a book for witnesses to look at, and can be colloquially referred to as a rogue's gallery.

Because mug shots are so firmly associated with the idea of criminality, and because the arrested person often does not look their best in these photos, the mug shot itself can lead the public, the press, and crucially, members of criminal juries, to assume that the presence of the mug shot means that the person is guilty. For that reason, many states have laws that are intended to discourage prosecutors from allowing juries to see the mug shot of the accused.

After O. J. Simpson was arrested for killing two people in 1994, *Time* magazine put a digitally altered mug shot on the cover, which made his face much darker and more sinister than it was in reality. Critics charged that *Time* was emphasizing the fact that Simpson was **African American** and preying on the racial fears of Americans. *Time's* editor later apologized. In a more recent case, Jared Loughner was charged with shooting 20 people outside of an Arizona supermarket and killing 6 in January 2011. His mug shot shows a bald man with wild eyes and a crazy smile on his face, and was released by the press under headlines like "face of evil" or "mad eyes of a killer." Most people who see the photo see a person who seems both insane and defiant, and, most importantly, evil. While at the time of this writing there are no plans to try Loughner in court (he has been declared mentally incompetent to stand trial), if there ever comes a time when he does face a jury for his alleged crimes, the widely disseminated mug shot may be considered prejudicial.

See also Slang Terms

Further Reading

Schlesinger, Arthur M., and S. J. Perelman. *1886 Professional Criminals of America.* New York: Lyons Press, 2000.

Mummery

Mummery is a type of folk performance, found in England, in which disguised actors perform rhymed verse sketches in streets, pubs, and other public places. Mummers' plays are typically performed in conjunction with a handful of holidays, including All Souls' Day, **Halloween**, Easter, and New Year's Day. Also known as guisers, mummers are traditionally men.

Play types include the hero/combat play, in which a hero and his enemy must fight, resulting in the death and cure by a quack doctor of one of the characters; the recruiting sergeant play, in which a farmer joins the army, leaving his beloved at home, who then marries a fool, is hurt, and must be cured by a doctor; and the sword dance play in which a fool is killed with a sword and then cured by again, a quack doctor. The theme of death and a magical cure is common to all of the plays. Characters and play types differ regionally across England, as do costumes. Characters are distinguished by their unusual headgear, which obscures the faces of the performers. Unlike the wearing of **masks**, which represent characters, mummers generally wear hats or hoods that obscure their faces but do not represent the characters they are playing. At other times, the performers wear **blackface** or red makeup. Mummers traditionally performed for money. (Cornwall England has its own celebration, known as Mummer's Day, but once called Darkie Day, in which participants wear blackface or masks as a celebration of winter.)

Mummery is related to the practice of trick-or-treating on Halloween. Mummery—dancing and cavorting in masks, sometimes door to door—dates back to Medieval England but the plays themselves may only be as old as the 18th century. Another related tradition is found during Carnival when masked people went house to house offering to play dice with the residents. Mummery is also related to souling, an English tradition in which the poor, wearing masks, would go door-to-door and beg for soul cakes in exchange for praying for people's dead relatives on All Saints'

Mummers plays and parades feature characters who act out skits and often disguise themselves with masks. In Philadelphia, a Mummers Parade is held each New Year's Day. (iStockPhoto.com)

Day. This is related to guising, in which children or adults dress up in costume and go door to door to ask for food or other treats. And on other saints' days, English villagers might visit a local manor and try to compete with the Lord in a singing competition; if the Lord lost, he had to give the singers food and drink. One reason for the wearing of face-disguising masks or headgear during any of these activities was that it preserved the anonymity of the people, who were, after all, begging. Sometimes, during door-to-door visits, mummers would encourage the residents of the house to guess the visitor's identities. Wandering guisers and mummers have been subject to a number of laws restricting their performances and behavior, because of concerns about criminality associated with the groups.

By the middle of the 20th century, mummers plays and performances had experienced a decline, but since that time have experienced a revival in England, although the performers today are drawn largely from the middle class, while in earlier centuries they were largely working class. Philadelphia also has a tradition of mummery, found in the annual Mummers Parade held each New Year's Day.

See also Blackface; Halloween; Theater

Further Reading

Nicoll, Allardyce. *Masks, Mimes and Miracles: Studies in the Popular Theatre.* New York: Cooper Square Publishers, 1963.

N

Native North America

The indigenous tribes of **North America** have a number of different practices that relate to the face, including tattooing, piercing, and the ritual wearing of **masks**.

A number of Native American tribes, for instance, once used facial tattooing. Tattoos were typically associated with tribal membership, social status, gender, and specific roles. Tattoos were probably brought over with one of the groups of Asian immigrants who came to the Americas from the Bering Strait, possibly between 5000 and 1500 BCE. On the west coast, for example, women often wore chin tattoos that indicated group membership or marital status. Eastern Indians, such as those who lived in Virginia, the Carolinas, and Ontario, often wore tattoos that represented social status, and that were often representational, rather than abstract. Techniques ranged from using sharpened bones or rocks to carve the tattoo into the skin, rubbing into it ash to make a permanent mark, to using porcupine quills dipped in ink, to the use of needles made of fish bones. Some tribes only tattooed women, while others only tattooed men. When men were tattooed, it was often given as a mark of adulthood or to commemorate an important event like a man's first time participating in a battle. Among other tribes, tattooing was used for spiritual, magical, or medicinal purposes.

The Ohlone Indians are a tribe who lived on the Pacific Coast between Baja California and the San Francisco Bay area. Tattooing was mainly done on women, and was mostly decorative. Ohlone tattoos were mostly found on the face but could also extend over the neck, breasts, and shoulders. Some tattoos had magical significance, and some had practical uses. Unlike many tribes, Ohlone tattoos were not just black but incorporated the juice from a number of plants to create green and blue pigment as well. Ohlone women got their tattoos when they reached puberty; they noted the girl's tribal affiliation and lineage, and marked her as marriageable.

The Cree used tattoos as charms to prevent illness, which was seen as being of a spiritual nature; for example an image tattooed on the cheek could protect against toothaches, while a tattoo on the forehead would keep headaches away. Cree women wore chin tattoos made up of black lines reaching from the lower lip to the chin, similar to a number of other groups such as the Ojibwa and Inuit. Tattoo methods included dipping a sharpened stick into pigment and carving the design into the skin, and a later method included the use of steel needles wrapped around the stick.

A number of Native American tribes pierced their noses and ears, and some wore not only earrings, nostril, and septum piercings, but lip plugs in stretched lip holes as well. The Seminoles of Florida,

Tlingit native woman in full potlatch dancing regalia, ca. 1906. Facial tattooing and facial piercing were once very common among a number of Native American tribes, and were especially common among women in the Pacific Northwest. (Library of Congress)

for example, wore multiple holes in their ears, into which they inserted small pieces of wood for decoration. Labrets, or piercings that are attached below the lower lip, are the most common form of facial piercing in Native America, including many Northwest Coast Indians, such as the Tlingit, Haida, Chugach, Inuit, and Tsimshian, among whom the labret was often a sign of status. High status Tlingit girls and women, for example, wore labrets as both decoration and to mark rank. The actual cutting or piercing of the labret was often done during the large community potlatches, and the holes were enlarged over the years. In some groups, men also wore labrets, and in Alaska and further north, men could double labrets, worn on either side of the

mouth. Like women, men received theirs as part of an initiation ritual. Materials for labrets included walrus ivory, abalone shell, bone, obsidian, and wood, and the labrets could be in the form of a long piece or a round stud. Labrets were also once worn by tribes in the Gulf Coast region of Florida and Texas.

Many Native American tribes make and use ceremonial masks, often as a part of **shamanism**. Along the Pacific Northwest coast, masks are carved of wood and sometimes have moveable jaws or other parts. These tribes engage in masked dances to promote hunting, wore masks during important community events like the potlatch, and wore masks during rites of passage and other communal rituals. The Tlingit, for example, made masks representing humans, dead ancestors, animals, and spirits, and utilized the same artistic styles found in other forms of art in the region such as totem poles. Women's masks included labrets. The Haida, another Pacific Northwest tribe, wore masks during rituals to commemorate ancestors, to celebrate cutting a lip for a labret, or to commemorate a new tattoo. The Kwaikutl used masks during initiation rituals. Here, initiates would go into the woods while possessed by cannibalistic spirits, while dancers, wearing the masks of the spirits, performed. Kwaikutl transformation masks were especially elaborate, and were made with movable parts to allow the mouth to open and close. These masks relate to the belief that humans and animals were at one time able to transform themselves into other beings; while wearing the masks, it is believed that that ability still exists, and humans can still transform into ravens or other animals. During these dances, the dancer would open the mouth, revealing another face inside. The Yup'ik of Alaska also used masks during their rituals, especially during the long, dark winters. Carved from wood and elaborately decorated, Yup'ik masks were used in ceremonial dances involving shamans who communicate with the spirits from other worlds.

The Great Lakes and Woodland tribes also use masks in both healing and hunting rituals. The Iroquois are known for their wooden false-face masks, which are a major part of the False Face Society, an organization devoted to healing. The masks represent gods and spirits and are carved from living trees, painted red or black, adorned with horse or buffalo hair, and decorated with a variety of twisted and gruesome facial expressions depending on the function of the particular mask. The spirits instruct the carvers to make their likenesses into masks, and when the mask is fed (often with burning tobacco), the maker will have the ability to cure illness. When wearing the false face, members of the society visit a sick person and perform a ritual involving turtle shell rattles and tobacco intended to cure him. Those who are cured then join the society. In this sense, the society serves as what anthropologists call a cult of affliction. Those who are afflicted with illness, interpreted spiritually, can then join the cult in order to assist others once they are able to overcome their illnesses. Today, some Iroquois make false-face masks to sell to collectors.

The Pueblo tribes of the Southwest also create elaborately decorated masks for use in ceremonial dances. The masks may be in the form of the gods and can be made of leather with fur, feather, and leaves as decorations. Pueblo groups like the Zuni and the Hopi also use masks in rituals to ensure the fertility of the crops; the masks represent the sun, moon, rain, and other natural and spiritual forces, which are called on to bring success to the planting and harvest.

Another important dance tradition involving masks is the Booger Dance of the Eastern Cherokee of North Carolina. This dance involves masked men wearing tattered clothes who engage in crazy behavior such as feigned seizures, mocking the spectators, and harassing the women. Each of the booger dancers performs a solo dance, which represents the crazy names of the boogers—for example, Big Testicles, Black Buttocks, Rusty Anus—with the women present. The masks represent people—either white men or Cherokee—and are made from wood, gourds, and even hornet's nests. They are painted and decorated to create a fantastic appearance and are used to mock the powerful. In recent years, the dances were primarily used to mock whites, but others could be targeted as well. Both the appearance of the mask and the dance itself is aimed to be a stereotypical representation of the worst, funniest, or strangest qualities of the targets. By mocking and humiliating their targets, the Cherokee are able to cope with the stress of oppression, illness, danger, or poverty.

See also Facial Piercing; Facial Tattoos; Inuit; Labrets, Lip Plugs, and Lip Plates; Masks

Further Reading

Mails, Thomas E. *The Great Sioux Piercing Tradition.* Tulsa, OK: Council Oak Books, 2003.

White, James, ed. *Handbook of Indians of Canada*. Published as an Appendix to the Tenth Report of the Geographic Board of Canada, Ottawa, 1913.

Neck Rings

Neck rings are rings worn around the neck of a girl or woman in order to make it appear that her neck has grown longer. Neck rings are worn by the Padaung of Myanmar as well as among the Ndebele of South Africa.

The Padaung, also known as the Kayan Lahwi, are a small tribe from Myanmar (or Burma), well known for the practice of

Elderly Padaung woman with neck rings in the Loikaw region of Myanmar, 1995. Today, most of the Padaung live in refugee camps in Thailand where they are a tourist attraction, thanks to their neck rings. (Eddy Van Ryckeghem/Dreamstime.com)

placing brass or bronze neck coils on the necks of their girls and women. Padaung girls traditionally had the coils wrapped around their necks and their calves from the age of about five. A village shaman originally applies the coils, first massaging the neck and applying protective ointment and cushions. Over the years, longer coils are added, until an adult Padaung woman's neck can carry more than 20 pounds of coils, which compress the collarbone and upper ribs, in turn making the neck appear to measure up to 10 to 15 inches in total length. The women are known as giraffe necks or giraffe-necked women, and are a major draw for tourists. It is often thought that without the support of the coils, the girls' heads would no longer be supported by their bodies, which is not true, although there is some temporary loss of muscle strength in the neck. In fact, the women periodically remove the coils in order to wash their necks. Long necks are a sign of female beauty and highly praised, which is most likely the reason for the wearing of the rings.

The use of neck coils among the Padaung has become controversial in recent years. Many younger women choose not to wear the coils, choosing instead to leave their villages and seek an education, and the Burmese government, too, has discouraged the use of the coils, in an attempt to appear more modern to the outside world. Since the 1980s, due to the oppression of the military government of Myanmar, many Padaung have fled their country and now live in refugee camps in Thailand. There the Thai government has encouraged women to wear the coils in order to bring in tourism. Tourists now flood to the Padaung villages in Thailand in order to take pictures of the women, creating a new form of dependency on tourism, and encouraging girls to wear the coils, not for cultural identity but for financial reasons. Because of travel restrictions placed on them by the Thai government, the Padaung are forced to live in human zoos with very little opportunity for advancement. Since 2008, however, a handful of Padaung refugees have been allowed to leave the country, and resettle in New Zealand.

The other cultural group that has historically worn neck rings (rather than coils) is the Ndebele of South Africa. Traditionally, women wore rings around their necks, arms, and legs. These rings, called *idzila*, were worn by married women, starting at about age 12, and symbolized a woman's faithfulness to her husband. The rings are made of copper or brass and are split in the middle, to allow them to be opened up and placed around the neck or limbs. Traditionally, the rings are worn in odd numbers, and the more rings that are worn, the greater the indication of status and wealth. *See also* Beauty; Gender

Further Reading

Chawanaputorn, D., V. Patanaporn, P. Malikaew, P. Khongkhunthian, and P. A. Reichart. "Facial and Dental Characteristics of Padaung Women (long-Neck Karen) Wearing Brass Neck Coils in Mae Hong Son Province, Thailand." *American Journal of Orthodontics and Dentofacial Orthopedics* 131, no. 5 (2007): 639–45.

New Guinea

New Guinea is a large Melanesian island, made up of the Indonesian provinces of Papua and West Papua on the east, as well as the independent country of Papua New Guinea on the west. Islanders practice a variety of adornments including **facial piercing**, tattooing, and **face painting**, and the wearing of **masks** is common during celebrations. In addition, **head hunting** was once a common practice in New Guinea.

Festivals were and are an important part of life for many highland tribes of Papua New Guinea. Many tribes wear elaborate headdresses made of shells, bark, wood, fiber, feathers—especially the bird of paradise—hair, and bones for ceremonial purposes, as well as face and body paint, in order to placate spirits and ensure prosperity. The types of decorations and paint demonstrated clan membership as well as rank, and at large gatherings such as the annual Mount Hagen Festival, serve to let other tribes know one's tribal affiliation.

Papuan people also pierce their septums and their ears, and men wear horns, bones, pearl shells, feathers, and tusks through the openings. The nose is pierced with a sharp object, such as the sharp end of the sweet potato plant or a cassowary quill. Piercings might first occur as early as 9 years old, or as late as the early 20s. The Kangi tribe, for example, wear bat bones and sweet potatoes in their noses, and other tribes favor pig tusks, which make the men look fierce for warfare. Tribes in other parts of New Guinea favor septum piercings as well, such as the Asmat tribe of West Papua who traditionally wear plugs made of pig bone, and historically, the bone from a human slain in battle, in their septums.

Tattooing is also a traditional Papuan practice, although it has been largely abandoned since the mid-20th century. Women were once tattooed with black geometric

This man from New Guinea wears a septum piercing, which is a traditional form of body modification in Melanesia. Animal bone, tusks, or horns are typical adornments to be worn in the opening. (Bernard Breton/Dreamstime.com)

markings like lines, dots, and stars over their entire bodies including their faces. Girls were tattooed throughout their childhoods; at each stage of their lives, they were tattooed on a different part of their bodies. Tattoo techniques were similar to those in Polynesia in which a wooden stick with one or more thorns sticking out of the end would be tapped into the skin with another stick. Tattooists were generally women and different women tattooed different parts of the body.

Masks are an important part of cultural tradition in New Guinea. They can be carved of soft wood or can be molded from clay. They are decorated with shells, pig tusks, and the feathers of cassowary birds. For instance, the tribes who live in the region of the Sepik River in Papua New Guinea use a variety of masks including dance masks, which are worn to ensure successful hunts, battles, or harvests; ancestral masks, which represent the spirits of the dead; *mwai* masks, which represent mythical relatives of the clan and are used during initiation rituals; and *savi* masks, which depict angry spirits and appear with their tongues sticking out in order to scare the enemies of the clan. Masks may depict important totem animals like pigs, crocodiles, and cassowaries, and may be as high as six meters tall. With the exception of those for dances, masks are not intended to be worn, and thus do not have eyeholes. Yam masks are made of wood or woven grasses and are used to decorate long yams that are highly prized and serve as a basis for the traditional system of exchange. The decorated yams represent ancestors called *nggwal*; the mask allows the spirit to possess the yam. Masks are kept in the village spirit house, and can only be accessed by men. If a mask appears to have lost its power, typically it will be destroyed.

The Tolai people of New Britain, an island in Papua New Guinea's Bismark archipelago, once formed secret societies known as *duk duk* societies that were focused around the spirit Duk Duk. The societies were used to maintain social control, and duk duk rituals were like legal proceedings in the West, with members deciding on the guilt of a member and meting out punishment. During the ceremonies, members wore duk duk masks made from sugar cane or barkcloth and decorated with leaves. Only men could be members of the society and women were punished if they even saw a ceremony or mask.

Head hunting was once a very common practice in New Guinea. Tribes were often at war with each other, and warriors would bring back the heads of the men that they killed. The head was thought to contain the spirit and the power of the dead man; keeping the skull meant that the spirit would help protect the clan. Heads would then be displayed in men's houses, or might be buried underneath them. Decorated skulls were also sometimes hung on skull racks known as *agiba*, which were carved boards painted to resemble anthropomorphic creatures. The racks were painted anew before each new skull was hung on it in order to re-infuse the rack with power. Skull racks, which were owned by the clan, could contain hundreds of skulls. Because head hunting is no longer practiced, trophy heads carved from wood or gourds now substitute for real human heads. They are displayed in men's houses or spirit houses, or used wherever real heads or skulls may once have been used.

See also Face Painting; Facial Tattoos; Masks; Nose Piercing

Further Reading

Kempf, Wolfgang. "The Politics of Incorporation: Masculinity, Spatiality and Modernity among the Ngaing of Papua New Guinea." *Oceania* (September 2002): 56–77.

Kirk, Malcolm. *Man as Art: New Guinea Body Decoration.* London: Thames and Hudson, 1981.

Newton, Douglas. *New Guinea Art in the Collection of the Museum of Primitive Art.* Greenwich, CT: The New York Graphic Society, 1967.

Strathern, Andrew, and Marilyn Strathern. *Self Decoration in Mt. Hagen.* London: Backworth, 1971.

North Africa

North Africa is refers generally to the area north of **Sub-Saharan Africa**, and more specifically to the countries of **Egypt**, Tunisia, Morocco, Libya, Algeria, Sudan, and Western Sahara. Culturally, the region shares a number of features in common with the **Middle East**, due to its close proximity and the influence of Islam, but also shares some features with Sub-Saharan Africa as well. Cultural practices associated with the face include **facial tattooing**, **nose piercing**, the use of **henna**, and **veiling**. For example, while not nearly as common in North Africa as the Middle East, a number of North African nomadic groups, including the Berber, the Beja, and the Bedouin, have worn nose piercings.

Henna is used in this region to decorate the face, the hands, and to color the hair. While it is much more common today to see henna used as an adornment on feet and hands, it was once a used as makeup for the face. For instance, in ancient Egypt,

women used henna paste to stain their lips, and today, henna is often used as a semi-permanent eyeliner. Henna has also been used as a prescription against the **evil eye**. In North African cultures with a belief in the evil eye, a variety of techniques have been developed to either protect against the evil eye, or to undo the damage done when one has been harmed by the evil eye. One of those protective devices has been henna.

Islam arrived in Africa in the mid-seventh century, bringing with it many of the practices associated with the Muslim countries of the north and east. One of those is veiling. While it is not as common in North Africa as in some cultures of the Middle East, nor is it mandated in

Many North African peoples wear veils, thanks to both the Muslim culture and the need to keep the harsh desert sand and sun from one's face. The Tuareg are often known as the "People of the Veil," because of the use of veils by Tuareg men. (Dreamstime.com)

North African countries, veils are still worn in North African countries. In fact, because of the presence of France in Tunisia, Morocco, and Algeria, veiling became associated with national identity and independence, strengthening its presence there. In Egypt, some women wear veils and others do not, and for those who do, it is often more of a fashion statement than a religious statement. In Morocco, some women who choose to veil face discrimination, and in Tunisia, the wearing of veils is largely discouraged by the government. In a handful of nomadic tribes in North Africa, women are not veiled but the men are. The men of the Tuareg tribe, for example, who roam the Saharan desert on camels, wear a blue scarf called the *alasho* over their lower faces to protect them from the desert wind and sand. Young men begin to wear the alasho after initiation, and it is a sign of manhood. The Berbers are another North African tribe in which the men traditionally cover their faces.

Since Christianity arrived in Egypt in the form of Coptic Christianity in the first century, Coptic Christians in Egypt (as well as Ethiopia and Eritrea) have gotten Coptic tattoos to demonstrate their faith. These tattoos are often put on the face; one of the most common is the cross on the forehead. This tattoo is both a visible marker of religious faith and is used to ward off evil.

See also Middle East; Veiling

Further Reading

Shirazi, Faegheh. *The Veil Unveiled: The Hijab in Modern Culture.* Gainesville: University Press of Florida, 2001.

North America

The United States and Canada are both multicultural countries with as many different beliefs and practices regarding the face as there are cultures within them. This section deals with the beliefs and practices associated with the colonists and immigrants who made their homes in North America, rather than the Native North Americans who are treated in a separate section.

The first colonists who arrived in North America in the 16th century were from Spain, but most of the United States and Canada are influenced far more by English beliefs and practices than by Spanish beliefs. For instance, rather than inheriting Spanish beliefs about the evil eye, they instead inherited northern European beliefs suggesting one's facial features indicate one's personal character. While the individual beliefs vary across North America, many regions include their own beliefs about the relationship between, for example, forehead size or chin size and intelligence or temperament.

The United States was founded, in part, on racial inequality and oppression. The English colonists formed the cultural core of the new United States (and Canada), and immediately created a racialized system in which Native Americans were to be used as labor or removed from their land, and Africans were to be used as a labor source. Economics drove the Atlantic slave trade and the demand for land, both of which then shaped the emerging racial picture in the United States. Racial difference justified exploitation, and racial difference was, in the 18th and 19th centuries, justified by newly developing fields in science. Biologists and eugenicists developed new theories to account for racial difference and inferiority, such as the idea that humans were created differently by God; or that humans evolved according to natural selection, but that some humans—the non-white races—degenerated over time. One 19th-century science that justified racial separation was craniometry. Dr. Samuel Morton collected hundreds of skulls to show that different skull sizes could be correlated to different racial groups and to different levels of intelligence. His data were manipulated and even faked to fit his hypothesis, which demonstrated that whites had the largest brains, and thus, the greatest intelligence. Later, a new science was developed that measured facial angles and associated the angles with intelligence, again *proving* by science that whites were superior to non-whites. By the second half of the 19th century, racial inferiority was a given.

Today, **African American**s and other minorities are still judged differently than whites in terms of beauty, intelligence, trustworthiness, and other characteristics, and these racialized judgments often have to do with their faces. American standards of **beauty** still emphasize European traits, such as light skin, petite facial features, and straight hair. Consequently, African Americans have been judged as less beautiful than Europeans, as have Native Americans, Latinos, and Asian Americans. As a result of these beauty standards, skin whitening or bleaching products have long been used by many minorities in order to lighten their skin, and cosmetic surgery has been used to make many minorities' **facial features** seem more European. For instance,

European-style round eyes are considered more attractive than the eye shapes found among many East Asians, making blepharoplasty, a cosmetic surgery procedure to insert a crease into the **epicanthic fold**, a very popular procedure among Asians in the United States today. In addition, **caricatures** that are based on stereotypes of minorities have long been common in this country: images of blacks with big lips and bug eyes, of Asians with thick glasses and buckteeth, and of Native Americans with long hair, big noses, and stoic expressions. These stereotypes were closely related to a popular form of entertainment involving white actors wearing makeup to darken their faces, known as **blackface**.

The United States is a relatively young country, and has long valued youth over age. In addition, the it has inherited a set of gendered beliefs and practices related to beauty from Europe. Because women in particular are valued in part by their appearance, **aging** is seen as negative for American women. Because of this, there is an enormously profitable American market in makeup, pharmaceuticals, and cosmetic surgery, which are intended to reverse or slow down the signs of aging on the face. Cosmetic surgery is not just about youth, however. It is also about women having to meet a relatively narrow standard of beauty. According to the American Society of Aesthetic Plastic Surgery, almost 10 million cosmetic procedures (surgical and nonsurgical) were performed in the United States in 2009, at a cost of $10.5 billion. Of those, women had more than 90 percent of the procedures, or more than 9 million procedures that year, in order to improve the appearance of their eyes, lips, chins, cheeks, foreheads, and other parts of their bodies.

> Age should not have its face lifted, but it should rather teach the world to admire wrinkles as the etchings of experience and the firm line of character.—*Clarence Day*

Makeup, too, is a heavily used commodity in the United States, and is another way that women attempt to meet an impossible (for most) standard of beauty. **Cosmetics** include products to color, shape, and enhance the lips; foundation, concealers, powders, and blush to even out and brighten the skin; and eye liners, eye shadow, mascara, and eyebrow liners to enhance and define the eyes. American women either try to lighten their skin (if naturally dark) or darken their skin, via suntanning and artificial bronzers, if naturally light. They try to make their eyes and lips both appear larger, and their noses appear smaller. They try to make their cheeks and lips appear as if they are flushed, and their eyes appear darker. Finally, American men and women both demand very white teeth, investing in a variety of **teeth whitening** products and procedures. But because of the American diet high in sweeteners, Americans must fight tooth decay as well, and wear braces and require dental surgery in greater numbers than other populations, both in order to fight decay and also to create artificially uniform, straight teeth.

For a country that demands conformity to artificial standards of beauty, there is also a sizeable movement in the United States challenging those same standards, and adopting different ways of presenting one's face to the world. For example, the United States leads the world in the modern primitives movement, which borrows body modification practices from non-Western cultures. **Facial piercings**, including nostril piercings, lip piercings, labrets, **tongue piercing**s, eyebrow piercings, and surface piercings on the cheek, dimples, and forehead, are becoming more common among young Americans who favor a primitive appearance.

As in so many other countries, the United States has its own traditions involving **masks** and masquerades. The two most important are **Mardi Gras** and **Halloween**. Mardi Gras is a celebration in many parts of the world that takes place during the final week before Ash Wednesday. In many countries, the celebrations are referred to as Carnival, but in the United States, most Americans associate Carnival with New Orleans' Mardi Gras. Masking during parades and masquerade parties are among the most important elements of Mardi Gras. In the United States, krewes are social organizations that operate year round, and play a central role in the Mardi Gras festivities by creating Mardi Gras floats and throwing parties. During the parades, krewe members wear masks and throw beads or gifts, and during the balls, society members come wearing formal wear and masks, as in the European masquerade balls. Key colors to be found on Mardi Gras masks are green, gold, and purple, and these are often elaborately decorated with feathers, beads, and jewels.

Halloween is another tradition that derives from Europe, but is well known in

Mardi Gras is a widely celebrated holiday in the southeastern United States. These men are members of the Zulu Rascals Krewe of New Orleans. (AP/Wide World Photos)

the United States and has taken on its own distinctive elements. In the United States, Halloween has lost all of its Roman, Celtic, and Irish elements, and any aspect of religion. Instead, it is a completely secular and commercialized holiday involving store-bought costumes and masks, horror films, haunted houses, trick-or-treating, and Halloween parties. While many of the costumes and masks are still of ghosts, devils, and spirits, keeping with the ancient practices of celebrants attempting to mimic and placate the spirits of the dead, or to frighten them off, Americans have developed entirely new costumes. Scary costumes are still popular, although today witches, vampires, and zombies have over-

taken ghosts and devils, but sexy costumes for girls and women now dominate the market. In addition, every year costumes are introduced to take advantage of popular figures in the media; in 2010, popular costumes were of singer Lady Gaga, reality TV star Snookie, and superheroes like Spiderman.

See also African American; Aging; Beauty; Blackface; Cosmetic Surgery; Halloween; Mardi Gras

Further Reading

Abrahams, Roger D. *Blues for New Orleans: Mardi Gras and America's Creole Soul.* Philadelphia: University of Pennsylvania Press, 2006.

Brunvand, Jan H. *American Folklore: An Encyclopedia*. New York: Garland, 1996.

Davis, Kathy. *Reshaping the Female Body: The Dilemma of Cosmetic Surgery*. London: Routledge, 1995.

DeMello, Margo. *Encyclopedia of Body Adornment*. Westport, CT: Greenwood Press, 2007.

Mullins, Paul R. *Race and Affluence: An Archaeology of African America and Consumer Culture*. New York: Plenum Press, 1999.

Russell, Kathy, Midge Wilson, and Ronald Hall. *The Color Complex: The Politics of Skin Color Among African Americans*. New York: First Anchor Books, 1993.

Santino, Jack. *Halloween and Other Festivals of Death and Life*. Knoxville: University of Tennessee Press, 1994.

Takaki, Ronald. *A Different Mirror: A History of Multicultural America*. Boston: Little, Brown, 1993.

Wykes-Joyce, Max. *Cosmetics and Adornment: Ancient and Contemporary Usage*. New York: Philosophical Library, 1961.

Nose Piercing

Nose piercing refers to the piercing of the skin or cartilage of the nose. Nose piercings are done primarily for decorative reasons.

In a nostril piercing, the most common kind of nose piercing, the wearer has one side of their nostrils pierced. **Jewelry** is generally a ring, which encircles the nostril from the outside to the inside, or a stud or jewel. Nostril piercings were worn by the ancient Hebrews; Genesis 24:47 notes that Abraham's servant gave Rebekah a gift of a nostril ring when he realized she would be the wife of Abraham's son Isaac. The practice of piercing the nostril in order

to wear jewelry probably spread from the **Middle East** to Asia in the 16th century by Mogul emperors. Since that time, it has become extremely common in **India** as both a marker of beauty and social standing for Indian girls. In more recent times, a Hindu girl often has her left nostril pierced on the night before her wedding. Both studs and rings are worn by Indian women, and sometimes the nose jewelry is joined to an earring by a chain. While some women do have both sides of their nose pierced, the left side is far more common, because the left nostril is associated in Indian medicine

Indian woman with a nose piercing, Calcutta. Nose piercing is almost ubiquitous among women and girls in India. It serves as both a marker of beauty and social standing. A Hindu girl often has her left nostril pierced on the night before her wedding. (Dreamstime.com)

with the female reproductive organs. Having one's left nostril pierced is said to make childbirth easier and lessen menstrual pain. Some women in India also pierce their noses to induce a state of submissiveness, by placing the piercing in an acupuncture point. Some Indian tribes also enlarge their nostril piercings, such as the Apa Tani of Northeastern India.

Nostril piercing is also practiced among the nomadic Berber and Beja tribes of Africa, and the Bedouin of the Middle East. In these cases, the size of the ring represents the wealth of the family. As jewelry, it is given by the husband to his wife at the marriage, and is her security if she is divorced. Nose piercing is still popular in Pakistan, India, and Bangladesh. It also remains popular today in Middle Eastern and Arab countries.

In the United States, nostril piercing did not become popular until it was introduced by hippies in the late 1960s and 1970s. Afterward, punks and other youth subcultures in the 1980s and 1990s adopted the nostril piercing, and today it is common with young people from a variety of backgrounds. Next to the earlobe piercing, it is the most popular form of piercing today. While some men have their nostrils pierced, it is far more common among women.

A nasal septum piercing, which is a piercing through the flesh that divides the nostrils, is less common in the West than nostril piercings. Septum piercings were worn by a number of traditional societies, but especially among men in warrior societies, probably because wearing a large bone or horn through the nose makes a person look very fierce. In those cases, the hole in the septum is enlarged to accommodate the bone. The use of septum tusks is common, for example on Borneo, New Guinea, and the Solomon Islands, as well as among some Australian Aboriginal groups. Typically, septums were pierced in these cultures as part of initiation rituals for boys. Ancient Mesoamericans like the Aztecs and the Mayans as well as the Incans also had their septums pierced, and wore elaborate jade and gold jewelry. The Cuna Indians of Panama still wear gold rings in their septums. Septum piercing was popular among some Native American tribes such as the Shawnee and many tribes of the Pacific Northwest Coast. Bones were often worn through the piercings, and sometimes beads were strung through the hole and hung in front of the mouth.

Today, septum piercings are popular among the modern primitives community. Jewelry includes captive bead rings (in which the ring encircles the septum, entering both nostrils, and the bead sits just below the tip of the nose), circular barbells (which look a bit like a horse shoe with both ends of the jewelry emerging from the nostrils), a septum retainer (which is shaped like a staple and can be worn inside the nostrils, in order to hide it from view), and for those who want to make a statement, an artificial tusk (which necessitates a stretched piercing). The septum piercing in which a ring is worn is often referred to as a bull-ring piercing because they are sometimes used to control bulls.

See also Facial Piercing; India; Middle East

Further Reading

Angel, Elayne. *The Piercing Bible: The Definitive Guide to Safe Body Piercing.* Berkeley, CA: Celestial Arts, 2009.

O

Oral Piercing

Oral piercings are piercings in and around the mouth. Inside the mouth, these include **tongue piercings**, tongue web or frenulum piercings, and, rarely, uvula piercings. Piercings inside and outside of the mouth are called lip and labret piercings. Oral piercings are worn in many traditional cultures, and have become common among the modern primitives community in the West.

Lip piercings are the most common form of oral piercing around the world. Lip piercings are either labrets, in which a stud or a spike is attached below the lower lip, or are piercings anywhere around the lip in which a ring encircles the lip. Labrets were commonly worn among a number of Pacific Northwest Native American tribes, as well as ancient Mesoamericans like the Maya and the Aztecs. A number of African tribes also wear lip plates in large stretched lip holes.

In Africa, lips are pierced with a thorn and enlarged by inserting a stalk of grass or other implement into the hole. Larger and larger plugs or plates are inserted as the hole gets bigger, with the sizes of the plates reaching six inches or more. Women who wear lower lip plates often have two or four of their lower teeth removed as well. It has been suggested that women in Africa may have originally worn lip plates in order to deform their faces, to protect them against

Arab slave traders. Whether that is true, the reason given today is that it beautifies a woman. In some tribes, however, men wore lip plates, too.

Labrets have been worn by a number of Native American tribes, including many Northwest Coast Indians, such as the Tlingit, Haida, Chugach, Inuit, and Tsimshian, among whom the labret was often a sign of status. High status Tlingit girls and women, for example, wore labrets as both decoration and to mark rank. In some groups, men also wore labrets, and men could wear single or double labrets, worn on either side of the mouth. (Different historical periods in the northwest are associated with either male or female wear, or both.) Like women, men received theirs as part of an initiation ritual.

Labrets were also commonly worn in pre-Columbian Mesoamerica. Among the ancient Aztecs and Mayans, labret piercings were only worn by elite men, who wore elaborately sculpted and jeweled labrets fashioned from pure gold in the shape of serpents, jaguars, and other animals.

In the West, the most common lip piercing is the ring around the lip. But the most common oral piercing in the West today is probably the tongue piercing. Tongue piercings are worn for decorative purposes and for sexual purposes. Tongues are usually pierced in the center of the tongue, and vertically, with the piercing going through the top and bottom of the tongue. Some people choose to get an off-center piercing, and very rarely is a horizontal, or side-to-side, piercing chosen. Other rare placements include tongue surface piercings. Related piercings include the tongue web piercing, which is a piercing through the frenulum, or piece of tissue that connects the tongue to the bottom of the mouth. The edges of the tongue can be pierced as well with a tongue rim piercing, which generally uses a ring to encircle the edge of the tongue. Jewelry for tongue piercings is usually a barbell.

While tongue piercings for decorative purposes are not common outside of the body modification scene, tongue piercings did play a role in ancient Mesoamerican blood rituals. Maya leaders in particular would cut or pierce a particular part of the body, in order to give a blood sacrifice to the gods. For instance, women were known to pull a thorn-covered rope through a hole in their tongues. Members of a number of Northwest Indian tribes such as the Haida, Kwaikiutul, and Tlingit also pierced their tongues as an offering to the gods. In addition, Fakirs and Sufis from the Middle East practiced tongue piercing as a form of sacrifice and as proof of trance state.

Some people have the tissue, or frenulum, that connects the upper or lower lips to the mouth pierced. Upper lip frenulum piercings, also known as smiley piercings, pierce the webbing underneath the upper lip, and can display the jewelry when the wearer smiles. Lower frenulum piercings, known as frownies, pierce the webbing connecting the lower lip to the inside of the mouth, but the jewelry is not normally visible when the wearer smiles. Jewelry is usually a captive bead ring or a circular barbell.

Finally, some people have the uvula, or the piece of tissue that hangs between the tonsils in the back of the throat, pierced. Because the uvula piercing cannot be seen as decorative (since it can not really be seen), motivations for getting such a piercing are generally much more personal. Because of the difficult to access location, and the tendency of most people to instinctively gag when an object is placed in the back of the throat, it is a difficult piercing to administer or receive. Jewelry is usually a captive bead or other type of ring.

See also Labrets, Lip Plugs, and Lip Plates

Further Reading

Angel, Elayne. *The Piercing Bible: The Definitive Guide to Safe Body Piercing*. Berkeley, CA: Celestial Arts, 2009.

P

Permanent Makeup

Permanent makeup, also known as cosmetic tattooing, refers to the practice of using tattooing to create the permanent effect of makeup on the face. Cosmetic tattooing is used to tattoo beauty marks, to create permanent eyeliner, lipstick, blush, eye shadow, or eyebrows and can be used to correct **scars** or disfigurements.

Permanent makeup is used by women who do not want to have to apply makeup

every day, or who are uncomfortable with the appearance of their eyes or lips without makeup. Some women get cosmetic tattooing if they are allergic to makeup, or have a physical condition that makes the application difficult. Others may have a

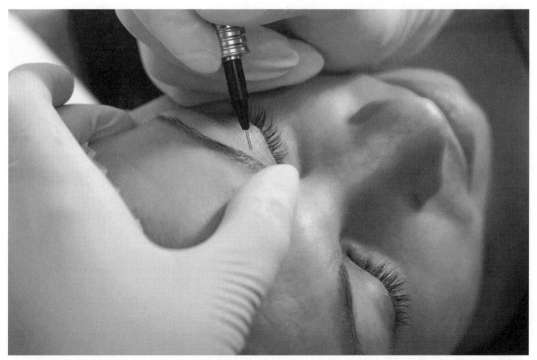

A cosmetologist applies permanent makeup to the eyebrows. Permanent makeup is also known as cosmetic tattooing, and is generally applied by cosmetic technicians rather than tattooists. (Alexey Zarodov/Dreamstime.com)

loss of pigment in their skin or sparse or no eyebrows or eyeliners. In these cases, permanent makeup can create the illusion of facial hair and can correct pigmentation irregularities. Permanent makeup is also used to camouflage scars, birth defects, and other skin disfigurements, and tattooing the scalp is a way to simulate hair when a person suffers from premature hair loss.

The drawbacks to permanent makeup include the fact that colors will fade over time, especially when exposed to sunlight. In addition, makeup trends change, so the shape of one's eyebrows, the color of the lips or eye shadow, or even the thickness and color of eyeliner, may go out of style well before the tattoos have faded.

Permanent makeup is done with a regular tattoo machine, although tattooists rarely offer it as a service. Instead, cosmetic technicians perform the procedures. Most states regulate cosmetic tattooing, but in general, the training—often no more than 40 hours—undertaken by cosmetic tattooists is far less than the training professional tattooists have.

See also Cosmetics

Further Reading

Hill, Pamela, and Judith Culp. *Permanent Makeup: Tips and Techniques.* Clifton Park, NY: Thomson Delmar Learning, 2007.

Physiognomy and Phrenology

Physiognomy and phrenology are two pseudo-sciences that claim that facial features or structures of the head are indica-

tive of personality or character. While both were once widely practiced, and are still used today in activities like face reading, they are, for the most part, not accepted as sciences anymore.

Physiognomy (from the Greek words for judge (gnomon), nature (physis), and law (nomos), refers specifically to discerning the character of a person from their facial features or body parts. It is based on a belief that the internal part of a human corresponds to the external part. It dates back to at least the Babylonians, where it was thought that the face could indicate not just personality or character but could also reveal a person's future, and was widely practiced in ancient Greece. The Babylonians, the Greeks, and the Romans also practiced astrological physiognomy, which suggests that our physical characteristics come to us through the signs of the zodiac or from the planets. Physiognomy was described at length in the fourth century BCE book, *Physignomica*, written by an anonymous philosopher, which covered both humans and animals. The Roman philosopher Polemon wrote *Physiognomy* in the second century, and counseled that it could be used to help pick suitable wives, to pick out slaves, and other practical purposes.

Physiognomy was also practiced in the Arab world. Polemon's *Physiognomy* was translated into Arabic, and Arab philosophers and doctors like Hunayn ibn Ishaq saw the physical features as having a humoural basis, and indicating temperament. In **India**, physiognomy also has a long history, and has primarily been associated with the upper castes, where it was used to help find a proper wife, and to determine

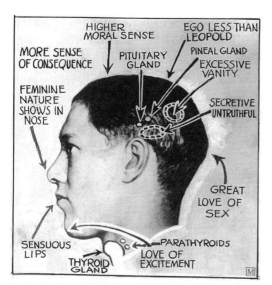

A phrenology diagram of Richard Loeb, one of the slayers of Robert Franks in Chicago. Practitioners of phrenology once believed that the characteristics of a person could be determined based on the shape of the skull, which corresponded to the shape of the brain. (Getty Images)

male succession in the family. Even today, it plays a role in Tibet in determining who will become the Dalai Lama.

Physiognomy also has been practiced in **China** for thousands of years. Chinese **face reading** is the Chinese practice of reading facial features and shapes in order to determine personality and health characteristics. Chinese medical practitioners, for example, have long relied on face reading to help understand the psychological, physical, and emotional state of a patient, while Chinese parents have called in face readers to help them to evaluate potential mates for their sons or daughters. Face reading was also a form of divination, in that a trained reader could see in the face, as with palm reading, the course that a person's life may take. Face reading spread,

starting in the 14th century, to **Japan**, **Korea** and **Southeast Asia** with the spread of Chinese culture.

In Medieval Europe, physiognomy was practiced and taught in universities until the 16th century when it was banned. It was revived in the 17th and 18th centuries when philosophers like Johann Caspar Lavater (who wrote *Physiognomische Fragmente* in the late 18th century) and Thomas Browne once again claimed that one can discern the heart and soul of a person by the appearance of the face. Lavater felt that a person's intellectual capabilities could be seen in the shape and form of the head, while the moral character was shown in the face. Beliefs in physiognomy shaped the new art of **caricatures** and influenced portrait artists, who drew portraits of politicians and other famous people that were intended to call attention not only to prominent physical features, but to the character traits of the subjects. Physiognomy reached its modern height in the 19th century, when a host of writers and thinkers used it in their writings. For example, in Oscar Wilde's *The Picture of Dorian Gray*, the portrait ages and becomes uglier with each of the main character's sins. The 19th century also saw the rise of a form of criminology that was based on physiognomy as well as phrenology, in which criminal tendencies could be seen in the face and/or the shape of the skull.

An Italian doctor named Cesare Lombroso was an advocate of this approach and examined the bodies of hundreds of criminals in the 19th century in order to ascertain the physical characteristics shared by criminals. He found that a number of traits, such as broad noses or fleshy lips, were found more commonly in criminals, and came up with a theory that said that these traits were associated with primitive man. Of course, these traits were also found more commonly among Africans, a group he claimed was inferior to whites. Another 19th-century theorist who subscribed to this theory was Francis Galton, who was also, not coincidentally, a leading eugenicist. In fact, during the Victorian era, the belief that character could be read from facial features was closely linked to the belief that character and racial characteristics are linked. Whether the subjects were Italians, Irish, or African-Americans, the result was the same—those groups deemed racially different were seen by the scientists at the time as racially inferior in character, intelligence, and morality.

As in ancient times, in modern times physiognomy has been used for everything from screening job applicants to finding a spouse to discerning the guilt or innocence of a person. How one reads and interprets facial characteristics differs with each culture, and generally, men's and women's faces are read differently. For instance, in the European tradition, a large nose on a man could signify endurance and strong character, while the same nose on a woman indicates dominance and aggression. In India, on the other hand, one begins interpreting a woman's body and face on her left side, while a man is investigated from his right side.

Physiognomy has also been practiced in the 20th century. For instance, the Nazis used calipers to measure the facial features of Jews and accused Jews; Nazis thought that Jews had larger, more animal-like facial features, so the size of a person's nose, ears, or brow ridge could mean the difference between life and death. More recently, evolutionary psychologist Satoshi Kanazawa has revived Lombroso's theories and claims that criminality really can be detected by facial features. He also suggests that women can tell which men would make good or bad fathers just by looking at them, and that we can tell nice from nasty people by their facial features; high or low levels of testosterone are thought to play a role in both shaping facial features and creating aggression. Other modern physiognomists say that even political orientation can be detected from looking at one's face. Sadly, as in the 19th century, physiognomy continues to be linked to racism, with many proponents continuing to find in non-white facial features evidence of criminality, aggression, or bad character.

On the other hand, a study came out in 2011 that suggested that men with wide faces are more likely to lie and cheat. The authors of the study claimed that wide faces are evolutionarily linked to dominance— a trait seen, for example, in male orangutans, where alpha males have the widest faces. The assumption in humans is that men with wide faces are more dominant and thus have more power, leading them to take advantage of others.

Phrenology is related to physiognomy, but focuses on the shape and size of the skull (and brain), rather than the facial features. It has a much more recent history than physiognomy, dating only to the 18th century when physician Franz Joseph Gall first proposed that different areas of the brain had different functions (a proposal that would be confirmed a century later by Paul Broca). Gall felt that the brain was broken into 27 sections, or what he called organs, each with a function like a tendency toward murder, pride, or religiosity. Further, each organ corresponded with a section of skull, so looking at the bumps on a person's skull (which have conformed to the different organs in the brain) could give insight into that person's abilities and character. In particular, a well-developed area of skull over a certain area of the brain, or organ, would indicate the importance of that area to the subject's temperament. In the 19th century, Orson Squire Fowler was America's leading phrenologist, preaching that one could not only know oneself through phrenology, but that one could improve oneself through the knowledge gained through phrenology, picking one's career, for example, based on this knowledge. Fowler ran a phrenology business in which people would pay to have their heads examined—quite literally—by him. Customers sought advice on finding spouses, making hiring decisions, and other mundane matters. Later, in the 20th century, phrenology was used both to determine criminality in people as well as to justify racial superiority and oppression.

Both phrenology and physiognomy share the basic idea that not only does the outward physical appearance correspond to the internal nature of a person (i.e., you can really read a book by its cover) but that one's nature—personality, temperament, character, intellect, etc.,—is innate. Today, a pseudo-science known as personology has revived the ancient art of physiognomy, and claims that there are 68 facial traits that correspond to personality characteristics.

See also Face Reading

Further Reading

Jenkinson, J. "Face Facts: A History of Physiognomy from Ancient Mesopotamia to the End of the 19th Century." *Journal of Biocommunication* 24, no. 3 (1997): 2–7.

Lombroso, Cesare. *Criminal Man.* Raleigh, NC: Duke University Press, 2006.

Pearl, Sharrona. *About Faces: Physiognomy in Nineteenth Century Britain.* Cambridge, MA: Harvard University Press, 2010.

Porter, Martin. *Windows of the Soul: The Art of Physiognomy in European Culture 1470–1780.* Oxford: Clarendon Press, 2005.

Stern, Madeleine. *Heads and Headlines: The Phrenological Fowlers.* Norman: University of Oklahoma Press, 1971.

Swain, Simon, ed. *Seeing the Face, Seeing the Soul: Polemon's Physiognomy from Classical Antiquity to Medieval Islam.* Oxford: Oxford University Press, 2007.

Zebrowitz, Leslie A. *Reading Faces: Window to the Soul?* Boulder, CO: Westview Press, 1997.

Prosopagnosia

Humans and other animals have brains that are specially designed to perceive the face, and have one part, the fusiform gyrus, that identifies individual faces (as well as other objects). Being able to perceive faces means not only understanding that one is looking at a face; in addition, we are able to identify the individual face that we are looking at. In addition, in order to truly recognize a person, the part of the brain that attaches emotions to images must be working as well. Without the emotional attachment to a face, we are unable to recognize the face. This is known as prosopagnosia, or face blindness.

Prosopagnosia is a brain disorder that is caused by damage to the fusiform gyrus.

It usually occurs after a brain injury, but can possibly be a congenital condition for some people. For instance, it is now thought that some forms of autism may be associated with prosopagnosia. Most people with prosopagnosia can identify other objects; the only thing that they cannot identify is the face (and for many, physical locations as well). For most people, when we look at a face, our minds are able to quickly capture the individual features of the face, and use that information to create a structural model of the face, which is then placed into our memory (and associated with information about that person's identity), and can be called upon when we see that person again. It is this set of abilities that is lacking in people suffering from prosopagnosia.

There is no known cure for the condition, but people living with it learn new techniques to help them to identify the faces of loved ones, which may involve focusing on people's voices, body shapes, or hair or clothing styles. People with this condition often cannot even recognize their own faces. There are different degrees of the disorder, with some sufferers unable to see differences between faces, genders, or ethnicities, while other people may be able to see these differences, but may simply be unable to recall faces or identify individual faces. Those who were born with the condition generally can cope well (and some do not even know that they have it), while those who develop it due to a brain injury often have a much harder time coping with no longer recognizing their loved ones.

Related to prosopagnosia is Capgras syndrome, another condition in which faces are misidentified. The difference is that in Capgras syndrome, a person can distinguish between faces, and can recognize people, but the sufferer has lost the emotional attachment to the face. This results in people who think that their loved ones have been impersonated by aliens or other imposters. Like prosopagnosia, Capgras syndrome usually occurs after a traumatic brain injury.

Among a number of famous people who suffer from prosopagnosia, primatologist Jane Goodall is an interesting case, because she has reported that she has no trouble distinguishing the faces of chimpanzees; only human faces are a problem for her. She has said that because chimpanzees don't change their hairstyles or clothing, she is more easily able to identify and remember them.

See also Face Perception

Further Reading

Harris, A. M., and G. K. Aguirre. "Prosopagnosia." *Current Biology* 17, no. 1 (2007): 7–8.

Sacks, Oliver W. *The Man Who Mistook His Wife for a Hat and Other Clinical Tales.* New York: Summit Books, 1985.

R

Race

Race is a system of inequality based on perceived biological differences between people. In particular, many people hold the belief that a handful of facial features combined with skin color can be used to classify people into different races, or subspecies, which can then be ranked.

While race was once thought to be a scientific classification system, scientists are, for the most part, agreed today that race does not exist in nature. Instead, it is a folk system that came to have scientific merit during an era where racial differences were used to justify colonialism and slavery. Race, however, has no scientific basis.

In humans, skin color is created through a combination of genes and environment. Variation in skin color is determined primarily by the amount of melanin in the skin cells. Melanin protects the skin from too much ultraviolet radiation, so people whose ancestors come from environments with a great deal of sunlight have darker skin than those whose ancestors come from areas with little sunlight.

Facial features, too, evolved in specific populations as a result of the environmental conditions in the region in which those people evolved. For example, longer noses develop in areas where temperatures are cold and dry; shorter noses where temperatures are hot and moist. The **epicanthic fold** of the eye developed in far northern climates like North Asia, North Europe, and the Arctic, because it protects eyes against harsh sunlight and cold.

With European colonialism, beginning in the late 15th century, and the Atlantic slave trade, Europeans began to develop ideas that highlighted the differences between those with different skin colors and facial features, and linked those physical differences to supposed cultural, intellectual, and emotional differences.

The reality is, however, that neither skin color, hair color or type, nor the handful of facial features—nose shape, eye shape, the size or shape of the lips, the width of the cheekbones—designated as racial features are correlated in any way with how smart a person is, whether a person is musically inclined, or even whether a person is athletic. Furthermore, there is no way to say that a whole population of people who share a number of physical characteristics also share intellectual or emotional characteristics. We simply know that there is no connection between external physical traits and other characteristics.

In addition, the traits that are designated as racial are arbitrary. One can just as easily create a classification system based on people who are tall and thin and people who are short and round. Furthermore, racial traits vary independently of other traits; one cannot predict one racial trait by knowing a different trait a person possesses. A person with dark skin can have a broad nose (a combination common in West Africa), a narrow nose (as many East Africans do), or even blond or red hair (seen in Australia and New Guinea). A person with dark skin can have curly hair (as in southern Africa and Australia) or straight hair (as in East India or South America).

Finally, racial classification is arbitrary, and changes from time to time and place to place. In the United States, African Americans have long been defined by hypodescent, or the one drop rule, which states that in the case of mixed race offspring, the child takes the racial classification of the socially subordinate parent, which is why Barack Obama, Tiger Woods, and Halle Barry are all considered to be black, even though all have parents from different backgrounds.

With the spread of European colonialism starting in the 15th century, came the idea that populations of people are fundamentally different from each other, and this difference implies inferiority and superiority. The rise of the African slave trade created a further incentive to categorize and rank human groups in this way to justify the barbarous treatment of African slaves. A set of folk beliefs took hold that linked inherited physical differences between groups to inherited intellectual, behavioral, and moral qualities. And later, at the end of the 19th century, the notion of race was incorporated by biologists and eugenicists, who made it scientific. This led to the rise of the race purity movements in the United States and Germany and ultimately enabled the Holocaust.

Today, racial differences are still important around the world, but especially in those regions of the world that once experienced either European colonialism or slavery. People with light skin are almost universally preferred over those with dark skin, even in countries where everyone has darker skin. European facial features, too, are considered more attractive, especially for women, than African and Asian facial features, in many places. Due to these preferences, which are the legacy of slavery and colonialism, there has long been a thriving market in skin whitening products, which are aimed at Africans and Asians, and the last few years have seen a rise in the prevalence of **cosmetic surgery** procedures aimed at making Asian or African faces seem more European, by reducing the size of the nose or changing the shape of the eyes.

See also African American; Cosmetic Surgery; Skin Colors and Disorders

Further Reading

Gallagher, Charles A. *Rethinking the Color Line.* Boston: McGraw-Hill, 2009.

Gould, Stephen J. *The Mismeasure of Man.* New York: W. W. Norton, 2008.

Gregory, Steven, and Roger Sanjek. *Race.* New Brunswick, NJ: Rutgers University Press, 1994.

Takaki, Ronald. *A Different Mirror: A History of Multicultural America.* Boston: Little, Brown, 1993.

Religious Beliefs

Religious beliefs about the face generally have to do with representations of gods, folk beliefs about the face that may derive from religious beliefs, and religious uses of or practices regarding the face.

It should not surprise us that the face and the head are central in many religions, because it is the major way in which humans identify and communicate with each other, and because in some cultures, the head is the center of a person's spiritual power. For example, in many Polynesian cultures, there is a belief in mana, which is a diffuse, impersonal force that lends supernatural power to things in which it is located: people, objects, plants, animals. It was believed that chiefs and nobles had more mana than ordinary people did, and it was primarily located in their heads. This is one reason for the large statues known as moia found on **Easter Island**, and for the practice of collecting the preserved heads of the chiefs among the Maori of New Zealand.

In Hinduism, too, the head is of spiritual importance. Men and women often wear a tilaka in the middle of their forehead, which signifies the third eye or the sixth chakra, known as Ajna. In Hinduism, the seven **chakras** refer to seven energy centers in the body, and the sixth chakra is where the body's latent or kundalini energy leaves the body. The red bindi worn on that spot retains that energy, increases concentration, and protects against bad luck. Today it is still common for priests to mark visitors to a Hindu temple with a mark on their forehead made of red powder.

> The face is the soul of the body.—
> *Ludwig Wittgenstein*

Some religions portray their gods or spirits in art, in religious icons, or in masks. Other religions do not allow representations of their gods. The earliest such representations may include the 25,000 year old *Venus of Brassempouy*, who may be a woman but perhaps may be a goddess. The cultures of the ancient classical world, like Egypt, Greece, and Rome, did represent their gods and goddesses in sculpture, painting, and other forms of art. Egyptians used a stylistic method of representation while Greek and Roman artists used a more naturalistic form of representation, although they did portray idealized images, rather than truly real people.

After the fall of the Roman Empire and the rise of Christianity in the West, Medieval European art emphasized biblical characters, representing Jesus, Mary, and other church leaders, using realistic styles, but also standardized forms of representation (i.e., a beard and long hair for Jesus), since there is no real way to know what Jesus, Mary, or any other biblical figure looked like. Many believers feel that we do in fact have a realistic likeness of Jesus. The **Shroud of Turin** is one of a number of images that were thought to be created miraculously by the hand of God, and is understood by the faithful to be a perfect likeness of the man himself. These images, and the representations of those images, are known as the Holy Face of Jesus, and collectively are worshipped by many Catholics.

Eastern religions like Buddhism and Hinduism also represent deities in art. For hundreds of years, there had been no images of the Buddha in art, but about 600 years after his death, those images began to appear, alongside sculptures and paintings of other Buddha figures. While no one knew what Buddha looked like, the images eventually became standardized and

This image of Jesus Christ shows his face as it is typically represented in religious art in the West—with light skin, long dark hair and a full beard, a crown of thorns, and blood dripping down his forehead. This statue is found in a Roman Catholic Church in Macau. (Jeremy Wee/Dreamstime.com)

and often grotesque, especially when representing demons and other evil spirits.

How the face is seen in religion differs greatly based on the religious tradition. In the Judeo-Christian-Islamic tradition, the term face carries a variety of meanings. A number of biblical references to the face mean the face of God, or the presence of God. Seeking God's face, for example, means to seek His presence or sometimes His forgiveness. On the other hand, when God hides His face, He literally turns His back on His followers, because of their sins, and no longer protects them. For the ancient Jews as well as other people in the **Middle East**, the face is also associated with intimacy and privacy. This explains why, even though numerous biblical passages encourage the faithful to seek God's face (i.e., presence), no one is actually allowed to truly see God's face. This is also one reason why **veiling** is so important in Middle Eastern cultures, because covering one's face both protects one's privacy and can also indicate humility.

Veiling is widely practiced by Muslim women, but veils can also be worn by Jewish or Christian women. Today, it remains Jewish practice for married women to cover their hair while in the synagogue, and many Orthodox women continue to cover their hair in public with a scarf or a wig; some have even taken the practice of veiling their faces in public as well. And while it is rare for Christian women to cover their heads during prayer, some Catholics still practice this, as do many nuns, and groups like the Amish and the Mennonites still require the wearing of head coverings for their women. And of course, in Islam, women are expected to cover their faces

are now easily recognizable. Hindu gods, on the other hand, have long been represented artistically, whether in human or animal form. Islam will not show the face of the prophet Mohammed in art. Sunni Muslims do not allow visual depictions of the prophet at all; other traditions allow for his depiction, as long as his face is concealed.

Gods are represented in other cultures. For instance, masks are used to represent the faces of gods, spirits, ancestors, and other deities in Africa, **Southeast Asia**, and in pre-Columbian Central and **South America**. In these areas, faces are highly stylized

and hair. In Muslim countries, women may cover their faces, a portion of their face, their hair, or, in the most extreme cases, their entire bodies. Veils can cover the entire face; they can cover the entire body, as in the burqa worn in Afghanistan and originating in Pakistan; or they can be worn around the head and under the chin, as in the hijab, the most popular form of head covering.

Christian traditions have often focused on the face or the head, perhaps because in many cultures and religions, the head is the seat of spiritual energy. For instance, **baptism** is a Christian ritual in which an infant or adult is sprinkled with or immersed in water; generally the head is the focus of the ritual, borrowed from other purification rituals, rather than the full body. Ash Wednesday, or the first Day of Lent, is also marked with a ritual involving the head; on this day, the faithful are anointed on their foreheads with the sign of the cross made of ashes mixed with oil and blessed to show the repentance of their sins.

Many religious traditions involve the wearing of masks that represent gods, spirits, animals, and other sacred beings. These are often associated with **shamanism**, a form of religious belief and practice in which part-time religious intermediaries known as shamans travel to the spirit world in order to provide healing and other services to community members. Shamanistic traditions have been found in Siberia, Mongolia, Europe, Africa, Central Asia, and **Native North America**, and often involve the wearing of masks, in which the masks represent the spirit that the shaman is calling. By wearing the mask, the shaman calls forth the power of the spirit, who then provides protection, good luck, or healing to the wearer or the person on whose behalf the shaman is acting. The masks of the Pacific Northwest, **Tibet and Nepal**, **Mongolia**, **Sub-Saharan Africa**, **Korea**, **China**, and Siberia are not only still used in shamanistic rituals, but many have become sought-after collectors' items for art collectors in the West.

Masks also play a role in religious rituals in cultures without shamanism. **India**, Mongolia, Tibet, and Nepal, for example, all have well-developed masking traditions in which the gods of the Buddhist and Hindu religions are depicted in dances and plays. Buddhist monks, for example, put on elaborate performances as part of annual festivals in which important heroic and religious stories are acted out by masked dancers. Hindu epics, too, are performed by actors wearing masks representing Hindu gods, demons, or heroes.

Finally, one religious and folk belief that spans a number of religions in both the East and the West is the belief in the **evil eye**. The evil eye is a belief that certain individuals can cause illness, misfortune, and even death to others through a look that is often unintentional. The evil eye belief probably derives from Indo-European, Mediterranean, and Middle Eastern cultures; its roots go back to the ancient civilizations of those regions. In Judaism, Christianity, and Islam, as in other traditions, those who are jealous or covetous possess the evil eye. Magico-religious remedies and preventatives for the evil eye abound in these traditions and include: placing a red thread around the wrist of a child as protection (Jews); saying inshallah, which means if God wills it or God willing (Muslims) after receiving a compliment; or if someone admires a child, the adult must touch the child and invoke God's protection (Christians). These beliefs, or the use of eyes as protective amulets, predate even the ancient Hebrews and were found in other cultures of the Middle East. For instance, the Eye of Horus served as a protection against evil in ancient Egypt, and eyes were used on amulets in Mesopotamia. Ancient Egyptians used **kohl** to draw lines around their eyes to protect themselves, and in modern India, women do as well, both to protect themselves, and to ensure that they do not inflict harm on others. Using mirrors to reflect the evil eye back on the perpetrator, is also a common strategy, leading to the development of small mirror charms worn on people or kept in houses or cars; for example, in India and in the Middle East, it is still common to find clothing, scarves, and decorative textiles made from mirrors crocheted into cloth.

See also Ash Wednesday; Baptism; Buddhism; Christianity; Evil Eye; India; Judaism; Middle East

Further Reading

Bailey, David A., and Gilane Tawadros, eds. *Veil: Veiling, Representation, and Contemporary Art.* Cambridge, MA: Massachusetts Institute of Technology Press, 2003.

Baskin, Judith. *Jewish Women in Historical Perspective.* Detroit: Wayne State University Press, 1991.

Dundes, Alan. *The Evil Eye: A Folklore Casebook.* Garland Folklore Casebooks 2. New York: Garland, 1981.

Editors of *Hinduism Today* Magazine. *What Is Hinduism?: Modern Adventures into a Profound Global Faith.* Kapaa, HI: Himalayan Academy, 2007.

Eliade, Mircea. *Shamanism: Archaic Techniques of Ecstasy.* Princeton, NJ: Princeton University Press, 2004.

Grabar, Andre. *Christian Iconography: A Study of Its Origins.* Princeton, NJ: Princeton University Press, 1968.

Heissig, Walther. *The Religions of Mongolia.* Berkeley: University of California Press, 1980.

Lewis, I. M. *Ecstatic Religion: An Anthropological Study of Spirit Possession and Shamanism.* Harmondsworth, England: Penguin Books, 1971.

McArthur, Meher. *Reading Buddhist Art: An Illustrated Guide to Buddhist Signs and Symbols.* London: Thames and Hudson, 2004.

Russia and Siberia

Russian prisoners have been practicing tattooing for at least 150 years; some of these tattoos are done on the face and are very distinctive. In addition, Siberia, the eastern region of Russia, still has many nomadic groups practicing **shamanism**. In fact, some of the first anthropological accounts of shamanism come from groups still living in Siberia.

Starting in the 19th century, tattooing became a common practice among prisoners in Russia, as a way to mark individual status and group membership. Vagrants, for example, were the highest class of prisoners in the Russian prison system, and developed a specific set of tattoo symbols for themselves. These 19th-century convicts served as the model for modern Russian convicts and outlaws. Tattoos for convicts in Russia today serve many of the same purposes as vagrant tattoos: they uphold traditions belonging to the group, signify group solidarity, and utilize a language kept secret from the authorities. Tattoos today, as in the past, are also given as a rite of passage for new convicts and serve as a calling card for other convicts. Today, tattoos are so common in Russian prisons that 75 percent to 85 percent of all Russian convicts are tattooed, and many are tattooed on the face. As with tattoos in prisons around the world, prison tattoos were once primarily handpicked, but are now often made with homemade machines made from electric razor parts, using ink from pens or even made from ashes mixed with water or urine.

Symbols used by Russian prisoners, like prison tattoos around the world, signify the convict's position vis-à-vis the criminal justice system, and often express his or her contempt for the system. In addition, tattoos symbolize the convict's wish for freedom and suffering under intense confinement. Tattooing oneself on the face, as with prison tattooing in other cultures, is the prisoner's way of telling other prisoners, the prison guards, and the world that they are permanent gangsters. **Facial tattoos** can include barbed wire—tattooed across the forehead it signifies a life sentence—words, skulls, stars, Nazi and white supremacist imagery, and crosses and other religious imagery. Other prisoners may also forcibly tattoo the word slave or other derogatory words on one's face as punishment; child molesters, for example, can be subject to this. Prisoners like this are called downcasts, and are often used sexually by other inmates.

Siberia is known as the location where Russian prisoners have long been sent for confinement and hard labor. It's also a region of the world long populated by nomadic herders, many of whom practice shamanism, a form of religious belief and practice in which part-time religious specialists travel to the spirit world in order to provide healing and other services to community members. Shamanistic traditions have been found in the Siberian cultures of the Soyot, Nganasan, Yakuts, Selkups, Nenets, Enets, and the Ket. While these cultures all have different practices, there are a number of features that are shared by many of them, including imitating a focus on animal spirits (like deer, bears, or birds), who act as helping spirits for the shaman, singing or mimicking the calls of animal spirits; the use of skeleton symbolism; and the wearing of **masks** and/or headdresses. Shamans here, as in other places, are called to shamanism by the spirits, who possess them while they are in a trance state; they do not choose their calling themselves, and it is believed that the calling is hereditary, and is passed down from ancestors who were shamans. Siberian shamans initially become sick; this sickness is interpreted as a sign that the spirits have called, and the shaman has a gift. The shaman then undergoes an initiation period during which he gathers his helping spirits. They are also given an extra soul that helps them to find spirit helpers and protects them on their spirit journeys. Finally, the shaman learns to control the spirits. Shamans in Siberia provide healing, divination, protection, and hunting magic to individuals but also keep the entire community in balance with the land and with the spirits.

Siberian shamans often wear a mask (or sometimes a handkerchief over the eyes), as well as a special cap during their rituals. Caps are made with animal skins, and may be decorated with feathers, buttons, and other items. Like Mongolian shamans, Siberian shamans also wear ritual coats, made of animal skins, which are decorated with metal items. One shaman's coat can have hundreds of copper or iron pendants, which represent animal spirits and serve as protection. Masks can be made out of animal skin, wood, or metal, and may be decorated with fur or feathers; they generally represent the shaman's primary animal spirit. It was believed that the mask itself is imbued with spirit, and it is that spirit that helps the shaman to go into a trance. Some masks have no holes for the eyes or the ears; this blocks out the outer world and helps the shaman better enter the trance state. Siberian shamans were buried with a custom death mask. These masks were created in the likeness of the shaman, and had the eyeholes blocked with bone, to keep the shaman's spirit (or other spirits) from returning to and invading the body.

Shamanism was banned by the Russian government in 1931, although it continued to be practiced. Today, while it is no longer prohibited, it is much less commonly practiced than it was in the past.

See also Facial Tattoos; Masks; Shamanism

Further Reading

Baldaev, Danzig, Sergei Vasiliev, and Alexei Plutser-Sarno. *Russian Criminal Tattoo Encyclopaedia.* London: Steidl Publishing, 2003.

Eliade, Mircea. *Shamanism: Archaic Techniques of Ecstasy.* Princeton, NJ: Princeton University Press, 2004.

Lambert, Alix. *Russian Prison Tattoos: Codes of Authority, Domination, and Struggle.* Atglen, PA: Schiffer Publishing, 2003.

Schrader, Abby M. "Branding the Other/Tattooing the Self: Bodily Inscription among Convicts in Russia and the Soviet Union." In *Written on the Body: The Tattoo in European and American History*, edited by Jane Caplan, 174–92. Princeton, NJ: Princeton University Press, 2000.

Siikala, A.L. *The Rite Technique of the Siberian Shaman.* Helsinki: FF Communications, 1978.

S

Scarification

In many African, Australian, and Melanesian cultures, smooth skin is seen as naked and unadorned. In these cultures, skin that has texture and design on it is much preferred. Scarification refers to the practice of slicing the skin in order to create **scars**, which are typically joined together into decorative patterns. Scarification can be done on both the face and the body.

Also known as cicatrisation, scarification is an analogous practice to tattooing, in that both mark individuals with important social information such as rank, genealogy, marital status, social status, and tribal or clan membership, and both are often performed as part of a rite of passage, generally enabling the wearer to move from youth into adulthood. Because both practices are painful, wearing a tattoo or scar is a sign of one's strength and bravery, usually for a man, but sometimes also for women. Finally, both scarification and tattooing are often seen as a form of beautification, without which the individual would be less attractive. Tattooing, however, tends to be practiced by people with relatively light skin, through which the tattoos can show, while scarification, tends to be practiced by people with darker skin.

There are a number of different techniques used to create scars. Some techniques involve cutting the skin deeply, either in long lines or short ones, to cre-

ate a scar. Indented scars are produced by slicing out a piece of skin, usually in a line. Others involve first pulling up a small amount of skin with a hook, and slicing off a piece of the elevated skin. This creates a raised welt, and, when multiple pieces of skin are raised and cut, creates an overall design that can be quite stunning. Another method is to cut the skin, and afterward insert mud or ash in the cuts, which can leave the scars colored, or can leave raised bumps, known as keloids.

In many cultures, especially in Africa, women are more commonly scarred and wear more elaborate designs than men. Often, women's scars are seen as an indication that she can withstand the pain of childbearing, making her well suited to be a wife. Girls are generally first scarred at puberty, and the face, the shoulders, the chest, and the abdomen are the most common locations.

Tribes in the Democratic Republic of the Congo, Nigeria, Sudan, the Ivory Coast, and Ethiopia use scarification, which has long been considered beautiful for women. For these tribes and other African groups, girls receive scars at puberty to demonstrate that they are ready to be married, and that they are strong enough to bear children. Of equal importance, the scars are seen as beautiful to touch and to look at. Children in the Fulani tribe of West Africa, for example, receive scars across their nose and forehead as a sign of beauty.

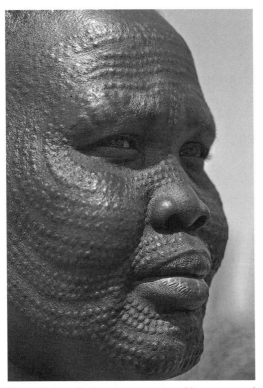

A southern Sudanese woman with a scarred face waits for food distribution by the World Food Programme (WFP) in Juba on January 6, 2011. Scarification is used throughout Africa as a form of adornment for women. (AFP/Getty Images)

Men in Africa often wear scars received during initiation, or sometimes after having killed an enemy, as a sign of bravery. Among the Barabaig of Tanzania, boys' heads are cut so deeply that the injuries sometimes show up on the skulls. Because scars are considered attractive, they are often cut in such a way as to emphasize the contour of the face or body. The Tiv of Nigeria, for instance, mark along the cheekbones with long, linear scars as an emphasis to the cheekbones.

Among the Nuba of southern Sudan, girls undergo scarification, usually from their breasts to their navel, a number of times during her life, in order to mark important events such as first menstruation or the birth of her first child, after which her back, legs, arms, and neck are scarred. Nuba men wear scars on their torsos and arms, usually as part of an initiation ritual. Men of the Dinka tribe of the south also scar themselves, generally on the forehead during a boy's rite of passage into adulthood.

The Tabwa, who live in Southwestern Congo and Northeastern Zambia, called their practice *kulemba*, which means to inscribe or beautify a blank surface. Women were once scarred on the cheeks and forehead plus back and shoulders, but today scars are limited to small lines on the forehead, nose, and cheeks. As with most African tribes, girls without scars were not considered marriageable. Tebwa men also practiced facial scarification, with a pattern known as face of the cross in which tiny dots were patterned into lines that made up a cross on the face.

The Ga'anda of northern Nigeria also use scarification, known as *hleeta*, to make girls marriageable. The process begins at age 5 or 6, with the final phase beginning at age 15 or 16 just before marriage, once she has been engaged. Girls are scarred on their forehead, shoulders, arms, belly, legs, back of neck, back, and buttocks, with an elaborate pattern of dots that form lines, curves, and diamonds. Forehead scars are given when the girl's future husband pays her parents her bride-price. The Ga'anda, like a number of other African tribes, are seeing scarification disappear due to disapproval from authorities and a declining interest in arranged marriages.

The Tiv of Nigeria view scarification as purely decorative. Men are scarred on the chest, face, arms, and legs. Scars can be geometric designs of animal representations. The Baule of Nigeria also practice scarification, known as *ngole*, as a way of beautifying themselves and pleasing others. In addition, scarification both orients an individual within society by marking tribal, clan, lineage, or other membership, and also denotes social information like marriageability or success in hunting. Finally, some scars were used to protect against magic and disease in that a small amount of poison was injected directly into the scar, known as a kanga mark. The Baule borrowed the Senofo pattern of lines radiating from the mouth, to protect young children from harm.

In Australia, scarring was once commonly practiced among a number of groups, but is very infrequent today. As with African scarification, Australian scars indicate strength, courage, endurance, social status, individual identity, and beauty. Both men and women were scarred, generally with lines, women between the breasts, men on the shoulders, chest, and belly, and both on the face. It was traditional that one needed to be scarred in order to engage in reciprocal trade relations, in order to marry, and in order to participate in rituals or didgeridoo playing. Non-scarred people were seen as unbranded, and if a person was unbranded, they were not allowed to do anything socially. Scarification began when a man or woman was around 16 or 17, and was carried out with a sharpened rock, followed by burnt wood in the wounds to stop the bleeding.

Some Native American tribes also once practiced scarification. For instance, Cree men once scarred their faces as signs of valor. They wore vertical lines on the forehead, the nose, the cheeks, and the chin. It also has a history in Melanesia; scarification was once commonly practiced in Papua New Guinea (but not on the face), and facial scarification was common in the Solomon Islands. Known as *segesege*, both boys and girls were scarred as part of their initiations into adulthood; for girls, this also involved full-body tattooing. In more recent years, however, scarification has been done on younger children, perhaps because it was easier to convince younger children to have the procedure performed on them. Having one's children scarred as part of an elaborate ceremony in which the parents give a variety of gifts to others both beautifies the children and raises the parents' status in the community.

In the modern primitives and body modification communities, scarification is also practiced, often as a rite of passage, although rarely as elaborately as in Africa. Typically in the West, scarification is created by cutting lines in the skin, and sometimes removing narrow strips of flesh, rather than cutting small raised welts to form an overall pattern. However, raised scars are still typically the goal.

See also Australia and New Zealand; Scars; Sub-Saharan Africa

Further Reading

Bohannon, Paul. "Beauty and Scarification amongst the Tiv." *Man* 56, no. 129 (1965): 117–12.

Camphausen, Rufus C. *Return of the Tribal: A Celebration of Body Adornment: Piercing, Tattooing, Scarification, Body Painting.* Rochester, VT: Park Street Press, 1997.

Drewal, Henry John, "Beauty and Being: Aesthetics and Ontology in Yoruba Body Art." In *Marks of Civilization: Artistic Transformations of the Human Body*, edited by Arnold Rubin, 83–96. Los Angeles: Museum of Cultural History, University of California, 1998.

Gay, Kathlyn. *Body Marks: Tattooing, Piercing, and Scarification.* New York: Millbrook Press, 2002.

Herle, Anita. *Pacific Art: Persistence, Change, and Meaning.* Honolulu: University of Hawaii Press, 2002.

Vogel, S. "Baule Scarification: The Mark of Civilization." In *Marks of Civilization,* edited by Arnold Rubin, 97–103. Los Angeles: Museum of Cultural History, UCLA, 1988.

Scars

Scars refer to areas of hardened tissue that form on the skin after an injury. They are generally formed after an accidental injury, but can be intentionally created, via scarification or other forms of body modification like cutting. They can be raised (hypertrophic) or sunken (atrophic).

Humans scar more than do other animals, as a consequence of humans' relatively quick healing process. Some scientists think that this ability may have evolved among humans as our intelligence grew; scars may be a visible reminder of dangerous mistakes, which help us to learn to not repeat those errors. Another hypothesis suggests that heavy scarring may be evolutionarily adaptive for men. Scars are often seen as masculine, and are associated with aggression, bravery, and injury. A recent study done in England, for example, found that women seeking short term sexual relationships were attracted to men with facial scars. It may be that our capacity to scar may be a form of sexual selection.

Having a scar on the face can cause a person considerable anxiety and even shame, especially for women for whom scars are often seen as ugly and masculine. In addition, scars received because of a traumatic injury are visible reminders to the wearer of that injury, and for that reason, may be especially traumatizing. Because of the concern that many people have about visible scars, there are a number of treatments available to reduce the appearance of scarring, such as chemical peels, injections with collagen or other fillers, laser treatments, and dermabrasion. Some scars can even be removed via surgery.

Because of the negative perception of scars, evil characters in literature and film are often marked with scars as a way visually to highlight their character. Examples include Tony Montana in *Scarface*, Scar in *The Lion King*, Darth Vader (under his costume) in *Star Wars*, and, especially, Freddy Krueger in *A Nightmare on Elm Street*. On the other hand, some film characters have scars as badges of honor and courage, such as Humphrey Bogart in *Casablanca* and Harry Potter in the Harry Potter books and films.

Scars are not always seen negatively, however. In the early 20th century, receiving scars during dueling was popular among upper-class Austrian and German students. Dueling was an important social practice and young men who engaged in duels, and received a scar, wore the scar as a badge of courage, as well as a mark of upper-class status and honor. To be invited to duel meant that one was included in the social circle. Participants protected their eyes and throat from injury, but intentionally left the rest of their face open to injury. Some men even poured wine in the wounds to emphasize them. Because of the significance of the scar, some men cut themselves on the face with a razor in order to create their own scars. On the other hand, Jews were often excluded from these duels and Jewish men who were found to create their own scars (by approaching doctors or even barbers) would be shunned. Among the Yanomamo tribe of Brazil, scars that result from warfare are accentuated via **face painting** in order to highlight the warrior's bravery. For both the German students and the Yanomamo warriors, having facial scars meant being socially acceptable and sexually attractive.

Some cultures create scars intentionally. **Scarification** refers to the practice of slicing the skin in order to create scars, which are typically joined together into decorative patterns. It is found primarily in areas with people with high amounts of melanin on their skin, like Africa, Australia, and New Guinea. In these regions, scarification is often done as a rite of passage, and as a form of beautification. Scarification is done either by deeply cutting the skin to create a scar, slicing out a piece of skin, or pulling up skin with a hook and slicing off the exposed skin. Another method is to cut the skin, and afterward insert mud or ash in the cuts, which can leave the scars colored, or can leave raised bumps, known as keloids.

See also Scarification

Further Reading

Gilman, Sander L. *Jewish Frontiers: Essays on Bodies, Histories, and Identities.* New York: Palgrave Macmillan, 2003.

Sex and Sexuality

The human face differs between men and women, and faces play a role in the sexual practices and sexuality of people around the world.

In the human species, men's and women's faces differ due to sexual selection. According to this theory, males and females of a species develop different traits that help them to become more reproductively successful. These traits develop through competition for mates—generally by males for females. In the human face, sexual selection has resulted in men who have bigger heads, bigger jaws, bigger noses, and a bigger brow ridge than women, and women who have smaller features. In addition, due to hormones, women have fuller lips, lighter skin, and more fat on the cheeks, and men have thicker eyebrows and facial hair. In women, these secondary sex characteristics, which appear after puberty, decline after menopause.

Men and women, according to evolutionary psychology, use these obvious sexual markers to identify potential sexual mates. Men who don't have strong jaws, thick eyebrows, or other markers of masculinity should have a harder time finding mates, while women with more masculine facial features should as well, thus the demand for cosmetics and cosmetic surgery to artificially create these features where they are lacking.

A woman knows the face of the man she loves as a sailor knows the open sea.—*Honore de Balzac*

It has long been assumed that men use their eyes in identifying potential sexual partners, and in enjoying sex, more than women do. After all, men seem to favor young and beautiful women while women often pick partners who are less objectively or subjectively attractive. In addition, men have long been avid consumers of pornography. However, at least one recent study has challenged this assumption by showing that women showed similar brain activity to men when viewing erotic imagery. It may well be that men's attraction to pornography is more cultural than it is biological, and in fact, in recent years, women's consumption of pornography in the United States has increased, as pornography has moved from the public space of the movie theater into the privacy of the home. Still, it is clear that women continue to put a great deal of attention into exaggerating (or creating) the facial markers associated with youth and fertility, by making their eyes appear larger and darker, their lips appear redder and fuller, their cheeks appear flushed, their noses smaller, and eliminating their facial hair.

Because of the importance of the face to one's gender and sexual identity, transgendered people must spend a great deal of effort to make sure that their faces match their sexual and gender identities. Transgendered people are men or women who adopt the behaviors, roles, and appearances not typically associated with the gender roles assigned to their birth sex. Transgendered people include transvestites who cross-dress, intersex people, those who choose to be androgynous in appearance and/or behavior, and biological men or women who feel that they are in the wrong body; this is known

Thailand has the world's largest known community of transgendered people, known as *kathoey*, or "lady boys." Yonlada Krerkkong Suanyot, shown here, has a face that looks as feminine as many women's faces, thanks to surgery and other cosmetic procedures, hormones, and makeup. (Getty Images)

as transsexualism. Most transsexuals want to not only want to live as a member of the gender with which they identify, but want to surgically and chemically alter their bodies so that their bodies match their internal gender identity. Doing so involves the taking of hormones to counteract the natural androgens or estrogens that are produced by the body, and for many, involves counseling and sex reassignment surgery as well.

Transsexuals often have an extremely difficult time transitioning from one sex and gender to the other, and when their faces do not reflect the feminine (or masculine) identity that they want to project, they can experience a great deal of stigma, discrimination, and suffering. For a male-to-female transsexual, testosterone and other androgens play a major role in the appearance of the face—in the size and shape of the jaw and brows, and in the amount of facial hair. Even after taking feminizing hormones, and the removal of the testicles, these features will not naturally go from masculine to feminine. Instead, transwomen must remove their facial hair, generally with electrolysis or laser hair removal. In addition, some transwomen choose to undergo facial feminization surgery as well. This refers to a set of procedures in which the facial bones are recontoured to make the face appear more feminine. Surgery may include a brow contouring in which the brow ridge is reduced and reshaped; a scalp advancement, which involves moving the natural hairline down to create a smaller forehead (and lifting the eyebrows at the same time); a mandible reduction, in which the jaw bone is filed down, making the jaw smaller and more pointed; and a nose job, in which the nose is reduced in size. Some transmen will also elect to have silicone implants placed into the cheeks, to have collagen injections in the lips, and to have their Adam's apple shaved down. Finally, wearing carefully applied cosmetics is one additional way in which transmen can make their faces appear as feminine as possible.

See also Beauty; Cosmetic Surgery; Cosmetics; Gender

Further Reading

Jackson, Linda A. *Physical Appearance and Gender: Sociobiological and Sociocultural Perspectives.* Albany: State University of New York Press, 1992.

Ousterhout, Douglas K. *Aesthetic Contouring of the Craniofacial Skeleton.* Boston: Little, Brown, 1991.

Perrett, D. I., and E. Brown. "What Gives a Face Its Gender?" *Perception* 22, no. 7 (1993): 829–40.

Rhodes, Gillian, and Leslie Zebrowitz, eds. *Facial Attractiveness: Evolutionary, Cognitive, and Social Perspectives.* Westport, CT: Ablex Publishing, 2002.

Shamanism

Shamanism is a form of religious belief and practice in which shamans, part-time religious intermediaries, travel to the spirit world in order to provide healing and other services to community members. Shamanism is most commonly found among foraging societies, but is also found in herding and horticultural cultures. It was most likely brought to the New World via Siberia by reindeer herders and hunters. Shamans often use masks during their rituals.

The shaman gets his or her power through direct communication with the spirit realm. His or her experience is direct, unlike practitioners from other religions, and communication is via trance, spirit possession, divination, dreams, healing, and glossalia, or speaking in tongues. These experiences are often brought about through drugs, fasting, lack of sleep, sexual abstinence, dancing, chanting, or meditation. Shamans travel between the profane world in which people live to the spirit world, via spirit possession and trance. Shamans ask, manipulate, or cajole spirits into doing things on behalf of their clients:

they ask them to heal, to provide good luck, to protect from misfortune. They also participate in important rites of passage and other communal and individual rituals.

Shamanism rests on a set of interlinked beliefs: the idea that the souls or spirits of the living and dead can inhabit the sacred realm, that shamans (and sometimes others) can travel to that world, and the idea that the shaman is particularly experienced in spirit travel and negotiating with the spirits. The spirits can be asked to aid the living with a variety of problems—health, luck, protection, and divination. The spirits themselves are generally classified by anthropologists as tutelary spirits, who are assigned to the shaman as guides and protectors, and helping spirits, who assist humans in particular tasks. Spirits can be anthropomorphic, taking the form of living or dead humans, or theriomorphic, taking the form of animals.

In many cultures, shamans came to their calling through illness, affliction, or disability. They generally do not choose to be shamans. Many shamans come from marginalized positions in society, and their afflictions, which are interpreted as spirit possessions, are in part a response to that social condition. Through shamanism, their marginal status is temporarily reversed, and if the afflicted become particularly good at controlling the spirits that afflict them, they can themselves become shamans, people of power. Shamans say that those whose lives flow smoothly are rarely summoned by the spirits.

While we typically think of shamanism with regard to contemporary tribal religions, evidence of shamanism goes back many thousands of years. Accounts that discuss people falling into trances, being ambushed by spirits, transforming into animals, being able to foresee the future or understand what occurred in the past, and healing the sick are all indications of beliefs in what we now call shamanism. Mircea Eliade's *Shamanism: Archaic Techniques of Ecstasy* is the classic piece on shamanism. Eliade suggests that shamanism is an early stage in the history of religious thought, which arose with nomadic populations and spread throughout the world. Archaeological evidence of shamanism includes rock and cave art that depicts people wearing what appear to be the heads of animals; those are most likely depictions of shamans who are possessed by animal spirits and/or wearing animal **masks**. Shamanistic traditions have been found in Siberia, **Mongolia**, Europe, and Central Asia, especially among the nomadic hunting cultures of those regions.

Masks play a central role in many shamanistic cultures, because the masks generally represent the spirit that the shaman is calling. The earliest uses of masks, in fact, most likely occurred in shamanistic rituals, as seen in the Upper Paleolithic cave paintings and rock art mentioned earlier. Thus masks may be created in the likenesses of important animal spirits, spirits of the ancestors, or other spirits, and even demons. Often the shaman's personal spirit is represented in the mask that he or she wears. Wearing the spirit's likeness helps the shaman to tap into that spiritual energy; it could also be to protect him or her from spiritual harm. Another interpretation of the use of animal masks by shamans is that shamans are often called upon to ensure success in a hunt. By wearing animal masks during these rituals, the shaman may be negotiating with the animals for their sacrifice. The mask may also be marked with symbols representing the clan or lineage of the shaman. Some masks, like some used among the tribes in the Pacific Northwest Coast, have two faces—the external animal spirit face, which then opens to reveal an internal, private, human face.

The Arctic region of the world has long been known by anthropologists for its shamanistic practices. In fact, the term shaman comes from the language of the Evenk, a northern Siberian people. **Inuit** shamans often wear masks as part of their rituals. For example, the Koryak, Evenk, and Yukaghir tribes wear masks made of leather during funeral rituals, and the Chukchi of Siberia wear masks representing evil spirits to scare children. Other tribes living near the Bering Sea wear masks of animals like bears during hunting rituals.

Many Native American tribes make and use ceremonial masks as a part of shamanistic rituals. Along the Pacific Northwest coast, masks are carved of wood and sometimes have moveable jaws or other parts. The Tlingit, for example, made masks representing humans, dead ancestors, animals, and spirits, and utilized the same artistic styles found in other forms of art in the region such as totem poles. Tlingit masks were asymmetrical and often had closed or missing eyes. The Haida, another Pacific Northwest tribe, wore masks during rituals to commemorate ancestors, to celebrate cutting a lip for a labret, or to commemorate a new tattoo. The Kwaikutl also used masks during initiation rituals. Here, initiates would go into the woods while possessed by cannibal spirits, while dancers, wearing the masks of the spirits, performed.

Shamanism has also been practiced in Asia—Siberians, Mongolians, Koreans, and Chinese all had shamanistic practices involving masks. In **Korea**, masks worn by shamans are made to be grotesque or horrifying, so as to scare off evil spirits, and are made of alder wood, elaborately painted, and include hinges to allow the mouth to open. Mongolian shamans traditionally wore masks that represented the animal spirits necessary for the shaman's journey,

Working to beat the devil—Eskimo medicine man exorcising evil spirits from a sick boy, ca. 1900–1930. Shamans, like this man, often wear masks representing the spirits that the shaman hopes to harness in his work. (Library of Congress)

and often wore antlers or eagle feathers to aid in the journey. Himalayan shamans, too, once wore masks to represent animal spirits, although this practice was largely abandoned with the rise of **Buddhism** and Hinduism into the region.

See also Buddhism; China; Inuit; Masks; Mongolia; Southeast Asia; Tibet and Nepal

Further Reading

Eliade, Mircea. *Shamanism: Archaic Techniques of Ecstasy.* Princeton, NJ: Princeton University Press, 2004.

Lewis, I. M. *Ecstatic Religion: An Anthropological Study of Spirit Possession and Shamanism.* Harmondsworth, England: Penguin Books, 1971.

Sarangerel. *Riding Windhorses: A Journey into the Heart of Mongolian Shamanism.* Rochester, VT: Destiny Books, 2000.

Vitebsky, Piers. *Shamanism.* Norman: University of Oklahoma Press, 2001.

Shroud of Turin

The Shroud of Turin is, to believers, the bloodstained burial shroud of Jesus. It was discovered in the 14th century and is kept at Turin Cathedral in northern Italy. Some consider the Shroud of Turin and the **Image of Edessa**, another piece of cloth that disappeared in the 13th century that was said to bear the image of Jesus Christ, to be the same thing. The Shroud of Turin is known as an acheiropoeta—an image made by God.

The shroud is a linen cloth, measuring 14 feet 5 inches by 3 feet 7 inches, which shows the full image of a naked man with long hair and a beard, with the front of the man on one side and the back on the other. The face and body show bloodstained wounds consistent with the historical and biblical account of Jesus's beating and crucifixion, including marks around the forehead that may indicate wearing a crown of thorns. While the image on the shroud itself is not very clear, in 1898 an Italian named Secondo Pia photographed the shroud, and his black and white negative of the image shows the details much more clearly. Pia's negative shows the image as a positive image, which implies that the actual Shroud is also a negative.

The shroud is thought to have been rediscovered in the 14th century by a French knight named Geoffrey de Charny. The shroud was first written about in 1390 when Bishop Pierre d'Arcis wrote to the pope to tell him that the shroud was a forgery. It was transferred from a chapel in Chambéry, France, where it was damaged in a fire in 1532, to the Turin Cathedral in 1578, where it has been ever since.

While the Shroud of Turin is a representation of the body of a man, and the Image of Edessa just the face, some people think that the Image of Edessa did in fact contain the full image of Christ's body, but that it was once folded in fourths, displaying only the image of Christ's face. In fact, an eighth century account of King Abgar's receiving the cloth shows him receiving a cloth with a full body image of Christ. Today, scholars and religious devotees are not in consensus about the relationship, if any, between the legendary Image of Edessa and the Shroud of Turin.

The shroud has been subject to a handful of scientific tests to determine its authenticity. In 1988 three universities performed

The Holy Shroud, a 14-foot-long linen revered by some as the burial cloth of Jesus, at the Cathedral of Turin, Italy. (AP/Wide World Photos)

radiocarbon dating on a sample of the fabric and concluded that the material dated to the 13th or 14th centuries, which, if correct, would make the shroud a forgery, although critics charge that the sample may have been taken from a piece of cloth used to repair the shroud. Other analyses have looked at the weave of the fabric, the proportions of the image, whether the image shows a realistic body after crucifixion, the minerals in the image, the makeup of the blood stains, images of flowers and pollen samples from the shroud, and even the dirt particles on it, and have come to competing conclusions about its authenticity. Other studies have focused on how the image could have been created—via painting, some type of early photography, dust transfer, bas-relief, or some other means, and these analyses have likewise been inconclusive. While the Catholic Church has not taken an official position as to whether the shroud is authentic, it has approved the use of images of the shroud as devotions.

See also Christianity; Image of Edessa; Veil of Veronica

Further Reading

Humber, Thomas. *The Sacred Shroud.* New York: Pocket Books, 1978.

Nickell, Joe. *Inquest on the Shroud of Turin: Latest Scientific Findings.* Amherst, NY: Prometheus Books, 1988.

Wilson, Ian. *Holy Faces, Secret Places: An Amazing Quest for the Face of Jesus.* New York: Doubleday, 1991.

Wilson, Ian. *The Shroud of Turin: The Burial Cloth of Jesus Christ?* rev. ed. Garden City, NY: Image Books, 1979.

Sign Language

Sign language refers to the languages used by deaf people, which use the movements of the hands and arms as a symbolic form of language. Sign language is not a simple translation of spoken language, however, and has its own grammar and syntax that governs its structure. And like spoken languages, signs are symbols, as are written letters and words. American Sign Language is the form of sign language used by the deaf (and people who communicate with them) in the United States.

Sign languages are manual languages. The meaning of a sign derives from a combination of features: the hand shape, the orientation of the hand, the location of the hand on or around the body, and the movement of the hand. In addition, sign language not only uses hands and arms to convey words, letters, and expressions, but **facial expressions** (as well as body posture) play a role in conveying meaning as well.

Sign languages depend on sight to work; those who are communicating with each other via sign language must be able to see the signs made by a person, and must be able to see their facial expression as well to truly interpret those signs.

Facial expressions, when used with signs, are akin to the tone of voice when speaking; they convey emotion, speaker intent, and add meaning to the signs as well. They are also used as an additional form of grammar. For instance, just as asking a question through speech involves raising the pitch of a voice, asking a question when signing involves either raising the eyebrows combined with opening the eyes wider (for yes/no questions), or lowering the eyebrows, combined with narrowing the eyes (for who/what questions). Negating a clause involves shaking one's head while signing. Some signs' meaning will change depending on the movement of the head, the position of the eyebrows, or when the tongue touches the lip. Clenching the teeth, puffing the cheeks, wrinkling the nose, and shifting the direction in which the eyes face also convey meaning.

In addition, mouthing words plays a role in signing as well. Mouthed words can act as adjectives or adverbs, qualifying or modulating the signed words, just as exaggerated facial expressions can. At other times, mouthed words are used during signing to help people learning to sign associate the signs with the words. And finally, some signs must be made in a specific location in space or on the body; for instance, the same sign means different things when the hand making the sign touches the forehead, the chest, or the chin. On the face, the areas that can impact the meaning of the sign is the forehead, the whole face or head, the eyes and nose, the lower face, and the side of the face.

Just as with speaking and hearing people, the deaf use facial expressions to convey emotions, so signs about being sad or angry are accompanied by the appropriate facial expressions. In addition, having an expressionless face while signing could tell people that the signer is not interested in the conversation.

For some women in the **Middle East**, deafness is more of a disability than it is elsewhere. It is impossible to read the lips of a woman who is wearing a veil, so deaf women who do not know sign language have a hard time communicating with other women. In addition, because the facial expression is so critical to the meaning of signs, a woman who signs while wearing a veil cannot convey the full range of meaning that would be possible without a veil.

See also Facial Expressions; Veiling

Further Reading

Grossman, Ruth B., and Judy Kegl. "To Capture a Face: A Novel Technique for the Analysis and Quantification of Facial Expressions in American Sign Language." *Sign Language Studies* 6, no. 3 (2006): 273–305.

Skin Bleaching and Tanning

Skin bleaching refers to using products, either internally or externally, to lighten dark skin temporarily or permanently. Tanning refers to darkening one's skin, either through exposure to the sun or other forms of ultraviolet light, or with artificial products.

In the West prior to the 20th century, lighter skin was a sign of status for Europeans and Americans, since it indicated that they did not have to work outdoors. This dates back to classical times, when women of ancient Greece and Rome used lead paints and chalks to whiten their faces. During the Middle Ages, European women used arsenic to lighten their skins, and during the Renaissance, white face powder was worn to lighten the skin, and parasols were carried at all times when outdoors.

Light skin is a sign of status in non-Western countries as well, as in **India**, where higher castes are lighter skinned than the lower castes. Even today, actors and actresses in Bollywood films tend to be lighter skinned than most of the Indian population. In Eastern Asian countries as well, pale skin has typically represented nobility and status. In **Japan**, **Geisha**s use thick white face powder to give the illusion of white skin, which represents **beauty** and sophistication. In **China** in the Middle Ages, women used skin whiteners made of mercury.

In parts of Latin America, the Arab world, and Africa, due to colonization, the lighter a person is, the more beautiful. In former slave nations like Jamaica, for example, a brown complexion is often considered more beautiful than a black one. It's not surprising, then, that skin whiteners are very popular in these countries.

In the United States, women of color have also invested in skin-whitening products, not so that they could pass for white (although those with more Caucasian features sometimes could), but because going back to slavery, lighter skinned **African Americans** received better privileges than darker skinned blacks. Skin whiteners were also used by darker skinned Eastern and Southern European immigrants to help them blend into mainstream American society.

People around the world have long used chemicals to lighten their skin; these practices are most common in cultures that were colonized by Europeans or that are otherwise affected by the European preference for light skin. Roadside vendor Sophia McLennan displays her selection of skin-bleaching agents near a pharmacy in downtown Kingston, Jamaica. (AP/Wide World Photos)

Even in the 20th century, skin whiteners have been marketed that contain dangerous ingredients, like mercury and hydroquinone. While the Civil Rights and Black Pride movements made a dent in the skin whitening industry by convincing many black women that dark skin was beautiful, skin whiteners are more popular than ever today, with hundreds of pills, soaps, creams, and lotions on the market in the United States, Asia, Latin America, Africa, and India. In Japan alone, the skin-whitening industry was worth $5.6 billion in 2001.

Skin whiteners generally work by breaking down the melanin in the skin, as well as providing sunscreen to protect the skin from the sun. However, some whitening products are just bleaches that temporarily lighten the skin. Exfoliants and lasers are more modern options.

While hydroquinone is considered the most popular and effective of the skin whiteners (often called a bleaching agent, it actually stops the production of melanin in the skin), its use has been banned in a number of countries, because of the damage that hydroquinone products have caused to skin. South Africa, for instance, banned products containing the chemical after countless black women were permanently disfigured. Other agents used are topical azelaic acid, tretinoin, kojic acid, glycolic acid, and a number of plant extracts.

Today, high-end skin whiteners are being marketed as anti-aging products, and primarily target well-to-do women overseas, primarily in Asia. Cheap, often dangerous products are still being sold, often illegally, to minorities in the United States and poor women overseas, however.

Sun tanning describes the process of human skin darkening due to exposure to ultraviolet radiation from sunlight (or a tanning bed). While tanning is often inadvertent and can occur anytime someone is in the sun for an extended period of time, it can also be an intentional act in which a person deliberately exposes the body to the sun in the hopes of receiving a tan. In the West, this process is often called laying out or sunbathing.

The ancient Greeks sunbathed, calling the act of laying in the sun heliotherapy; they felt that natural sunlight could cure certain illnesses. In the West prior to the modern era, however, light skin was preferred for Europeans and Americans, as light skin was seen as a sign that a person did not have to engage in outdoor labor. In ancient Rome, for example, women deliberately lightened their skin with **cosmetics** in order to appear well off, and throughout Europe during the Renaissance, elite women lightened their untanned skin even further with makeup and face powder. Having fair skin meant that one not only did not have to work outdoors, but that she was wealthy enough to hire other people to work for her. Elites in the United States prior to the 20th century also worked to protect their skin from the sun and wore makeup to lighten their already light skin.

In the 20th century, however, with fewer people engaged in agricultural or other outdoor labor, most work moved indoors, and men and women of all classes were less exposed to the sun. In the 1920s, French fashion designer Coco Chanel acquired a suntan during a vacation on the French Riviera, and helped to popularize suntans among the wealthy; suntans at this point became a sign of status for men and women who could afford to travel to sunny or tropical climates for a holiday.

> Nature gives you the face you have at twenty; it is up to you to merit the face you have at fifty.—*Coco Chanel*

Starting in the mid-20th century, tanned skin also became associated with a new outdoor lifestyle—not of work, but of leisure. As clothing styles (especially for women) allowed for the display of more skin, and as many men and women began hiking, picnicking, or engaging in sports for relaxation, tanned skin became more popular still, as well as more available to the average American and European.

Sunbathing became a pastime in and of itself in Europe and America, and, by midcentury, cosmetic products were created to simulate the look of a suntan, and suntanning oils were marketed to encourage a better tan.

Another development in the 20th century was the indoor tanning industry, first popularized in the 1970s and by the 1980s, tanning salons became ubiquitous in suburban America. Tanning salons are places in which a person relaxes in a tanning bed that emits ultraviolet radiation in order to achieve a suntan in a short amount of time regardless of the climate.

In the late 1970s, however, the link between exposure to ultraviolet radiation and skin cancer became apparent, and men and women who had sunbathed extensively began developing melanomas. In the late 1970s, the Federal Drug Administration developed the first sunscreen rating system that measured the product's sun protection factor or SPF. Not until the 1980s, however, was the public aware of the dangers of overexposure to the sun, either through sunbathing or lying in a tanning bed.

Today, artificial bronzers and sunless tanning products are popular with celebrities and the general public, which create the suntanned look without the associated dangers. These products can be applied at home, in the form of gels, lotions, mousses, sprays, and wipes; and airbrush spray tans are applied by professional technicians, who also operated sunless tanning spray booths in which artificial bronzers are sprayed over the entire body.

Another reason for the popularity of sunless tanning products has to do with the time needed to receive a conventional tan. Because getting a tan requires a commitment of time (whether laying out in the sun or going to a tanning booth), and many modern Americans no longer have the time necessary for idle sunbathing, skin bronzers have become popular.

See also Beauty; Cosmetics

Further Reading

Allison, Kevin, and Dr. Faye Z Belgrave. *African American Psychology: From Africa to America.* Thousand Oaks, CA: Sage Publications, 2005.

Mullins, Paul R. *Race and Affluence: An Archaeology of African America and Consumer Culture.* New York: Plenum Press, 1999.

Russell, Kathy, Midge Wilson, and Ronald Hall. *The Color Complex: The Politics of Skin Color among African Americans.* New York: First Anchor Books, 1993.

Sikes, Ruth G. "The History of Suntanning: A Love/Hate Affair." *Journal of Aesthetic Sciences* 1, no. 2 (May 1998): 6–7.

Skin Colors and Disorders

In humans, skin color is created through a combination of genes and environment—specifically, exposure to the sun or other forms of ultraviolet light. Skin color can range from very light to very dark, and having light or dark skin has great cultural implications around the world.

Variation in skin color is determined primarily by the amount of melanin in the skin cells, which are inherited in the genes from one's parents. Melanin protects the skin from too much ultraviolet radiation, so people whose ancestors come from environments with a great deal of sunlight have darker skin than those whose ancestors come from areas with little sunlight. Because humans evolved in **Sub-Saharan Africa**, where exposure to the sun is very high near the Equator, the original skin color of the earliest human being was most likely very dark. (Prior to that time, our pre-human ancestors most likely had light skin covered by hair. With the disappearance of our body hair, the natural selection caused the skin of our ancestors to lighten, as a protection against too much sunlight.) That only began to change when modern humans left Africa, probably about 50,000 years ago, and began to settle in northern climates in Europe and Asia. Over time, due to natural selection, the skin of those European and Asian populations got lighter, in order to allow in more sun, which brings in Vitamin D.

Skin color also changes due to environmental conditions. Exposure to the sun will temporarily change the color of one's skin, either burning or tanning the skin. Exposure to a small amount of ultraviolet light causes a tan to develop; exposure to too much ultraviolet light over a brief period of time can cause a sunburn. Both conditions can lead to the eventual development of skin cancer. In addition, artificial tanning products can provide the appearance of tanned skin without the dangers of exposure to the sun. While (slightly) darker skin is desirable among European-Americans today, for many centuries, light skin was preferred over dark skin. The result of that is that since the time of the ancient Romans, women in particular have invested in products that were intended to lighten their skin, either temporarily or permanently. White makeup and skin-whitening products, many containing dangerous substances like lead, have been used in cultures ranging from **Japan** to Africa to **India** to Latin America.

Finally, skin color can change due to genetic disorders. For example, albinism is a genetic disorder in which melanin is not produced, and the skin (and hair and eyes) thus has no pigment at all. The result is that people and animals with albinism, known as albinos, have very light skin, very light hair, and pink eyes. Albinos are vulnerable to sunburns because their skin is so light, and are thus in danger of contracting skin cancer. They may also have problems with vision. Because albinos are so distinctive looking, they have been stigmatized in a number of cultures throughout history. For instance, in the East African countries of Tanzania and Burundi, albinos are thought to be witches and are often killed; since 2007, there have been more than 60 documented killings in both countries associated with this belief. It is also believed by some that the body parts of albinos carry supernatural powers and can bring luck or wealth, or that having sex with an albino girl can cure AIDS. In Mali, it is thought that albinos are born because of the deviant behavior of the parents, and are linked to a supernatural being named Faro who maintains equilibrium in the world, and who also rules twins and hermaphrodites. In Mozambique, as in other areas of Africa, it is believed that albinos do not die; instead they vanish. It should not be a surprise to learn that throughout Africa, giving birth to an albino is an unhappy event.

Vitiligo is another disorder of the skin. Unlike albinism, vitiligo does not cause an overall lightening of the skin; instead, it causes the skin to lose pigment in patches. Michael Jackson famously suffered from the condition; before he publically admitted that he had vitiligo, it was rumored that the singer lightened his skin in order to appear white. His response was that he wore light makeup in order to even out the patchy appearance of his skin.

With European colonialism, beginning in the late 15th century, and the Atlantic slave trade, Europeans began to develop ideas that highlighted the differences between those with different skin colors and facial features, and linked those physical

Julieta Chilombo, mother of Rosa Paulo, age 4, an albino child, waits to be helped at a hospital in Kuito, some 310 miles southeast of Luanda, Angola, on June 12, 2002. Albinism is a genetic disorder in which melanin is not produced, and the skin (and hair and eyes) thus has no pigment at all. Because albinos are so distinctive looking, they are often stigmatized and in some African countries are thought to be witches. (AP/Wide World Photos)

differences to supposed cultural, intellectual, and emotional differences. This system became known as a racial system, and formed the basis for a system of racial inequality that changed the world and the fate of its people for centuries.

One result of classifying and ranking people by skin color is that around the world, light skin is almost universally preferred over dark skin. Especially in countries that once experienced race-based slavery, those with lighter skin have higher status than those with darker skin. Light-skinned African American women are thought to be more beautiful than darker-skinned blacks, and lighter-skinned African American men tend to experience more success in the business world than those with darker skin. Even during the period of African slavery in the New World, slaves with lighter skin (due to their mixed parentage) were granted greater privileges, serving, for example, as house slaves rather than field slaves. Today, in countries like Brazil, there are hundreds of racial classifications that depend on slight variations in hair color, hair texture, skin color, and eye color. Those with facial features considered more European, and lighter hair and skin, are socially more desirable than others. This pattern tends to be repeated throughout Latin America, and is also found in India and other parts of Asia. Due to this preference, skin-whitening products continue to be in wide demand throughout much of the world. Even among people who already have relatively light skin, like Europeans and Asians, lighter skin has traditionally been preferred over darker skin, because darker skin indicated outside work and lower social status. Protecting the skin from the sun, then, is one way to ensure that one looks, at least, to have higher status, and wearing makeup and skin whitening products is another.

See also Race; Skin Bleaching and Tanning

Further Reading

Glenn, Evelyn N. *Shades of Difference: Why Skin Color Matters.* Stanford, CA: Stanford University Press, 2009.

Hall, Ronald E. *Racism in the 21st Century: An Empirical Analysis of Skin Color.* New York: Springer, 2008.

Russell, Kathy, Midge Wilson, and Ronald Hall. *The Color Complex: The Politics of Skin Color among African Americans.* New York: First Anchor Books, 1993.

Slang Terms

The face is not known for the variety of slang terms associated with it, but there are a few terms that indicate the importance of the face to our personal identities.

For instance, the mouth can be called the grill (i.e., he's got an ugly grill), but it can also refer to the face as a whole. "Get out of my grill" means to get out of my face, and being "up in one's grill" means being right in a person's face. This can also be a metaphorical usage of the term, because being up in one's grill can also mean being involved in someone else's business. Grill could also mean teeth that are adorned with jewels, as in the hip-hop community. The term derives from the grill of a classic American car, which can look like a face. Another term that is used instead of face is map. Here the map refers to the ways in which the face is indicative of the overall person; by looking at one's face, or map, one can get a sense of the whole person. Another term to refer to the face is mug, but this is usually just used in a negative sense. A person can be said to have an ugly mug, and a **mug shot** is a photo of a person arrested for a crime. Mug can also mean to stare at someone. Puss is another term for face, and, like mug, it is usually used negatively. A sour-puss is a person with a negative facial expression.

See also Face Folklore; Mug Shot

Further Reading

Partridge, Eric, Tom Dalzell, Terry Victor, and Eric Partridge. *The New Partridge Dictionary of Slang and Unconventional English.* London: Routledge, 2006.

South America

South America, colonized by the Spanish and the Portuguese beginning in the late 15th century, is a collection of 12 countries with mixed cultures that include indigenous cultures and Latin American cultures. This part of the world has a number of traditions related to the face, including **facial piercing**, **ear piercing**, ear stretching, **head hunting**, and the use of **masks** for rituals and celebrations.

In pre-Columbian Peru, a variety of cultures from the Chavin civilization to the Inca created art featuring human faces. The Moche, for instance, who lived from the second to the ninth centuries, made ceramics with lifelike, individual human portraits on them, probably representing elites, warriors, and famous craftsmen, and the Chimú, another Peruvian culture that predated the Inca, created portraits in gold and other precious metals.

A number of pre-Columbian cultures in South America made and used masks. One of the most common uses for masks in these cultures was for burial. The Quimbaya, an ancient Columbian civilization, made death masks in hammered gold. These masks were adorned as a human in that culture would be, with filed teeth, **nose piercing**s, and **jewelry**. As with the masks of other cultures, the eyes of the Quimbaya masks are closed, perhaps to represent seeing into the spiritual realm. Similar masks were also used in funerary complexes in the Chimú culture of northern Peru a thousand years ago; some were sized to fit over the face of the dead, and others much larger, to be buried with the deceased along with treasure. The Inca also used masks to bury their dead; the royalty had masks made of gold, while commoners might have masks made of wood or clay.

We know from masks, ceramics, textiles, and other images that the Inca practiced facial piercing; in particular, they had their septums pierced and their ears were not just pierced but stretched. They wore elaborate jade and gold jewelry in both their ears and noses. In their ears, they wore engraved spools of gold, silver, copper, sometimes inset with stone or shells, and these were most likely reserved for the elites. We also know that they practiced **head binding**, at least for royals. Head binding was also once practiced in other South American cultures like Venezuela, Colombia, Ecuador, Chile, Argentina, and Guyana.

South America has a number of indigenous tribes that live either in the highlands or in the Amazonian region, some of whom still practice their ancient customs, and, especially for those in the rainforest, have resisted Spanish interference. These groups still practice facial piercing. For example, the Kayapo, hunter-gatherers and horticulturalists who live in the Amazon Basin in Brazil, wear large plates and plugs in their lips, and the Yanomamo of Brazil and Venezuela pierce their septums and cheeks and wear sticks in the openings.

The men and women of the Suya tribe, horticulturalists who also live in Brazil, once wore both lip plates and ear plugs in ear openings stretched as far as 8 centimeters. The Suya called the piercing of the ears *opening* and this ritual occurred at adolescence when a boy was expected to open his ears and listen to his elders. Eventually, he would wear, on ceremonial occasions, large ear discs made of wood or palm leaves, painted white, in his stretched ear lobes. Lips were pierced several years later, at age 15 or 20, as confirmation of adulthood, and men would not go out in public without the lip plate, which is painted with red and black dye. Where ear discs were associated with hearing, lip discs were associated with oration and song.

Men of the Canela tribe of Brazil must also have their ears opened at adolescence. The action is performed by a ritual piercing specialist who pierces the ear with a hardwood awl, and then places wooden pins into the holes. Over the next few weeks, the boy replaces the first wooden pins with a series of larger pins that will enlarge the hole.

Tribal people in the Amazon region of South America have also practiced head hunting. For example, the Jivaro, who live in Ecuador and Peru, not only collected human heads as part of their battles but shrunk and preserved them. According to a witness in the 1920s, after the heads were severed from the bodies, the warriors peeled the flesh from the skulls, and then sewed together the skin of the face, closing the holes of the eyes, mouth, ears, and nose. The skin heads are then filled with sand and placed into a pot of water, which is brought almost to a boil, at which point the heads are pulled out, having shrunk to one-third their original size. The process of

Makajau, an elder of the Suya ethnic group, rests in the shade of his hut at the border of Xingu Indian Reservation in the northern state of Mato Grosso, Brazil, November 28, 2003. The men and women of the Suya tribe once wore both lip plates and ear plugs in ear openings stretched as far as 8 centimeters. (AP/Wide World Photos)

filling the heads with sand and shaping the face continues for another couple of days until the heads were said to look just like their former inhabitants.

After the Spanish and the Portuguese arrived in South America, they introduced their own cultural traditions, including Carnival festivals. Known elsewhere as Mardi Gras, they are the final celebrations for Catholics just prior to the fasting associated with Lent. Carnival celebrations involve the use of elaborate costumes, music, parades, and masks. While every South American country celebrates Carnival, Brazil is known around the world for its celebrations. It began in the mid-17th century and borrowed from the masquerade balls held in Paris at that time. Later, Brazilian Carnival incorporated elements from the Afro-Brazilian and Spanish cultures. Another South American festival incorporating masks is the Fiesta Virgen del Carmen, held in a village outside of Cusco, Peru in July. This festival celebrates the patron saint of the local population, and participants wear masks; some have faces on them, while others are blank. It is said that the masks are leftovers from the Incan culture, and were once worn to protect the Incans from being recognized by the Spanish when they rebelled. Other dancers wear masks representing the slaves who once served the Spanish.

See also Death Masks; Ear Spools and Plugs; Labrets, Lip Plugs, and Lip Plates

Further Reading

Henshen F. *The Human Skull: A Cultural History.* New York: Frederick A. Praeger, 1966.

Turner, Terence. "Social Body and Embodied Subject: Bodiliness, Subjectivity and Sociality among the Kayapo." *Current Anthropology* 10, no. 2 (1995): 143–70.

Southeast Asia

Southeast Asia is a collection of countries that sit both on the mainland of the Asian continent, south of **China** and east of **India**, and on the islands in the vicinity. It includes Vietnam, Cambodia, Laos, Thailand, Indonesia, and the Philippines. These countries all have a number of distinctive practices pertaining to the face, including facial tattooing, the use of **masks**, the wearing of **neck rings**, **teeth filing**, and **teeth painting**.

Altering the teeth has long been a common practice in Southeast Asia. Teeth painting is a practice that involves using dyes made of a combination of acids, minerals, tannins, and vegetable material to blacken the teeth. It has been practiced in Vietnam, Laos, Indonesia, Thailand, and the Philippines. Vietnamese girls typically had their teeth dyed after puberty, which made them marriageable. In Vietnam, it was once thought that to be civilized, and human, meant that one had dark teeth; only animals, savages, and evil spirits had white teeth. Another reason for blackening the teeth is to keep them from being seen. As in other Asian cultures, the Vietnamese control their facial expressions, and often do not like to smile or laugh in such a way that the teeth show. Other Southeast Asian

cultures that practice or practiced teeth painting include the Si La of Laos, whose women paint their teeth black but whose men paint them red, and a number of tribes in the Philippines, who only blacken their teeth after marriage.

Another Southeast Asian practice that seems odd to Westerners is tooth filing. Some Vietnamese hill tribes practice tooth evulsion in which one or both of the front incisors are chipped, knocked, or pulled out. Other groups file their teeth into sharp points, such as the Mentawai of Sumatra. In Bali, teeth are filed not for decorative reasons but because canines symbolize negative emotions like anger, jealousy, and greed, which can be controlled through filing the teeth. The Iban of Borneo filed their teeth, blackened them, and inserted a brass stud into a drilled hole.

Another practice associated with Southeast Asia is the wearing of neck rings by the Padaung of Burma (or Myanmar). Padaung girls traditionally had the coils wrapped around their necks from the age of about five. Over the years, longer coils are added, until an adult Padaung woman's neck can carry more than 20 pounds of coils, which compress the collarbone and upper ribs, in turn making the neck look as long as 15 inches. Long necks are a sign of female beauty and highly praised, which is most likely the reason for the wearing of the rings.

Some cultures of Southeast Asia also practice facial tattooing. For instance, the Chin tribe of northwest Burma once tattooed the faces of their girls in order, it was said, to keep the girls from being kidnapped, but it was most likely considered a sign of beauty and marriageability. The

Khon masks are worn by actors in the classical dances of Thailand known as *khon*, which are based on the *Ramakien*, the Thai version of the *Ramayana* of India. (Surabky/Dreamstime.com)

tattoos were elaborate, covering the entire face, including eyelids, with a design of curved and straight lines, but have almost entirely stopped since the 1960s. The older women in Burma who still carry the tattoos can make money from allowing themselves to be photographed by tourists who travel to see them.

Finally, due to the influence and spread of both **Buddhism** and Hinduism into Southeast Asia, many Southeast Asian cultures have a well-developed tradition of mask-making and performances using masks. For instance, the Balinese are Hindu, and they use masks to tell Hindu Sanskrit stories about gods, heroes, and demons; the masks represent humans, animals, gods and demons. Some of the masks are huge, made of wood, and elaborately painted and decorated with metal and horse hair, and can take months to make. Common dances in which these masks are used include the *Topeng* dance, which tells of ancient kings and noblemen, and the *Barong* dance, which depicts a fight between good and evil.

In Thailand, which has a long tradition of performing classical dance dramas, known as *Khon*, masks also play a central role. Khon masks, made of papier-mâché, are used to portray characters in the Thai versions of Indian stories, and represent monkeys, demons, and other animals; other characters are portrayed by actors wearing makeup. Some Southeast Asian cultures still practice **shamanism**, and thus their masks are of an older tradition. For instance, the tribes from the remote hilly region of Vietnam still make traditional masks out of wood and colored paper; the shaman places new paper onto the mask for each ritual, and tears off the old paper from the previous one.

See also Facial Tattoos; Masks; Neck Rings; Shamanism; Teeth Filing; Teeth Painting

Further Reading

Chawanaputorn, D., V. Patanaporn, P. Malikaew, P. Khongkhunthian, and P. A. Reichart. "Facial and Dental Characteristics of Padaung Women (long-Neck Karen) Wearing Brass Neck Coils in Mae Hong Son Province, Thailand." *American Journal of Orthodontics and Dentofacial Orthopedics* 131, no. 5 (2007): 639–45.

Huard, Pierre, and Keith Botsford. *The Blackening of Teeth in Eastern Asia and in Indochina.* New Haven, CT: Human Relations Area Files, 1970.

Zumbroich, T.J. "Teeth as Black as a Bumble Bee's Wings: The Ethnobotany of Teeth Blackening in Southeast Asia." *Ethnobotany Research and Applications* 7 (2009): 381–98.

Sub-Saharan Africa

The people who live on the African continent south of the Sahara desert have long practiced **scarification**, both on the body and on the face, have a number of cultural practices related to the mouth, and have well-developed artistic and ritual traditions involving making and using **masks**. In fact, the masks of many African tribes include the scarification patterns of those cultures, demonstrating a close link between two different artistic practices.

For example, among the tribes of the Ivory Coast, scarification was primarily a decorative practice in that it added to the **beauty** of the face and body. In addition, scarification is seen as a critical way to demonstrate that a person is a cultural being; without scars, a person is not considered civilized. The Dan, who live in the western part of the country as well as Liberia, wear facial scars that emphasize bilateral symmetry, which is seen as beautiful. Dan dance masks also show scarification patterns. The Senofo, who live in the northern part of the Ivory Coast and southern Mali, practiced facial scarification, with the most common pattern being lines that radiate outward from the mouth. Carved Senofo ancestor figures and ritual masks also show scarification, sometimes on the face and other times on the body.

The Baule, a neighboring tribe of the Senofo who migrated from Ghana in the 18th century, also practice scarification, known as ngole, as a way of beautifying themselves and pleasing others. In addition, scarification both orients an individual within society by marking tribal, clan, lineage, or other membership, and also denotes social information like marriageability or success in hunting. Finally, some scars were used to protect against magic and disease in that a small amount of poison was injected directly into the scar, known as a kanga mark. While scarification designs were like hairstyles in that they varied through place and time, with raised scars more common in the past and indented cuts more popular in recent years, one common pattern was a series of small scars on the forehead and at the base of the nose. The Baule also borrowed the Senofo pattern of lines radiating from the mouth, to protect young children from harm. Baule ceremonial masks and carved statues also show scarification patterns as well as the elaborate hairstyles favored by the Baule.

Like many Sub-Saharan African tribes, most tribes in Nigeria traditionally practiced scarification. The Tiv view scarification as purely decorative although the designs also denote the wearer's generation since patterns change over the course of a person's lifetime, from flat shiny scars to raised lumpy scars, to flat dull scars, to deep cuts rubbed with charcoal. The decorative function of the scars is most important because the Tiv consider scars necessary for a person to be beautiful. The Tiv also oil their skin, use elaborate forms of **jewelry** and makeup, and chip their teeth, all to beautify the face and body.

These two performers, members of the Dogon tribe of Mali, dance wearing antelope masks. The mask represents an antelope god known as Walu. The Dogon use the Walu masks to commemorate the origin of death. (Michele Alfieri/Dreamstime.com)

Men are scarred, generally on the chest, face, arms, and legs. Scars can be geometric designs of animal representations.

The Ga'anda of northern Nigeria also use scarification, known as *Hleeta*, to make girls marriageable. The process begins at 5 or 6, with the final phase beginning at 15 or 16 just before marriage, at which time the girl will also have her ears pierced for earrings and her lip pierced to insert a labret. Elderly women perform the procedure, which is done, like many other tribes, with a fishhook to raise the skin and a razor to slice the skin, leaving a raised welt. Girls are scarred on their forehead as well as the body, with an elaborate pattern of dots that form lines, curves, and diamonds.

The Yoruba are another tribe whose women are traditionally scarred, as a test of a woman's bravery and to ensure that she will be strong enough to withstand childbirth; she must be scarred prior to marriage. Yoruba scars, known as *kolo*, are carved with a y-shaped double blade knife, followed by rubbing charcoal into the wounds to ensure a strong scar. The small scars are then combined into lines along the face and body, and into elaborate images. Some marks have a specific meaning, like the *osilumi* mark on the face worn for mourning. Men can be scarred too, but it's not as important culturally, and they do not have the wide variety of designs that women have.

The Lulua of the Congo use scarification as a form of beautification, to attract benevolent spirits, and to signal marriageability. The Tabwa, who live in the Congo and Northeastern Zambia, called their practice *kulemba*, which means to inscribe or beautify a blank surface. Women were once scarred on the cheeks and forehead plus back and shoulders, but today scars are limited to small lines on the forehead, nose, and cheeks. The method for scarification was to use a hook or thorn to pull up the skin, after which it is sliced off with a razor, and the incisions rubbed with soot. As with most African tribes, girls without scars were not considered marriageable. Men in the Congo also undergo scarification. Kongo men, for example, undergo facial scarification. Tebwa men also practiced facial scarification, with a pattern known as face of the cross in which tiny dots were patterned into lines that made up a cross on the face.

Some African cultures have a number of cultural practices related to the mouth, and in particular, the teeth and lips. For instance, the Nuer of Sudan practice tooth avulsion in which one or both of the front incisors are chipped out. Other groups, such as the Masai and Waarusha of Tanzania, remove the lower incisors of adolescents, and the Masai and the Shilluk of Sudan also remove the baby canine teeth of children. These practices are related to cultural beliefs that suggest that the presence of the teeth can cause, or exacerbate, illnesses. And still other cultures file their teeth into sharp points, such as the Efe of the Democratic Republic of the Congo, or the Dinka of Sudan. Some African tribes pierce or slice the lips in order to insert plugs or plates into them. Lip plates are usually no larger than three centimeters in width, but the women of southern Chad wear extremely large plates, often as large as 24 centimeters. Tribes that are known for their traditional lip plates include the Mursi and Surma of Ethiopia, the Makololo of Malawai, the Makonde of Tanzania, and the Sara and Djinja of Chad. The Lobi women of Ghana and the Ivory Coast and the Kirdi people of Cameroon use lip plugs to protect the women from evil spirits who enter via the mouth.

Masks represent an important part of the cultures throughout Sub-Saharan Africa. Made from wood, animal skins, feathers, fabric, and metal, these are elaborately decorated and, while still used in rituals throughout Africa, are also highly sought after collectors items in the West. Some masks were worn on the face, some were worn as helmets, covering the entire head; some were worn like a headdress upon the head, and many were carried, rather than worn. For instance, Yoruba dance masks may be carried or may be worn over the top of the head; these masks could be as high as four feet tall, and because of their weight, rest upon the wearer's shoulders. Most are used during ritual dances, which involve drumming, chanting, and dancing, both by the wearer as well as others in the community. Masks may represent specific ancestors, totem animals, or gods and spirits. They may also represent a combination of characteristics or can even be abstract rather than representational—especially when depicting spirits. Wearing a mask of an animal that is thought to have power conveys that power to the wearer and protects him or her from dangerous spirits. Other masks are worn to ward off sorcery or witchcraft. Ancestral masks are often worn during initiation rituals; the ancestor represented by the mask protects and provides for the initiates. Among the Pende tribe of the Congo, for example, young men who have finished their initiation into adulthood emerge into the community wearing a mask that represents their new status as adults. Other masks are worn during harvest ceremonies, fertility rituals, or funerals.

Masks may be worn during public ceremonies at which members of the community participate, or during private ceremonies as part of a secret society. During many ceremonies, the wearer of the mask goes into a trance and may communicate with the ancestor, animal totem, or spirit; wearing the mask representing that being allows for that communication to happen, and for the spirit to come alive during the ritual.

The Senufo of the Ivory Coast wear masks called Kpelie masks, which combined both human and animal features on the mask, during male initiation rituals, harvest festivals and funerals. These are carried in front of the wearer's head rather than worn on the face. The Nuna of Burkina Faso create masks that represent powerful animal spirits like the hawk or the crocodile. The spirits are called on and asked to protect the families and clans that own the masks, and are worn during initiation rituals, funerals, and market days. The dancer wearing the mask will often mimic the behavior of the animal during the dance. For instance, the Dogon people of Mali wear antelope masks while imitating the antelope pawing the ground. These masks are worn by members of a secret society called Awa at funerals and end of mourning ceremonies in order to chase the spirits of the dead from the village.

While most cultures reserve the use of masks for men, some masks in Africa are made especially to represent women. For instance, the Punu tribe of Gabon makes white-faced masks that represent ideal female beauty, while the Nimba Baga of Guinea symbolizes female fertility. The Dogon have a mask that represents an ancient female ancestor named Yasigi; because of her importance, the Yasigi mask, called the sister of the masks, is present at all ceremonies involving masks. Another mask representing a female ancestor is found among the Chokwe tribe of the Congo and Angola; this mask represents the scarified face of a woman who died at a young age, and is used during initiation rit-

uals. These masks, however, are not worn by men, but are worn by male performers.

Some masks are worn exclusively by kings, and even today, African kings may continue to wear masks during ceremonial occasions. For instance, in the Congo, the Kuba king wears a *moshambwooy* mask, which represents the mythical first king of the Kuba kingdom. He wears the masks during royal ceremonies, and upon his death, kings are typically buried with their mask. The Pende people of the Congo also had a number of masks that were only worn by Pende kings, such as the fearsome Pumbu mask, worn during times of social crisis in order for the chief to reassert his authority.

Finally, the Baule of the Ivory Coast have a tradition of creating portrait masks, known as *mblo* masks, which represent actual living people. They are carved to represent both the person as well as Baule values; for example, the eyes are typically depicted as pointing downward, because in many African cultures, it is a sign of respect to not look into the eyes of an elder or a person of higher status. They also typically feature scarification along the cheeks and forehead, on both the male and female masks, representing the ideal form of male and female beauty. These masks are worn during non-ritual dances known as *Gbagba* dances, in which the subject of the mask dances next to a dancer wearing the mask.

Maskmaking is a highly skilled art. In making a wooden mask, the maskmaker first chooses the proper tree, sometimes consults a diviner and offers a sacrifice to the spirit of the tree, because it is believed that the spirit of the tree may be transferred to the mask, increasing its power. Masks are carved, rubbed with palm oil, and then painted or stained. Afterward, the mask is decorated with natural fibers, leaves, feathers, skins, nuts, shells, beads, and other natural or manmade items. Because the masks represent the spirits of people, animals, or non-anthropomorphic spirits, they are considered sacred and can not be handled or worn by anyone. Wearing the mask temporarily transforms the wearer into the spirit, making him very powerful.

See also Masks; Scarification

Further Reading

Adams, Sarah. "Praise Her Beauty Well: Ùrì from the Body to Cloth." In *Call and Response: Journeys into African Art.* New Haven, CT: Yale University Art Gallery, 2000.

Berns, Marla C. "Ga'Anda Scarification: A Model for Art and Identity." In *Marks of Civilization: Artistic Transformations of the Human Body*, edited by Arnold Rubin, 57–76. Los Angeles: Museum of Cultural History, University of California, 1998.

Bohannon, Paul. "Beauty and Scarification amongst the Tiv." *Man* 56, no. 129 (1956): 117–21.

Cornet, J. *A Survey of Zairian Art.* Raleigh: North Carolina Museum of Art, 1978.

Drewal, Henry John. "Beauty and Being: Aesthetics and Ontology in Yoruba Body Art." In *Marks of Civilization: Artistic Transformations of the Human Body*, edited by Arnold Rubin, 83–96. Los Angeles: Museum of Cultural History, University of California, 1998.

Fisher, Angela. *Africa Adorned: A Panorama of Jewelry, Dress, Body Decoration, and Hair.* New York: Henry Abrams, 2000.

Roberts, Allen F. "Tabwa Tegumentary Inscription." In *Marks of Civilization: Artistic Transformations of the Human Body,* edited by Arnold Rubin, 41–56. Los Angeles: Museum of Cultural History, UCLA, 1988.

Vogel, Susan M. *Baule: African Art, Western Eyes.* New Haven, CT: Yale University Press, 1997.

Vogel, Susan. "Baule Scarification: The Mark of Civilisation." In *Marks of Civilization: Artistic Transformations of the Human Body,* edited by Arnold Rubin, 97–103. Los Angeles: Museum of Cultural History, UCLA, 1988.

Sumptuary Laws

Sumptuary laws are laws that place restrictions on clothing, food, or luxury consumption. They are often used to maintain class distinctions in stratified societies by restricting certain luxury items to elite classes. While clothing is a common target for sumptuary laws, they also sometimes extended to other forms of adornment, like **jewelry** and makeup. They were common in Europe from the 13th century into the 18th century, in Imperial **China** and **Japan**, and pre-colonial Africa, and even in colonial America. One of the earliest documented sumptuary laws dates from the third century BCE in Rome, and restricted the amount of gold that women could wear and the color of their tunics.

One reason for laws that aim to restrict the wearing of certain clothing and shoes is that governments (and the Church in Medieval Europe) often saw excessive spending on lavish fabrics to be both a sign of moral decay and vanity, but also a waste of money. The English in particular worried that the excessive spending on foreign materials like silk was problematic for society, and for the local economy. Another reason for these laws is that prices could be regulated by establishing restrictions on the amount of fabric that can be used in a product. Finally, the laws ensured that the lower classes did not appear to be striving to be above their station. Of special concern, evidently, was that prosperous merchants or craftsmen might be able to dress in clothing finer than members of the nobility.

While makeup was not always included in sumptuary laws, it was sometimes found in such laws. In Renaissance Italy, upper-class women lightened their skin, bleached their hair, and painted their eyes, lips, and cheeks, which was seen as an affront to God's creation as well as an unseemly focus on luxury. Another reason, however, for laws that restricted the type of makeup worn by women was that it was thought that women used cleverly applied makeup in order to deceive men into marrying them, and once married, to force their husbands to submit to them.

For instance, in 1670, the colony of New Jersey passed a law that prohibited women from using "scents, paints, cosmetics, washes, artificial teeth, false hair, Spanish wool, iron stays, hoops, high-heeled shoes, or bolstered hips" to "betray into matrimony" any man. Those who were convicted of such an offense would pay the penalty administered to those convicted of witchcraft (generally a year in prison for a minor offense; major offenses would be punished by hanging), and their marriages would be annulled.

See also Cosmetics

Further Reading

Kovesi Killerby, Catherine. *Sumptuary Law in Italy 1200–1500*. New York: Oxford University Press, 2002.

Wiesner, Merry. *Early Modern Europe, 1450–1789*. Cambridge: Cambridge University Press, 2006.

T

Teeth Filing

Altering the teeth for aesthetic reasons is a practice that has been found in cultures around the world.

Some cultures file their teeth into sharp points, such as the Mentawai of Sumatra, the hill tribes of Vietnam, the Dogon of Mali, the Efe of the Congo, and the Dinka of Sudan. In Bali, teeth are filed not for decorative reasons but because canine teeth symbolize negative emotions like anger, jealousy, and greed, which can be controlled through filing the teeth. For the Balinese, tooth filing is also an important rite of passage for adolescents, and helps to ease their transition into adulthood. Upper-class Mayans also filed their teeth, and sometimes etched designs onto the surface of the teeth; they also drilled holes into the teeth for the purposes of inserting jewels, a practice that would have been limited to the elites. Some cultures stained and filed the teeth to make them more beautiful; in

A Mentawai woman with filed teeth. Tooth filing, or *Pasi Piat*, is a beauty tradition and is practiced from adolescence. Due to pressure from the Indonesian government, this tradition is slowly losing its importance. (Corbis)

Vietnam, for example, black, filed teeth were preferred to white, straight teeth; and the Iban of Borneo not only blackened their teeth, but filed them and inserted a brass stud into a drilled hole. Throughout **Southeast Asia**, in fact, the practice of filing and blackening the teeth at puberty was a commonplace phenomenon.

Today in the contemporary body modification community, teeth sharpening is a relatively rare practice but is used by some people, including those who want to mimic the look of an animal, such as Eric Sprague or Stalking Cat. Tooth filing is done at a dentist's office, although some people have filed their own teeth at considerable risk. *See also* Dental Care; Teeth Painting

Further Reading

Alt, K., and S. Pichler. "Artificial Modifications of Human Teeth." In *Dental Anthropology Fundamentals, Limits and Prospects*, edited by K. Alt, F. Rosing, and M. Teschler-Nicola, 387–415. New York: Springer-Wien, 1998.

Hillson, S. *Dental Anthropology.* New York: Cambridge University Press, 1996.

Milner, G., and C. Larsen. "Teeth as Artifacts of Human Behavior: Intentional Mutilation and Accidental Modification." In *Advances in Dental Anthropology*, 357–78. New York: Wiley-Liss, 1991.

Teeth Painting

Teeth painting, or teeth blackening, refers to a custom whereby people intentionally blacken their teeth. It is most well known in Imperial Japan, but has been practiced elsewhere as well.

In Japan, tooth blackening is known as *ohaguro*. Practiced since ancient times, teeth painting was only discontinued in the 19th century. Originally it was practiced only by the elites; eventually royalty, samurai, and those who worked in the royal palaces and temples darkened their teeth after puberty. Until all warriors adopted the practice, soldiers could differentiate between their own side and the enemy based on who blackened their teeth and who did not. For the general population, married women and Geishas also blackened their teeth, as did others at ceremonial times such as at funerals. Beggars, outcasts, and the poor were forbidden from blackening their teeth. After the end of the Edo period in the 19th century, only the aristocrats continued the practice for a time, until it was officially banned in 1870. The dye was a combination of acids, iron, mineral powders, and tannins, usually steeped in tea, and was applied every few days. While one benefit of teeth painting was that the dye helped to prevent tooth decay, that was not the original intention. Instead, blackening the teeth was one way to ensure that they would never be seen, which was one way to disguise one's emotions. It was also a way to distinguish married from single women, protecting them from the advances of men, and, because the color black is considered very beautiful in Japan, ultimately came to be seen as a sign of feminine beauty. In addition, the blackness of the teeth, eyebrows, and hair set off the artificial whiteness of a lady's skin. One final reason was that it was said that white teeth reminded people of the white tiles that were used to venerate the ancestors. Today, it is still possible to see some Geisha who dye their teeth black.

Teeth painting has been practiced in other Asian cultures as well. For instance, it has long been practiced in Vietnam. Girls typically had their teeth dyed after puberty; the process took a few applications over the course of a week. Once a girl had her teeth dyed, she was able to be married. The dye can be made of a number of ingredients, including tree resin, iron, copper, tannin, or burnt coconut husks, and can either be reapplied to keep the teeth dark and shiny, or else many women chew betel nuts, which maintains the color. In Vietnam, it was once thought that to be civilized and human, it meant that one had dark

A Lahu woman in the Karen tribe of Thailand smiles, showing black teeth caused by chewing herbs. The Lahu tribes are a minority in Thailand, surviving mainly by opium cultivation. (Guido Vrola/Shutterstock)

teeth; only animals, savages, and evil spirits had white teeth. In fact, blackening the teeth helps keep one from being mistaken for such a spirit. Another reason for blackening the teeth is to keep them from being seen. As in other Asian cultures, the Vietnamese control their facial expressions, and often do not like to smile or laugh in such a way that the teeth show. Other **Southeast Asian** cultures that practice or practiced teeth painting (which has largely fallen out of fashion in recent years, due in part to the influence of the French in Indochina) include the Si La of Laos, whose women paint their teeth black, but whose men paint them red; and a number of tribes in the Philippines, who only blacken their teeth after marriage. The Chinese, for example, called the area black teeth country because of the prevalence of the practice. In Sumatra, teeth are filed both for aesthetic reasons and also because filing the teeth removes the enamel and makes it easier for the dye to take. Among the tribes of Thailand, darkened teeth were so highly prized that love poems compared the black teeth of beloved women to ebony and other woods, and the 19th century Thai king, Mongkut, had a set of false teeth made after he lost his teeth, which were carved of dark red Sappan wood. Finally, the people of many of the Pacific Islands such as Palau, the Mariana Islands, and the Caroline Islands also stained their teeth black.

It was also a trend, for a time, in Europe for people to stain their teeth dark. During the Elizabethan era, when sugar was both highly prized and highly expensive in Europe, elites were able to eat so much sugar that their teeth would rot, while the poor, who did not have access to expensive sugar, had relatively healthy teeth. Queen Elizabeth, the fashion trendsetter of the time, had black teeth due to her love of sugar, which caused a brief fad among middle class women to blacken their teeth as well. *See also* Dental Care; Japan; Teeth Filing; Teeth Whitening

Further Reading

Huard, Pierre, and Keith Botsford. *The Blackening of Teeth in Eastern Asia and in Indochina.* New Haven, CT: Human Relations Area Files, 1970.

Louis, Frederic. *Daily Life in Japan at the Time of the Samurai, 1185–1603.* New York: Praeger, 1972.

Zumbroich, T.J. "Teeth as Black as a Bumble Bee's Wings: The Ethnobotany of Teeth Blackening in Southeast Asia." *Ethnobotany Research and Applications* 7 (2009): 381–98.

Teeth Whitening

In the West, but especially in the United States, white, straight, even teeth are desired by both men and women, and cosmetic dentistry practices are geared toward achieving this ideal.

It is difficult to know exactly how long people have been attempting to clean and whiten their teeth, but researchers know that people around the world have been using sticks made from roots or branches to clean their teeth for thousands of years. In some parts of Africa, chewing sticks are still used to clean teeth, and scientists have found that these sticks, when chewed and frayed and then used to scrub the teeth, are effective in inhibiting the growth of microbes in the mouth.

The first bristle toothbrushes were developed in the 15th century in **China**. They were made with hog bristles, which were inserted into handles made of bone or bamboo. At that time, upper-class Europeans were using brushes made of softer horsehair, or used toothpicks made of brass or silver to clean their teeth. The poor continued to use chewing sticks. Artificial toothbrushes did not emerge until after the invention of nylon in 1938. The first nylon bristled toothbrush was the Dr. West's Miracle Tuft Toothbrush, introduced in 1938, and ultimately replaced the hog's hair brushes, especially after softer nylon was introduced in the 1950s.

The first toothpaste may have been developed by in Egypt some 4,000 years ago, and was made from powdered pumice mixed with vinegar, and brushed on with a chew stick. The Greeks and the Romans added in additional abrasives to help scrub the teeth, like crushed oyster shells. The Romans developed a paste containing human urine to clean their teeth; they realized, correctly, that ammonia can whiten teeth. In fact, ammonia continued to remain an ingredient in tooth cleaning pastes for hundreds of years. In the 19th century, tooth powders made of crushed chalk or brick became popular in Europe, and by the 20th century, tooth paste using hydrogen peroxide and baking soda became the standard formula for cleaning and whitening the teeth. Today, toothpaste continues to be made with cleaners like baking soda, abrasives like silica (which also help to whiten teeth), whiteners like peroxide, and fluoride to fight cavities.

From the Middle Ages until about the 19th century, people went to barber-surgeons for both limb removal and tooth removal, and those same barbers could also whiten teeth, by filing down the enamel and applying a corrosive acid to the surface of the teeth. Later, chlorinated lime combined with acid was also used, as was spraying chlorine gas into the mouth. At the end of the 19th century, hydrogen peroxide was discovered to whiten teeth, and in 1918, some dentists began shining intense lights onto teeth during the bleaching process to intensify the process.

In the 1980s, teeth whitening became a more prominent part of cosmetic dentistry as Americans began to demand whiter teeth. Dentists developed new whitening techniques that could be done at the dentist's office. In fact, teeth whitening procedures are the fastest growing aspect of cosmetic dentistry today. By the 1990s, companies like Procter and Gamble developed the first at-home teeth bleaching kits, which used bleaching agents in mouth trays or on strips that are affixed to the teeth for a period of time.

Techniques for whitening the teeth at the dentist's office include gel bleaching, in which a bleaching agent like carbamide peroxide or hydrogen peroxide is squirted into a tray that is fitted to the patient's mouth. Another method of whitening is laser bleaching or power bleaching in which halogen light or another high intensity light source is used to accelerate the bleaching process during a peroxide treatment.

At home, techniques are similar to those performed by cosmetic dentists, but the concentration of bleaching agent is much lower, in order to reduce the risks of chemical burn or overbleaching, and the trays are kept in the mouth for longer periods of time.

Another method for at-home treatment is to use whitening strips on which the bleaching agents have been applied. The strips are worn for 10 to 30 minutes at a time.

None of the above methods of whitening are permanent, and especially for people who drink a lot of red wine or coffee, stains will eventually return. Some people elect to have porcelain veneers applied to the teeth, which is a permanent way of making the teeth appear whiter by covering up the stained teeth.

While it's difficult to imagine today, white teeth have not, however, been universally popular. It is true that the many people work hard to whiten their teeth, but other cultures have preferred black teeth to white. Some Native American tribes prior to colonization, such as the Natchez, stained their teeth black with tobacco and wood ash. In **Japan**, women and many men once intentionally blackened their teeth, as did women in Renaissance Europe, to simulate the effect of rotten teeth from eating too much sugar. And throughout South and **Southeast Asia**, men and women both blackened their teeth.
See also Dental Care

Further Reading

Kwon, So-Ran, Seok-Hoon Ko, Linda Greenwall, and Ronald E. Goldstein. *Tooth Whitening in Esthetic Dentistry*. London: Quintessence, 2009.

Theater

Theater refers to a type of performance art in which actors portray a story, sometimes with music or dance, in front of an audience.

Many cultures' theatrical traditions did not begin as entertainment, but probably evolved out of ritual performances such as **shamanism**. Because the audience needs to see the faces of the actors, in order to understand the emotions that they are conveying, the practices of wearing makeup or **masks** date back to the earliest performances. Makeup and masks also allow the actor to melt into the character that he or she is portraying.

In the West, theater dates to the ancient Greeks, but dramatic performances are much older than that. For instance, every culture that has an oral storytelling tradition has a performative history in which performers acted or danced a story in front of an audience, or with a group of participants. The wearing of masks in some theatrical tradition no doubt dates to these performances, which have also been religious in nature. The shaman, for instance, when wearing a mask depicting a god, totemic animal, or ancestor spirit, embodied that spirit for the other participants or audience members. This same form of embodiment through the wearing of a mask is found in many forms of theater. African story telling traditions, for example, thus fit neatly into a history of theatrical performances.

In the West, theater originated in the city-state of Athens where political events and religious festivals and rituals of all types were common, and involved every level of the population. Greek actors performed dramas, tragedies, and comedies, all of which originally evolved, as did other theatrical traditions, from earlier religious ceremonies. The practices associated with the Cult of Dionysus, for example, including animal and human sacrifice, the use of

masks, and ecstatic dancing and trances, were ultimately formalized through dramatic performances that were played in front of audiences, complete with music, dancing, and singing. Because the Greeks acted in large amphitheaters that could seat thousands, it was critical that the audience could see the faces of the actors. To that end, actors carried or wore large masks with exaggerated **facial expressions** to convey the feelings of each character. The members of the chorus wore identical masks (since they acted collectively as a single character) that were different from those worn by the lead actors, all of whom were male, and wore female masks to portray women. Masks were made of wood, linen, or leather, decorated with human or animal hair, and covered the whole head and face. Masks had holes for the eyes and holes for the mouth, and some scholars have suggested that one function of the mask was to act as a resonance chamber for the voice of the actors. Greek theatrical styles influenced Roman theater and later, European theater, and the Romans borrowed the Greek practice of having the actors wear masks to convey their characters to the audience.

Large theatrical performances disappeared after the fall of the Roman Empire. No large theaters existed in Europe, and the Church frowned on the excesses of Roman theater. Street performers and traveling bards emerged and proliferated through the Middle Ages. One type of play performed during this period was known as a mystery play, which told stories out of the Old and New Testaments and were performed by actors wearing masks who depicted demons, sins, or dragons.

It was not until the Renaissance that theater grew once again in Europe, with new forms of masked theater like the commedia dell'arte, and it was also at this time that theatrical makeup replaced the use of masks. Actors (who were still male), wore makeup to highlight the personalities of their characters. Lead, soot, burnt cork, and other materials were used to make faces lighter or darker and to highlight facial features.

In the East, theater also goes back thousands of years. Chinese theater dates back to the Shang Dynasty, between the 18th and 12th centuries BCE, with the most popular form, Chinese opera, dating to about the third century. Chinese performances may derive, however, from ancient religious rituals called *nuo* in which masked performers frightened off evil spirits. Chinese opera performers traditionally wore elsaborately painted masks to represent their

characters but today primarily wear makeup that allows for individual facial expressions to be seen. The makeup represents the moral qualities and disposition of the character and use standardized features and colors that are well understood by the audience; for instance, black symbolizes fierceness, red courage, yellow ambition, and white treacherousness. When complete, the made up face looks like a mask.

In **India**, Sanskrit dramatic performances depicted tales about heroes, fantastic creatures, love stories, and Hindu gods. In the classical plays, actors tended to wear makeup, while in the folk performances in villages and temples around the country, actors often wore masks representing the animals, demons, gods, and heroes of Indian epics like the Ramayana. Today, Chou,

Chinese opera performer in elaborate costume. The use of masks is common in Chinese opera. (Corel)

Kathakali, and Gambhira dancers all wear masks representing the gods, goddesses, and other characters from Hindu mythology.

Japanese theater is one of the more recent theatrical forms, dating to the 14th century. Kabuki theatre, the most well known form, is one of dance drama in which actors (originally female, but later male) told stories from Japan's past. Actors do not wear masks but wear carefully applied makeup. The application process is known as *kao o tsukuru*, which means making a face, and allows the actor to get into character. Makeup, known as *kumadori*, is highly stylized and represents gender, age, character type, and personality. Wrinkles and lines are drawn onto very white faces, exaggerating the facial features and highlighting the emotions. As in Chinese theater, the colors used in Kabuki makeup are symbolic of personality traits.
See also China; Cosmetics; India; Japan; Masks; Shamanism

Further Reading

Beacham, Richard C. *The Roman Theatre and Its Audience*. Cambridge, MA: Harvard University Press, 1996.

Brooke, Iris. *Costume in Greek Classical Drama*. London: Methuen, 1962.

Shaver, Ruth M. *Kabuki Costume*. London: Simon & Schuster, 1991.

Yarrow, Ralph. *Indian Theatre: Theatre of Origin, Theatre of Freedom*. London: Routledge, 2001.

Tibet and Nepal

The Himalayan region of Tibet and Nepal shares cultural beliefs and practices with **China** to the north and **India** to the south, including nostril piercing and the use of masks, which is informed by **shamanism**, Hinduism, and **Buddhism**.

Like women in India, women in Tibet and Nepal often get their nostrils pierced as a form of decoration. Unlike India, however, septum piercing is also common for tribal women in this region.

The Himalayan region has a long tradition of shamanism involving masks, most likely borrowed from the nomadic peoples of Central Asia. The local form of shamanism was known as Bonism, which still influences Tibetans today. These traditions go back thousands of years and have shaped the use of masks in dramatic and dance performances in the region. In more recent centuries, both Buddhism and Hinduism have influenced the appearance and use of masks.

The Magar and Gurung tribes in the highland regions of Nepal create hardwood masks while those of the lowland areas, such as the Tharu, create masks made of softwood. Both types are elaborately decorated with paint, clay, fur, and some masks have nose rings. Other masks are created from goat skin, felt, and even tree fungus. These masks represented animal spirits like goats, yaks, tigers, and lions, and were worn during ritual dances. Masks were also hung on walls to protect homes from evil spirits.

With the influence of Buddhism and Hinduism, masks began to be created to represent the heroes, demons, and gods of these religions, and are today worn in dance performances throughout the region, in which Hindu epics like the Ramayana and the Mahabharata are performed. Buddhist masks are used in dances to invoke guardian spirits and to scare off evil ones. For instance, Tibetan monks practice Chham dances that commemorate a Buddhist guru and second Buddha known as Padmasambhava. This dance includes characters who wear wood and papier-mâché masks representing the eight aspects of Padmasambhava as well as the Lord of Death and his demons; they are also known as devil dances, and are thought to exorcise evil spirits. The masks used in these dances are kept in monasteries between performances. Another common Tibetan drama is the Dance of the Red Tiger Devil, in which lamas wearing masks representing demons and gods exorcise demons from the community. Local village rituals and performances may borrow from the Hindu

and Buddhist characters, but also incorporate deities from their local myths.

Later, with the rise of opera, masks began to be used in a strictly performative, entertaining form, although they derive from the shamanism and bonism of the past. Today, masks are primarily made of clay, plaster, or wood, combined with animal skins and cloth and are painted with colors that symbolize emotions and virtues. For example, black masks represent cruelty, purple jealousy, and white peace.

See also India; Masks; Nose Piercing; Shamanism

Further Reading

Bradley, Lisa, and Eric Chazot. *Masks of the Himalayas*. New York: Pace Primitive, 1990.

Monks perform a sacred masked dance, or Cham dance, at a festival in a temple courtyard in central Tibet, 2008. Masks are worn during ritual dances in cultures around the world as a way to symbolically turn the performers into gods, animals, or spirits. (iStockPhoto.com)

Chazot, Eric. "Tribal Masks of the Himalayas." *Orientations* 10 (October 1988): 52–64.

Tongue Piercing

Tongue piercing is a piercing of the tongue, the most common oral piercing in the modern West, and one of the most popular **facial piercing**s. Tongue piercings are worn for decorative purposes and for sexual purposes. Women also often report feeling empowered by wearing a tongue piercing.

While tongue piercings for decorative purposes are not common outside of the body modification scene, tongue piercings did play a role in ancient Mesoamerican blood rituals. Maya leaders in particular would cut or pierce a particular part of the body, in order to give a blood sacrifice to the gods. For instance, women were known to pull a thorn-covered rope through a hole in their tongues. Members of a number of Northwest Indian tribes such as the Haida, Kwaikiutul, and Tlingit also pierced their tongues as an offering to the gods. In addition, Fakirs and Sufis from the **Middle East** practiced tongue piercing as a form of sacrifice and as proof of a trance state.

Tongues are usually pierced in the center, with the piercing going through the top and bottom of the tongue. Some people choose to get an off-center piercing, and very rarely is a horizontal, or side-to-side, piercing chosen. Other rare placements include tongue surface piercings. Related piercings include the tongue web piercing, which is a piercing through the frenulum— the piece of tissue that connects the tongue to the bottom of the mouth. The edges of the tongue can be pierced as well with a

Pierced tongues are becoming a more common form of body modification among young people in the West. (Andrei Malov/Dreamstime.com)

tongue rim piercing, which generally uses a ring to encircle the edge of the tongue. Jewelry for tongue piercings is usually a barbell.

See also Facial Piercing; Oral Piercing; Tongue Splitting

Further Reading

Angel, Elayne. *The Piercing Bible: The Definitive Guide to Safe Body Piercing.* Berkeley, CA: Celestial Arts, 2009.

Tongue Splitting

Tongue splitting is an extreme body modification that involves the splitting of the tongue from the tip backward; the result is a literal forked tongue. While still rare, tongue splitting is growing in popularity within the body modification community in the West. Reasons for having the procedure done include aesthetics (as some people enjoy the way that they look) as well as sexual enhancement.

Some people, with practice, can independently move and control the two halves of their tongue. For others, there is a personal or spiritual benefit from it, while for still others, it simply looks and feels different. Like many modern body modifications, tongue splitting is also done because people simply want the ability to shape their bodies according to their own desires.

In the West, tongue splitting was first documented in 1997, and is so far best associated with people who attempt to transform their bodies into animals, such as Erik Sprague, who goes by the name Lizardman. Snakes, for example, have forked tongues, which allow them to smell from two different sides at once.

Tongue splitting is mentioned in a number of ancient Indian texts on yogic practices. Khechari mudra describes a practice in which the tongue is split like a serpent, washed with a mixture of milk, ashes, and clarified butter, and is flipped into the back of the throat where the two forks of the tongue block the nostril cavities. The yogi is encouraged to remain like this for several days in a semi-unconscious state.

Because tongue splitting is a surgical procedure, it is illegal in many localities for a nonlicensed doctor to perform it, so those who want a split tongue must either convince a surgeon to do it, or they do it

James Keen, a 19-year-old from Scottsville, Kentucky, shows off his split tongue at his home, May 7, 2003. James got his tongue split in December by a piercer after a surgeon declined to do it for him. He says the piercer used a scalpel heated by a blow torch and no anesthetic. (AP/Wide World Photos)

themselves or with friends. Do-it-yourself surgeries pose substantial health risks including blood loss, nerve damage, and affected speech. Other than the risks, however, the process is relatively simple: the tongue is sliced down the middle with a scalpel, heated blade, or laser, and allowed to heal in a split state. Other methods include using a tongue piercing in order to tie off the tongue with a piece of string, tightening it gradually until the tongue separates. This evidently is quite a painful procedure.

See also Tongue Piercing

Further Reading

Schwenk, K. "Why Snakes Have Forked Tongues." *Science* 263, no. 5153 (1994): 1573–77.

U

Unibrow

The term *unibrow* indicates a pair of eyebrows that are so bushy that they appear to be one eyebrow, rather than two. Synophrys is the medical term that refers to the fusion of the eyebrows, a condition that in some cases can be indicative of developmental disorders such as Cornelia de Lange syndrome.

In the West, having a unibrow is considered unattractive, especially for women, but there are some cultures in which it has been favored. In general, men are expected to have more facial hair and bushier eyebrows than women, but some cultures go further and see very thick eyebrows as a sign of virility for men. On the other hand, 19th-century psychiatrist and criminologist Cesare Lombroso saw heavy eyebrows and strong jaws as the two most important indicators of criminality in a man. Even today, many people interpret a person's character by their facial features, and eyebrows play a major role in determining what we think about a person. Very thick, bushy eyebrows, and eyebrows that appear to grow together, can make a person seem angry, fierce, or intense. In general, eyebrows make faces much more expressive, so having prominent eyebrows makes a face more expressive—good or bad.

In the West, and in cultures in which unibrows are considered unattractive, bushy brows can be controlled via hair removal

Frida Kahlo was a Mexican artist who painted her image in a number of portraits, all of which emphasized, and exaggerated, her unibrow. Frida Kahlo, *Self-Portrait with Curly Hair*, 1935, oil on tin, 7-¼ x 5-¾ inches. (AP/Wide World Photos)

techniques like plucking, waxing, threading, or shaving. Even men with unibrows may resort to such measures, especially when faced with social pressure to do so.

Unibrows are favored for both men and women in some Central Asian countries. For example, in Tajikistan, unibrows are considered to be so attractive that some women try to mimic their appearance via makeup or dying the skin with herbal concoctions like usma. In Iran, unibrows are also considered beautiful for women, as it was in ancient Greece, where it signified both beauty and intelligence, and was emphasized with kohl.

Euro-American folklore has a number of beliefs, some contradictory, about unibrows. For example, thick eyebrows are considered to be a sign of a bad temper or disposition, but having eyebrows that grow together could indicate anything from deceit, jealousy, stinginess, a short life, or wealth.

The Unibrow Club is a Web site that celebrates people with unibrows, and features such celebrity unibrow wearers as Bert from Sesame Street, George W. Bush, Noel Gallagher from the group Oasis, and Leonid Brezhev. But perhaps the most famous wearer of a unibrow was Mexican artist Frida Kahlo, who not only had bushy eyebrows, but in her self-portraits, she exaggerated them, making them a fundamental part of her public image.

See also Eyebrow Grooming; Facial Hair and Removal; Physiognomy and Phrenology

Further Reading

Cosio, Robyn, and Cynthia Robins. *The Eyebrow*. New York: Harper Collins, 2000.

V

Veil of Veronica

The Veil of Veronica is, according to legend, a piece of cloth that was used by a woman named Veronica (or Bernice in Greek legend) to wipe the sweat and blood from the face of Jesus Christ while he was en route to his crucifixion at Golgotha. The cloth was then imprinted with the image of Jesus's suffering face, and is now considered to be an important relic associated with Jesus. This episode is immortalized in the Sixth Station of the Cross.

Like the Shroud of Turin and the Image of Edessa, the Veil of Veronica is known as an acheiropoeta—an image made by God, but many scholars and Christians alike consider the veil to simply be a legend. In fact, the name Veronica is simply a combination of the Latin word vera (true or authentic) and the Greek word for icon, meaning an authentic icon of Christ. The Veil of Veronica is thought by believers to be able to cure a number of ailments such as blindness and even death.

A woman by the name of Veronica first appears in print in the apocryphal Acts of Pilate in 380 CE (but may date to the mid-second century). She was identified as the woman mentioned in the New Testament who experienced 12 years of hemorrhaging but was cured by touching Jesus's clothes (Mark 5:24–34; Matt. 9:18–26; and Luke 8:40–56). The first known written account of the veil dates to the late seventh century when a story called the Avenging of the Saviour tells of how a woman named Veronica was in possession of the cloth, and when Tiberius saw the cloth, he (and the others present) were all cured of their illnesses. At some point, it was said to have been transported to Camulia, in modern Turkey, and then to Constantinople, the seat of the Byzantine Empire, by the end of the sixth century, where it was used to protect the city from harm. From there, it was sent to Rome for temporary safekeeping at the turn of the eighth century. There, Pope John VII built a chapel called the Oratory of St. Mary of the Veronica to hold the relic. The veil was first displayed in the year 1300 by Pope Innocent III and became known as a Mirabilia Urbis or wonder of the city for pilgrims who traveled to Rome.

Many people feel that the veil was destroyed in the 16th century when Rome was sacked by Charles V, but others claim that it was hidden and saved in Saint Peter's Basilica; still others suggest that it was either stolen or destroyed during the rebuilding of Saint Peter's in 1608. In fact, in 1618, the Vatican commissioned an inventory of the objects held in Saint Peter's, and the list included the reliquary in which the veil had been contained, but no veil itself. Some scholars feel that the veil was indeed destroyed because of a law that was passed by Pope Urban VIII in 1629 that prohibited the making of replicas of the veil, and that ordered all existing replicas to be destroyed. On the other hand, the official Catholic position is that the veil is housed at the Vatican today. It is said to be kept within a statue of Veronica next to the altar. It, or a replica, is displayed briefly every year on the Sunday before Palm Sunday, but no scientific analyses of the cloth have ever been made.

In 1999 a Jesuit art historian named Heinrich Pfeiffer announced that he had found the original Veil of Veronica at the Sanctuary of the Sacred Face in Manoppello, Italy. Unlike the other stories of the veil, which come from Jesus's journey to his crucifixion, believers in the Manoppello veil suggest that this was instead the cloth that was laid over Jesus's face after the crucifixion, when he lay in his tomb. In other words, it may be the Image of Edessa. This veil is a piece of transparent linen measuring 17 centimeters by 24 centimeters, which clearly shows the face of a man on it. The face, featuring wide, open eyes, contains bruises and scars, as well as clotted blood, and observers say that the image appears on both sides of the cloth. (Prior to the 17th century, images of the veil showed Christ with his eyes open; later copies showed him with his eyes closed.) The linen is displayed in a wood and glass frame. The veil was allegedly given to the sanctuary in 1638 by a man who bought it from a woman, who herself had received it as a dowry in 1608; sometime prior to this, the veil would have been stolen from Saint Peter's.

The Manoppello veil was examined by scholars in 1977, who claim that the veil, made of a rare silk called Byssus, could not have been painted nor woven with colored fibers. More recent analysis shows that the image is identical in size and appearance to the Shroud of Turin, although the shroud shows Jesus with his eyes closed, while the veil shows him with his eyes open; even the facial features and tufts of hair are thought to be of the same dimensions on both relics. On the other hand, the Manoppello veil looks much more like a stylized Renaissance painting than an image of a person, and does not resemble any of the well-known replicas that were thought to be made from the original veil. Those replicas include the Holy Face of Alicante, which dates to the mid-15th century and is kept in the Monastery of the Holy Face in Alicante, Spain; the Holy Face of Vienna, made as a copy of the original in 1617 and kept in the Hofburg Palace in Vienna; and The Holy Face of Jaén, which dates to the 14th century and is kept in the Cathedral of Jaén in Spain.

See also Christianity; Image of Edessa; Shroud of Turin

Further Reading

Badde, Paul. *The Face of God: The Rediscovery of the True Face of Jesus.* San Francisco: Ignatius Press, 2010.

Kuryluk, Eewa. *Veronica and Her Cloth: History, Symbolism and Structure of a True Image.* Cambridge, MA: Blackwell, 1991.

Wilson, Ian. *Holy Faces, Secret Places: An Amazing Quest for the Face of Jesus.* New York: Doubleday, 1991.

Veiling

Veiling refers to the practice of covering the hair, face, or body with a cloth. Veiling is widely practiced by Muslim women, but veils can also be worn by Jewish or Christian women. In the West, many people see the veil as a sign of oppression toward women, but in cultures that practice veiling, the veil is seen much more positively.

Veils have long been worn by women in a variety of cultures. For example, in the Middle East, where Judaism, Christianity, and Islam developed, privacy is a highly valued concept for women, and seeing a woman's face is often seen as a sign of intimacy, to be reserved only for family. Hiding one's face both protects one's privacy, but can also indicate humility. For example, in the Bible, when men hide their faces before God (Exod. 3:6; Isa. 6:2; or 1 Kings 19:13 when Elijah wrapped his face in his mantle), it means that they are showing humility and reverence before Him, as in the traditions of many cultures that demand social inferiors not make eye contact with those who are superior to them.

But while there are traditions in which men cover their heads or hair, especially during prayer, those traditions typically distinguish between men and women. In the Jewish tradition, men are expected to cover their hair during prayer as a sign of respect for God, but in the Orthodox tradition, married women are expected to cover their hair at all times. Christianity also distinguishes between men and women. For instance, in 1 Corinthians 11:4–7, men are to uncover their heads in prayer, since they were made in the image of God, while women must cover their heads, since they reflect only the glory of man. Today, it is rare for Christian women to cover their heads during prayer but some Catholics still practice this. Some orders of nuns mandate the wearing of a veil or other head covering, and groups like the Amish and the Mennonites still require the wearing of head coverings for their women. Finally, in Islam, only women are expected to cover their faces and hair.

While the veil is most strongly associated with Islam, veiling predates Islam by thousands of years. Veiling for women was a sign of prestige in the Assyrian, Greek, Persian, Indian, and Byzantine cultures. In these cultures, elite women covered their hair or face, but in ancient Rome, servants covered their hair as a sign of respect. Because veiling was a sign of status, many cultures prohibited the wearing of veils by prostitutes, although lower-class women often did wear veils in order to appear as if they were of a higher class. The practice may have traveled to Arab countries, before the time of Muhammad, via the Byzantine and Persian Empires. But during Muhammad's own life, veiling was still not a fundamental part of Islam—his own wives, for example, did not wear the veil nor were they secluded, until the end of his life. Eventually, however, Islam embraced the veil, and as Islam spread from Saudi Arabia to other cultures, the wearing of veils spread along with it, becoming common by the eighth century—first by elites, and later by lower-class women. Rural and nomadic cultures, however, often did not veil their women. By the 10th century, many countries began instituting laws restricting the behavior of women, and mandating veiling or seclusion.

In Muslim countries, women may cover their faces, a portion of their face, their hair, or, in the most extreme cases, their entire bodies. Veils can cover the entire face; they can cover the entire body, as in the burqa worn in Afghanistan and originating in Pakistan, or the niqab, worn in the Gulf States; or they can be worn around the head and under the chin, as in the hijab, the most popular form of head covering. The chador is a full-length body shawl that is held together in the front with a pin or by hand and is common in Iran.

Veiling is an example of purdah—the seclusion of women. It is also a response to the Qu'ranic demand that women dress modestly in public (although veiling itself is not explicitly discussed in the Qu'ran). To be veiled is to be protected and secluded, and to have one's anonymity maintained. In cultures that have a strong honor-shame complex, as in the Middle East, a woman can bring shame onto her entire family by her personal conduct. If she were to be violated, her whole family, but especially the men, would be shamed. But veiling oneself when appearing in

Afghan women, one in a burqa, stand on a rubble-strewn street. The burqa, worn in many regions of the country, covers a woman's body from head to toe, leaving only a panel of netting over the eyes. Other cultures favor other types of veils, which may only cover the hair or part of the face. (Lizette Potgieter/Shutterstock)

public protects a woman from the gaze of men, protecting her honor, and that honor is then extended to the members of her family. Because men respect the veil, they will be less likely to prey upon a woman who is veiled. The veil then represents respect, modesty, humility, and obedience—to religion, to culture, and to the family. It also shows that she protects her chastity or her fidelity to her husband, thus guaranteeing virginity upon marriage and paternity to her husband.

In addition, as in the past, the veil represents wealth and status. In stratified societies, elite women often experience the greatest amount of control over their sexuality. The veil is one way to protect the wealth, status, and honor of well-to-do families by ensuring that the women in those families do not have sexual relations with lower-class men. In addition, in the past, only wealthy families could afford to seclude their women, so veiling is a sign of status and prestige as well.

Each culture has different rules about the wearing of the veil. Some cultures have the law of hijab, a mandatory code for women to veil in public. This was the case in Afghanistan under the Taliban, in Saudi Arabia, and in Kuwait and Iran today. Failure to comply can result in imprisonment, harassment, or physical punishment. The veil then represents, ironically, freedom because women can use their veils to go out in public; here it acts as a form of portable seclusion. Some countries, like Tunisia and Turkey, prohibit the wearing of veils in public buildings or schools. Most Muslim countries do not have mandatory veiling laws, so women can voluntarily choose to wear the veil. However, to veil or not to veil is often not truly a woman's choice but is constrained by her family.

Starting in the late 19th century, some in the Middle East began to encourage a move away from veiling and other symbols of traditional life. The first country to ban the veil was Iran, which prohibited

Hijab Lawsuits

Abercrombie and Fitch is an American retailer of casual clothing for young people. The company has been sued for their look policy, which mandates that employees working in their retail stores uphold certain standards of appearance. According to a 2004 lawsuit, those standards of appearance were discriminatory toward non-white employees, and according to a 2009 suit, against disabled employees. And in both 2009 and 2010, female Muslim employees and potential employees were told that they could not wear their headscarves, which were said to be in violation of the look policy. These women sued the company and enlisted the help of the Equal Employment Opportunity Commission, who ruled that the company could not legally fire nor refuse to hire them. In June 2011, a judge ruled against the company in the case of the first woman's lawsuit, and in July, she was awarded $20,000 in damages. In the meantime, the other lawsuits are moving forward as well.

the wearing of the veil in the 1930s. Egypt, while not banning the veil, began to move away from it in the 1920s so much so that the veil became, until recently, almost nonexistent in that country. Later in the 20th century, however, the veil and other markers of modesty for women have seen a revitalization. Veiling is now associated with Islamic nationalism, and is seen as a challenge to Western values, colonization, and modernization.

Today, due to the conflicts between Western Christian societies and Islamic cultures, veiling has become increasingly controversial. In early 2011, France banned the wearing of face coverings, after a contentious public debate. Those in support of the law see it as a way to protect Muslim women from control by their husbands and to force the assimilation of Middle Eastern populations into French society. Those opposed to the law see it as a sign of the increasing stigmatization of Muslims in France.

See also Christianity; Judaism; Middle East

Further Reading

Abu-Lughod, Lila. *Remaking Women: Feminism and Modernity in the Middle East.* Princeton, NJ: Princeton University Press, 1998.

Bailey, David A., and Gilane Tawadros, eds. *Veil: Veiling, Representation, and Contemporary Art.* Cambridge, MA: Massachusetts Institute of Technology Press, 2003.

Fernea, Elizabeth W., and Basima Q. Bezirgan. *Middle Eastern Muslim Women Speak.* Austin: University of Texas Press, 1977.

Shirazi, Faegheh. *The Veil Unveiled: The Hijab in Modern Culture.* Gainesville: University Press of Florida, 2001.

W

Warts

Warts are small benign tumors that grow on the skin. They are generally caused by the human papilloma virus, and because they are contagious, can be caused by touching another person's warts. They can appear on the hands, on the feet, on the face, on the genitals (genital warts), or on the soles of the feet or hands (plantar warts).

Warts are generally considered to be unattractive, especially when they are on the face (this is probably why European witch lore always finds witches have warts on their faces), and are the subject of a wide variety of cultural beliefs and practices. For example, it was once a common belief in Europe that touching a toad can give a person warts. This is because some toads have bumps on their skin, so it was long assumed that touching those bumps would transmit warts to the human. It has also been commonly believed that warts are caused by magic, and that witches can curse a person with warts. One of the reasons for the wide variety of beliefs about warts is that warts appear to come and go with no obvious cause.

Warts can be treated effectively depending on the type of wart. For instance, a new vaccine can prevent infection with the human papiloma virus (HPV), and thus can prevent genital warts and other warts caused by HPV. Warts can also be removed with salicylic acid, silver nitrate, or even duct tape; can be frozen off with liquid nitrogen; can be sliced off; or can be removed with laser treatments.

There is also a wide variety of folk remedies for warts. In the European tradition, warts can be given away, sold, and even given to the dead. For instance, rubbing a penny over a wart is one way of selling that wart to someone else. You can give a wart to the dead by rubbing the mud from funeral mourners on a boot, or by throwing a rock at a funeral procession, when chanting a magical phrase such as "wart, wart, follow the corpse." You could give it to someone else by rubbing the wart with your hand and then wishing it upon someone else, and you can bury it buy rubbing a beet over a wart and then burying it in the garden. In fact, rubbing the wart onto something, and then burying it or throwing it away is considered to be an effective cure, regardless of the item used. But watch where you throw it away! If the item that the wart touched is thrown away where someone else can pick it up, then you've given the wart to him. Because toads and frogs are thought to cause warts, it should not be surprising that they can cure them. Allowing a toad to urinate on one's wart can make it go away, and killing a frog and rubbing the still-twitching leg on the wart will also get rid of it. It was believed that rubbing menstrual fluid, sunrise dew, dishwater, lemon, sow's urine, mashed potato bugs, or cow manure over a wart also would cause it to disappear. Finally, the number three is a magical number, so reciting a prayer three times over a wart, or reciting three holy names, can cure a wart, as can letting a Negro kiss it three times. In addition, in Wales there were once wart charmers who could remove one's warts for a fee.

See also Face Folklore

Further Reading

Burns, D. A. "'Warts and All'—the History and Folklore of Warts: A Review." *Journal of the Royal Society of Medicine* 85 (1992): 37–40.

Bibliography

Aarne, Antti, and Stith Thompson. *The Types of the Folktale: A Classification and Bibliography.* Helsinki: Academia Scientiarum Fennica, 1961.

Abrahams, Roger D. *Blues for New Orleans: Mardi Gras and America's Creole Soul.* Philadelphia: University of Pennsylvania Press, 2006.

Abu-Lughod, Lila. *Remaking Women: Feminism and Modernity in the Middle East.* Princeton, NJ: Princeton University Press, 1998.

Adams, Sarah. "Praise Her Beauty Well: Ùrì from the Body to Cloth." In *Call and Response: Journeys into African Art.* New Haven, CT: Yale University Art Gallery, 2000.

Aihara, Kyoko. *Geisha: A Living Tradition.* London: Carlton Books, 2000.

Allison, Kevin, and Dr. Faye Z. Belgrave. *African American Psychology: From Africa to America.* Thousand Oaks, CA: Sage, 2005.

Alt, K., and S. Pichler. "Artificial Modifications of Human Teeth." In *Dental Anthropology Fundamentals, Limits and Prospects,* edited by K. Alt, F. Rosing, and M. Teschler-Nicola, 387–415. New York: SpringerWien, 1998.

Ammer, Christine. *The American Heritage Dictionary of Idioms.* Boston: Houghton Mifflin, 1997.

Angel, Elayne. *The Piercing Bible: The Definitive Guide to Safe Body Piercing.* Berkeley, CA: Celestial Arts, 2009.

Anocona, George. *Pablo Remembers, The Fiesta of The Day of the Dead.* New York: Lothrop, Lee, and Shepard Books, 1993.

Badde, Paul. *The Face of God: The Rediscovery of the True Face of Jesus.* San Francisco: Ignatius Press, 2010.

Bailey, David A., and Gilane Tawadros, eds. *Veil: Veiling, Representation, and Contemporary Art.* Cambridge, MA: Massachusetts Institute of Technology Press, 2003.

Baldaev, Danzig, Sergei Vasiliev, and Alexei Plutser-Sarno. *Russian Criminal Tattoo Encyclopaedia.* London: Steidl Publishing, 2003.

Balsamo, Anne. "On the Cutting Edge: Cosmetic Surgery and the Technological Production of the Gendered Body." *Camera Obscura* 28 (1992): 206–37.

Barker, John H., Niki Stamos, and Allen Furr. "Research and Events Leading to Facial Transplantation." *Clinical Plastic Surgery* 34 (2007): 233–50.

Baskin, Judith. *Jewish Women in Historical Perspective.* Detroit: Wayne State University Press, 1991.

Beacham, Richard C. *The Roman Theatre and Its Audience.* Cambridge, MA: Harvard University Press, 1996.

Beck, Emily M., and John Bartlett. *Familiar Quotations: A Collection of Passages, Phrases, and Proverbs Traced to Their Sources in Ancient and Modern Literature.* Boston: Little Brown, 1980.

Beijing College of Traditional Chinese Medicine. *Essentials of Chinese Acupuncture.* New York: Pergamon Press, 1981.

Bellinzoni, Arthur J. *The Old Testament: An Introduction to Biblical Scholarship.* Amherst, NY: Prometheus Books, 2009.

Bendersky, Gordon. "Tlatilco Sculptures, Diprosopus, and the Emergence of Medical Illustrations." *Perspectives in Biology and Medicine* 43, no. 4 (2000): 477–501.

Berns, Marla C. "Ga'Anda Scarification: A Model for Art and Identity." In *Marks of Civilization: Artistic Transformations of the Human Body*, edited by Arnold Rubin, 57–76. Los Angeles: Museum of Cultural History, University of California, 1998.

Bogdan, Robert. *Freak Show.* Chicago: University of Chicago Press, 1988.

Bohannon, Paul. "Beauty and Scarification amongst the Tiv." *Man* 56, no. 129 (1956): 117–21.

Bond, Michael Harris. *Beyond the Chinese Face: Insights from Psychology.* New York: Oxford University Press, 1991.

Bond, Selena, and Thomas F. Cash. "Black Beauty: Skin Color and Body Images among African-American College Women." *Journal of Applied Social Psychology* 22, no. 11 (1992): 874–88.

Bradley, Lisa, and Eric Chazot. *Masks of the Himalayas.* New York: Pace Primitive, 1990.

Brandes, Stanley H. *Skulls to the Living, Bread to the Dead: The Day of the Dead in Mexico and Beyond.* Malden, MA: Blackwell, 2006.

Bray, Warwick. *Everyday Life of the Aztecs.* New York: Dorset Press, 1968.

Bridges, Lillian. *Face Reading in Chinese Medicine.* St. Louis, MO: Churchill Livingstone, 2004.

Brooke, Iris. *Costume in Greek Classical Drama.* London: Methuen, 1962.

Brown, C. S., B. Gander, M. Cunningham, A. Furr, D. Vasilic, O. Wiggins, J. C. Banis, M. Vossen, C. Maldonado, G. Perez-Abadia, and J. H. Barker. "Ethical Considerations in Face Transplantation." *International Journal of Surgery* 5 (2007): 353–64.

Bruce, V., and A. Young. *In the Eye of the Beholder: The Science of Face Perception.* Oxford: Oxford University Press, 2000.

Brunvand, Jan H. *American Folklore: An Encyclopedia.* New York: Garland, 1996.

Brush, Pippa. "Metaphors of Inscription: Discipline, Plasticity and the Rhetoric of Choice." *Feminist Review* 58 (1998): 22–43.

Burns, D. A. " 'Warts and All'—the History and Folklore of Warts: A Review." *Journal of the Royal Society of Medicine* 85 (1992): 37–40.

Cahlon, Baruch, and Sam S. Rakover. "Face Recognition: Cognitive and Computational Processes." *Advances in Consciousness Research* 31. Amsterdam: John Benjamins Publishing Company, 2001.

Camphausen, Rufus C. *Return of the Tribal: A Celebration of Body Adornment: Piercing, Tattooing, Scarification, Body Painting.* Rochester, VT: Park Street Press, 1997.

Carmichael, Elizabeth, and Chole Sayer. *The Skeleton at the Feast: The Day of the Dead in Mexico.* Austin: University of Texas Press, 1992.

Chawanaputorn, D., V. Patanaporn, P. Malikaew, P. Khongkhunthian, and P. A. Reichart. "Facial and Dental Characteristics of Padaung Women (long-Neck Karen) Wearing Brass Neck Coils in Mae Hong Son Province, Thailand." *American Journal of Orthodontics and Dentofacial Orthopedics* 131, no. 5 (2007): 639–45.

Chazot, Eric. "Tribal Masks of the Himalayas." *Orientations* 10 (October 1988): 52–64.

Chevalier-Skolnikoff, Suzanne. "Facial Expression of Emotion in Nonhuman Primates." In *Darwin and Facial Expression: A Century of Research in Review*, edited by Paul Ekman, 11–89. Cambridge, MA: Malor Books, 2006.

Cicero. *The Nature of the Gods.* Trans. P. G. Walsh. New York: Clarendon Press, 1997.

Cleese, John, and Brian Bates. *The Human Face.* New York: Dorling Kindersley, 2001.

Cockrell, Dale. *Demons of Disorder: Early Blackface Minstrels and Their World.* Cambridge: Cambridge University Press, 1997.

Cordain, Loren, Staffan Lindeberg, Magdalena Hurtado, Kim Hill, S. Boyd Eaton, and Jennie Brand-Miller. "Acne Vulgaris: A Disease of Western Civilization." *Archives of Dermatology* 138 (2002): 1584–90.

Cornet, J. *A Survey of Zairian Art.* Raleigh: North Carolina Museum of Art, 1978.

Corson, Richard. *Fashions in Eyeglasses from the 14th Century to the Present Day.* London: Peter Owen, 1980.

Cosio, Robyn, and Cynthia Robins. *The Eyebrow.* New York: Harper Collins, 2000.

Coss, Richard G., and Brian T. Schowengerdt. "Evolution of the Modern Human Face: Aesthetic and Attributive Judgments of a Female Profile Warped Along a Continuum of Paedomorphic to Late Archaic Craniofacial Structure." *Ecological Psychology* 10, no. 1 (1998): 1–24.

Dain, Bruce R. *A Hideous Monster of the Mind: American Race Theory in the Early Republic.* Cambridge, MA: Harvard University Press, 2002.

D'Ambrosio, Antonio. *Women and Beauty in Pompeii.* Los Angeles: J. Paul Getty Museum, 2001.

Daniels, Cora L. M. *Encyclopedia of Superstitions, Folklore, and the Occult Sciences of the World: A Comprehensive Library of Human Belief.* Detroit: Gale Research, 1971.

Dart, Raymond. "The Waterworn Australopithecine Pebble of Many Faces from Makapansgat." *South African Journal of Science* 70 (1974): 167–69.

Darwin, Charles. *The Expression of the Emotions in Man and Animals.* Chicago: University of Chicago Press, 1965.

Davis, Kathy. *Reshaping the Female Body: The Dilemma of Cosmetic Surgery.* London: Routledge, 1995.

DeMello, Margo. *Bodies of Inscription: A Cultural History of the Modern Tattoo Community.* Durham, NC: Duke University Press, 2000.

DeMello, Margo. *Encyclopedia of Body Adornment.* Westport, CT: Greenwood Press, 2007.

Diamant, Anita. *The New Jewish Wedding.* New York: Simon and Schuster, 2001.

Didron, Adolphe N. *Christian Iconography: The History of Christian Art in the Middle Ages.* New York: F. Ungar, 1965.

Downer, Lesley. *Women of the Pleasure Quarters: The Secret History of the Geisha.* New York: Broadway Books, 2001.

Drewal, Henry John. "Beauty and Being: Aesthetics and Ontology in Yoruba Body Art." In *Marks of Civilization: Artistic Transformations of the Human Body*, edited by Arnold Rubin, 83–96. Los Angeles: Museum of Cultural History, University of California, 1998.

Dundes, Alan. *The Evil Eye: A Folklore Casebook.* Garland Folklore Casebooks 2. New York: Garland, 1981.

Dundes, Alan. "Wet and Dry: The Evil Eye: Am Essay in Indo-European and Semitic Worldview." In *Interpreting Folklore,* edited by Alan Dundes, 93–312. Bloomington: Indiana University Press, 1980.

Editors of *Hinduism Today* Magazine. *What Is Hinduism?: Modern Adventures into a Profound Global Faith.* Kapaa, HI: Himalayan Academy, 2007.

Ekman, P. "Cross-Cultural Studies of Facial Expression." In *Darwin and Facial Expression: A Century of Research in Review*, edited by P. Ekman, 1–83. New York: Academic, 1973.

Ekman, P., W. V. Friesen, and P. Ellsworth. *Emotion in the Human Face.* New York: Pergamon Press, 1972.

Eliade, Mircea. *Shamanism: Archaic Techniques of Ecstasy.* Princeton, NJ: Princeton University Press, 2004.

Ellingson, Stephen, and M. Christian Green. *Religion and Sexuality in Cross-Cultural Perspective.* New York: Routledge, 2002.

Ellis, Andrew, Nigel Wiseman, and Ken Boss. *Fundamentals of Chinese Acupuncture.* Brookline, MA: Paradigm Publications, 1991.

Evans, J. *A History of Jewellery 1100–1870.* London: British Museum Publications, 1989.

Fagen, Brian M. *Kingdoms of Gold, Kingdoms of Jade: The Americas Before Columbus.* New York: Thames and Hudson, 1991.

Fernea, Elizabeth W., and Basima Q. Bezirgan. *Middle Eastern Muslim Women Speak.* Austin: University of Texas Press, 1977.

Fisher, Angela. *Africa Adorned: A Panorama of Jewelry, Dress, Body Decoration, and Hair.* New York: Henry Abrams, 2000.

Flenley, John, and Paul G. Bahn. *The Enigmas of Easter Island: Island on the Edge.* Oxford: Oxford University Press, 2003.

Foster, Lynn V. *Handbook to Life in the Ancient Maya World.* New York: Facts on File, 2002.

Fraser, Antonia. *Faith and Treason: The Story of the Gunpowder Plot.* New York: Doubleday, 1996.

Fridlund, Alan J. *Human Facial Expression: An Evolutionary View.* San Diego: Academic Press, 1994.

Friedlander, Marti, and Michael King. *Moko: Maori Tattooing in the Twentieth Century.* Auckland, New Zealand: David Bateman, 1999.

Fulbeck, Kip. *Permanence: Tattoo Portraits.* San Francisco: Chronicle Books, 2008.

Gallagher, Charles A. *Rethinking the Color Line.* Boston: McGraw-Hill, 2009.

Gardiner, Alan H. *Egypt of the Pharoahs: An Introduction.* New York: Oxford University Press, 1966.

Garland Thompson, Rosemary, ed. *Freakery: Cultural Spectacles of the Extraordinary Body.* New York: New York University Press, 1996.

Gathercole, Peter. "Contexts of Maori Moko." In *Marks of Civilization,* edited by Arnold Rubin, 171–78. Los Angeles: Museum of Cultural History, UCLA, 1988.

Gay, Kathlyn. *Body Marks: Tattooing, Piercing, and Scarification.* New York: Millbrook Press, 2002.

Gilman, Sander. "Imagined Ugliness." In *The Body Aesthetic: From Fine Art to Body Modification,* edited by Tobin Siebers, 199–216. Ann Arbor: University of Michigan Press, 2000.

Gilman, Sander L. *Jewish Frontiers: Essays on Bodies, Histories, and Identities.* New York: Palgrave Macmillan, 2003.

Glenn, Evelyn N. *Shades of Difference: Why Skin Color Matters.* Stanford, CA: Stanford University Press, 2009.

Gould, Stephen Jay. *The Mismeasure of Man.* New York: Norton, 1996.

Grabar, Andre. *Christian Iconography: A Study of Its Origins.* Princeton, NJ: Princeton University Press, 1968.

Greenwald, Laura. *Heroes with a Thousand Faces: True Stories of People with Facial Deformities and Their Quest for Acceptance.* Cleveland, OH: Cleveland Clinic Press, 2007.

Gregory, Steven, and Roger Sanjek. *Race.* New Brunswick, NJ: Rutgers University Press, 1994.

Griffin, Joy. "Labrets and Tattooing in Native Alaska." In *Marks of Civilization,* edited by Arnold Rubin, 181–90. Los Angeles: Museum of Cultural History, UCLA, 1988.

Grimshaw, Beatrice. *Fiji and Its Possibilities.* New York: Doubleday, Page & Co, 1907.

Grossman, Ruth B., and Judy Kegl. "To Capture a Face: A Novel Technique for the Analysis and Quantification of Facial Expressions in American Sign Language." *Sign Language Studies* 6, no. 3 (2006): 273–305.

Guscin, Mark. *The Image of Edessa.* Leiden: Brill, 2009.

Hall, Ronald E. *Racism in the 21st Century: An Empirical Analysis of Skin Color.* New York: Springer, 2008.

Harris, A. M., and G. K. Aguirre. "Prosopagnosia." *Current Biology* 17, no. 1 (2007): 7–8.

Hauser, Marc D. *The Design of Animal Communication.* Cambridge, MA: MIT Press, 1999.

Heissig, Walther. *The Religions of Mongolia.* Berkeley: University of California Press, 1980.

Henshen, F. *The Human Skull: A Cultural History.* New York: Frederick A. Praeger, 1966.

Herle, Anita. *Pacific Art: Persistence, Change, and Meaning.* Honolulu: University of Hawaii Press, 2002.

Herring, Cedric, Verna Keith, and Hayward Derrick Horton. *Skin Deep: How Race and Complexion Matter in the "Color Blind" Era.* Chicago: University of Illinois Press, 2004.

Hill, Pamela, and Judith Culp. *Permanent Makeup: Tips and Techniques.* Clifton Park, NY: Thomson Delmar Learning, 2007.

Hillson, S. *Dental Anthropology.* New York: Cambridge University Press, 1996.

Hobson, Jeremy. *Curious Country Customs.* Newton Abbot, UK: David & Charles, 2007.

Huang, A., D. Yen, and X. Zhang. "Exploring the Potential Effects of Emoticons." *Information and Management* 45, no. 7 (2008): 466–73.

Huard, Pierre, and Keith Botsford. *The Blackening of Teeth in Eastern Asia and in Indochina.* New Haven, CT: Human Relations Area Files, 1970.

Humber, Thomas. *The Sacred Shroud.* New York: Pocket Books, 1978.

Izard, C. E. *The Face of Emotion.* New York: Appleton-Century-Crofts, 1971.

Jackson, Linda A. *Physical Appearance and Gender: Sociobiological and Sociocultural Perspectives.* Albany: State University of New York Press, 1992.

Janik, Vicki K. *Fools and Jesters in Literature, Art, and History: A Bio-Bibliographical Sourcebook.* Westport, CT: Greenwood Press, 1998.

Jenkinson, J. "Face Facts: A History of Physiognomy from Ancient Mesopotamia to the End of the 19th Century." *Journal of Biocommunication* 24, no. 3 (1997): 2–7.

Johnson, Paul. *A History of Christianity.* New York: Simon & Schuster, 1995.

Jonaitis, Aldona. "Women, Marriage, Mouths and Feasting: The Symbolism of Tlingit Labrets." In *Marks of Civilization*, edited by Arnold Rubin, 191–205. Los Angeles: Museum of Cultural History, UCLA, 1988.

Juettner, Bonnie. *Acne.* Detroit: Lucent Books, 2010.

Kaw, E. "Opening Faces: The Politics of Cosmetic Surgery and Asian American Women." In *In Our Own Words: Readings on the Psychology of Women and Gender*, edited by M. Crawford and R. Under, 55–73. New York: McGraw-Hill, 1997.

Kempf, Wolfgang. "The Politics of Incorporation: Masculinity, Spatiality and Modernity among the Ngaing of Papua New Guinea." *Oceania* (September 2002): 56–77.

Kirk, Malcolm. *Man as Art: New Guinea Body Decoration.* London: Thames and Hudson, 1981.

Kirkpatrick, David. *The Facebook Effect: The Inside Story of the Company That Is Changing the World.* New York: Simon and Schuster, 2011.

Kleiner, Fred. *Gardner's Art through the Ages,* vol 1. Eastbourne, UK: Gardners Books, 2010.

Knauft, Bruce M. *South Coast New Guinea Cultures: History, Comparison, Dialectic.* Cambridge: Cambridge University Press, 1993.

Korzenny, Felipe, and Stella Ting-Toomey. "Cross-cultural Interpersonal Communication." *International and Intercultural Communication Annual* 15. Newbury Park, CA: Sage, 1991.

Kovesi Killerby, Catherine. *Sumptuary Law in Italy 1200–1500.* New York: Oxford University Press, 2002.

Kraus, Michael, and Dacher Keltner. "Signs of Socioeconomic Status: A Thin-slicing Approach." *Psychological Science* 20, no. 1 (2009): 99–106.

Krohn, F. "A Generational Approach to Using Emoticons as Nonverbal Communication." *Journal of Technical Writing and Communication* 34, no. 4 (2004): 321–28.

Kupka, Karel. *Dawn of Art: Painting and Sculpture of Australian Aborigines.* Sydney: Angus and Robertson, 1965.

Kuryluk, Eewa. *Veronica and Her Cloth: History, Symbolism and Structure of a True Image.* Cambridge, MA: Blackwell, 1991.

Kwon, So-Ran, Seok-Hoon Ko, Linda Greenwall, and Ronald E. Goldstein. *Tooth Whitening in Esthetic Dentistry.* London: Quintessence, 2009.

Lambert, Alix. *Russian Prison Tattoos: Codes of Authority, Domination, and Struggle.* Atglen, PA: Schiffer Publishing, 2003.

Lewis, I. M. *Ecstatic Religion: An Anthropological Study of Spirit Possession and Shamanism.* Harmondsworth, England: Penguin Books, 1971.

Lip, Evelyn. *Your Face Is Your Fortune: An Introduction to Chinese Face Reading.* Singapore: Marshall Cavendish Editions, 2009.

Littlejohn, Stephen W., and Kathy Domenici. *Facework: Bridging Theory and Practice.* Thousand Oaks, CA: Sage, 2006.

Livingston, R., and N. Pearce. "The Teddy-Bear Effect: Does Having a Baby Face Benefit Black Chief Executive Officers?" *Psychological Science* (October 2009): 1229–36.

Lombroso, Cesare. *Criminal Man.* Raleigh, NC: Duke University Press, 2006.

Lopez Sorensen, Lone. *Facial Reflexology.* Paharganj, New Delhi: Health Harmony, 2008.

Lott, Eric. *Love and Theft: Blackface Minstrelsy and the American Working Class.* New York: Oxford University Press, 1993.

Louis, Frederic. *Daily Life in Japan at the Time of the Samurai, 1185–1603.* New York: Praeger, 1972.

Lust, Annette. *From the Greek Mimes to Marcel Marceau and Beyond: Mimes, Actors, Pierrots, and Clowns: A Chronicle of the Many Visages of Mime in the Theatre.* Lanham, MD: Scarecrow Press, 2000.

Macdonell, Arthur Anthony. *A Practical Sanskrit Dictionary: With Transliteration, Accentuation, and Etymological Analysis Throughout.* Delhi: Munshiram Manoharlal, 1996.

Macgregor, Alexander. *Highland Superstitions: Connected with the Druids, Fairies, Witchcraft, Second-Sight, Hallowe'en, Sacred Wells and Lochs, with Several Curious Instances of Highland Customs and Beliefs.* Stirling, UK: E. Mackay, 1922.

Maheswaraiah, H.M. "Caste Mark." In *South Asian Folklore,* edited by Peter J. Claus, Sarah Diamond, and Margaret Ann Mills, 99–100. New York: Routledge, 2003.

Mails, Thomas E. *The Great Sioux Piercing Tradition.* Tulsa, OK: Council Oak Books, 2003.

Mascetti, Daniela, and Amanda Triossi. *Earrings: From Antiquity to the Present.* London: Thames and Hudson, 1999.

McArthur, Meher. *Reading Buddhist Art: An Illustrated Guide to Buddhist Signs and Symbols.* London: Thames and Hudson, 2004.

McCormick, James P. "Japan: The Mask and the Mask-Like Face." *Journal of Aesthetics and Art Criticism* 15, no. 2 (1956): 198–204.

McNab, Nan. *Body Bizarre Body Beautiful.* New York: Fireside, 2001.

Meggitt, M.J. *Desert People: A Study of the Walbiri Aborigines of Central Australia.* Sydney: Angus and Robertson, 1986.

Métraux, Alfred. "Ethnology of Easter Island." *Bernice Bishop Museum Bulletin* (Honolulu) 160 (1940).

Mieder, Wolfgang, Stewart A. Kingsbury, and Kelsie B. Harder. *A Dictionary of American Proverbs*. New York: Oxford University Press, 1992.

Milner, G., and C. Larsen. "Teeth as Artifacts of Human Behavior: Intentional Mutilation and Accidental Modification." In *Advances in Dental Anthropology*, 357–78. New York: Wiley-Liss, 1991.

Mogilner, Victoria. *Ancient Secrets of Facial Rejuvenation: A Holistic, Nonsurgical Approach to Youth and Well-Being*. Novato, CA: New World Library, 2006.

Mohapatra, R. P. *Fashion Styles of Ancient India: A Study of Kalinga from Earliest Times to Sixteenth Century A.D.* Delhi: B. R. Publishing, 1992.

Moller, A. P., and R. Thornhill. "Bilateral Symmetry and Sexual Selection: A Meta-analysis." *American Naturalist* 151 (1998): 174–92.

Morris, Desmond. *The Naked Woman: A Study of the Female Body*. New York: Thomas Dunne Books, 2005.

Mullins, Paul R. *Race and Affluence: An Archaeology of African America and Consumer Culture*. New York: Plenum Press, 1999.

Newton, Douglas. *New Guinea Art in the Collection of the Museum of Primitive Art*. Greenwich, CT: The New York Graphic Society. 1967.

Nicholas, Thomas, ed. *Tattoo: Bodies, Art and Exchange in the Pacific and the West*. Durham, NC: Duke University Press, 2005.

Nickell, Joe. *Inquest on the Shroud of Turin: Latest Scientific Findings*. Amherst, NY: Prometheus Books, 1988.

Nicoll, Allardyce. *Masks, Mimes and Miracles: Studies in the Popular Theatre*. New York: Cooper Square Publishers, 1963.

Nunley, John, and Cara McCarty. *Masks: Faces of Culture*. New York: Harry N. Abrams, in Association with the Saint Louis Art Museum, 1999.

Ostier, Marianne. *Jewels and Women: The Romance, Magic and Art of Feminine Adornment*. New York: Horizon Press, 1958.

Ousterhout, Douglas K. *Aesthetic Contouring of the Craniofacial Skeleton*. Boston: Little, Brown, 1991.

Packer, Sharon. *Superheroes and Superegos: Analyzing the Minds Behind the Masks*. Santa Barbara: Praeger/ABC-CLIO, 2010.

Parani, Maria G. *Reconstructing the Reality of Images: Byzantine Material Culture and Religious Iconography (11th–15th Centuries)*. Leiden: Brill, 2003.

Parry, Carol, and Joseph Eaton. "Kohl: A Lead-Hazardous Eye Makeup from the Third World to the First World." *Environmental Health Perspectives* 94 (1991): 121–23.

Partridge, Eric, Tom Dalzell, and Terry Victor. *The New Partridge Dictionary of Slang and Unconventional English*. London: Routledge, 2006.

Pearl, Sharrona. *About Faces: Physiognomy in Nineteenth Century Britain*. Cambridge, MA: Harvard University Press, 2010.

Perrett, D. I., and E. Brown. "What Gives a Face Its Gender?" *Perception* 22, no. 7 (1993): 829–40.

Peterkin, Allan. *One Thousand Beards: A Cultural History of Facial Hair*. Vancouver: Arsenal Pulp Press, 2001.

Picton, Janet, Stephen Quirke, and Paul C. Roberts. *Living Images: Egyptian Funerary Portraits in the Petrie Museum.* Walnut Creek, CA: Left Coast Press, 2007.

Pontynen, Arthur. *For the Love of Beauty: Art, History, and the Moral Foundations of Aesthetic Judgment.* New Brunswick, NJ: Transaction Publishers, 2006.

Porter, Martin. *Windows of the Soul: The Art of Physiognomy in European Culture 1470–1780.* Oxford: Clarendon Press, 2005.

Price, Ed Simon, and Emily Kearns. *The Oxford Dictionary of Classical Myth and Religion.* Oxford: Oxford University Press, 2003.

Price, Weston A. *Nutrition and Physical Degeneration: A Comparison of Primitive and Modern Diets and Their Effects, Etc.* New York: P. B. Hoeber, 1939.

Proffit, William R., and Henry W. Fields. *Contemporary Orthodontics.* St. Louis, MO: Mosby, 2000.

Quigley, Christine. *The Corpse: A History.* Jefferson, NC: McFarland, 1996.

Rauser, Amelia Faye. *Caricature Unmasked Irony, Authenticity, and Individualism in Eighteenth-Century English Prints.* Newark, DE: University of Delaware Press, 2008.

Reaves, Wendy Wick, and Pie Friendly. *Celebrity Caricature in America.* New Haven, CT: National Portrait Gallery, Smithsonian Institution, in association with Yale University Press, 1998.

Reynolds, Reginald. *Beards: Their Social Standing, Religious Involvements, Decorative Possibilities, and Value in Offence and Defence through the Ages.* New York: Doubleday, 1949.

Rhodes, Gillian, and Leslie Zebrowitz, eds. *Facial Attractiveness: Evolutionary, Cognitive, and Social Perspectives.* Westport, CT: Ablex Publishing, 2002.

Robb, David. *Clowns, Fools and Picaros: Popular Forms in Theatre, Fiction and Film.* Amsterdam: Rodopi, 2007.

Roberts, Allen F. "Tabwa Tegumentary Inscription." In *Marks of Civilization*, edited by Arnold Rubin, 41–56. Los Angeles: Museum of Cultural History, UCLA, 1988.

Rodriguez-Morales, Edda L., Maria S. Correa-Rivas, and Lillian E. Colon-Castillo. "Monocephalus Diprosopus, a Rare Form of Conjoined Twins, and Associated Congenital Anomalies." *Puerto Rico Health Sciences Journal* 21, no. 3 (2002): 237–40.

Rogers, Nicholas. *Halloween: From Pagan Ritual to Party Night.* Oxford: Oxford University Press, 2002.

Roper Starch Worldwide, Inc., and AARP. *Public Attitudes toward Aging, Beauty, and Cosmetic Surgery.* Washington, DC: AARP, 2001.

Rose, Christine. "The Democratization of Beauty." *The New Atlantis* 5 (Spring 2004): 19–35.

Rose, Jerome C., and Richard D. Roblee. "Origins of Dental Crowding and Malocclusions: An Anthropological Perspective." *Compendium of Continuing Education in Dentistry* 30, no. 5 (2009): 292–300.

Rosenberg, Sarah. "Face." Beyond Intractability Knowledge Base Project. Conflict Research Consortium, University of Colorado, 2004. http://www.beyondintractability.org/essay/face/.

Russell, James A. "Is There Universal Recognition of Emotion From Facial Expression? A Review of the Cross-Cultural Studies." *Psychological Bulletin* 115, no. 1 (1994): 102–41.

Russell, Kathy, Midge Wilson, and Ronald Hall. *The Color Complex: The Politics of Skin Color among African Americans.* New York: First Anchor Books, 1993.

Sacks, Oliver W. *The Man Who Mistook His Wife for a Hat and Other Clinical Tales.* New York: Summit Books, 1985.

Samovar, Larry A., and Richard Porter. *Communication between Cultures.* Belmont, CA: Wadsworth, 2009.

Sands, Rosita M. "Carnival Celebrations in Africa and the New World: Junkanoo and the Black Indians of Mardi Gras." *Black Music Research Journal* 11 (1991): 75–92.

Santino, Jack. *Halloween and Other Festivals of Death and Life.* Knoxville: University of Tennessee Press, 1994.

Sarangerel. *Riding Windhorses: A Journey into the Heart of Mongolian Shamanism.* Rochester, VT: Destiny Books, 2000.

Schlesinger, Arthur M., and S. J. Perelman. *1886 Professional Criminals of America.* New York: Lyons Press, 2000.

Schrader, Abby M. "Branding the Other/Tattooing the Self: Bodily Inscription among Convicts in Russia and the Soviet Union." In *Written on the Body: The Tattoo in European and American History*, edited by Jane Caplan, 174–92. Princeton, NJ: Princeton University Press, 2000.

Schulz, Regine, Matthias Seidel, Betsy Morrell Bryan, and Christianne Henry. *Egyptian Art.* Baltimore: Walters Art Museum, 2009.

Schwenk, K. "Why Snakes Have Forked Tongues." *Science* 263, no. 5153 (1994): 1573–77.

Scott, A.C. *The Flower and Willow World; The Story of the Geisha.* New York: Orion Press, 1960.

Scranton, Philip. *Beauty and Business: Commerce, Gender, and Culture in Modern America.* New York: Routledge, 2001.

Scruton, Roger. *Beauty.* Oxford: Oxford University Press, 2009.

Sebesta, Judith L., and Larissa Bonfante. *The World of Roman Costume.* Madison: University of Wisconsin Press, 1994.

Shaver, Ruth M. *Kabuki Costume.* London: Simon & Schuster, 1991.

Sherrow, Victoria. *For Appearance' Sake: The Historical Encyclopedia of Good Looks, Beauty, and Grooming.* Phoenix, AZ: Oryx Press, 2001.

Shirazi, Faegheh. *The Veil Unveiled: The Hijab in Modern Culture.* Gainesville: University Press of Florida, 2001.

Siikala, A.L. *The Rite Technique of the Siberian Shaman.* Helsinki: FF Communications, 1978.

Sikes, Ruth G. "The History of Suntanning: A Love/Hate Affair." *Journal of Aesthetic Sciences* 1, no. 2 (May 1998): 6–7.

Simmons, D.R. *Ta Moko: The Art of Maori Tattoo.* Auckland, New Zealand: Reed Books, 1986.

Stark, Richard B. *Aesthetic Plastic Surgery.* Boston: Little, Brown and Company, 1992.

Starkey, David. *Monarchy: From the Middle Ages to Modernity.* London: HarperPress, 2006.

Stern, Madeleine. *Heads and Headlines: The Phrenological Fowlers.* Norman: University of Oklahoma Press, 1971.

Strathern, Andrew and Marilyn Strathern. *Self Decoration in Mt. Hagen.* London: Backworth, 1971.

Strausbaugh, John. *Black Like You: Blackface, Whiteface, Insult and Imitation in American Popular Culture.* New York: Jeremy P. Tarcher/Penguin, 2006.

Strickland, Carol, and John Boswell. *The Annotated Mona Lisa: A Crash Course in Art History from Prehistoric to Post-Modern.* Kansas City, MO: Andrews and McMeel, 1992.

Strouhal, Eugen. *Life of the Ancient Egyptians.* Norman: University of Oklahoma Press, 1992.

Swain, Simon, ed. *Seeing the Face, Seeing the Soul: Polemon's Physiognomy from Classical Antiquity to Medieval Islam.* Oxford: Oxford University Press, 2007.

Tait, H. *Seven Thousand Years of Jewellery.* London: British Museum Publications, 1986.

Takaki, Ronald. *A Different Mirror: A History of Multicultural America.* Boston: Little, Brown, 1993.

Thevóz, Michel. *The Painted Body.* New York: Rizzoli International, 1984.

Tilney, Nicholas L. *Transplant: From Myth to Reality.* New Haven, CT: Yale University Press, 2003.

Turner, Patricia A. *Ceramic Uncles and Celluloid Mammies: Black Images and Their Influence on Culture.* New York: Anchor Books, 1994.

Turner, Terence. "Social Body and Embodied Subject: Bodiliness, Subjectivity and Sociality among the Kayapo." *Current Anthropology* 10, no. 2 (1995): 143–70.

Up de Graff, F. W. *Head Hunters of the Amazon: Seven Years of Exploration and Adventure.* New York: Duffield and Co, 1923.

Vadetskaya, E. "Painting on Tashtyk Burial Masks." *Archaeology, Ethnology and Anthropology of Eurasia* 29, no. 1 (2007): 46–56.

Van Cutsem, Anne. *A World of Earrings: Africa, Asia, America.* New York: Skira International, 2001.

Van den Beukel, Dorine. *Traditional Mehndi Designs: A Treasury of Henna Body Art.* Berkeley, CA: Shambhala Publications, 2000.

Van Stone, James W. *An Early Archaeological Example of Tattooing from Northwestern Alaska.* Chicago: Field Museum of Natural History, 1974.

Van Tilburg, JoAnne. *Easter Island: Archaeology, Ecology, and Culture.* Washington, DC: Smithsonian Institution Press, 1994.

Vatsyayan, Kapila. *Buddhist Iconography.* New Delhi: Tibet House, 1989.

Vitebsky, Piers. *Shamanism.* Norman: University of Oklahoma Press, 2001.

Vogel, Susan. "Baule Scarification: The Mark of Civilization." In *Marks of Civilization,* edited by Arnold Rubin, 97–103. Los Angeles: Museum of Cultural History, UCLA, 1988.

Vogel, Susan M. *Baule: African Art, Western Eyes.* New Haven, CT: Yale University Press, 1997.

Vollmann, William T. *Kissing the Mask: Beauty, Understatement and Femininity in Japanese Noh Theater: with Some Thoughts on Muses (especially Helga Testorf), Transgender Women, Kabuki Goddesses, Porn Queens, Poets, Housewives, Makeup Artists, Geishas, Valkyries, and Venus Figurines.* New York: Ecco, 2010.

Vuillier, Gaston. *A History of Dancing from the Earliest Age to Our Own Times.* Boston: Milford House, 1972.

Wen, H. "Face Acupuncture." *International Journal of Clinical Acupuncture* 7, no. 3 (1996): 301.

White, James, ed. *Handbook of Indians of Canada.* Published as an Appendix to the Tenth Report of the Geographic Board of Canada, Ottawa, 1913.

White, Randall. "The Women of Brassempouy: A Century of Research and Interpretation." *Journal of Archaeological Method and Theory* 13, no. 4 (2006): 250–303.

Wiesner, Merry. *Early Modern Europe, 1450–1789.* Cambridge: Cambridge University Press, 2006.

Williams, Carol. *Framing the West: Race, Gender, and the Photographic Frontier in the Pacific Northwest.* New York: Oxford University Press, 2003.

Wilson, Ian. *Holy Faces, Secret Places: An Amazing Quest for the Face of Jesus.* New York: Doubleday, 1991.

Wilson, Ian. *The Shroud of Turin: The Burial Cloth of Jesus Christ?* rev. ed. Garden City, NY: Image Books, 1979.

Worland, Rick. *The Horror Film: An Introduction.* Malden, MA: Blackwell Pub, 2007.

Wright, Edward F. *Manual of Temporomandibular Disorders.* Ames, IA: Blackwell Munksgaard, 2005.

Wykes-Joyce, Max. *Cosmetics and Adornment: Ancient and Contemporary Usage.* New York: Philosophical Library, 1961.

Yang, Henning H.L. *Mian Xiang: The Chinese Art of Face Reading.* London: Vega, 2001.

Yarrow, Ralph. *Indian Theatre: Theatre of Origin, Theatre of Freedom.* London: Routledge, 2001.

Zebrowitz, Leslie A. *Reading Faces: Window to the Soul?* Boulder, CO: Westview Press, 1997.

Zumbroich, T.J. "Teeth as Black as a Bumble Bee's Wings: The Ethnobotany of Teeth Blackening in Southeast Asia." *Ethnobotany Research and Applications* 7 (2009): 381–98.

Index

About the Author

Margo DeMello has a BA in Religious Studies from U.C. Berkeley and earned her PhD in Cultural Anthropology in 1995 from U.C. Davis. She currently lectures at Central New Mexico Community College, teaching sociology, cultural studies, and anthropology.

Her books include *Bodies of Inscription: A Cultural History of the Modern Tattoo Community* (2000), *Stories Rabbits Tell: A Natural and Cultural History of a Misunderstood Creature* (2003), *Low-Carb Vegetarian* (2004), *Why Animals Matter: The Case for Animal Protection* (2007), *The Encyclopedia of Body Adornment* (2007), *Feet and Footwear* (2009), the edited collection, *Teaching the Animal: Human Animal Studies Across the Disciplines,* and *Animals and Society: An Introduction to Human-Animal Studies* (2012).

She has had her work published in journals such as *Anthropology Today, Journal of Popular Culture*, and *Anthrozöos*, and contributed essays and chapters to *Pierced Hearts and True Love: A Century of Drawings for Tattoos* (edited by Ed Hardy, 1995), *Cultural Anthropology: The Human Challenge* (edited by William Haviland, 2004), *Encyclopedia of Human-Animal Relationships* (edited by Marc Bekoff, Greenwood Publishing, 2007), and *A Cultural History of Animals: The Modern Age* (edited by Randy Malamud, 2007).